First Do No Harm

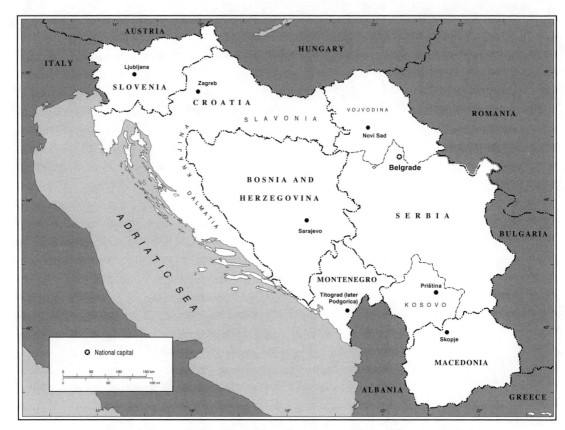

Republics and Autonomous Provinces of Yugoslavia, 1990

First Do No Harm

Humanitarian Intervention and the Destruction of Yugoslavia

David N. Gibbs

Vanderbilt University Press • Nashville

© 2009 by Vanderbilt University Press
Nashville, Tennessee 37235
All rights reserved
Third printing 2011

Frontispiece: Based on "The Former Yugoslavia" (map) from
the United Nations Department of Peacekeeping Operations,
Cartographic Section.

Library of Congress Cataloging-in-Publication Data

Gibbs, David N.
First do no harm : humanitarian intervention and the
destruction of Yugoslavia / David N. Gibbs.
p. cm.
Includes bibliographical references and index.
ISBN 978-0-8265-1643-5 (cloth : alk. paper)
ISBN 978-0-8265-1644-2 (pbk. : alk. paper)
1. Humanitarian intervention—Bosnia and Hercegovina.
2. Humanitarian intervention—Serbia—Kosovo. 3. Yugoslav
War, 1991–1995—Participation, Foreign. 4. Kosovo
(Serbia)—History—Civil War, 1998–1999—Participation,
Foreign. 5. United States—Foreign relations—Yugoslavia.
6. Yugoslavia—Foreign relations—United States. I. Title.
JZ6369.G53 2009
949.703—dc22
2008039277

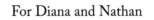

For Diana and Nathan

Contents

Preface

This book is the product of my long-standing interest in foreign intervention. As I grew up during the 1960s and 1970s, the unfolding disaster of US intervention in Vietnam sparked my interest in this topic. I remember well when I heard in 1969 the first details of the My Lai massacre and was disturbed to realize that US troops were capable of such actions. I was similarly shaken by the effects of US bombing, the use of chemical weapons, and the advent of "free fire" zones, among other horrors of that war. What impressed me even more was the extent to which official lies and deceptions helped to justify the war and to mislead the public (a point underscored by the publication of the *Pentagon Papers* in 1971, when I was thirteen). As a graduate student and a young professor, I pursued these interests in extended studies of foreign interventions in the Congo Crisis of the early 1960s, and then in Afghanistan after 1978.

I am thus writing from a position that is fundamentally skeptical about the merits of intervention and, to some extent, of war more generally. I agree that there have been a handful of wars that produced positive results (and yes, US involvement in World War II was one such example). But I would see these "positive" cases as rare. In most instances, the legacy of military intervention has been appalling, and I have found nothing in my studies of Yugoslavia to challenge this basic assumption.

Another influence on this book has been the continuation of US militarism following the demise of the USSR. The basic paradox was succinctly stated by Chalmers Johnson in a recent interview:

> In 1989, Mikhail Gorbachev makes a decision. [He] could have stopped the Germans from tearing down the Berlin Wall, but [instead] . . . he just watches them tear it down and, at once, the whole Soviet empire starts to unravel. . . . [W]hat startled me almost more than the Wall coming down

was this: As the entire justification for the military-industrial complex, for the Pentagon apparatus, for the fleets around the world, for all our bases came to an end, the United States instantly ... began to seek an alternative enemy. Our leaders simply could not contemplate dismantling the apparatus of the Cold War.[1]

The lack of any basic change in US Cold War policy was indeed a remarkable fact.

What was even more remarkable was the absence of any real public debate about the direction of US policy after the Cold War. This lack of debate was fully accepted by Democrats and Republicans alike, and most of the media. In a now famous speech to the US Senate, Robert Byrd stated: "This Chamber is, for the most part, silent—ominously, dreadfully silent. There is no debate, no discussion. . . . There is nothing."[2] These comments were made in February 2003 regarding the lack of debate on the impending war against Iraq, but the same could be said regarding the lack of debate more generally.

The obvious questions are, Why was there so little change in American policy after the end of the Cold War, and why was there so little discussion on this topic? My tentative answer is that alleged humanitarian interventions in the Balkans helped establish a new rationale—however spurious—for militarism. The Yugoslav case served to define US intervention as a benevolent and even altruistic activity, and this image has proven useful as a justification for virtually all overseas action. I explore those issues more fully in later chapters, but I want to emphasize here that my interest in Yugoslavia stems from a larger concern with the persistence of US militarism—and the lack of serious discussion of militarism—after 1989.

This study is written from the standpoint of the political Left, an ideological identification I have always held and have seen no reason to change. However, I have learned much from such conservative writers as Christopher Layne, Paul Craig Roberts, Ted Galen Carpenter, and Jude Wanniski. I hope that this book will appeal to readers on both sides of the spectrum.

In writing this book, I have been helped by many friends and colleagues, including Ronald Cox, Bruce Cumings, Jerri-Lynn Scofield, Julia Clancy-Smith, Thomas Christiano, Gary Gaynor, Milan Brdar, Mark Zepezauer, Peter Gowan, Jovan Babić, Oscar Martinez, Susan Zakin, Laura Tabili, Ido Oren, Lisa Adeli, Sandy Thatcher, Nicola Ramsey, David Wilkins, Richard Falk, Paul Shoup, Jeremy Scahill, Robert Hayden, William Gaston, Michael Schaller, and Sandra Halperin. Thomas Ferguson, Jacqueline Sharkey, and Lucie Greenblum deserve special thanks. Several of these persons disagreed with elements of my analysis, and their criticisms have sharpened my arguments. At Vanderbilt University Press, it has been a pleasure to work with Michael Ames. Heather Cottin allowed me to use the research materials of her late husband, Sean Gervasi, who died before he could publish his own book on Yugoslavia.

With regard to quotations from the International Criminal Tribunal for the Former Yugoslavia (ICTY): Some of these come from witness testimonies that were originally presented in various Balkan languages. In these cases, I have used the official court translations as they appeared on the ICTY's English-language Web site. With regard to translations from newspapers and other media materials: Roland Lechner, a University of Arizona student, made the German translations for me; the French translations are mine. Research support was provided by the Udall Center for Studies in Public Policy, the Office of the Vice President for Research of the University of Arizona, and the George H. W. Bush Foundation. Portions of Chapters 2 and 3 previously appeared in "Washington's New Interventionism: US Hegemony and Inter-Imperialist Rivalries," *Monthly Review* 53, no. 4 (2001), and (in Serbian translation) in "Origins of the Yugoslav Conflict," *Sociološki Pregled* 35, nos. 3–4, 2001.

This book is dedicated to my wife, Diana, and my son, Nathan.

First Do No Harm

1

The Rise of Humanitarian Intervention

> We must act to save thousands of innocent men, women, and children from humanitarian catastrophe, from death, barbarism, and ethnic cleansing.
> —*Tony Blair on humanitarian intervention*

> The echoes of 19th century imperialism are there whether you like it or not.
> —*David Rieff on humanitarian intervention*

The period following the end of the Cold War proved less stable and potentially less benign than many had hoped. Conflicts in Haiti, Afghanistan, the Balkans, and several regions of sub-Saharan Africa suggested that civil wars and ethno-religious hatreds had replaced East-West tensions as the principal pivot of world politics. These conflicts often led to atrocities and humanitarian emergencies. In light of these new concerns, the idea of humanitarian intervention has emerged as a major source of hope. Advocates of intervention argue that armed action by major powers, led by the United States, can attenuate the most destructive effects of local conflicts and might also help to prevent future ones. The doctrine has been applied in a range of cases. By far the most important cases of humanitarian intervention occurred in the former Yugoslavia, notably in Bosnia-Herzegovina and Kosovo. It is the Yugoslav cases, more than any others, which have influenced both the discussion and the practice of humanitarian intervention.

This book provides a detailed examination of external intervention in these Yugoslav wars, and it proceeds from the premise that previous studies have seriously misrepresented these conflicts. Much of the discussion of humanitarian intervention is therefore predicated on a basic misunderstanding of what happened in these key cases. My purpose in writing this book is to correct the record, and to address this misunderstanding. The book also takes a critical view of the concept of humanitarian intervention, both in general and as it was applied in the Yugoslav case. We will see that external intervention was one of the principal *causes* of the conflict. Interventions helped to trigger the breakup of Yugoslavia and the various wars that followed the breakup; later intervention served to intensify the war, and to spread the fighting. External intervention did not resolve or attenuate the conflict; it helped create the conflict in the first place.

In making this argument, I contest a large portion of the existing literature on this subject. Thus far, the dominant interpretation of the Yugoslav wars downplays the role of external intervention. According to this view, Yugoslavia's breakup resulted entirely from internal factors, while international powers—notably the United States, Western Europe, and the United Nations—stood aside; initially the international community made little effort to resolve the war or to protect its victims. As a result of international inaction, this view holds, the world allowed major acts of genocide to occur. Samantha Power succinctly stated this overall view in her widely influential book *"A Problem from Hell": America and the Age of Genocide*. With regard to the Balkans, she claims: "US policymakers did almost nothing to deter the crime. Because America's 'vital national interests' were not considered imperiled by mere genocide, senior US officials did not give genocide the moral attention it warranted. . . . The key question . . . is: Why does the United States stand so idly by?"[1] Journalists and academics have widely accepted this view of US and Western inaction in the Yugoslav wars. In addition, when the United States finally intervened with military force in 1995 in Bosnia and in 1999 in Kosovo, this was seen (by Power and others) as a positive step that led to resolution of the humanitarian emergencies in both cases.

In the context of widespread interest in the Yugoslav events, there has emerged a substantial literature on the doctrine of humanitarian intervention.[2] As mine is primarily an applied rather than a theoretical study, what follows elucidates only the main points of the interventionist paradigm before I turn to the specifics of the Yugoslav case.

The Paradigm of Humanitarian Intervention

The advocates of interventionism have included some of the major intellectuals in the United States and Europe. In addition to Power, this group includes such prominent figures as Todd Gitlin, Mary Kaldor, Bernard-Henri Lévy, Václav Havel, Richard Perle, Susan Sontag, Paul Wolfowitz, Joshua Muravchik, Anne-Marie Slaughter, Stanley Hoffmann, William Shawcross, Elie Wiesel, Bernard Kouchner, Jean Bethke Elshtain, Christopher Hitchens, Michael Ignatieff, Michael Walzer, and Paul Berman.[3] Some of these figures had, in earlier periods, expressed suspicion or even hostility toward the idea of intervention, which was associated with such disastrous actions as the Vietnam War, or the overthrow of the elected Allende government of

Chile. In the new conditions that attended the end of the Cold War, however, the situation has been transformed (so the argument goes) in ways that make intervention appear a far more benign force, one that genuinely reflects universalistic values, such as the protection of minority groups from persecution. At the same time, the interventionist intellectuals insist that they are not supporters of official policy. On the contrary, they view themselves as dissident figures, isolated from power circles and even from the mainstream of intellectual life, who make their case for intervention by arguing against establishment viewpoints.

The central idea behind humanitarian intervention is the salience of human rights, which are to be given precedence over the rights of states and governments.[4] In the view of interventionist intellectuals, earlier discourses had overemphasized state sovereignty and the associated right of state officials to act as they wished—without external interference. This discourse gave too little consideration to the rights of individual citizens to be free from oppression. External intervention by purportedly disinterested powers is considered a solution to these problems, acceptable in order to liberate the oppressed and alleviate human suffering.

The interest in humanitarian intervention is closely connected with a renewed attention to the crime of genocide. The advocates of intervention emphasize that several recent wars—in Rwanda, the Sudan, and former Yugoslavia—have entailed genocidal action perpetrated by one ethnic group against a subordinate group. The gravity of this crime underscores the need for decisive action. In this context, interventionists draw attention to the importance of the internationally recognized Genocide Convention of 1948, which states that genocide exists whenever certain acts are committed "with intent to destroy, in whole or in part, a national, ethnical, racial or religious group." The Convention enumerates specific acts defined as genocidal, including:

a. Killing members of the group;
b. Causing serious bodily or mental harm to members of the group;
c. Deliberately inflicting on the group conditions of life calculated to bring about its physical destruction.[5]

There remain some unresolved questions about how the Genocide Convention should be interpreted: Should ethnic killing "in whole or in part" automatically be considered genocide, without regard to how many are killed? Should any number of killings be considered genocide? In response to these questions, there is no clear consensus. On the one hand, some authorities insist that the number of victims does in fact matter in determining whether a particular incident qualifies as genocide. Thus, the International Criminal Tribunal for the Former Yugoslavia determined that "it is widely acknowledged that the intention to destroy must target at least a *substantial* part of the group" in order to qualify as genocide.[6] Accordingly, to kill a relatively small number of persons, even as part of a calculated racist campaign, would not be sufficient.

On the other hand, some disagree with the judgment of Yugoslav Tribunal and insist that the number of victims is irrelevant. Mirsad Tokača of the Sarajevo Research and Documentation Center states: "*Genocide is not a matter of numbers.* . . . The Convention on Genocide . . . does not specify numbers" (emphasis added). Tokača goes further and states that even nonfatal forms of ethnic oppression also might qualify: "[The Genocide Convention] speaks of the intention to destroy or kill a specific group, or indeed to expose it to conditions leading to its demise. Such demise moreover does not mean that the victims must be physically exterminated, but that they are forced to leave their habitat."[7] From this standpoint, genocide occurs whenever an ethnic group is forced to leave its homeland, even if no one is killed. Whatever the differences in interpretation, many recent studies emphasize the contemporary significance of the Genocide Convention, and view it as a guide to interventionist action.[8]

In practice, at least some ethnic conflicts are morally complex, for instance, where both sides (or sometimes multiple sides) engage in cycles of atrocity and vengeance. Establishing clear-cut aggressors and victims may seem an impossible task in such cases. However, the interventionists insist that this moral complexity is not present in all cases. There are certain conflicts where the burden of guilt is not shared among warring parties. This latter class of conflicts, it is claimed, involves asymmetric violence: There *are* clear-cut aggressors and perpetrators of violence, as well as victims of violence.[9] The eight thousand victims of the 1995 Srebrenica massacre are frequently cited as examples of violence that is both genocidal and asymmetric: The Muslims who perished at Srebrenica were powerless to defend themselves against their Serb attackers. For the interventionist intellectuals, it is wrong to present such cases as "morally complicated," since the claim is factually inaccurate, as well as insulting to the memory of the victims.

The need to prevent a recurrence of genocide—the crime of crimes—is thus a key argument in favor of military intervention. Other justifications for intervention include alleviating the effects of famine and other natural disasters (this was of course the principal basis for the 1992 intervention in Somalia, the first major act of humanitarian intervention in the post-Soviet era). But it is genocide that now forms the main argument for intervention.

The new emphasis on genocide naturally evokes images of Adolf Hitler and the Third Reich, combined with the infamous efforts by British officials to appease Hitler during the 1938 Munich meeting. Advocates of humanitarian intervention often draw parallels between these World War II events and more recent ethnic conflicts, such as Kosovo. Thus Jean Bethke Elshtain states that the NATO campaign in Kosovo was, "for many, a paradigmatic instance of humanitarian intervention in the very name of humanity itself" that called to mind "the Nuremberg precedents and 'crimes against humanity.'" And Elshtain implies additional parallels: Just as Hitler resisted compromise and responded only to force, "Milošević was immune to diplomatic overtures."[10] The interventionists argue that the world community has been too quick to "appease" aggressors like Milošević, and too slow to use force.[11]

With regard to contemporary conflicts, the interventionists often stress the importance of specific personalities, whom they describe as being similar to Hitler; they emphasize such personalities as causes of recent genocides in the same way that Hitler is remembered as the cause of an earlier genocide. This tendency toward personalization is evident in both academic and journalistic accounts. Thus, Milošević is often held to be the primary cause—or even the sole cause—of the violence in the former Yugoslavia.[12] There have been efforts to personalize other crises as well, such as the Darfur conflict in the western Sudan. Thus Franklin Foer states: "A lot of the perpetrators and the victims [in Darfur] are . . . relatively nameless and faceless. But I think that, who is the Milošević? Who is the Hitler of this genocide? These people exist in Khartoum, and I think it's incumbent upon journalism to let people know who these figures are."[13] It has become difficult to imagine a humanitarian emergency without some Hitler-like figure who assumes the role of organizer. During the 2003 US intervention in Iraq, commentators emphasized the personality of Saddam Hussein as the sole cause of Iraq's problems. And in the more recent US conflicts with Iran and Venezuela, discussion has focused on the personalities of Mahmoud Ahmadinejad and Hugo Chávez. Whether historically accurate or not, these personalized accounts serve an important function: They establish that certain conflicts are morally and analytically simple, since they are caused by pathological personalities, and such simplicity presents a strong basis for legitimate intervention.

From a strictly legal standpoint, the practice of humanitarian intervention is problematic, as the UN Charter forbids intervention in the domestic affairs of member states (except when it is authorized by the Security Council).[14] The legal prohibition against intervention was reaffirmed in a 1981 General Assembly resolution which reads: "No state has the right to intervene, directly or indirectly, for any reason whatsoever, in the internal or external affairs of any other state."[15] The idea of state sovereignty was strongly privileged in international law, partly because great power intervention was seen at the time as the quintessential act of realpolitik, illegitimate virtually by definition.[16] Since 1990, however, intervention has come to be viewed in a far more positive light, and this has produced a legal quandary, since the practice remains legally tenuous. And this quandary has practical implications: It is often difficult to achieve Security Council consensus on the need for armed force, and so in some cases, interventionists see a need to act without Council approval. Humanitarian intervention that results from these circumstances and that circumvents the Security Council may fall into the unfortunate category of illegality and even criminality. The response from the advocates of intervention is twofold. First, there are increasing calls for changing international law to adjust to the new Western consensus, and to make it easier for the United States and its allies to intervene.[17] Second, more and more voices emphasize the importance of intervening even without a clear legal basis, since such intervention serves a moral purpose. Thus, postmortem analyses of the 1999 Kosovo bombing campaign view the action as morally justified, even though it was technically illegal.[18]

The growth of interest in armed intervention results in part from dissatisfaction with more traditional ways of resolving humanitarian crises, especially through UN peacekeeping forces. Peacekeeping forces are intended (at least in principle) to operate on the basis of strict impartiality. While the nature of impartiality has been long debated, it implies at least some degree of reluctance, on the part of the peacekeepers, to take sides in specific conflicts.[19] Peacekeeping operations themselves are predicated on the idea that military aspects of the operation are of secondary importance; the primary focus is on separating the combatants while mediation and negotiations achieve a reconciliation of the warring sides through a political settlement. Accordingly, peacekeepers are in most cases lightly armed, and their weapons are used primarily for self-defense; they are supposed to resist using force as a technique of conflict resolution. During the 1990s, there was growing impatience with these practices. Strategies that relied on diplomatic pressure and negotiations to resolve crises—and thus avoided force—were considered overly hesitant and even cowardly by the interventionist intellectuals.[20] In the case of Bosnia-Herzegovina, they argue, extended efforts by the United Nations and the European Union to seek a negotiated settlement failed completely, and served to encourage Serb aggression.[21]

The difference between these two strategies—impartial UN peacekeeping, on the one hand, and humanitarian intervention, on the other—recalls the competing perspectives on how to view internal political conflicts and civil wars. From the standpoint of UN peacekeepers, such conflicts involve extreme complexities, whereby all sides bear at least some blame. As we have seen, advocates of humanitarian intervention often criticize such "complex" perspectives on ethnic conflict, arguing that these views whitewash the actions of *génocidaires*, while they perpetuate the misery of victims. Efforts to mediate and negotiate involve simple appeasement of murderous armies. What is needed, instead, is decisive military action to stop genocide and to punish those who direct it. A *New Republic* editorial stated the matter this way: "In the response to most foreign policy crises, the use of military force is properly viewed as a last resort. In the response to genocide, the use of *military force is properly viewed as a first resort*" (emphasis added).[22]

With these assumptions, the advocates of intervention often look to the world's principal source of military power, the United States, which must lead these humanitarian efforts. Thus Michael Reisman states: "Everyone likes to criticize US pretensions to being the constable of the world. But when people need the cops, guess who they call?"[23] Inevitably, the humanitarian intervention paradigm requires US hegemony. The United Nations and smaller states also have a role to play, but they must do so under the guidance of the one country with the military wherewithal to direct the operations, the United States.

A key issue for the advocates of humanitarian intervention is that of choosing which conflicts should be candidates for intervention. Clearly, even the vast military resources of the United States would be insufficient for intervention in more than a few conflicts at any given time. And as a practical matter, of course, brief interventions are usually insufficient. In many of the more complex communal conflicts, it would be necessary to have an extended occupation force to separate hostile ethnic groups in order to establish a more viable form of government, and to some extent, to reorder the societies in order to foster the resolution of underlying tensions and the prevention of future outbreaks of violence. In the case of Bosnia-Herzegovina, for example, there has been an occupation force on the ground since 1995, and in Kosovo since 1999. Afghanistan has been effectively occupied since 2001. If interventions are cut short (as occurred in Somalia in 1995), the result can be a return to civil war and chaos. To have any real effect, humanitarian interventions must be of long duration. It seems straightforward that such expensive and time-consuming operations cannot be performed for every ethnic conflict in the world, given limited resources.

The issue of deciding which conflicts merit outside intervention has been a difficult one for the advocates of intervention. Some recognize the problem of limited resources and call for a form of triage, according to which the intervening powers will decide where to intervene based on a number of criteria (such as the severity of the humanitarian emergency, the potential expense of such intervention, or the logistical problem of dispatching troops).[24] Governments, it is argued, will inevitably engage in triage determinations when deciding to intervene, so it is necessary to make sure that the criteria according to which these determinations are made will be reasonable. Other advocates of intervention, however, tend to ignore the issue of practicality altogether and simply insist that the United States must intervene whenever a conflict threatens to destroy a particular population group, "in whole or in part."[25]

Another divisive issue concerns how to weigh the possibility that humanitarian interventions may themselves cause harm and thus increase suffering. All wars entail some degree of human cost, in combat casualties and (inevitably) civilian casualties as well. There is also the danger that interventions can cause unpredictable results. Direct military action—however well intended—may intensify rather than reduce ethnic tensions, and it may serve to heighten violence, including possibly genocidal violence. In response, some interventionists do consider these potential costs of military action, and they argue (or imply) that states must be careful to weigh costs and benefits before committing themselves to the use of force. Michael Walzer argues as a general point that interventionists should assume a stance of restraint, and they must avoid destructive "crusades," including ones that aim for humanitarian objectives.[26] Others, however, disregard the issue of assessing the costs of intervention, and the associated danger that intervention can in some cases make the situation worse.[27] In general, most studies downplay the potential costs of humanitarian intervention and simply assume that intervention will have a positive impact.

A Self-Interested Motive?

One possible objection to humanitarian intervention is that it makes intervention easier to undertake, and certainly easier to justify. There is an obvious danger here: The United States can use humanitarianism as a pretext to justify aggressive actions that serve to advance its economic and geostrategic position in the world. After all, great powers have long justified their self-interested acts in terms of a higher moral purpose.[28] Perhaps the doctrine of humanitarian intervention is merely a way of excusing US aggression, and it should be viewed with the same cynicism that we now view Britain's "white man's burden," France's "*mission civilisatrice*," the Soviet Union's "defense" of the Afghan people, or other great power rationalizations from previous eras.

In response to such criticisms, it is often emphasized that most recent interventions did *not* serve US or Western interests in any significant way. The major interventions during the 1990s occurred in remote regions that are inherently unimportant from the standpoint of great power interests. According to Martha Finnemore, many recent interventions occurred in areas of "negligible strategic or economic importance." She adds: "The recent pattern of humanitarian interventions [during the 1990s] raises the issue of what interest intervening states could possibly be pursuing. In most of these cases, the intervention targets are insignificant by any usual measure of geo-strategic or economic interest."[29] Paul Berman makes a similar point when he laments that "massacres in the Balkans or anywhere else threatened the fundamental interests of not one of the great powers."[30] From the standpoint of US interests, the most logical response to ethnic conflicts involving genocide is not to intervene at all, and to let the conflicts fester.

Yet major interventions have occurred despite the supposed lack of great power interest. To address these interventions, two sets of explanations are offered. Some writers suggest that governmental structures themselves have been transformed and that "idealistic" norms have indeed influenced the foreign policy bureaucracies of major states, including the United States.[31] The intervening powers have set aside the Cold War norms of realpolitik, at least to some degree, and their motivations really do include a desire to protect victims of persecution. A second and more typical view is that the post–Cold War interventions result from pressures outside the governmental structure. Power, for example, emphasizes the importance of continual prodding by journalists, human rights activists, and dissident foreign service officers, who embarrass the United States and other states into assuming an interventionist stance.[32] In the absence of such external pressure, however, no interventions would have occurred. Thus Michael Ignatieff writes: "Left to themselves most political leaders in the post–Cold War era would have avoided the political risks of intervention if they could."[33]

The claim that interventions are undertaken reluctantly and that they do not serve national interests is a highly significant one, since it increases the legitimacy of the interventionist project. As noted, some key interventions (notably Kosovo) were clear violations of the UN Charter, and therefore illegal. In the absence of legality, it is especially important to endow intervention with extralegal legitimacy. The contention that the United States and its allies do not wish to intervene (and have to be shamed into doing so) helps to furnish this legitimacy.

The purported reluctance to intervene convinced some openly leftist figures, such as Christopher Hitchens, to favor intervention. This is surely a surprising turn of events, since the Left has traditionally viewed intervention as a predatory, imperialist activity.[34] Among some on the Left, however, the position gradually shifted, and their argument went as follows: In the post–Cold War period, intervention is no longer a predatory activity, since contemporary interventions are undertaken with great reluctance, and since they do little to further the interests of the intervening states. The "disinterested" character of these interventions seems reassuring to the Left. The basic argument was well stated by Hitchens himself in a cleverly entitled essay: "Never Trust Imperialists (Especially When They Turn Pacifist)."[35] It is the alleged "pacifism" of the imperialist states—their reluctance to intervene—that leftists should now protest against. If the imperialists were eager to project their power into ethnic conflicts, then we should be suspicious of their motives; but they are not eager to project it, and accordingly we have no basis for suspicion. This lack of eagerness shows that when the imperialist states finally overcome their hesitation and *do* intervene, they genuinely seek to alleviate human suffering; and they do so with few ulterior motives or hidden agendas.

The 2003 US invasion of Iraq and the extended war that followed has proven a vexing issue for the interventionist intellectuals. Some pro-interventionist figures have supported the Iraq war, since it was conducted against an obvious tyrant with a murderous record, Saddam Hussein. Longstanding neoconservative supporters of humanitarian intervention, notable among them Paul Wolfowitz, played a key role in organizing the Iraq War from within the Bush administration. And several Left-leaning (or perhaps formerly Left-leaning) figures also supported the war, on the grounds that this was an authentic humanitarian action in defense of the Iraqi people.[36] Other interventionists, however, have opposed this particular intervention, partly because they distrusted the motives of the Bush administration.[37] And needless to say, the Iraq intervention occurred in a region, the Persian Gulf, that was of obvious strategic and economic importance. The earlier arguments that humanitarian interventions do not involve selfish, great power interests are inapplicable in the Iraq case. As the Iraq War has dragged on and has produced negative effects from a humanitarian standpoint, the whole operation has become more controversial for the general public and also for intellectual advocates of intervention.[38] Overall, it seems fair to conclude that the argument in favor of humanitarian intervention in general has been weakened by the Iraq experience. However, recent calls for intervention in Darfur and Burma/Myanmar suggest that support for humanitarian intervention is far from dead.

My Critique of Humanitarian Intervention in the Former Yugoslavia

This study assesses the foregoing claims in a case study of intervention in the Yugoslav conflict. As noted, Yugoslavia has always been viewed as the most important and most influential case of humanitarian intervention ever undertaken. By examining intervention in this case, it should be possible to draw at least some tentative conclusions regarding the plausibility of the humanitarian intervention paradigm more generally. A special point of focus will be claims (by Power and others) that the Western powers were reluctant to intervene in the Yugoslav conflict, throughout the course of that conflict; that Western intervention in Bosnia and Kosovo, when it finally did occur, was motivated primarily by humanitarian concerns, rather than by power politics; and that these interventions improved human rights conditions in the region and were therefore positive steps. I contest all these points.

First, let us consider the question of motivation: The substantive portions of this book argue that purported acts of humanitarian intervention in Yugoslavia were perfectly consistent with the geo-strategic interests of the United States and other key states, as well as of private interest groups within those states. My basic argument is that during the post–Cold War period the United States was seeking to reaffirm and then strengthen its position of worldwide dominance. US policy makers resolved to take advantage of the new opportunities offered by the collapse of the Soviet Union in 1991: They sought to use this circumstance to establish a new order of unilateral US hegemony with no challengers, and to perpetuate this dominance as far into the future as possible. A closely related US objective was to find a new role for the North Atlantic Treaty Organization, which was considered a key instrument of US hegemony. The unilateralist US vision collided with the ambitions of the European Community\Union, whose member states sought to establish the Union as a major international actor, independent of the United States. Among the EU states, Germany played an especially assertive role. The United States, in turn, sought to contain these European assertions, which were increasingly viewed as a threat.

The Yugoslav conflict of the 1990s thus occurred in the context of heightened tension between the United States and Western Europe. Each sought to use the Yugoslav war to showcase its respective capabilities and to legitimate its power position. Yugoslavia was to be the principal arena in which these US-European tensions would be played out and ultimately resolved.

We will see that it was not the United States but Germany that first intervened in Yugoslavia. I present new evidence that at least several months before warfare began, Germany encouraged the republics of Slovenia and Croatia to secede from the Yugoslav federation. The European Union followed the German lead (albeit reluctantly) and acquiesced in the collapse of Yugoslavia that resulted from this action. At first, the United States was distracted by Operation Desert Storm and the breakup of the Soviet Union—both of which occurred in 1991—and was thus unable to play a decisive role in the first phases of the Balkan conflict. It was the absence of US leadership that allowed Germany (by default, to some extent) to act as the intervening power. The initial US quiescence would soon prove embarrassing, however, since it presented an image of weakness. As a result, the Bush administration shifted its policy and resolved to play a lead role in the Balkan conflict. With this policy shift, the United States would become the premier external power in the conflict. In assuming this new role, the United States sought to upstage Germany and other European states.

The main focus of this new US policy in the Balkans would be the emerging conflict in the Republic of Bosnia and Herzegovina, where war began in April 1992. Most studies claim that the Bush administration was reluctant to intervene in the Bosnia conflict and remained inactive. I argue that, on the contrary, the administration was actively involved in this conflict from its earliest phases, even before war broke out. Specifically, US officials urged Bosnian leaders to leave the Yugoslav federation and to form an independent state. At the same time, the United States undercut a series of European efforts that aimed at resolving ethnic conflict in Bosnia and preventing war.

Beginning in 1993, the incoming Clinton administration faced a dilemma with regard to Bosnia. On the one hand, the new administration sought (like its predecessor) to use the conflict as a means of reaffirming US power; on the other hand, it was reluctant to accept the risk of direct military intervention, which might have led to casualties. This phase of the war, I show, was marked by extended contention between the United States and the European Union. The main issue was whether the United States or the European Union ultimately would receive credit for ending the conflict. The European Union wished to use the conflict as a way to establish itself as an international force capable of acting independently from the United States. The United States sought to undercut these efforts and to terminate Europe's quest for an independent role. During 1993–1994, US officials continued their earlier policy of opposing EU peace plans—which sought a compromise agreement among Bosnia's ethnic groups—and effectively blocked their implementation. Partly due to US opposition, the EU mediation efforts failed. At the same time, the United States furnished military equipment to its Muslim and Croat allies in the Bosnia conflict through a large-scale covert operation. In late 1995, US officials brokered the Dayton Accords, which finally did end the war. The implementation of these Accords took place under the aegis of a NATO-directed peacekeeping force, thus accomplishing the long-standing US objective of finding a new function for NATO. At a substantive level, however, the Dayton Accords were not much different from the earlier EU-sponsored peace plans that the United States had opposed. In short, the US insistence on acting in an adversarial fashion vis-à-vis the European Union may have prolonged the Bosnia war by several years.

During 1998–1999, the United States used the Kosovo conflict to reaffirm its hegemonic role in Europe. US officials deliberately undercut a potential diplomatic solution to the Kosovo war; instead of using diplomacy to resolve the conflict, the United States sought a military solution in which NATO power could once again be demonstrated. The resulting air war, in 1999, succeeded in fully establishing the continued relevance of NATO, thus affirming US hegemony in Europe and undercutting European proclivities for foreign policy independence.

Thus, this book presents a history of external intervention in the Yugoslav conflict that differs significantly from the one presented by Samantha Power and other advocates of intervention. Contrary to Power's claims, the United States and Europe did not stand "idly by" and allow atrocities to proceed in the Balkans. On the contrary, the Western powers were deeply involved in the conflict from its very earliest phases.

The interventionist intellectuals are partly correct in their contention that the powers were reluctant to use direct *military* intervention in the Balkans, especially forms of intervention that entailed the use of ground troops in combat situations. All the major international actors—including the United States and the EU states—were wary of taking actions that might have entailed combat casualties. Despite this caution, the Western powers were willing and even enthusiastic about using diplomatic pressure, covert action, and other forms of nonmilitary intervention to achieve their objectives. And in key instances, the United States and to some extent Europe were willing to use air strikes as an additional means of advancing their interests. If we define intervention broadly, as the deliberate manipulation of the internal politics of one state by another state, then external intervention in the Yugoslav case was extensive, and it commenced early in the conflict. Previous analyses not only understate the extent of Western intervention but also fail to recognize the self-interested character of this intervention.

From a humanitarian standpoint, external involvement in Yugoslavia had negative and even disastrous consequences. Indeed, Western intervention was a major factor in triggering the country's breakup in the first place and thus set the stage for war. Successive waves of intervention that followed the initial breakup helped spread the fighting and augment the level of suffering. Intervention in the Balkan crisis did not help alleviate the humanitarian emergency.

Some will be surprised by my contentions, since they go against a widely accepted consensus about what happened in Yugoslavia. Serious readers will of course insist on substantiation for my claims, based on reasonable sources. I present such substantiation in subsequent chapters. For now, I simply remind readers that our understanding of many past conflicts has been revised based on new source materials, as well as on new interpretations of these materials. Historical interpretation is always evolving, and many previous consensus viewpoints have been reconsidered or debunked altogether. There are many examples: The traditional view of the Korean War as a clear-cut case of communist aggression is now considered overly simplistic, given new evidence regarding the origins of that conflict presented by Bruce Cumings and other scholars.[39] The image of the US role in Vietnam changed fundamentally following the 1971 publication of the Pentagon's secret study of the war's origins.[40] Evidence of CIA covert operations in Guatemala, Iran, Lebanon, and the former Belgian Congo has altered our perceptions of US policy with regard to these cases.[41] New documents released from the ex-Soviet archives cast doubt on long-standing interpretations of the 1979 Afghanistan invasion that viewed the action as a threat to the Persian Gulf.[42] Israeli historians such as Ilan Pappé and Benny Morris have brought forth new interpretations regarding the origins of the Israeli-Palestinian conflict that differ considerably from traditional views.[43] In all these instances, what once passed for a generally accepted interpretation has been dispelled. I hope that this book contributes to our understanding of Yugoslavia—and dispels some of the myths that have too long been accepted in popular and academic discussion.

Sources of Information

In researching this book, I have relied on five basic categories of primary source material. First, I have used testimony from the war crimes trial of Slobodan Milošević, which took place at the International Criminal Tribunal for the Former Yugoslavia in The Hague during the period 2001–2006.[44] Many of the key figures who were involved in the various aspects of Yugoslavia's demise testified at length, often over the course of several days, and they provide valuable insights unavailable elsewhere.[45] As one might expect, the prosecution witnesses often presented the situation in stark, black-and-white terms, arguing that Milošević was the cause of virtually all problems. However, the prosecution case also contained some surprising evidence that suggests far more complex causes for Yugoslavia's breakup and the subsequent wars.

Second, I have used published memoirs. The Yugoslav episode has produced a rich collection of memoirs, and I have made extensive use of these, especially accounts written by US and European officials. Naturally, these accounts are quite biased, and they present events from the unique standpoint of the writer. In using these sources, I have tried to remain alert to the inevitable distortions and efforts at self-promotion or exculpation that appear in memoirs.[46]

Third, my research entailed a survey of the world's press. Periodical sources too contain hidden biases, and they often reflect the foreign policy interests of the states they represent.[47] To compensate for such biases, I have used sources from a wide range of countries and perspectives, including articles in French- and German-language publications, as well as in English. I have used both general interest periodicals and more specialized publications such as business and military journals. I cite more than one hundred periodicals and media sources.

A fourth source of information is legislative hearings and investigations from the United States, Britain, and the Netherlands. The British reports were especially useful for understanding the 1999 NATO war over Kosovo. In several instances, British officials expressed their views with unexpected candor. I have also consulted the Dutch report *Srebrenica—A "Safe" Area*, which (despite its title) provides a detailed account of all aspects of Yugoslavia's breakup and the various wars that followed, through the year 1995. The six-thousand-page *Srebrenica* report was authorized by the Dutch parliament, though the investigation itself was undertaken by the Netherlands Institute for War Documentation.[48]

A fifth source is official documents from the United States, Europe, and the United Nations. While large-scale declassification of the Yugoslavia materials has not yet occurred (and is probably at least a decade in the future), some documents are already accessible to researchers through the George H. W. Bush Presidential Library, the National Security Archive, and other sources. David Owen, who served as EU mediator during the Bosnia war, has made available a sizable number of private documents pertaining to the EU and UN mediation efforts in Bosnia. The public diplomatic records of the Yugoslav crisis are now readily accessible in a series of published compilations.

A Note on Terminology

Throughout this study, I use the term "humanitarian intervention" when referring to any intervention that is widely *believed* to spring from humanitarian motives. I do this despite my suspicions that the principal motives of the intervening states are not in fact humanitarian. I use this term because alternative descriptions—such as "purported humanitarian interventions"—are stylistically awkward.

2

US Predominance and the Logic of Interventionism

> Think hard about it. I'm running out of demons. I'm
> running out of villains.
> —*Colin Powell*

One of the main functions of this book is to refute the notion that US and Western intervention in the Yugoslavia conflict was not based on any concrete interests or considerations of realpolitik. On the contrary, external intervention in Yugoslavia was based on traditional considerations of national interest, as seen in both economic and geo-strategic terms. The specific aspects of Western intervention in Yugoslavia will be explored in detail in later chapters. In this chapter, I assess the larger international context in which the conflict played out. The basic argument here is that the United States has grown accustomed to its position as the world's dominant power and has sought to preserve this status, which provides major political, economic, and prestige benefits. During the Cold War, the threat of communism served to legitimate US hegemony over other capitalist democracies; with the end of the Cold War, the United States sought to use humanitarian intervention as the principal rationale for its hegemony. True, the terrorist attacks of September 11, 2001, have provided a newer and even more potent rationale. During the 1990s, however, it was humanitarian intervention that formed the main justification for US hegemony.

A major assumption underpinning my argument is that the post–Cold War era has triggered increased tensions among the advanced capitalist democracies, which in turn required these "humanitarian" military assertions to affirm the United States' dominant position. This may sound an odd argument, given the wide assumption that America's allies have always welcomed US hegemony. Geir Lundestad referred to US hegemony over Europe during the Cold War as a case of "empire by invitation," the result of cooperative, mutually beneficial activity between the Americans and Europeans.[1] Irving Kristol popularized this view in a 1997 *Wall Street Journal* article: "One of these days, the American people are going to awaken to the fact that we have become an imperial nation. . . . It happened because the world wanted it to happen."[2] Such views are untenable. First, they ignore the ambivalence with which allies of the United States have always viewed their subordinate position. And they also ignore that US hegemony has been maintained at least in part through forceful behavior, which has undercut efforts by America's allies to establish an independent foreign policy. These challenges to US hegemony from among the ranks of its allies had always been present to some extent even during the Cold War; with the end of the Cold War, these challenges increased considerably. There was also a rise in US efforts to resist these challenges.

US foreign policy thus entailed a measure of double containment—to simultaneously contain the communist nations and America's capitalist allies in Europe. With the demise of communism, after 1989, the containment of allies remained a major US objective, although it became more difficult to achieve. Overwhelmingly, the United States sought to reassert its power through a revitalization of the Cold War institutional structures; above all, this meant a renewed US interest in the North Atlantic Treaty Organization, widely regarded as the most successful alliance structure in history. Humanitarian interventions—particularly in the Balkans—emerged as NATO's principal mission.

A Predatory Hegemon?

The theme I am developing—that rivalry among the advanced industrial states became a central issue of the early post–Cold War period—may seem anomalous, given the long period of amity that had prevailed among capitalist states. During the Cold War, the communist enemy served to unite the capitalist powers for a fixed period. It is important to note however, that the period 1945–1989 was in some sense a historical aberration. When surveying the course of international relations over a somewhat longer period—let us say the past two hundred years—one could easily conclude that conflict and adversarial relationships rather than cooperation have been the norm among capitalist states; these latent conflicts were masked and held in check for an extended period during the Cold War. As David Calleo notes, the "Cold War seems a vacation from normal history—from the economic and political problems of the modern capitalist world."[3] As a result of this vacation, the major capitalist powers were able to set aside their long-standing mutual suspicions and join together for common political and military purposes. The agent that facilitated this cooperation was, of course, US hegemony.

During the late 1960s and early 1970s, a wave of self-identified radical scholars, such as Joyce and Gabriel Kolko, argued that the United States followed an imperialist strategy after World War II that aimed at dominating Western Europe and Japan; marginalizing political tendencies (of various ideological stripes) that opposed US dominance; and dismantling European and Japanese spheres of influence in the Third World, which impeded US economic expansion.[4] Anticommunism, it was argued, legitimated these US efforts to subordinate rival capitalist powers. Much of this New Left scholarship fell from favor as intellectual fashion shifted and a period of American triumphalism appeared.[5] However, the New Left interpretation reemerged in new guises. Essentially the same arguments have been advanced by such mainstream figures as Christopher Layne and Benjamin Schwarz, who in 1993 wrote as follows:

> Two paradoxes have shaped American foreign policy. First, although the Soviet Union was the immediate focus of US security strategy, it was really quite incidental to America's liberal internationalist policy. Second, the Soviet Union's existence, ironically, was indispensable to that policy's success. . . . After World War II, Washington sought an international order based upon—to quote NSC 68's primary author, Paul Nitze—"preponderant [US] power." That objective had very little to do with any existing or projected Soviet actions; in fact, American statesmen knew that their wide-ranging objectives would increase Soviet insecurity and thereby the risk of war; . . . the basic aspiration of US security policy since the Second World War has not been to contain the Soviets.[6]

Thus, the goal was to establish a liberal order led by the United States *justified* as a response to alleged Soviet aggression. Similar views have been advanced by a range of writers, including Kees Van Der Pijl, who is a Marxist; Calleo, cited earlier, a relatively centrist figure closely connected with the Washington establishment; and Ted Galen Carpenter, affiliated with the libertarian Cato Institute.[7] Layne and Schwarz, whom I quote, were affiliated respectively with the Cato Institute and the Rand Corporation.

The Layne/Schwarz notion of an aggressive US strategy, though still a minority view, has emerged as an important intellectual current during the post–Cold War period. This interpretation does indeed explain many facets of twentieth-century history that are left unaddressed by more mainstream views that place almost exclusive emphasis on the Soviet threat and the "voluntary" character of the US-led alliance structure. The latter views gloss over the considerable resistance to US hegemony that has always been just beneath the surface in both Western Europe and Japan. This resistance emanated from two main sources. The first source was the political Left, both communist and noncommunist, which enjoyed unprecedented popularity worldwide after the end of the Second World War. Communist parties were, in the late 1940s, major forces in the political systems of Italy and France (and in Japan as well); in addition, socialist groups—of varied orientations—were also influential. Advocates of a socialist Europe were suspicious or outright hostile toward US foreign policy, which was viewed as a conservative force.

And this type of anti-US sentiment extended well beyond communist circles. In this respect it is worth considering a 1947 essay by George Orwell that advocated a European form of democratic socialism independent of both superpowers. Orwell started from the premise that a socialist system "seems to me the only worthwhile political objective today." Of the potential barriers to socialism, one of most formidable was "American hostility. If the United States remains capitalist and especially if it needs markets for exports, it cannot regard a socialist Europe with a friendly eye." To combat this US hostility, Orwell advocated a pan-European socialist federation, with spheres of influence in parts of the Middle East and Africa, presumably linked together as a common currency and trading bloc.[8] The political Left in Europe was a key impediment to US designs, and was dealt with through direct political manipulation. Samuel Huntington notes that "the United States expended billions of dollars each year attempting to influence government decisions, elections, and political outcomes in other countries," including considerable sums spent to defeat communist parties and other radical elements in Western Europe.[9] In addition, US intelligence operatives used a variety of additional means, including alliances with the Catholic Church, conservative labor unions, and organized crime networks, all to undermine radical parties and unions during the late 1940s.[10]

A second major impediment to US aspirations in Europe came from the political Right, which had a long tradition of protectionist measures, state regulation, and colonial spheres of influence. This was especially true of Great Britain, whose Imperial Preference system (in effect a sterling trade zone) placed sizable areas of the globe off limits to US economic penetration. US efforts to dismantle some of these spheres of influence caused many Europeans to wonder aloud whether the United States or the Soviet Union was really the greater threat. The normally sober *Economist* noted in 1947:

Not many people in this country believe the communist thesis that it is the deliberate and conscious aim of American policy to ruin Britain and everything Britain stands for in the world. But the evidence can certainly be read that way. And if every time that aid is extended, conditions are attached which make it impossible for Britain ever to escape the necessity of going back for still more aid, to be obtained with still more self-abasement and on still more crippling terms, then the result will certainly be what the Communists predict.[11]

There can be no question that US policy both during and after World War II sought to open previously closed European spheres of influence to trade and investment, and that such policies were a key feature of US strategy. As an illustration of the overall approach, I cite a 1943 document, written by the State Department's leading Africa specialist:

> Overseas trade will be more important than ever before to this nation in maintaining our vaunted standard of living . . . our country will not be able to maintain our heretofore standard of living or even to approximate it unless we can produce more, export more, and help by our overseas trade to all lands to raise the standard of living of backward people so that they may absorb more and more of the products of American agriculture and industry . . . We have therefore the most vital national interest in this matter. In my opinion it is not sufficient that there be a condition of joint world leadership by Great Britain and the United States . . . [The US cannot tolerate] agreements which would relegate *in any area of the world* American influence . . . to a secondary position. [emphasis added][12]

Another US official, more succinctly, stated that "the British empire as it existed in the past, will never reappear and . . . the United States will have to take its place."[13] The result was a considerable measure of friction. The benign hegemony argument—which emphasizes the European eagerness for external leadership—ignores the fact that important segments of European opinion, from a range of political perspectives, did not share US objectives. The argument also overlooks strenuous US efforts to undermine opposition and manipulate outcomes.

The Cold War was on the surface a bipolar conflict, but the image obscured a considerable measure of complexity. The later fissures in the communist bloc became well known. However, there were also important fissures within the US-led alliance—fissures that appear considerably more important in hindsight than they appeared at the time. The French tendency to challenge American leadership during and after the presidency of Charles de Gaulle was especially noteworthy in this respect. De Gaulle criticized US domination of NATO, leading to a French departure from the joint military command and the permanent removal of NATO headquarters from Paris to Brussels (although France remained a part of the alliance's political structure). France jealously protected its influence in sub-Saharan Africa from perceived US incursions; De Gaulle's special advisor on Africa policy, Jacques Foccart, became "virtually the main enemy of United States diplomacy in Africa." Foccart's staff "saw the United States, not China or Russia, as the main enemy."[14] The international role of the dollar, and alleged US abuse of its privileged monetary position, was an additional object of Gaullist criticism ("The Americans only used the atom device twice on Asia . . . but they use the dollar on Europe every day").[15]

Criticism of US leadership was not confined to France. Not a single European country was willing to assist America's lackluster war effort in Vietnam, and this lack of allied support was a source of bitterness among US officials; from Europe, the war was regarded as misguided and irresponsible.[16] During the 1970s, the Nixon-Kissinger tendency to undertake unilateral actions without consulting America's allies—such as the 1971 decision to devalue the dollar and to abandon free convertibility into gold—was widely resented.[17] Further unilateralist US actions in the area of energy policy during the gasoline shortages of 1973–1975 generated additional grievances.[18]

Thus, the Pax Americana was far from an unambiguous benefit to America's allies, who continued to harbor significant reservations about the whole project. However, these reservations had always been held in check by three factors: First and most obviously, the Americans presented "free" security against the possibility of a Soviet invasion. Few seriously believed that direct Soviet aggression was a probability;[19] however, it was widely considered a hypothetical possibility throughout the Cold War, owing to the numerical superiority of Warsaw Pact conventional forces in central Europe.[20] The Atlantic alliance offered an additional advantage, at least for more conservative Europeans: The United States was a reliable bulwark against the possibility of radical social change, and there was an understanding that the Americans would work behind the scenes against any prospective government by the Far Left.[21] Many upper-class Europeans (and also some conservative trade unionists) slept better at night as a result. This aspect of the Cold War represented a tacit alliance between European elites and US foreign policy, which shared a deep apprehension of the political Left. Third, US hegemony was, at least for most of the Cold War, associated with economic prosperity, especially on the European continent, as indicated by the figures in Table 2.1.

Economic growth during the early period of the Cold War was far above historical averages; throughout the industrialized world, there was full or near full employment, combined with advanced welfare states. And the economic growth was beneficial to nearly every segment of society, with major improvements in the material conditions of the working classes. Whether this prosperity was actually caused by the US hegemony is debatable; the

Table 2.1. Average Annual Growth Rates (%) in Total Output for France, Germany, and Italy

	1870–1913	1913–1950	1950–1959	1960–1969
France	1.6	0.7	4.6	5.8
Germany*	2.9	1.2	7.8	4.8
Italy	1.4	1.3	5.8	5.7

Source: Statistics from Herman Van Der Wee, *Prosperity and Upheaval: The World Economy, 1945–1980* (Berkeley: University of California Press, 1987), 50.

*West Germany after 1945.

fact that prosperity coincided with US hegemony contributed to the political legitimacy of the project.

European leftists could still fantasize about the prospect of a "Europe without America," but during the Cold War this was never a serious possibility.[22] In recent decades, however, each of the three factors which undergirded the legitimacy of US hegemony has gradually eroded. First, the period of economic prosperity clearly came to an end during the 1973–1975 recession, and it never returned. Thereafter, economic conditions in Europe have entailed much slower rates of growth, combined with permanently high unemployment in many countries. Second, the radical Left parties, rather than benefiting from the new, more rigorous economic conditions, gradually declined or, alternatively, diminished the radical content of their programs. This process was already far advanced during the 1980s and has accelerated since then. Tony Blair's neoliberal "Third Way" was only the most obvious public manifestation of a more basic trend.[23] Although there were some contrary tendencies—such as the surprising resiliency of the former East German Communist party and the 1995 French general strike—the basic picture was one of an increasingly domesticated Left. And of course in 1989 the military threat posed by the Warsaw Pact ceased to exist as a realistic possibility. By 1991, with the final breakup and dissolution of the Soviet Union, the danger of an invasion from the East could no longer be entertained by anyone.

US Hegemony Triumphant, 1989–1991

The initial reaction to the end of the Cold War was an augmentation in American prestige, which reached remarkable heights during 1989–1991.[24] Many saw the victory over communism as not only a political victory, but also an ideological and even cultural victory for free market capitalism and the US way of life. What has now been termed "American triumphalism" was briefly shared by much of the world, in Western Europe and practically everywhere else as well. The US-led victory over Iraqi forces in the Gulf War of 1991—achieved with an unprecedented degree of international consensus—increased US prestige still further. And there can be little doubt that the popularity of US consumer culture translated into some measure of "soft power," which was advantageous for US foreign policy.[25]

It is also important to note that the transatlantic unity that characterized this period was based on a common policy agenda. US and European elites were in agreement that the formerly communist states of Eastern Europe were to be restructured as new outposts for the free market. The capitalist powers sought to privatize the Eastern economies as quickly as possible; to open them to foreign investment; and to ensure that these changes would be permanent and that there would be no going back to a socialist system. On the other hand, there were clear impediments to this objective: Socialist (or partially socialist) economic models retained residual popularity in Eastern Europe, even in states where the Communist parties themselves had been discredited. In the context of the 1989 Velvet Revolution, a poll found that 47 percent of Czechoslovaks still favored a state-controlled economy, and another 43 percent wanted a mixture of state and private control; only 3 percent said they wanted unfettered capitalism.[26] And it should not be forgotten that in several Eastern European states—Bulgaria, Albania, and parts of Yugoslavia—the former Communist parties won reasonably free elections during 1989–1990.

Thus, it was not immediately clear that the Eastern Europeans themselves would welcome the rapid introduction of a market economy. Nevertheless, both the United States and Western Europe were determined to implement their neoliberal agenda in the East, and they used all means of diplomatic pressure and economic leverage to achieve this objective. The United States and Europe sought to maintain the Cold War system of export controls as a source of influence over the new postcommunist states. It also was made clear to the new Eastern governments that economic aid and debt relief—through the IMF or other institutions—would be conditioned on rapid implementation of market reforms.[27] In the next chapter, we will see that these policies had a major impact on political developments in Yugoslavia and contributed to its disintegration as a unified state.

In all these initiatives, it was the United States that led the way, but it did so with considerable support from Western Europe. The efforts to create a neoliberal Eastern Europe, and to achieve this objective quickly, were joint projects by the United States and Western Europe, which acted in concert to a considerable degree. Even the social democratic parties collaborated with the efforts to impose laissez-faire, as noted by Peter Gowan:

Particularly striking has been the acquiescence and collusion of the social democrats of Western Europe. . . . Much of this drive [for a capitalist
Eastern Europe] has passed through a European Union in which the Left
controls a majority within the European Parliament and in whose Commission the presiding genius is a French socialist [Jacques Delors]. The
Social Democrats along with the Christian Democrats [have expressed
some reservations] . . . yet they have not raised their voices against the
demand that entry into the world economy be conditional upon sweep-
ing privatizations.[28]

These policies were predicated upon a widely held ideological objective that
German chancellor Helmut Kohl succinctly stated: "We have won; . . . Socialism, communism are dead."[29] The years 1989–1991 thus represented a
brief period of consensus among Europeans, and also between Europe and
the United States. It was the high point of transatlantic unity. This unity
would be short-lived, however, and it would be replaced by a new phase of
conflict.

Renascent Challenges to US Hegemony

In the triumphalist atmosphere of the early 1990s, most Europeans were eager to forget their old quarrels with the United States. What is interesting is
how quickly this atmosphere evaporated. By the middle of the decade, a new
era of anti-US sentiment emerged worldwide, especially in Europe. There
are many indications of this sentiment, but let us begin with a poll taken in
France in 1996.[30] In that year, a plurality of French adults viewed the United
States with antipathy. When asked which words they most associated with
the United States, the answers were mostly negative: The top associations
with America were "violence" (59 percent), "power" (57 percent), "inequalities" (45 percent), and "racism" (39 percent). There was, however, one segment
of French society that was consistently favorable toward the United States,
but disturbingly, these were supporters of the extreme right-wing, racist National Front Party. The association of the United States with xenophobia and
racism seemed complete, and it was true even among right-wing admirers of
the US way of life.

It is easy to dismiss this poll as simply another example of a distinctive
French brand of anti-Americanism, but clearly this is an insufficient analy-
sis. In fact, the French have *not* always harbored anti-American sentiments.
In a 1988 poll, a majority of French adults held favorable views of the United
States.[31] The main conclusion must be a substantial growth of anti-American
sentiment following the end of the Cold War. And it is clear that the rise

of anti-Americanism was not confined to France. Writing in 1995, British economist Susan Strange criticized the "natural (but destructive) unilateralist tendency in the US political system. Today . . . the only way to remove the present hegemonic, do-nothing veto on better global governance [exercised by the United States] is to build, bit by bit, a compelling opposition based on European-Japanese cooperation but embracing wherever possible the Latin Americans, Asians, and Africans."[32] In 1998, a British diplomat stated: "One reads about the world's desire for American leadership only in the United States. Everywhere else one reads about American arrogance and unilateralism."[33] Even the *Economist* lamented how "successive American governments have seen the corpus of international law as a useful device to restrain or vilify other nations, while refusing to let it apply to their own. . . . How can the United States get away with this?"[34] Though we have been focusing on Western Europe, it is worth noting the rise in anti-US sentiment in Russia (despite the strongly pro-US sentiments that appeared immediately after the dissolution of the Soviet Union). By early 1999, the liberal Moscow weekly *Moskovskiye Novosti* reflected on the growing hostility toward the United States in Russian novels, and offered this assessment:

> The depiction of our overseas neighbor [the United States] in the Soviet era was more sympathetic. The object of hatred was the fat capitalist with the cigar or the hawkish general with an atomic bomb under his arm rather than the ordinary American. But in today's novels, the right class origin will not save anyone. On the contrary, it is held against all Americans. "They were earth diggers, and they're still earth diggers," writes [Yuri] Nikitin. "Now they have just picked up university diplomas and degrees and run banks and trusts." The American is seen as a cunning, independent peasant—a loafer and a parasite.[35]

In recent years, it has become fashionable to assume that George W. Bush created much of the world's hostility toward US leadership. It should not be forgotten, however, that anti-Americanism was already rising during the 1990s, several years before Bush came to power.

The increasing tendency to doubt the value of US hegemony, to regard it as a mere expression of self-interest and exploitation, received little attention from the US press at the time; the more benign view of US power, exemplified by the quote from Irving Kristol noted earlier, was much more typical. But there were some interesting exceptions. Samuel Huntington, who for a generation epitomized the close connection between academia and US hegemony, adopted a reassessment that was decidedly noncelebratory in tone. Writing in *Foreign Affairs* in 1999, he ridiculed official rhetoric:

"American officials ... boast of American power and American virtue, hailing the United States as a benevolent hegemon." He quotes Madeleine Albright, who "has called the United States 'the indispensable nation' and said that 'we stand tall and hence see further than other nations.' This statement is true in the narrow sense that the United States is an indispensable participant in any effort to tackle major global problems. It is false in also implying that other nations are dispensable ... and that American indispensability is a source of wisdom."[36] Huntington then goes on to demolish the image of a benign America:

> [The United States has] attempted or been perceived as attempting more or less unilaterally to do the following: ... promote American corporate interests under the slogans of free trade and open markets; shape World Bank and International Monetary Fund policies to serve those same corporate interests; intervene in local conflicts in which it has relatively little direct interest; bludgeon other countries to adopt economic and social policies that will benefit American economic interests; promote American arms sales abroad while attempting to prevent comparable sales by other countries; force out one UN secretary-general and dictate the appointment of his successor; expand NATO initially to include Poland, Hungary, and the Czech Republic and no one else; undertake military action against Iraq and later maintain harsh economic sanctions against the regime; and categorize certain countries as "rogue states," excluding them from global institutions because they refuse to kowtow to American wishes.[37]

It would go beyond this discussion to assess whether and to what extent these charges were accurate. What I will note is the increasing *perception* that the United States had become a predatory hegemon, using its power to advance its own parochial interests and to do so at the expense of other countries. It must be recognized that, for better or worse, such perceptions were widely accepted, even among America's allies.

The US Reaction

From the very beginning, US officials saw these transatlantic strains as a threat to their continuing hegemony, and they sought to contain the resulting tensions. In essence, US officials responded to the new threats by seeking to retain the main institutions of the Cold War for as long as possible, on the assumption that this would be the most efficacious way to maintain US political power in Europe. Recreating the Cold War, or at least some plausible substitute for it, was a general theme of US foreign policy during the 1990s, as implied in the epigraph from Colin Powell with which we began this chapter. American officials, both uniformed and civilian, very much missed the legitimacy that the struggle against communism conferred on US hegemony on the one hand, and the concomitant subordination of America's allies which resulted from this hegemony on the other. When President Bill Clinton admitted, "I miss the Cold War," he was no doubt expressing a widely held sentiment.[38] There was thus an effort to revive the complex system of alliances that the United States had forged in the course of the Cold War.

There was a special effort to retain the North Atlantic Treaty Organization, which was considered the most important of these alliances. NATO was regarded as a key structure for maintaining US hegemony in Europe, and the importance of the Atlantic alliance cannot be overstated: Henry Kissinger wrote in 1994 that the alliance was "the prize for victory in the Cold War. . . . In the process, America was tied to Europe by permanent consultative institutions and an integrated military command system." NATO was the linchpin of US hegemony in Europe or, in Kissinger's words, "the principal institutional link between America and Europe."[39] In Europe, officials were less restrained. Gabriel Robin, former French representative to NATO, wrote that the alliance's "real function, which surpasses all others, is to serve as the chaperon of Europe. . . . [It is] the means to prevent [Europe] from establishing itself as an independent fortress and perhaps one day . . . a rival."[40] It was through the alliance that America was not only a European power, but the dominant European power. NATO thus emerged as a paradoxical institution during the post–Cold War era: It was nominally a military alliance to guard against external military threats. But its real function was to maintain US predominance in Europe.

And it was also in Europe that US hegemony faced its most potent, concrete threat: the increasing importance of the European Community/Union, as well as the Union's proclivity for independent action. The EU threat was threefold: First, its size—measured in terms of total GDP—made the Union one of the largest economic units in the world. The economic strength of the European Union made it a threat to US hegemony, potentially more formidable at least in the medium term than any other power center, including China. Second, political changes were underway within the European Union that threatened to increase its independence from the United States. During the period of the Cold War, it was in fact France that was the most recalcitrant of America's allies, but French anti-Americanism was easily caricatured and dismissed in Anglophone circles as a mere eccentricity of French political culture. During the post–Cold War period, however, Germany began to join France in openly advocating European independence. Undoubtedly, the German assertiveness was influenced by the new opportunities that attended reunification in 1990. It was clearly the dominant power within the European Union, and Germany, in close cooperation with France, became a forceful advocate for increased European autonomy. Josef Joffe, foreign editor of Munich's *Süeddeutsche Zeitung*, observed that "the old days when Germany was tied to the United States by a distinct security dependence, are irretrievably gone."[41] And this German assertiveness evoked considerable hostility from US officials during the early 1990s.[42]

Third, the European Union began to adopt specific measures to implement a more independent policy, termed the Common Foreign and Security Policy (CFSP).[43] For the member states of the Union, the CFSP seemed a natural progression. The European Union had after all begun in the 1950s as an organization that dealt with relatively narrow economic and technical issues, and had gradually matured into a multifaceted organization with a broad range of functions. A common foreign and military policy seemed a next logical step. And, more germane to our discussion, it offered the Europeans a chance to establish an independent world role more commensurate with the size and economic weight of the combined European states. In early 1991, French president François Mitterrand and German chancellor Helmut Kohl began exploring new ways of pooling Europe's military resources. The two leaders proposed that the Western European Union (WEU) should be established as a key element of an integrated foreign and military policy.[44] The EU members approved this idea in 1992 at the historic Maastricht conference. In addition, France and Germany—traditionally the centers of power within the European Union—announced that they would step up bilateral military relations. Thus began the formation of a Franco-German army corps. Though the new corps was strictly speaking a bilateral measure undertaken outside the EU structure, it was presented as the nucleus of a pan-European army that other EU members would be expected to join in time. The new military force was provocatively termed the "Eurocorps." The possibility of an independent European foreign and military policy was immediately viewed—on both sides of the Atlantic—as a potential threat to NATO. European governments, especially the French, were openly seeking to reduce US influence on the continent (even while they emphasized that they did not seek a complete break with the Americans). French officials, especially in the Foreign Ministry, frankly stated that the objective of establishing these pan-European military instruments was to dilute US influence in Europe.[45]

As early as 1991, European Commission president Jacques Delors wrote (with characteristic understatement): "There are also friendly powers, which seem to fear the development of a European identity."[46] European military integration was singled out for criticism and led to a series of incidents during 1991–1992: The State Department's senior Europeanist, Reginald Bartholomew, bluntly warned European governments "not to set up any kind of caucus which might preempt NATO decisions," while former defense secretary Casper Weinberger stated that the Eurocorps was "an attempt to undermine NATO."[47] National Security Advisor Brent Scowcroft wrote directly to Chancellor Kohl and complained about German "ingratitude, despite American support for reunification."[48] And President George Bush himself issued a delicately worded threat: "Our premise is that the American role in the defense and the affairs of Europe will not be made superfluous by European union. If our premise is wrong, if my friends, your ultimate aim is to provide individually for your own defense, the time to tell us is today."[49] The United States began to actively undermine European military integration. US officials lobbied European governments to oppose the French-German initiative, especially with regard to the proposed Eurocorps. According to one account: "Senior German officials say they continue to feel intense US pressure to back off plans for a European army corps and to make unspecified but apparently unending displays of their commitment to NATO.... US officials [are] lobbying smaller European countries to stay out of the developing German-French Eurocorps."[50]

Increased European assertiveness in the military field was matched by new initiatives in the area of financial policy. Specifically, the 1991 Maastricht conference ratified a plan for increased financial integration, with the eventual aim of a single, unified European currency, the euro, to be launched in January 1999. Though the euro was advanced as a technical means to achieve an integrated European market, it was clear from the start that it would also have major political implications: The euro would almost certainly pose a threat to the status of the US dollar as the international reserve currency. Since the dollar had long been regarded as a major source of US power in world affairs, the advent of the euro posed a more general threat to America's predominant position. In addition, the euro posed a threat to the important seigniorage advantages that accrue to the United States as the issuer of the world's key currency.

C. Fred Bergsten would later note: "The euro is likely to challenge the international financial dominance of the dollar." Bergsten also predicted a considerable increase in the scale of transatlantic economic disputes: "The end of the Cold War has sharply reduced the importance of the US military might for Europe and pulled aside the security blanket that often allowed both sides to cover up or resolve their economic disputes for the greater good of preserving the anticommunist alliance."[51] The *New Republic* called the advent of the euro one of "the most significant challenges to American foreign policy since the end of the Cold War." It was being pushed by the French who sought to "convert a united Europe into an alternative world power to the United States."[52] And the Europeans advanced some inflammatory accusations of their own: In 1992–1993, key European leaders claimed that the United States was undermining European financial cooperation by orchestrating speculative attacks against key currencies.[53] To many Europeans, it seemed that the United States sought to sabotage the euro even before it was launched.

The Pentagon's Reassessment of US Hegemony

> Without the Cold War, what's the point
> of being an American?
>   —*John Updike*

In early 1992, these latent tensions caused US officials to reassess US strategy.[54] The new strategic logic was presented in the 1992 Defense Planning Guidance (DPG) document, drafted under the direction of Paul Wolfowitz, the undersecretary of defense, and Zalmay Khalilzad, then a young protégé of Wolfowitz, with strong support from Secretary of Defense Dick Cheney.[55] This document offered a comprehensive reassessment of world politics for the post-Soviet era, and its influence was considerable. A draft of the DPG was leaked to the *New York Times*, which published excerpts on March 8, 1992.[56]

In essence, the Defense Planning Guidance argued that the United States should establish permanent global dominance, and that all potential challengers—even if they emerged from the ranks of US allies—must be restrained:

> Our first objective is to prevent the re-emergence of a new rival either on the territory of the former Soviet Union or elsewhere. . . . This is a dominant consideration underlying the new regional defense strategy. . . . There are three additional aspects to this objective: First, the US must show the leadership necessary to establish and protect a new order that holds the promise of *convincing potential competitors that they need not aspire to a greater role* or pursue a more aggressive posture to protect their legitimate interests. Second, in the non-defense areas, we must account sufficiently for the interests of the advanced industrial nations to discourage them from challenging our leadership or seeking to overturn the established political and economic order. Finally, we must maintain

the mechanisms for *deterring potential competitors from even aspiring to a larger regional or global role.* [emphasis added][57]

Although there was the conciliatory statement that the United States would take account of "the interests of the advanced industrial nations," the document contained a belligerent tone. The DPG outlined an offensive, even imperial, strategic stance.

Perhaps the most controversial aspect of the DPG document was the frankness with which it sought to find new enemy states as replacements for the USSR. Russia and China were of course singled out as potential threats, but the search for enemies did not stop with these two states. The document drafters also observed that Germany and Japan might rearm, which could lead to "military rivalry" with the United States.[58] The document implied—in all seriousness—that Germany and Japan might emerge as military threats to the United States. The European Union was regarded with suspicion as yet another potential adversary. While the DPG expressed support for some degree of European military integration, presumably on grounds of economy, the United States would actively block European efforts to establish an independent foreign and military policy: "*we must seek to prevent the emergence of Europe-only security arrangements* which would undermine NATO, particularly the alliance's integrated command structure" (emphasis added).[59] The document also emphasized the need to strengthen NATO as an institutional alternative to the European Union.

In recent discussions, it has become fashionable to view Wolfowitz and his neoconservative followers as idealists who seek to export US values abroad. Little of this alleged idealism is visible, however, in the Defense Planning Guidance document. In the sections that have become public, the DPG made only the most cursory mention of democracy promotion or human rights. The basic thrust of the document was hyperrealist: The United States now had the opportunity to become a unilateralist hegemon without restraints. US policy makers should seize this opportunity and perpetuate America's power. Other countries would have no choice but to accept their subordinate status.

In retrospect, the DPG strategy has brought mixed success (at least when it is viewed from the standpoint of its neoconservative drafters). On the one hand, it has not been particularly effective in restraining the power of Russia or China, which have emerged as even more effective challengers to US dominance since the time when the DPG was written. On the other hand, the strategy has been far more effective in restraining America's allies, most notably Western Europe, and preventing them from adopting an independent foreign policy. The document's effectiveness in this regard has been amply demonstrated by recent events: Even the very unilateralist actions of the George W. Bush administration and the controversy relating to the 2003 Iraq invasion have not threatened the basic integrity of the Atlantic alliance or NATO.[60] And it should also be noted that several European governments (including some that opposed the Iraq war) have cooperated to a significant degree with Bush's larger "war on terror"—including the more unsavory aspects of that war.[61] For better or worse, the Wolfowitz doctrine helped preserve the structure of America's Cold War alliance system.

Whatever its long-term effects, the DPG document itself was indeed provocative. Academics who read the document expressed unease at both the content and the tone. John Lewis Gaddis commented in 1992, "I was a little surprised somebody would put this kind of thing down on paper," while two political scientists saw the need to quote the DPG at length because "we feared that we would not be believed if we put all of this in our own words."[62] After criticism from the press, Congress, and allied governments, Bush administration officials distanced themselves from the document and sought to minimize its importance.[63] It is clear, however, that the document reflected the basic thrust of post–Cold War US policy during the first Bush presidency and to some extent during the Clinton presidency as well. Journalist James Mann, who interviewed many of the key figures involved in the DPG controversy, provides this account:

> Wolfowitz [later] argued that the ideas his office drafted in 1992 [in the original DPG document] had turned into the consensus, mainstream view of America's post–Cold War defense strategy. That claim may have been an exaggeration, but only a slight one. Over the following eight years of the Clinton administration, the Democrats did not specifically embrace the vision that America should operate as the world's sole superpower or that it should work to block other nations from emerging as rivals to the United States. Yet the Democrats' rhetoric and policies conformed in many respects to the ideas put forward by Wolfowitz's staff in 1992.[64]

The 1992 DPG may be seen as a blueprint for a bipartisan foreign policy, one that favored unrestrained US dominance.[65] These ideas seem inconsistent with a "benign" US hegemony, universally welcomed by its allies.

The controversy over the Defense Planning Guidance was to have a direct impact on US-European tensions. The publication of the document probably intimidated European leaders and caused them to doubt the wisdom of challenging US leadership. Several additional factors restrained the European

Union. First, long-standing fissures among the EU members intensified during this period. Britain had always been the most reliably pro-US element in Europe, and the "special relationship" initially seemed to grow stronger with the end of the Cold War. Britain became a forceful advocate of the US position and acted as a counterpoint to the German-French efforts aimed at greater independence.[66] Second, smaller European countries continued to feel jealousy toward the German-French tendency to dominate decision making within the European Union. And, third, there was the long-standing fear of a reunited Germany. Many Europeans preferred some degree of US influence to offset the prospect of German or possibly German-French dominance within the European Union. Finally, European officials throughout the Union wished to avoid a complete termination of the Atlantic alliance; some propitiation of the United States was clearly necessary.[67]

The idea of an independent European foreign policy was thus weakened somewhat during the period 1992–1994. European leaders now began to emphasize that the WEU was intended to complement and not compete with NATO. The new strategy was formalized at the January 1994 NATO summit, where NATO and the WEU were to be integrated through Combined Joint Task Forces. The following year, the French agreed in principle to resume its participation in NATO's military command structure, from which France had been absent since 1966.[68] The Eurocorps was activated, as planned in 1995. In addition to France and Germany, it was joined by units from Belgium, Luxembourg, and Spain, and had a full strength of fifty thousand troops. However, the Eurocorps too had been modified to conciliate the Americans. The Europeans agreed to an accord which provides "for the Eurocorps' subordination to SACEUR"—the Supreme Allied Commander, Europe, invariably a US officer.[69] In an interview, the first commander of the Eurocorps, Germany's Lt. Gen. Helmut Willmann, went out of his way to link the Eurocorps to NATO: The Eurocorps would "complement US assets and this will benefit NATO. Any idea of competition would be wrong and has to be excluded."[70] At the same time, the United States continued to jealously guard its dominance within NATO and firmly refused French suggestions that a European should be appointed chief of NATO's southern command.[71] Thus, early efforts at a foreign and military policy that was substantially independent of NATO were undermined. US efforts to domesticate the WEU and the Eurocorps were initially successful. We will see that the more basic transatlantic rift that had undergirded the specific dispute regarding EU military posture was far from settled. But for the moment at least, the Americans had succeeded in their efforts to undermine European military independence.

Eastward Expansion

These undertakings to protect NATO against European actions constituted the "reactive" side of US strategy. Another strategy—a more affirmative one, it might be said—has been to find new, additional functions for NATO to give the organization a new lease on life. The most important of these efforts has been to expand NATO and to incorporate portions of Eastern Europe under the US military umbrella. The concept of eastward expansion was broached as early as 1992, in the Defense Planning Guidance document. In 1999, expansion was implemented and Poland, Hungary, and the Czech Republic joined NATO as full members.

Eastward expansion served a vital function by giving NATO a new purpose—preserving order in Eastern Europe—which could serve at least as a partial replacement for the older and now obsolete objective of preventing a Soviet invasion. Expansion also served to alienate postcommunist Russia, thus generating a new threat to the stability of central Europe.[72] It may seem paradoxical that US policy actually has created new threats; but finding threats and enemies was a basic theme for post–Cold War foreign policy. And finding threats in Europe was salutary for preserving NATO and establishing a plausible function for the alliance.

Officials during this period were anxious about the *lack* of threats and the lack of any plausible function for NATO. In 1992, Senator William Roth called for a major reevaluation of the alliance and warned that if a plausible function were not found, "then it is our duty as US legislators to point out that this emperor has no clothes, that, tragically, NATO has degenerated into an alliance in name only and sadly, it is no longer deserving of our support or membership." (This quote appeared in an article entitled, "NATO Seeks Significance in a Post–Cold War Climate.")[73] In 1995, a French diplomat ridiculed NATO's military activities as mere "amusements of a strategic fiction."[74] The initial lack of any obvious function was becoming an embarrassment, and something had to be done. Secretary of State Warren Christopher noted that "the alliance faced a 'historic choice.' It could 'embrace innovation' and find a new purpose, or it could go on as it had for almost fifty years and 'risk irrelevance' and perhaps break up."[75] Eastward expansion helped forestall the possibility of irrelevance and breakup.

In addition, eastward expansion reinforced one of the alliance's original functions: to maintain—and indeed to augment—the US role as the dominant power on the European continent. Expansion reinforced US hegemony and precluded an independent Europe. According to an article in *Air Force Magazine*:

It is this prospect—the specter of Europe without NATO—that deeply troubles US leaders. . . . For Washington, an important if unstated goal is to ensure continued US influence in the affairs of Europe and to have a major say in Eastern European security developments. . . . For half a century NATO has served as a mechanism for exerting that influence, providing Washington's all important bridge to the continent. Eastward expansion would ensure that the US would be able to play a similar role in the nations emerging from the old Soviet empire.[76]

Thus, expansion helped reinforce NATO's central mission, that is, to serve as an instrument for subordinating Europe to US interests.

It is worth recalling the opinion of Christopher Layne and Benjamin Schwarz that the Cold War enabled the United States to contain simultaneously both the Soviets and the Europeans. The United States, they argue, used the context provided by the Cold War to establish itself as the dominant power in Europe. One can see that during the post–Cold War period, eastward expansion provided a new rationale for US dominance. To be sure, the new strategic logic had its flaws: The defense of Eastern Europe against a series of hypothetical and ill-defined threats lacked the legitimacy and instant public support that "defense against the communist threat" conferred upon US hegemony in an earlier era—but at least it was something.

NATO expansion accomplished several additional objectives. Expansion was strongly supported by vested interests in the United States, most obviously that cluster of interests known as the military-industrial complex. According to a 1998 article in the *New York Times*: "American arms manufacturers who stand to gain billions of dollars in sales of weapons, communication equipment, and other military equipment if the Senate approves NATO expansion, have made enormous investments in lobbyists and campaign contributions to promote their cause in Washington."[77] One lobbyist commented succinctly, "We want them [the Eastern Europeans] to buy American."[78] And the military-industrial complex favored NATO in other ways, apart from direct lobbying. Such military contractors as Boeing, Motorola, TRW, and United Technologies each paid $250,000 for the privilege of participating in NATO's fiftieth anniversary in 1999 as official corporate hosts. And many other corporate interests, including Eastman-Kodak, Ford, and General Motors, also emerged as public promoters of NATO, presumably because of the political entrée that NATO provides for US corporations in both Eastern and Western Europe.[79]

The uniformed military too benefited from the alliance's reinvigoration, which attended eastward expansion. Certainly, US officers did not wish to lose NATO, which was the crown jewel of the military's overseas establishment. In 1993, a retired US admiral stated:

> Let me tell you one of the reasons you hear so many contrived arguments for continuing the NATO alliance. It has been very, very good for the militaries of the countries involved. . . . [In] the United States alone, for example, almost 25 percent of all of the admirals and generals on duty today owe their stars to their NATO assignment. If NATO goes away, all those jobs go away, all those lovely chateaus, and chauffeurs, and railroad cars go away. It's something that has been very enjoyable for a good many years and the fact that there's no longer any requirement for it doesn't mean they don't want to keep a good thing going.[80]

It is well understood that bureaucracies do not wish to go out of business, even after their purported functions cease to exist.[81] Instead institutions seek new functions—and with eastward expansion, NATO had found its new function. Expansion facilitated NATO's bureaucratic self-preservation, and this was an important end in itself. Thus, a range of vested interests benefited from NATO's continued existence, and also its expansion.

Finally, eastward expansion served to consolidate the US position in a new sphere of influence, and to check the influence of competitor states. It initially appeared that the Europeans, and especially the Germans, might become dominant in the East—and this prospect evoked jealousy in Washington.[82] It would also seem likely that US business interests viewed this German assertiveness in a negative light. The expansion of NATO ensured that German influence would at least be diluted to a certain degree, especially in the key countries of Poland, Hungary, and the Czech Republic. NATO expansion was thus a major component of the overall US strategy of reaffirming its hegemonic status through a revival of Cold War institutional structures.

And so, NATO had a new function. Nevertheless, the view of NATO as an instrument of US domination remained widespread among European analysts.[83] And the conflicts between Europe and the United States were not altogether resolved. On the contrary, US-European discord in the area of military affairs continued through the end of the decade. Despite their previous commitments, the French never fully rejoined NATO's joint military command, and they continued to criticize perceived US arrogance.[84] As late as 1999, the *Economist* noted: "Many French politicians and businessmen . . . want to create not just a defense identity for the European Union but also a common front against the English-speaking world. It is in that context that they—and quite a few Germans—see such events as the recent merging of their defense-manufacturing giants."[85] The US establishment viewed with considerable apprehension the successful launch of the euro as a pan-European currency in January 1999.[86] The underlying transatlantic tension remained an active feature of the international relations in this era.

The disputes between the United States and Europe just outlined provide vital context for understanding our larger topic, humanitarian intervention. As we have seen, the revival of NATO was a central objective of US policy during the 1990s. The problem was that NATO remained essentially a *military* alliance, with a military function. The fact that its military role remained extremely vague was a source of frustration for both uniformed and civilian officials. Some specific military task was required to legitimate NATO's post–Cold War existence. We shall see that humanitarian intervention in the Balkans helped furnish this legitimacy, and provided the alliance with a plausible function.

The Threat of Trade Blocs

To this point, our focus has been primarily on political disputes among the advanced capitalist countries, especially between the United States and Western Europe. Overwhelmingly, these disputes have been presented as disagreements among various states and their respective governments, each seeking to advance their relative power and prestige. In this section, the scope of analysis broadens to consider how politically driven disputes between the US and Europe interacted with the international political economy.

The basic issue was this: International economic relations during the 1990s were characterized by high levels of multilateral trade and investment, mediated by a series of institutions that were global in scope—a set of conditions that denotes the phenomenon of globalization. Contrary to popular belief, the process of globalization has not always been associated with improved macroeconomic performance.[87] However, there is no doubt that globalization benefited certain elite business groups, especially though not exclusively in the United States. Indeed, recent research emphasizes that the dominant factions of US business, especially in banking and certain sectors of manufacturing, have had an internationalist bent, and they are promoters of globalization.[88]

US domination of international economic institutions—which undergirded globalization—provides asymmetrical benefits to US investors, a point that was well understood by the investors themselves. As one banker noted in testimony to Congress: "I think that one of the tremendous advantages of the IMF to the United States is the *appearance* of a somewhat arm's-length relationship that has helped us to get a lot of things done because it is not the United States imposing standards. . . . That has worked to our advantage, and I just would like to emphasize that we at least attempt to project that arm's-length relationship, because it will serve our purposes quite well" (emphasis added).[89] Expressing a similar view, economist Rudiger Dornbusch described the IMF as "a tool of the United States to pursue its policy offshore."[90] And the US government benefited from globalization in another way: The liberalization of international finance freed up capital and helped finance chronic US international accounts deficits. US Treasury bonds and other dollar-denominated debt service instruments were more attractive to foreign purchasers due to the unique function of the dollar in the international economy.[91]

Thus, a wide range of interest groups within both the public and private sectors of the United States favored the continuation of economic globalization. However, there was growing fear, throughout the 1990s, that tensions among the advanced industrialized countries might result in a breakdown of globalization and lead to a new, more protectionist system. Renascent isolationist tendencies within the United States, indicated by the intermittent popularity of Patrick Buchanan, were an additional concern. There was a direct connection between these economic issues and the more "political" disputes discussed earlier: NATO was widely viewed as assurance that the economic ties which had bound Europe and America in the past would continue, and that the prospect of protectionism could be forestalled. The US-Japan security treaty served a similar function in the Far East.

Before examining these issues in depth, however, I emphasize that there was indeed apprehension in establishment circles that the globalized economic relationships that had been so painstakingly built up over a period of decades would gradually break down. Clearly the United States intended to preserve the globalized world economy and parry possible threats to its existence. Another objective was to ensure that the United States would be able to dictate the course of globalization, and that globalization proceeded on terms that would favor both the US state and private sector.[92]

One worrying scenario was that a new economic system might emerge, comprising three mercantilist, semi-enclosed trading and currency blocs: Western Europe, with Germany and France at its core and based on the euro; North America, with the United States as its core and based on the dollar; and East Asia, with Japan as its core and based on the yen. In this scenario, trade and investment would proceed relatively freely *within* each of these three economic zones, but would be subject to significant barriers *among* the three zones. The idea of trading blocs was anathema to internationalists, but a sizable body of opinion viewed this as a realistic possibility. These concerns were regularly expressed throughout the early post–Cold War period. A 1991 article in the *Banker* stated: "By 2000 there could be three regional powerhouses—North America, West Europe, and East Asia—all of equal economic strength."[93] A 1992 study sponsored by the Brookings Institution was more explicit: "Three major trading blocs will face one another in the next century."[94] The European Union was often singled out for criticism, and Michael Aho noted the "growing danger that the [European Union] could turn inward and isolate itself."[95] These fears were also noted in the *Economist*: "American businesses . . . fear [that a] fortress Europe remains very much alive. . . . This American disquiet about European union will be the thing to watch."[96]

A particular point of concern was the growth of regional free trade areas, the most famous of which are of course the European Union and the North American Free Trade Agreement (NAFTA). These organizations were invariably presented as advances for free trade and investment, since they broke down barriers among countries within regions; the problem was that such agreements included, as a concomitant of integration, clauses that reduced trade and investment flows among regions. It seemed that regional trade organizations could become the institutional cores of future trading blocs. Indeed, one study of NAFTA concluded that many of its US backers were industries seeking integration with Mexico and Canada as a way to *increase* barriers against imports from competitor industries emanating from Europe and Asia.[97] Fearing their more protectionist features, many liberal economists turned critical: Jagdish Bhagwati condemned free trade agreements, which "have become a pox on the world trading system."[98]

In addition, Japan was considering a yen-based bloc for East Asia. In 1994, Chalmers Johnson, president of the Japan Policy Research Institute, observed: "I believe Japanese officials and the mass media are preparing the public for disengagement from the United States in favor of the United Nations and Asia. . . . Japan's beginning to find its place in Asia and its talk of Greater East Asian Coprosperity Sphere—not built at the point of bayonet but on true prosperity—is as idealistic as the European Union."[99] Enthusiasm for such a Coprosperity Sphere increased during the 1997–1998 East Asian economic crisis, which saw the temporary collapse of many economies in the region. In the context of this crisis, the US strongly supported the imposition of a disastrous series of IMF-directed austerity programs, which worsened the situation.[100] The US was increasingly viewed as an "imperialist" power, antagonistic toward Asian interests.[101] These factors all helped undermine US credibility and made many Asians receptive to an increased regional role for Japan as a potential counterweight to the United States.

The idea of a Japanese-led "yen bloc" now seemed a reasonable possibility. By 1999, Japan's vice minister of finance, Eisuke Sakakibara, foresaw a "genuine yen bloc emerging in about 10 years."[102]

The growing economic tensions among Europe, the United States, and Japan led to increased competition for privileged access to prospective markets in underdeveloped countries, with each player seeking to "steal" spheres of influence from the other. The United States sought to gain access to German spheres of influence in Eastern Europe and French spheres in Algeria and sub-Saharan Africa, often resulting in political frictions among these nominally allied powers.[103] US oil companies actively competed with their Russian counterparts for access to the lucrative oil and gas fields of Central Asia, again with strong political overtones.[104] Economic influence in South America was a special point of contention. The United States assiduously promoted the expansion of NAFTA to encompass the entirety of North and South America under a "Free Trade for the Americas" initiative. The United States pressured several Latin states to adopt the US dollar as their official currency to accelerate their incorporation into a US-led sphere of influence, and also to make them less accessible to European competitors. The Europeans countered with economic initiatives of their own. In 1997, *Business Week* noted with apprehension that "while the Congress and the Clinton Administration dither over moves to create a free-trade bloc covering the hemisphere by 2005, the European Union is barging in and bolstering its economic links with the region."[105] Amidst Japanese efforts to deepen ties with East Asian neighbors, both the United States and Europe sought privileged access to Asian markets. The United States for its part helped establish the America-Pacific Economic Conference; in March 1996, the European Union countered with a "Euro-Asian summit"—only to meet strong US resistance.[106] According to *Le Monde,* there were "underhanded US efforts to sabotage" these European initiatives in Asia.[107] Increasingly, intelligence agencies in both the United States and to some extent in Europe focused their activities on industrial espionage undertaken against prospective economic rivals.[108]

Thus, the capitalist allies were beginning to act like adversaries with regard to both political and economic matters. Internationalists feared that such tensions could get out of hand and lead to a breakdown of multilateral economic relationships. Needless to say, none of these scenarios came to pass. A fortress Europe or fortress Asia did not in fact develop to any significant extent. Viewed in retrospect, the dangers of a breakdown in globalized trade and investment may have been overstated. At the time, however, the dangers seemed real enough. As late as 1999, the London *Times* noted the possible "evolution of the world economy into three important trading blocs, clustered around three important currencies: the dollar, the yen, and the euro."[109] Such fears—justified or not—had a marked influence on policy.[110]

Economic Tensions and NATO

To contain these interallied tensions and to ensure that they stayed within certain bounds, US foreign policy turned, once again, to the North Atlantic Treaty Organization. The reinvigoration of NATO had, perhaps by default, become an all-purpose panacea for virtually all types of tensions between the United States and Europe, whether economic or political. It was after all the alliance against communism that had kept tensions in check during the Cold War; during the 1990s, the alliance retained its basic function of keeping tensions in check. Robert Hutchings, a member of the National Security Council staff during the Bush presidency, stated that a permanent military presence in Europe "had an economic as well as a security dimension and indeed was acquiring an increasingly economic logic and rationale. As the military dimensions of security receded, trade issues loomed larger—and now would be played out without the galvanizing element of the Soviet threat. It was as [George] Bush put it in a speech in the Netherlands before the Maastricht summit, 'the dangers that old Cold War allies will become new economic adversaries—cold warriors turned to trade warriors,'"[111] Former NATO commander Alexander Haig stated: "A lot of people forget that [the US troop presence in Europe] . . . keeps European markets open to us. If those troops weren't there, those markets would be more difficult to access."[112] And Michael Lind implied that during the Clinton presidency, the United States was seeking to prevent "Euro-American rivalries by preserving US hegemony in Europe through the refurbishment of NATO."[113]

In addition, NATO enabled the United States to exert influence over European economic policy and served as a conduit for US commercial power. This source of influence was highly prized by both US government officials and private sector investors. According to one analyst:

> Continuing strong American backing for the alliance is further assured by the fact that NATO remains the principal institutional vehicle through which the United States can influence West European policies. . . . And active American engagement, including the presence of US forces on the continent, endows the United States with considerable leverage. Indeed, the influence provided by its NATO involvement may even extend to other bilateral and multilateral issues, including those in the economic field. One American diplomat reportedly stated that by exerting its military weight in Europe through NATO, the United States is able to "tell

the Europeans what we want on a whole lot of issues—trade, agriculture, the [Persian] Gulf, you name it."[114]

US policy makers lamented that they had no ex officio voice in European economic affairs of any consequence. According to Jonathan Clarke: "A multilateral NATO-like institution between the United States and Europe has never existed. The General Agreement on Tariffs and Trade with its global membership is a pale shadow of NATO."[115] In the absence of a direct transatlantic economic link, NATO served this function. Thus, NATO had an implicit economic role that was widely recognized, though seldom discussed openly.[116]

Let us consider these facts in context. It was suggested during this period that US military strategy lacked any economic rationale, and that purely political, prestige, or cultural factors must account for continued interventions after the end of the Cold War. This is in essence a restatement of the globalization argument, and it asserts the following: As business interests achieved unfettered access to world markets, old-fashioned military power had become an anachronism. The continued US interest in military alliances, foreign interventions, and the like were viewed as atavistic phenomena devoid of material logic.[117] This argument is mistaken. As we have seen, US foreign policy during the 1990s did have a material logic, which was to preserve an open economic system against perceived threats of regionalization through the institutional structure of military alliances. As Layne and Schwarz have argued, "Threats to economic interdependence have replaced Marxism-Leninism as America's global bête noir."[118]

And continued US military power provided other advantages as well. As we have seen, the military-industrial complex remained an important economic actor, even after the Cold War, and this interest group benefited from US hegemony in Europe and elsewhere. And a range of business interests both military and nonmilitary favored the expansion of NATO. In short, a wide variety of economic interest groups supported an aggressive US military posture, despite the advent of globalization—or indeed because of it. As US investments became more globalized over time, these interest groups depended to a greater extent than before on military power to protect these investments, especially in unstable regions such as Africa or the Middle East.[119] In 1999, Thomas Friedman memorably noted: "The hidden hand of the market will never work without a hidden fist—McDonald's cannot flourish without McDonnell-Douglas, the designer of the F-15. And the hidden fist that keeps the world safe for Silicon Valley's technologies is called the United States Army, Air Force, Navy, and Marine Corps."[120] The politics of post–Cold War US hegemony rested on an economic base.

Conclusion: US Hegemony and the Search for Enemies

> How can we deny the central role of the enemy in our history?
> —*Robert Nozick*

We have seen that preserving the Cold War alliance structure, especially NATO, was one of the central objectives of US foreign policy during the 1990s.[121] Yet there remained the problem of justification. The considerable expenditure of resources that NATO required had to be justified to legislatures and voting publics in both the United States and Europe, while other treaty obligations (e.g., the US-Japan treaty) also had to be justified. To achieve these objectives quite simply required enemies. Yet the search for enemies failed to yield anything that even remotely resembled communism, in terms of either its ideological potency or its overall plausibility.

There was thus a large void in the international relations of that era. On the one hand, little had changed: NATO and other key alliances remained virtually intact; the US military that undergirded these alliances had almost the same level of strength (at least on paper) that it had during the height of the Cold War. Few of the major weapons procurement programs begun during the Cold War had been cancelled.[122] On the other hand, the purported threat that had justified the creation of these structures in the first place, that of communism, had virtually disappeared. What was required was a new threat to replace communism, as Irving Kristol suggested: "With the end of the Cold War, what we really need is an obvious ideological and threatening enemy, one worthy of our mettle, one that can unite us in opposition."[123]

The need for threats and enemies—the note on which this chapter began—thus became an overarching theme of US policy during the 1990s.[124] The idea of preserving stability in Eastern Europe was surely helpful, but by itself was insufficient as a general justification for US hegemony. Efforts to generate new military strategies based on new threats and enemies suffered from inherent implausibility, often to the point of being plainly ridiculous.[125] Terrorism would eventually emerge as a potent threat and also as a new justification for US power, but before 2001, terrorism was not available as a core rationale.[126] Something else was required.

The role of humanitarian intervention in this context is clear: It provided a rationale for US hegemony during the 1990s, as well as the Cold War institutions on which this hegemony was based. Indeed, it gave these institutions a new lease on life, and also a new set of enemies. Humanitarian operations drew the capitalist democracies together in a glorious moral crusade that was rhetorically similar to the Cold War and helped surmount the various issues that divided these states and strained their unity. And the crusade was led by a seemingly benign US hegemon, which furnished the military and logistical support that these operations required.

Humanitarian intervention offered additional advantages: It appealed to influential segments of the US public, especially political liberals, thus forging new constituencies for intervention.[127] But this strategy also had its shortcomings. The US military itself was cool to the idea and went along with some measure of reluctance. From the standpoint of the professional soldier, humanitarian operations did not offer the technical challenges of traditional warfare. The lack of clear-cut military objectives or exit strategies—conditions that typify humanitarian intervention—concerned military elites, who sought to avoid any repetition of the debacle suffered in Vietnam. The continued effect of the "Vietnam Syndrome" on the US military was a significant limitation.[128] Even the civilian elements of the foreign policy bureaucracy, which were more supportive, held ambivalent views about making humanitarian intervention the basic justification of US hegemony. But no strategy is perfect, and the lack of adequate alternatives at that time moved humanitarian missions onto center stage. Humanitarian interventions thus served to justify continued US hegemony over its allies, with attendant political and economic benefits to the United States. In subsequent chapters, we will see how this quest for unilateral hegemony shaped US intervention in Yugoslavia.

3

Origins of the Yugoslav Conflict

> I would be Serb, Bosnian, anything—Uzbekistani. I'd make
> my eyes slanted if I could have money.
> —*A Belgrade taxi driver, 1988*

Before we discuss in detail the international politics of the Yugoslav conflict, we will assess its origins at the domestic level. This chapter accomplishes two goals. First, it debunks several myths about how the conflict started. Most assessments of the Yugoslav wars overemphasize the salience of Serb aggressiveness. Some variants of this explanation emphasize alleged aggressive, racist, and unscrupulous tendencies among Serbs in general; a surprising number stress the importance of a single individual—Slobodan Milošević.[1] Aryeh Neier, for example, offers the following analysis:

> The Serb leader [Milošević] rose to power a dozen years before the Kosovo war by playing the card of nationalism and ethnic hatred against the Kosovar Albanians; *he* cemented his authority by unilaterally canceling their autonomy and the autonomy of another territory with a large population of non-Serbs, Vojvodina, precipitating the breakup of Yugoslavia; *he* launched wars in 1991 against Slovenia and Croatia; and *he* launched a particularly devastating war in Bosnia in 1992. The last of these alone resulted in some two million refugees and two hundred thousand deaths, the great majority at the hands of forces *created by Milošević*. Atrocities reached genocidal proportions. [emphases added][2]

Thus, Milošević himself caused the breakup of Yugoslavia; the wars in Slovenia, Croatia, and Bosnia-Herzegovina; and virtually all the death and human suffering that has resulted from these events. Similarly, Noel Malcolm begins his widely acclaimed study by stating without qualification: "Milošević first plunged the former Yugoslavia into war in 1991."[3] In the memoirs of Madeleine Albright, a chapter is entitled " 'Milošević Is the Problem.'"[4] Richard Holbrooke states: "This man [Milošević] wrecked the Balkans."[5] And social theorist Slavoj Žižek claims that "Yugoslavia . . . was all over the moment Milošević took over Serbia."[6]

What is noteworthy about the foregoing analyses is the extent to which they personalize social conflict and place all the blame on a single group—the Serbs—or even on a single person. It signifies a revival of the "great man" theory of history in a new guise. Such historical simplifications helped legitimate later interventions by NATO, which have been directed entirely against the Serbs. However, we will see that the Serbs were only one party to the breakup of Yugoslavia, and that other ethnic groups bear at least as much of the blame. Milošević was surely a villain, but he was not the only villain, nor was he the only cause of the breakup.

Second, in this chapter I examine the way international financial conditions—specifically the international debt crisis of the late 1970s and early 1980s—influenced Yugoslavia's breakup. More specifically, I discuss the role of the International Monetary Fund, which imposed a series of structural adjustment programs on the federation. It becomes apparent that intervention by the IMF and the Western financial community was a major factor leading to a collapse in living standards and helping create the conditions under which nationalist demagogues—of which Milošević was only one example—were able to flourish. The long-term effects of structural adjustment were ethnic rivalry, national disintegration, and ultimately war.

Historical Background to War

Yugoslavia was created in 1918 as the Kingdom of the Serbs, Croats, and Slovenes, comprising independent Serbia as well as portions of the defunct Austro-Hungarian and Ottoman empires. There can be no doubt that the union (renamed Yugoslavia in 1929) provided disproportionate benefits to the Serb ethnic group, which was the largest of the constituent national groupings. Indeed, Serbs formed the largest group among the military officer corps, as well as in senior positions in the government and civil bureaucracy, throughout most of the interwar period. The perception of Serb domination of interwar Yugoslavia was a major factor that circumscribed the legitimacy of the multinational project.[7] Despite these problems, the Yugoslav union provided at least some significant benefits for each of the principal nationalities. The uniting of ethnic units presented obvious military advantages; a multiethnic state could field a much larger army, to guard against the possibility of future aggression by the principal regional power, Germany. It was in fact the need to create a bulwark against German expansion in southeastern Europe that had led the victorious powers after World War I to support the creation of Yugoslavia in the first place.[8]

The anti-German character of Yugoslavia was thus established at its creation. The advent of Yugoslavia also reduced Germany's economic influence in the region. Before 1914, Germany had clearly been the dominant economic power and the largest source of foreign investment in southeastern Europe; by 1937, Germany's foreign investment position in Yugoslavia fell to fifth place, behind France, Great Britain, the United States, and Switzerland.[9] Germany was thus deprived of potential markets, as well as political allies in any future conflict. Reversing this state of affairs became a key objective of German policy: During the Third Reich, Germany made concerted efforts to expand both its political and economic sway in the Balkan region.[10]

In 1941, Germany as well as Italy, Hungary, and Bulgaria simultaneously invaded Yugoslavia and established occupation zones. The Axis occupation forces shrewdly sought allies among the Croats, who had been chafing under perceived Serb domination.[11] The occupying powers created the Independent State of Croatia, which comprised present-day Croatia, as well as most of Bosnia-Herzegovina; it was led by Ante Pavelić and a small Croatian fascist group, the Ustaša movement. Though the Ustaša government functioned essentially as a puppet of the Axis powers, it enjoyed at least some measure of popular support. (We will later see that in the 1990s, Croat nationalists would openly glorify the Ustaša period.) The Ustaša regime followed a violent, openly racist ideology that sought to "cleanse" Croatia of Serbs, Jews, Roma, and other racial undesirables, and achieved this in part through a mass extermination campaign. It is important to note that the extermination campaign was not, for the most part, undertaken by the forces of the SS or the Wehrmacht, but by Ustaša militias. Fred Singleton observes:

> The process of extermination which was later judged at Nuremberg to have amounted to genocide started at once in the areas of Croatia where Serbs were concentrated. . . . The exact number of Serbs who were killed in the [Independent State of Croatia] is not known. . . . The behavior of the *Ustaša* . . . even shocked the SS, according to a German security police report of February 1942: . . . "The *Ustaša* units have carried out their atrocities not only against Orthodox males of military age, but in particular in the most bestial fashion against unarmed old men, women, and children."[12]

German authorities estimated that the Ustaša murdered some 350,000 Serbs.[13] In addition to the atrocities committed against Serbs, large numbers of Roma and the majority of Yugoslavia's once sizable Jewish community were killed off.[14] Despite their concern about the possibly "excessive" nature of Ustaša atrocities, it is clear that the Germans had found a reasonably reliable proxy in the Independent State of Croatia. In addition, the Germans sought other allies within occupied Yugoslavia, and they tended to find them among ethnic groups that had some measure of rivalry with the Serbs. Specifically, Muslims in Bosnia-Herzegovina were recruited into a new Waffen-SS division, while an additional division was formed by ethnic Albanians residing in Kosovo.[15] The significance of these events for the recent wars in the former Yugoslavia is clear: Serb fears—some might say paranoia—about the potential of persecution at the hands of other ethnic groups has a measure of historical foundation. And we will see later in the chapter that the post-Yugoslav state of Croatia, which became independent in 1991, had important historical links with Pavelić's puppet state.

The Axis powers and their local collaborators were of course opposed by the communist Partisans, led by Josef Broz Tito (among other groups). The Partisans were the only major political grouping in wartime Yugoslavia that was explicitly multiethnic in its ideology and, to a large extent, in its practices as well. Tito himself is believed to have descended from mixed Croatian and Slovene parentage, while many of the Partisan fighters were Serb minority inhabitants from Croatia and Bosnia-Herzegovina; in time, especially toward the end of the war, the Partisans gained support among all major ethnic groups.[16]

The communist regime that emerged from World War II was undoubtedly popular and had strong indigenous roots within Yugoslavia. Nevertheless, the Yugoslav communist party was considered one of the most hardline and thoroughly Stalinized in Eastern Europe. Immediately following World War II, the victorious Partisans pointedly meted out revenge against Ustaša supporters and other collaborators. The period of repression and terror that inaugurated the new Yugoslav government was fortunately of relatively brief duration. By 1948, Tito had broken with Stalin, and Yugoslavia became the first genuinely independent communist state.[17] Though still a one-party state, censorship was relatively mild, and from the mid-1950s, Yugoslav citizens were free to engage in foreign travel, including to Western countries.[18] Yugoslavia also became, in 1958, the first communist country to tolerate strikes.[19]

One of the central challenges throughout Yugoslavia's history was of course the ethnicity question. The country was since its founding one of the most ethnically diverse states in Europe, and the danger of mass violence was dramatically demonstrated by the events of World War II, which entailed a considerable measure of civil war among the various ethnic groups, as well as a war against foreign occupation. In communist Yugoslavia, the official policy with regard to nationalities was at least on paper somewhat comparable to that of another multiethnic communist state, the Soviet Union. As in the

USSR, Yugoslav policy emphasized the simultaneous development of separate ethnic cultures and languages combined with a cosmopolitan Yugoslav identity that transcended nationality. In the national census, individuals were encouraged to self-identify according to their specific ethnic group; a small number, mostly from ethnically mixed marriages, chose to identify themselves as "Yugoslav," without any specified ethnicity.[20] A concomitant of Yugoslavia's nationalities policy was a federalized institutional structure. Once again, the federal structure had a surface similarity to the Soviet Union's; but in contrast with the USSR, whose federalization was largely for appearances, Yugoslavia was in fact highly decentralized, and most aspects of policy making were delegated to the republics and autonomous provinces (listed in Table 3.1).

The eight administrative units—six republics and two autonomous provinces—developed considerable autonomy from the central government and, after a constitutional revision in 1974, Yugoslavia's became one of the most decentralized political systems in the world.[21] And the two autonomous provinces, Kosovo and Vojvodina, though nominally subunits of Serbia, were given levels of authority virtually at the level of the six full republics. Since each of the eight units contained a predominant nationality (with the exception of Bosnia-Herzegovina), the decentralization afforded the major ethnic

Table 3.1. Administrative Regions of Yugoslavia

Administrative unit	Population, 1981	Percentage of total population
Bosnia-Herzegovina	4.1 million	18.4
Croatia	4.6 million	20.5
Macedonia	1.9 million	8.6
Montenegro	0.6 million	2.6
Serbia (excluding autonomous provinces)	5.7 million	25.3
Kosovo (autonomous province of Serbia)	1.6 million	7.1
Vojvodina (autonomous province of Serbia)	2.0 million	9.1
Slovenia	1.9 million	8.4
Total	22.4 million	100.0

Source: Richard F. Nyrop, ed., *Yugoslavia: A Country Study* (Washington, DC: US Government Printing Office, 1982), 274.

groups a large measure of self-governance. Smaller ethnic minorities—Roma, Czechs, Jews, Romanians, Russians, Bulgarians, Turks, Italians, Hungarians, and Vlachs—were granted explicit protections and cultural rights. Appeals to "national, racial, or religious hatred" were legally proscribed.[22] The Yugoslav National Army along with the federal League of Communists became the principal institutions that were truly national in scope; virtually all other activities were handled at the republic level. Even in the area of military defense, there was significant decentralization, as each republic organized a Territorial Defense Force of reservists as a supplement to the regular army. Each Territorial Defense Force was under the operational authority of the respective republic.[23]

In recent years, it has become fashionable to view Yugoslav communism as an economic failure whose eventual collapse was inevitable.[24] Such interpretations are contradicted by basic statistics. In fact, Yugoslav communism was associated, for most of its history, with economic dynamism. The figures on macroeconomic performance are noted in Table 3.2. Yugoslavia sustained a respectable rate of GDP growth, which averaged 8.8 percent during the period 1956–1964, and 6 percent during 1965–1972. Growth was both extensive, in terms of investment in physical and social infrastructure, and intensive, as reflected in improved labor productivity.[25] Though these macroeconomic performance figures would later decline and then regress—a matter I will discuss shortly—the earlier period was strongly positive.

Titoist communism brought major benefits to all classes of the population. British historian Basil Davidson commented that, under communism, "schooling flourished for the first time. Health and other public services got amazingly better than anything imaginable before."[26] A study by the Royal

Table 3.2. Macroeconomic Performance in Yugoslavia, 1956–1984

	Average annual growth rates (%)			
	1956–1964	1965–1972	1973–1979	1980–1984
Gross domestic product (GDP)	8.8	6.0	6.1	0.4
GDP per capita	7.7	5.0	5.1	–0.3
Labor productivity in the public sector	4.8	4.3	2.7	–2.0
Real personal income	6.3	6.1	2.7	–2.0

Source: Lenard J. Cohen, *Broken Bonds: Yugoslavia's Disintegration and Balkan Politics in Transition* (Boulder, Colo.: Westview, 1995), 31.

Institute of International Relations also acknowledged that communism produced dramatically improved living standards: "For individual Yugoslavs, social change in the 1960s was measured . . . in the arrival of clean, piped water in one's village, or . . . an indoor bathroom and toilet in anticipation of piped water next year or the year after. . . . It might be measured in terms of a cottage on the coast or on the banks of the Sava [River], or of a trip abroad which was no longer just to Trieste . . . but further and as a real tourist. It certainly meant, even in remote provincial towns by the mid-1960s, the marvel of a supermarket or a self-service 'superette.'"[27] A system of self-management was introduced in factories and economic enterprises throughout the country, which despite flaws afforded some measure of worker influence at the factory level. Though worker self-management was part of the official rhetoric in virtually all communist states, it was actually practiced to some extent in Yugoslavia. The self-management system was sufficiently impressive that political theorists such as Robert Dahl, Charles Lindblom, and Carole Pateman argued that the Yugoslav system contained democratic features from which Western democracies could learn.[28] The Yugoslav system was widely admired as a veritable "third way" between central planning and capitalism. At the international level, Yugoslavia gained considerable prestige as a center of independence from both major power blocs, and as a leader of the nonaligned movement of Third World states.

During the period 1945–1991, the various ethnic groups lived reasonably peacefully. For better or worse, communism proved an effective ideological bond. The Serbo-Croatian language was a source of national unity and was the primary language of more than 80 percent of the population.[29] The Serbian and Croatian variants of this language, though they used different scripts, were similar in speech. On the one hand, the Serbs constituted the largest single ethnic group, and Serbs tended to dominate the officer corps of the military. On the other hand, a number of factors reduced the Serbs' political sway within the federation. Major federal appointments were made, until the very end of the country's existence, with an eye to parity among the various administrative units and ethnic groups.[30] Even within the military, the senior commanders were ethnically mixed. And Yugoslavia's leader for most of the postwar period, Tito, was of Croatian/Slovene descent.[31]

The Yugoslav system, despite its manifest successes, also contained several major flaws that contributed significantly to the eventual demise of the country. The first flaw was constitutional. The 1974 constitution required a high degree of consensus among the eight republics and autonomous provinces in order to operate effectively. The constitution gave each of the eight regional governments "a veto over any legislation that might affect it negatively."[32] Any change in constitutional structure required unanimity among the regional units. The requirement of consensus would seem to have virtually guaranteed an element of immobility in policy making. However, the shared historical experience of World War II, the personal popularity of Tito, and the institutional structure of the League of Communists all provided a basis for national unity.[33] The rapidly improving living standards also contributed to political stability and helped facilitate consensus. After Tito's death in 1980, however, the inherent weaknesses became more apparent. The cumbersome and highly complex system of federalized—or virtually confederalized—governance would eventually become unworkable.

A second weakness was persistent regional inequality. Slovenia and Croatia constituted the most developed republics, owing to their proximity to the highly industrialized regions of central and Western Europe. The less developed regions, notably Kosovo, Montenegro, Macedonia, and Bosnia-Herzegovina, were located in the southeast, at greater distance from the industrial centers. The economic distance that separated the richest from the poorest regions was indeed considerable: By 1988, Slovenia's per capita output was eight times that of Kosovo.[34] The regional disparity also was evident in the much lower levels of health care and education that prevailed in the southeastern regions. To rectify these inequalities, the federal government of Yugoslavia provided subsidies and preferential access to credit for less developed regions, as part of a national development program; these were largely financed by the more developed republics, especially Slovenia and Croatia.[35] In general, efforts to redress regional economic disparities are common throughout the world. In the European Union, for example, Spain, Portugal, Greece, and southern Italy have long received subsidies, generally at the expense of the more developed countries of northern Europe. In Yugoslavia, however, the regional subsidy programs contained significant flaws. In the first place, they were used to fund projects that were notoriously capital intensive, thus having a reduced impact on employment; and perhaps inevitably, a certain amount of the transfers were diverted into prestige infrastructure projects—often of dubious developmental value—or into simple corruption.[36] Moreover, the economic transfers, though considerable, were insufficient to rectify regional disparities, which increased significantly during the 1980s.[37]

The deepening inequality augmented the traditional sense of grievance in Kosovo and other underdeveloped regions. At the same time, Slovenia and Croatia resented the subsidy program altogether, since it represented a drain on their resources. Indeed the subsidies had long been a source of political agitation. Nationalist upsurges in Slovenia in 1969 and then in Croatia during 1970–1971 resulted at least in part from protests against the subsidy program.[38] In Croatia nationalist demonstrators chanted, "Keep our foreign currency at home."[39] Overall, regional inequality remained one of the weakest features of Yugoslav communism. Still, the strong rate of economic growth—which benefited all regions to some extent—held these tensions in check during the period 1945–1972. Once macroeconomic performance began to falter, however, regional economic disparity would prove an explosive issue.

A third basic weakness was the import dependence of the Yugoslav economic model. Though self-sufficiency constituted an official developmental objective, the rapid industrialization of the country was made possible by massive and sustained imports of capital equipment and technology, especially from the West.[40] In addition, the Yugoslav economy imported most of its petroleum.[41] During much of its history, Yugoslavia had gained economic benefits from its neutral diplomatic status, as it could trade equally with Eastern and Western Europe, as well as the nonaligned states of the Third World. It also received economic aid from the United States, especially during the 1950s, due to its tensions with the Soviet Union, as well as remittances from the significant number of Yugoslavs who worked as *gastarbeiter* in Western Germany and elsewhere.[42] Such economic dependence, while initially beneficial, would leave the country exceptionally vulnerable to externally generated economic shocks. Such shocks would later shatter the stability of the Yugoslav political system.

Some studies have cited additional deficiencies. John Roemer notes that the socialist economic structure of Yugoslavia contained numerous pathologies, including pervasive soft budget constraints; lack of competition; inadequate accountability for managers of specific firms; generalized indiscipline of the labor force; various microeconomic distortions that resulted from these factors; and reduced macrolevel performance as a result.[43] As a general point, the basic inefficiencies of socialist economic systems have been widely noted. It is of course hypothetically possible that such problems reduced economic performance in Yugoslavia, which might have been higher had the alleged inefficiencies been corrected. All this should not obscure a key point: Despite the limitations noted by Roemer and others, economic performance in Yugoslavia from 1945–1972 was among the most impressive in the world, exceeded by few nations. In 1967, the *Economist* noted that Yugoslavia's economic growth "has been hardly less fast than Japan's."[44] And the rapid increase in productivity—which occurred in spite of the job security that prevailed in most enterprises—suggests that this performance was potentially sustainable. The fruits of Yugoslavia's economic experience benefited virtually all classes of the society, in every region (though admittedly to varying degrees). The main factors that led to the demise of the Yugoslav socialist model did not originate in the inadequacies of the model itself or from domestic factors, but from an unfavorable *international* climate.

Economic Crisis

> Traveling in Yugoslavia just before its breakup . . .
> [I asked] influential people the same question: "Which is
> the most serious problem facing Yugoslavia today[?]" . . . All
> (except the Kosovars) said, usually without hesitation, "the
> economy."
> —*John B. Allcock, University of Bradford*

> It was the International Monetary Fund
> that tore the Yugoslav federation to pieces.
> —*Jude Wanniski, former associate
> editor,* Wall Street Journal

The trade-dependent economic model worked quite well, as demonstrated by its rapid growth rates.[45] During the mid-1970s, however, international trends turned in a sharply disadvantageous direction, which gradually undermined the vaunted Yugoslav economic model and, later, the entire political system as well. The economic crisis began with the rapid rise in oil prices during 1973–1974, and the world economic recession that followed. For Yugoslavia, these events had two basic effects. First, the import bill increased rapidly, as energy import prices escalated. Second, export markets for goods, especially in Western Europe, deteriorated, owing to reduced consumer demand in light of the world recession. Yugoslav guest workers who sought employment in Europe were repatriated in large numbers, which stepped up competition for increasingly scarce jobs.[46] In addition to aggravating unemployment in Yugoslavia, the repatriation deprived the country of the salary remittances that had been an important source of hard currency inflow. Thus, Yugoslavia sustained a rapid deterioration in terms of trade, along with diminished capacity to finance imports.

The Yugoslavs were faced with a basic dilemma: To make up for the trade deficit, they had to augment their exports and develop new export lines, especially in more expensive, higher-end manufactured products. To achieve these objectives, however, they required continued and even increased importation of capital goods and technology as well as petroleum. The only alternative—extended austerity through "adjustment"—was at that time considered politically unpalatable. Yugoslavia, like many countries in Eastern Europe and also in the Third World, addressed this dilemma by bor-rowing heavily on international markets. The mid-1970s was a period when major commercial banks had excess liquidity, in part because of the recycling of petrodollars from Middle East oil-producing countries, and they were actively seeking new borrowers.[47] Yugoslavia borrowed heavily from West-ern banking consortia to finance the importation of new technology and to upgrade their productive capacity—without having to impose unpopular austerity measures. However, these loans were predicated on the assumption that the disadvantageous international economic conditions were transitory; this was an assumption that would later prove unfounded. By the end of the decade, export markets in Western Europe and elsewhere remained sluggish, and the demand for Yugoslav exports was insufficient. Yugoslavia was unable to meet its repayment schedule and was headed for default. A second major oil price increase, coinciding with the Iranian Revolution in 1979, further exacerbated the trade deficit.[48] The rise in oil prices was especially serious for Yugoslavia, which unlike most other Eastern European countries did not re-ceive Soviet oil at subsidized rates. Yugoslavs had to obtain their oil imports on commercial terms. In addition, increases in the US interest rate, also be-ginning in 1979, raised the effective debt burden, since the country's debt was mostly denominated in dollars. And there was an element of simple bad luck: The country suffered from a major earthquake along the Adriatic coast in 1979.[49]

The prospect of economic adjustment became unavoidable, and Yugo-slavia accepted assistance from the International Monetary Fund.[50] It is a basic feature of IMF policy that countries undergoing financial distress, bal-ance of payments problems, or both must "adjust"—that is, they must lower their living standards to reduce imports and amass sufficient capital to pay off their debts. Adjustment began in 1979 and continued in intensified form throughout the 1980s, up until the breakup of the country in 1991. The ef-fects were considerable, as consumer goods were removed from domestic consumption and shifted into exports. David Dyker describes the effect that such policies had on domestic consumption: "Imports of consumer goods were cut by 18 percent between 1981 and 1982, and by the end of 1982 ra-tioning had been introduced for key consumer goods, including petrol, sugar, detergent, cooking oil, and coffee. A survey done by the Business Cham-ber of Yugoslavia for 1982 found a 50 percent aggregate deficit in detergent supply, with corresponding figures for coffee and lard of 70 percent and 25 percent. Milk, butter, and meat were in serious shortage and coal and tires were totally unavailable."[51] In addition, "Food subsidies were eliminated in 1981. Prices for energy, food, and transport were raised by one-third in 1983. All new investment for social services, infrastructure, and other governmental projects was banned."[52] Living standards declined by one-third during the period 1979–1988, with concomitant increases in unemployment, as well rising strikes and work stoppages.[53] By 1989, after a decade of economic crisis and structural adjustment, "an estimated 60 percent of Yugoslav workers lived at or below the minimum income level guaranteed by the state, and the standard of living had fallen by 40 percent since 1982—[which returned] that indicator to the level of the mid-1960s."[54]

The rate of debt repayment ensured that Yugoslavia was, in the words of Dyker, "*exporting capital to the developed West,* apart from interest payments. In doing so, she has fitted in only too well with the pattern of 'perverse transfer of resources' from the poor to the rich, which has dominated the profile of relationships between creditor and debtor countries since 1982."[55] Growth of living standards—a major source of regime legitimacy—thus came to a definitive end. For the first time since the 1940s, Yugoslavs were forced to accept substantially lower standards of living. We will see shortly that the new, more difficult economic conditions of the 1980s were major factors in triggering the political and ethnic conflicts that ultimately resulted in the disintegration of the country. By 1990, after more than a decade of adjustment, Yugoslavia's foreign debt still stood at $16.5 billion, while the debt-service ratio (calculated as a percentage of GNP) was 19.3 percent.[56]

More recently, structural adjustment has come under considerable criticism, often from economists who had previously championed such policies.[57] At the time of the Yugoslav debt crisis, however, debt forgiveness was never seriously entertained as an option. The Western financial community—led by the IMF and the US Treasury Department—clearly opted for the imposition of austerity measures to ensure at least some measure of repayment. This strategy of insisting on repayment reflected technical concerns, specifically the need to preserve the stability of the international financial system and to avoid the risks of outright default. In addition, there was an important political motivation for IMF strategy: Adjustment was intended to dismantle statist economic systems to make them more accessible to multinational investors. A former official with the Inter-American Development Bank commented: "[To] the US Treasury staff . . . the debt crisis afforded an unparalleled opportunity to achieve, in debtor countries, the structural reforms favored by the Reagan Administration. The core of these reforms was a commitment on the part of the debtor countries to reduce the role of the public sector as a vehicle for economic and social development and rely more on market forces and private enterprise, domestic and foreign."[58] Similarly, a World Bank official noted that the debt crisis was "a blessing in disguise," since it enabled international organizations to alter the economic structure of a large portion of the globe to achieve freer movement of capital across borders.[59]

It would thus seem likely that US and possibly other Western officials viewed the Yugoslav debt crisis as an opportunity to fundamentally change that country's economic system in a neoliberal direction. Former *Wall Street Journal* editor Jude Wanniski would later wonder whether the IMF had imposed austerity in Yugoslavia "at the instigation of [the US] foreign policy establishment, which did not like the fact that Yugoslavia was making a success of market socialism."[60] A 1988 State Department document stated hopefully that Yugoslavia was "susceptible to Western pressure for policy changes" due to its "financial dependence on the West."[61] Certainly the United States was in a position to influence the situation, given the domineering role that it traditionally played with regard to the IMF.[62] Adjustment in Yugoslavia (and elsewhere) was invariably presented as a technical solution to a technical problem, but there was always a political objective just beneath the surface that aimed at subverting statist and socialist economic systems.

The Effects of Adjustment

Let us consider how the economic crisis affected Yugoslavia's performance (see Table 3.2 for statistics). A statistically visible decline in macroeconomic performance began in 1973 and accelerated considerably after 1979. Labor productivity had been growing at 4.3 percent per year during 1965–1972. During 1973–1979, however, productivity continued to grow at only 2.7 percent—a substantial decline from the earlier period. The growth rate of real personal income, though positive, also shows a considerable decline over the earlier period. GDP growth continued to increase steadily during the 1973–1979 period, but the rate was not sustainable, as it resulted from accumulation of debt. The real turning point in macroeconomic performance came after 1979. During the period 1980–1984, growth was virtually stagnant, and it never recovered; GDP, labor productivity, and real personal income showed a sustained decline, the first in the history of communist Yugoslavia.[63] A 1988 State Department assessment noted that Yugoslavia's "foreign debt severely restricts the economy's ability to expand for the foreseeable future."[64]

The key dates correspond closely to external stimuli. The decline during and after 1973 corresponded to the world increase in petroleum prices that began in that year, combined with the deepest world recession since the 1930s. The (more dramatic) economic downturn after 1979 corresponded to the second oil shock, combined with the international debt crisis of that era, which spread through much of Eastern Europe, Latin America, and Africa. The timing is significant: It suggests that the decline in performance seen after 1972, and especially after 1979, was related to events in the *global* economy, more than to anything that was occurring internally.

The new conditions of negative growth ensured that Yugoslav politics would assume the character of a zero sum game in which diverse interest groups would seek to shift the burden of adjustment onto competing groups. Much of the competition was in time fought out on a regional level, as long-standing inequalities intensified. The Republic of Slovenia adopted a strategy of export diversification, with some success; and during the course of the 1980s, the Slovenes became increasingly integrated into the world economy (particularly vis-à-vis the countries of the EC), and less integrated into the economy of Yugoslavia.[65] The economics of adjustment produced an incipient unraveling, at the economic level, of the Yugoslav federation. In addition, the adjustment policies caused the underdeveloped regions, notably Kosovo, to decline to an even greater extent. In personal income per capita, gross investment per capita, and infant mortality rates, Kosovo fell further and further below the national average.[66] It would not be quite accurate to say that the rich were getting richer while the poor were getting poorer; it is probable that every region saw a decline in living standards after 1979. The general economic decline, a concomitant of the debt crisis, affected all regions to some extent. But it is clear that there was considerable differentiation in the extent to which living standards declined. The four poorest regions—Bosnia-Herzegovina, Kosovo, Macedonia, and Montenegro—saw the most dramatic declines, while the richest republic, Slovenia, improved its relative standing after 1970.[67] As the regions were pulled apart in economic terms, their respective inhabitants felt increasingly estranged from one another. On the one hand, the richer republics chafed at the obligation to finance federal development schemes for the poorer regions. Indeed, the regional subsidy program had always been unpopular in the richer republics; under the new conditions of austerity, however, they came to view the subsidies as an intolerable burden. On the other hand, the inhabitants of the poorer regions bitterly resented their second-class status and resisted efforts to reduce the federal subsidies.

In 1989, a public opinion survey found high levels of ethnic, racial, and religious intolerance throughout Yugoslavia. The most interesting finding of the survey was that the *highest* levels of intolerance corresponded with extremes of economic inequality: Intolerance reached especially high levels in relatively rich Slovenia, as well as in the two poorest regions, Kosovo and Macedonia. Kosovo showed the highest intolerance levels of the eight regional units, while the Albanian communities within Kosovo and Macedonia—the very poorest group in the federation—showed the highest intolerance of all.[68] Apparently, the rising level of ethnic tensions tended to correlate with regional economic inequality.[69] The general atmosphere in Yugoslavia became one of increasing economic and political desperation. The Yugoslav population after all had become highly urbanized and accustomed to a degree of material comfort; the new conditions of austerity required a major change of attitude. These economic factors may not have guaranteed the violence that followed, but they surely made violence more likely.[70]

Austere economic conditions have throughout history produced popular obsessions with the finding of scapegoats, especially from seemingly "exotic" ethnic or religious groupings. Anti-Semitism often flourishes under these conditions, and indeed, there was some increase in anti-Semitic attitudes (especially in Croatia). This was not however a viable option for the most part, since the massacres during World War II had virtually emptied the country of Jews. Instead, Yugoslav politics began to take the form of increasingly virulent tensions among the major constituent ethnic groups that collectively constituted the Yugoslav federation.

The first major political upheaval in the new era of economic austerity was in Kosovo. In 1981, an upsurge of tension led to major riots. A state of emergency was declared, and federal troops were dispatched to restore order.[71] This was the first in a series of violent upheavals in the province, which gradually accelerated over the next decade. Ethnic tension in Kosovo would become a major destabilizing force for the whole federation. In other areas of the federation, intellectual and literary circles began to promote a renewed nationalism, especially in Slovenia, Croatia, and Serbia, that was often exclusionary and separatist in character. In addition, the number of strikes and work stoppages increased considerably throughout the country. In 1987 alone, some 365,000 workers participated in some form of work stoppage.[72]

A new era of mass politics and de facto democratization had begun—albeit under the worst possible circumstances. As the League of Communists grew weaker, the leadership became fearful of losing their monopoly of power. The increasing number of strikes was particularly embarrassing for the League. A matter of special concern to the League was the threat of national labor unions modeled on the famous Solidarność union of Poland. To avert that eventuality, the authorities used repression, "often crudely, with the special aim of trying to prevent alliances of intellectuals, workers, and potential leaders *across republic lines*."[73] This tactic had the foreseeable effect of further channeling latent tensions in a regional and ethnic direction, thus intensifying the decline of national-level politics. In the end, of course, the tactic was unsuccessful in maintaining one-party rule, and in 1990, multiparty elections were held in each of the Yugoslav republics.[74] In retrospect, however, these elections magnified the intensity of the conflict and accelerated national disintegration. The voting was conducted *only* at the republic level; no election took place at the federal level. These circumstances were bound to strengthen the individual republics, since they were now endowed with democratic legitimacy, while they concomitantly weakened the central government.

With the incipient arrival of mass politics toward the end of the 1980s, the long-standing taboos against public displays of ethnic hatred were lifted. A new class of politicians that rose in prominence was able and willing to mobilize supporters based on ethnic appeals, often with a strongly intolerant strain. Two of the principal figures among political personalities who emerged during this period were Slobodan Milošević and Franjo Tudjman.

The Political Role of Slobodan Milošević

Overall, Milošević made a central contribution to Yugoslavia's demise by pioneering a new style of political leadership—that of the racist demagogue.[75] Milošević certainly was not the only Yugoslav politician to play the ethnic card, nor was he necessarily the most divisive. But undeniably, he was the first major Yugoslav politician to seek power primarily on the basis of ethnic appeals. Milošević had begun his career innocuously enough. As a communist official with expertise in economic policy, he eventually became director of the Beogradska Banka, a Belgrade financial institution. His economic views, at least initially, favored free-market reforms; a later economic commission which he supervised, in 1988, advocated market policies that were similar to those being advocated by the IMF.[76] Western officials who knew Milošević as a banker and economic official during the 1980s were generally impressed by his economic competence, his smooth demeanor, and his command of the English language.[77] He was especially effective with visiting Americans, for whom Milošević seemed the "right" kind of Eastern European leader, one who "ordered scotch instead of slivovitz."[78]

However, Milošević gradually recognized—earlier than most—the new potential of ethnic politics. During 1986–1987, he reinvented himself as a populist and a Serb nationalist.[79] Milošević also employed a new oratorical style that dispensed with traditional communist phrases. According to a Yugoslav observer from that period:

> He's not exactly a born speaker; his delivery is somewhat rapid and it is obvious that he is more accustomed to reading his speeches than to ad-lib. However, what he reads is something new in Yugoslav political practice. Milošević has simply "stepped out" of the bounds of the iron political

jargon of our politicians, a jargon that has continued to assert and petrify itself for decades. His speeches include no long and involved sentences whose meaning is grasped by the audience only after it has worked its way through five or six subordinate clauses. In his speeches there is none of that compulsive theorizing that appears in every speech—even on the most banal occasions. . . . His speeches are delivered in short and simple sentences that are filled with metaphors, comparisons, and slogans that are easily understood by everyone and therefore can quickly turn into "folk sayings."[80]

Milošević also cultivated a relationship with Serb intellectuals, many of whom (particularly in the Serbian Academy of Sciences and Arts) were moving in a nationalist direction. The Academy intellectuals were becoming incipiently right wing and anticommunist; this did not dissuade the ever-pragmatic Milošević from encouraging them, despite his nominal communist affiliation.[81] Later, Milošević would willingly collaborate, from time to time, with the unsavory right-wing nationalist Vojislav Šešelj.[82]

Armed with his new and highly effective oratorical style, Milošević proceeded to consolidate his power within the Serbian League of Communists. In 1986, Milošević managed to outmaneuver his opponents and became leader of the Republic of Serbia. During and immediately after his rise to power, Milošević emerged as an advocate for the rights of ethnic Serb minorities who lived outside the Serbian Republic proper, especially in Kosovo. He gained considerable support for his very public role in championing the rights of Serbs against transgressions (both real and imagined) perpetrated by the Albanian majority.[83] On June 28, 1989, Milošević delivered a major speech in Kosovo on the Field of the Blackbirds. This field was the location of a much-celebrated 1389 battle, during which invading Muslims defeated Serb forces. The field held great importance to Serbs throughout the federation as a symbol of Serb victimization (and its importance was especially great in the year 1989, the six-hundredth anniversary of the battle). In his speech, Milošević extolled the memory of Serb nationhood, though he used relatively mild language to make his points. The most rousing phrases came in the conclusion of the speech: "Let the memory of Kosovo heroism live forever! Long live Serbia! Long live Yugoslavia! Long live peace and brotherhood among peoples!"[84]

The text of this speech does not conform to the stereotype of ranting extremism with which Serb nationalists have often been associated in the media. Milošević carefully praised Yugoslav unity, as well as Serb unity; and in a display of political correctness, Milošević entered a plea for peace and brotherhood across ethnic lines. In the context of Yugoslav politics during this period, however, the speech was incendiary, as it subtly appealed to Serb chauvinism in a manner that had long been taboo among Yugoslav communists. It had the effect—and was surely intended to have the effect—of electrifying Serbs throughout the federation. This speech has rightly been viewed as a political turning point for Kosovo, and for Yugoslavia as well.

Beginning in 1989, Serbia gradually dismantled the independent status of Kosovo; Albanians were subjected to discrimination and harassment by both federal and Serb security forces, which effectively governed Kosovo through martial law. Noel Malcolm provides a description of the atmosphere of intimidation that prevailed in Kosovo as martial law was imposed: "On 23 March 1989, the provincial assembly of Kosovo met under unusual circumstances, with tanks and armored cars parked in front of it.... Kosovo's 'autonomy' was now reduced to a mere token.... The reaction was immediate and intense.... The official death toll by the end of March was twenty-one demonstrators and two policemen; by the end of April it may have been as high as 100.... Many members of the Albanian elite—intellectuals, officials, directors of enterprises—were arrested and more than 200 were held in solitary confinement, without access to defense lawyers, for several months."[85]

The Serb minority in Kosovo no doubt appreciated the external protection that Milošević provided (even as the Albanian majority despised him). Milošević also enjoyed some popularity in Vojvodina, where Serbs constituted a majority, as well as in Montenegro, which had a historically close relationship to Serbia. Milošević was highly successful during 1988–1989 in directing mass protests against relatively moderate communist governments in Montenegro and Vojvodina. Compliant, pro-Milošević communist factions were installed in both regions (as well as in Kosovo).[86] Throughout this process, massed groups of demonstrators advanced Milošević's objectives; their anger and frustration were at least partly the result of economic austerity measures associated with the debt crisis and the "reforms" of this period (many of which had been supported or even directed by Milošević). According to Misha Glenny: "Unemployed young men were paid to travel around Serbia, Kosovo, and Vojvodina to participate in these [pro-Milošević] rallies."[87] At the same time, Milošević's image as an antibureaucratic man of the people elicited some genuine popular support, not just in Serbia, but also in Vojvodina and Montenegro.

In addition, Milošević used bullying tactics against the federation's richest republic, Slovenia. In late 1989, he sought to transport thousands of his supporters to Slovenia's capital, Ljubljana, for a mass demonstration. The stated purpose of this demonstration was to persuade the Slovenian population that the ongoing repression in Kosovo was justified. Many Slovenes had expressed sympathy with the Kosovar Albanians, and they opposed the Serb repression there; with the mass demonstration, Milošević sought to quiet these criticisms. Slovenian officials, however, regarded the planned demonstration as an affront to their authority, and they prohibited it, leading to a series of tit-for-tat acts of retaliation and counterretaliation between Slovenia and Serbia.[88] Such incidents surely exacerbated the political tensions of this period and contributed to the wars that followed.

Milošević as Authoritarian Democrat

In December 1990, in response to the general climate of international (and Yugoslav) democratization, Milošević held multiparty elections in Serbia. Residents of the autonomous provinces of Vojvodina and Kosovo voted as part the Republic of Serbia. Milošević transformed the local branch of the League of Communists into the newly created Socialist Party, which he used as his own electoral vehicle. He won overwhelmingly. Milošević was thus recreated as a nominally democratic figure, and he became the elected president of the Serb Republic. The elections were marred by Milošević's appeal to ethnic hatreds, his efforts to exclude opposition parties from access to the official media, the repression in Kosovo, and the general atmosphere of intimidation that prevailed throughout Serbia during this period. The majority of the Albanian residents of Kosovo boycotted the election as a protest against the prevailing repression.[89] But the election was not altogether fraudulent. Opposition parties actively participated in the campaign and were given some (admittedly limited) access to the official media. The opposition also participated in the counting of ballots.[90]

Though generally hostile toward Milošević, Western newspapers recognized that the voting had been fair. The *Washington Post* acknowledged that Milošević had "survived free elections."[91] According to the *New York Times*, the Serbian elections constituted "the first free vote in the republic in five decades."[92] Even a lobbyist for Slovenia noted the "completion of the first democratic elections in all of the Yugoslav republics," including Serbia.[93] Misha Glenny, who remains the most skeptical, states: "Nobody really doubted Milošević's victory, but many doubted its extent."[94]

It has become commonplace to refer to Milošević as a dictator in the mold of Iraq's Saddam Hussein or North Korea's Kim Il Sung, but such views exaggerate. In fact, Milošević combined repression and pluralism, using the two in combination to a significant degree. Opposition parties and media were from time to time harassed and intimidated, but they were not banned outright. There is no doubt that Milošević rigged certain elections during the course of his rule.[95] But such rigging was an intermittently used technique of rule, not a consistent one. Up until his overthrow from power in 2000, Milošević operated with some degree of legitimacy and public support.

Regarding Milošević's methods more generally, let us consider the 1998–1999 country report from Freedom House, a think tank with close ties to the US policy establishment. The Freedom House report is scathingly critical of the human rights situation in Milošević's Serbia; the overall country scores on political and civil liberties are only slightly higher than those for North Korea. Yet, if one reads the narrative discussion, one finds a good deal of information that does not fully accord with the negative rating. The Freedom House report acknowledges that opposition parties existed, and that "Serb parliamentary elections were generally 'free and fair.'"[96] Overall, the most accurate characterization of Serbia under the Milošević regime would be an authoritarian democracy, which incorporated elements of both authoritarian and democratic rule.[97] The result was hardly Jeffersonian—but it was not North Korean either.

With regard to economic policy, Milošević's views have shown considerable flexibility. As noted, Milošević began as a free-market enthusiast who enjoyed excellent relations with Western financial circles. By the end of the 1980s, however, he had reincarnated himself as a champion of socialism and an opponent of market reforms. In 1989, while endorsing political pluralism, Milošević added: "If this so-called political pluralism is used as another term to supplant Yugoslavia and socialism, then we in Serbia are against it."[98] Milošević's party was pointedly named the Socialist Party. Within Serbia, Milošević and his followers developed a reputation as "incorrigible communists."[99] Also, Milošević's wife, Marjana Marković, held strongly Marxist views, and in 1990 she helped found a new neocommunist party, the League of Communists–Movement for Yugoslavia; Marković founded this party in close cooperation with senior army generals.[100]

Why the leftward shift in economic philosophy? One possibility is that Milošević sensed the unpopularity of the structural adjustment package (combined perhaps with a certain nostalgia for the happier days of Tito). It also seems likely that Milošević sought to curry favor with the Yugoslav National Army, a bastion of communist traditionalism and a key power center. Finally, Milošević was able to use what remained of Serbia's socialist system as an instrument of corruption, and a small coterie of Milošević followers and family members profited handsomely.[101]

Overall, Milošević's ever-shifting ideological positions fit nicely with the opportunism that was a central feature of his campaign style.[102] Perhaps the best distillation of his method was the following statement from journalists with the publication *Vreme*: Milošević "managed to trick both the Communists and the nationalists; the Communists thought that he was only pretending to be nationalist, and the nationalists thought that he was pretending to be Communist."[103] At base a politician, Milošević positioned himself as all things to all people, thus broadening his base of support while maximizing his room to maneuver.

Whatever the underlying motivation, Milošević had by 1990 become a strong advocate of maintaining both Serbia and Yugoslavia as socialist. His decision to position himself as a socialist was decisively important, since this earned Milošević the enmity of the Western press. From 1990 onward, Milošević was singled out for attack, with all the standard phrases reserved for the international villain du jour: The *Washington Post* referred to Milošević as "a hard line socialist"; to the *Los Angeles Times* he headed a "hard line communist government." From Canada, the *Toronto Star* referred to "communist President Slobodan Milošević."[104] The words "hard-line" and "communist" were nearly ubiquitous in press descriptions of Milošević. The London *Independent* provided a particularly colorful portrait: "They don't make leaders like Slobodan Milošević anymore. Square headed, chunky faced, narrow eyed, the Serbian president reads text speeches to rhythmically clapping crowds just like the old communist bosses who, elsewhere in Eastern Europe have slunk into the woodwork."[105] From Germany, an editorial in the *Frankfurter Allgemeine Zeitung* evoked the language of the Cold War and referred to Serbia as "the last bastion of Leninism in Europe." Serbia would in time become "a fortress of communism, out of which it would be possible one day, with the cooperation of a resurgent Soviet Union, to spread Leninism-Stalinism throughout the eastern half of Europe once again."[106] Even in France, traditionally the most pro-Serb country in Western Europe, much of the press adopted the standard rhetoric. According to *Le Monde*, Yugoslav politics offered a "choice between the democratic pluralism established in Slovenia and Croatia, as opposed to the unreformed socialist authoritarianism of the Serbs."[107]

It is tempting to assume that this negative press coverage resulted from Milošević's strident nationalism, his authoritarian tendencies, and the violent crackdown in Kosovo, rather than from any ideological bias. However, human rights considerations cannot account for the Western hostility. We will see that the international press openly supported Balkan political figures who were just as unsavory as Milošević. The principal reason for the hostility toward Milošević was that he advanced views and to some extent specific policies that were anticapitalist, and he was widely perceived as a constraint on the full incorporation of Yugoslavia into the capitalist West. That the press attacks on Milošević were combined with harsh antisocialist and anticommunist language underscores the ideological character of these attacks. Thus, the image of a "red" Serbia was established early on and was continually reinforced and embellished through the familiar phenomenon of pack journalism.[108] This image was to play a decisive role in influencing the course of external involvement in the Balkan conflict.

Authoritarian Democracy in Croatia

A second nationalist figure who emerged during the opening of the late 1980s was Franjo Tudjman of Croatia. Tudjman had begun his career as a communist and a Partisan fighter during World War II and later achieved the rank of general in the Yugoslav National Army. However, during the 1960s, he left the army and moved in a stridently nationalist direction. He later authored a revisionist historical tract, alleging that official accounts of World War II had overstated the numbers of Serbs and Jews who had been killed. Tudjman was active during the nationalist upsurge in Croatia during 1970–1971. In the late 1980s, he was one of the principal organizers of the Croatian Democratic Union (HDZ), one of several nationalist parties that emerged in Croatia during this period. Tudjman rapidly became the leading figure of the HDZ, owing to his long association with historical revisionism, as well as strong support for him among the sizable and influential Croatian expatriate communities in the United States, Canada, and Germany. The latter would prove helpful as a source of funding for the HDZ.[109] From the very beginning the HDZ fostered an atmosphere of intolerance, as some party activists openly extolled the historical legacy of Ante Pavelić's Ustaša movement during World War II. Pavelić became an object of veneration in spite of—or perhaps because of—his close association with Nazi Germany.

It would be fair to say that Tudjman was another example of an illiberal democrat who came to power via an election that was free and fair (at least in the limited sense that multiple parties were able to organize, the suffrage was universal, and the vote counting was reasonably accurate). At the same time, Tudjman fostered an atmosphere of intimidation that was reminiscent of the tactics used by Milošević. According to a study by Jill Irvine: "Extremists within the HDZ and [Tudjman] himself display a hostility toward the opposition that ranges from denunciations of political opponents as 'enemies of the Croat people,' to harassment of opposition leaders and parties, to outright physical intimidation and possibly the assassination of political opponents. At the very least, the common practice of maligning political opponents for allegedly 'betraying' the Croatian cause has created an inhospitable atmosphere for the democratic exchange of views."[110] Tudjman and his supporters adopted a virulent brand of nationalism that openly claimed that the Republic of Croatia was to be a state of the ethnic Croats, with an attitude of suspicion (at best) toward the sizable minority of non-Croats, especially

Serbs. And Tudjman was not above using inflammatory rhetoric: In 1990, he praised the Ustaša regime, noting that it "reflected the centuries-old aspirations of the Croat people," and he later boasted: "Fortunately my wife is neither Serbian nor Jewish." With regard to the Jews: "Genocidal violence is a natural phenomenon, in keeping with the human-social and mythological-divine nature. It is not only allowed, but even recommended."[111] Tudjman later nominated an aging former Ustaša commander as ambassador to Argentina (the nomination was withdrawn due to negative responses from the Argentines). Tudjman also allowed the renaming of a school in honor of another pro-Nazi figure from the Ustaša period.[112]

In the highly charged atmosphere that resulted, the Serb ethnic minority was subjected to discrimination, harassment, and violence. These attacks commenced even before Croatia became independent. Bogdan Denitch writes that "the new Croat authorities [under Tudjman] did little or nothing to protect law-abiding Serbian citizens as they were 'disappeared' in Hospic, Zagreb, Zadar, and other cities. The perpetrators of a massive 'crystal night' in Zadar in the spring of 1991 and other outrages against the Serbian minority were never brought to justice."[113] Misha Glenny goes further and suggests at least some measure of official complicity in these murders: "From about May 1991 onwards, Serb property, especially in the crisis regions under Croat control, became the target of regular bomb attacks. . . . Even before the war began, the [Croatian] government was concerned to hush up nationalist motivated crimes against its Serb population while . . . *its police and soldiers were involved in the slaughter* of innocent Serbs; . . . urban Serbs were among the greatest victims of the war, whose plight, however, is one of the least well known. Tens of thousands were hounded from their homes" (emphasis added).[114] As Serb atrocities in the various Yugoslav wars have received so much attention, it is useful to bear in mind that Serbs have also been the victims of atrocities and, indeed, they were among the very first victims. Serb minorities living in Croatia had excellent reasons to oppose the HDZ government. And they had even better reasons to oppose an independent Croatia, which would be freed from any constraints on the persecution of minorities that the Yugoslav central government might have imposed. In the words of David Gompert, who served on the US National Security Council during this period: "Croats gave ethnic Serbs every reason to fear for their safety."[115]

Provocative statements by Tudjman were reported in the Western press from time to time—for those willing to read very carefully—but they were not emphasized. The specific atrocities against Serbs passed without notice. One had to wait until Tudjman's death in 1999 for the press to openly acknowledge the darker aspects of Croatian nationalism (Tudjman's obituary in the London *Sunday Telegraph* was entitled, "Yes, He Was a Monster, But He Was Our Monster").[116] At the time of Yugoslavia's breakup, however, Tudjman received overwhelmingly positive press coverage, and in June 1990, the *New York Times* furnished space on its opinion page for a promotional article written by Tudjman himself entitled "All We Croatians Want Is Democracy." In the article, Tudjman used familiar phrases calculated to appeal to Western audiences: "It is we, the Croatian people, who have risked our lives to put forward a democratic party and to vote our conscience. And it is we who continue to risk our lives in defiance of totalitarian communism."[117] Readers were sufficiently impressed with these banalities that, in 1991, the *Washington Post* also published an article by Tudjman.[118] In general, Tudjman was presented in the West as a fine example of the type of democratic and free-market liberal that the United States favored, in contrast to the hidebound, neocommunist Milošević.[119] Tudjman's later efforts aimed at secession were also portrayed in a flattering light.

Even the human rights community jumped on the prosecessionist bandwagon: In 1990, Jeri Laber, executive director of Helsinki Watch, coauthored an article—"Why Keep Yugoslavia One Country?"—that virtually advocated the breakup of Yugoslavia. The article contained harsh condemnation of Serb repression against Albanians in Kosovo but made no mention of Tudjman's provocations against Serbs in Croatia.[120] The image of unremitting Serb aggression as the driving force behind conflict in the Balkans was established early, and it has proven indelible.

In addition to the events in Serbia and Croatia, democratization in other republics produced ethnically based parties and ethnically based governments. All republics (with the sole exception of Bosnia-Herzegovina) eventually adopted constitutions that privileged the dominant ethnic group at the expense of ethnic minorities. This was true even of liberal Slovenia: By 1991, the Slovenian constitution referred to the "Slovene nation"—with the word "nation" clearly assuming an ethnic connotation. An organic link between the "nation" and the Slovene ethnic group was suggested, a situation that implicitly excluded non-Slovene ethnic groups who happened to reside in Slovenia. Accordingly, non-Slovene minorities were subjected to petty discrimination and harassment. Some 30 percent of non-Slovenes were refused citizenship, apparently on ethnic grounds.[121] The one exception to this trend, the Republic of Bosnia and Herzegovina, had a constitution that was ethnically neutral and did not privilege any specific ethnic group at the expense of others. But even Bosnia was led by what was in effect a Muslim chauvinist government that sought to advance Muslim communal interests—despite what the constitution said (a matter discussed at length in Chapter 5). In general, the harsh judgments of Robert Hayden, written in 1992, may be only a mild overstatement: "Virtually throughout the territory of ex-Yugoslavia, the levels of individual freedom and freedom of the press are far less under the new 'democratic' regimes than they were in the last several years of communism; . . . the ready acceptance of the results of a single set of hurriedly called elections as affording democratic legitimacy to the winners made it easy for parties and politicians with no democratic inclinations whatever to wrap themselves in the trappings of the new post-socialist cult of the politically sacred."[122]

The Road to War

Overall, the various 1990 elections were major setbacks for Yugoslav unity. Successors to the League of Communists were victorious only in Serbia and Montenegro, and even in these republics, the new Socialist parties were effectively vehicles for Milošević and Serb nationalism. And perhaps inevitably, the elections also set the stage for the final political rupture. The move to break up Yugoslavia was led by the two richest republics, Slovenia and Croatia.

Their motives in doing so were these: First, both republics had an economic interest in secession. This was probably the main motivation. Slovenia and Croatia had always been the richest republics in Yugoslavia, and their residents resented the mandatory payments to the federal government in Belgrade, which were used to finance investment in the underdeveloped republics and provinces in the southeast of the country. Long-standing popular resentment against the subsidy programs was a major factor in the earlier nationalist upsurges in Slovenia and Croatia, during 1969–1971 and again became a focus of agitation during the period 1990–1991. German publications—which were exceptionally friendly toward the secessionist movements—were nevertheless clear eyed about the secessionists' actual motives. According to *Die Zeit* of Hamburg: "Slovenia and Croatia want to leave the federated Yugoslavia *because they see the eastern republics as hindrances to their prosperity.* Above all the Slovenians . . . feel that they are being kept from achieving a European standard of living. And they believe that they have contributed a disproportionately high amount to the federal budget and to the national fund used to develop backward regions" (emphasis added).[123] From Munich, the *Süddeutsche Zeitung* made a similar point: Slovenia "assumed enormous burdens, contributing 22 percent of the national budget, as well as development funds for the other republics. *This was the main reason that so many Slovenians supported independence*" (emphasis added).[124] And from Croatia, Stjepan Mesić later acknowledged that his republic sought independence mainly because "its hard currency was being siphoned off."[125] In short, economic self-interest was a significant motivating factor.

Second, there was an ideological motivation for Slovenian and Croatian secession. The 1990 elections brought to power neoliberal parties that were determined to speed up privatization, to abandon the last vestiges of socialism, and to join the capitalist West as soon as possible. It was feared that the more socialist-oriented republics, led by Serbia, would serve as a brake on rapid privatization; a desire to prevent this scenario served as an additional incentive to secede. Prominent Slovenes were quite open about this objective. Slovenian economists Janez Prasnikar and Zivko Pregl advocated a free-market economy for Yugoslavia in an article published in the *American Economic Review* in May 1991. Near the end of the article, they added: "Some republics are working toward independence, in the belief that they can more successfully enact a stabilization program on their own than in the [Yugoslav] union."[126] And President Tudjman believed that "Croatia's moral superiority over Serbia lay in its fervent commitment to free market economics."[127]

Third, the leaders of Slovenia and Croatia were assured of external support from the governments of Germany and Austria; the Vatican; important segments of the international financial community; and most of the Western press.[128] Assurances of foreign support—which were offered before the republics seceded—undoubtedly influenced the decision-making process that led to the breakup of Yugoslavia. (The international politics of secession are discussed in the next chapter.)

A fourth motive was the excessive power and disproportionate influence of the Republic of Serbia within the federation. There is little doubt that Milošević's successful effort to end the autonomy of the Kosovo and Vojvodina provinces, as well as his meddling in the internal politics of Montenegro, caused apprehension throughout the federation. His unsuccessful efforts to hold a mass demonstration of Serbs in Slovenia contributed further to this apprehension. More generally, Milošević's willingness to use unscrupulous methods to advance his interests, and his apparent success in doing so, contributed to the climate of tension. On balance, however, the Milošević factor has been overstated as a specific cause of secession. A pro-Milošević coup was never a realistic possibility in Slovenia and Croatia, given the small number of ethnic Serbs that lived in those republics. And clearly, Milošević was *not* the only figure in Yugoslavia to use unscrupulous methods during this period. Nevertheless, the aggressive tactics of Milošević and his allies must count among the various factors that influenced the decisions of Slovene and Croat leaders to opt for a secessionist route.

The institutional structures that formed the central government in Belgrade—which had never been very strong to begin with—began to wither. The League of Communists had been gradually losing prestige and membership since the death of Tito. During the period 1980–1989, the number of youths who held membership in the League declined by more than half (and in Croatia and Slovenia, the membership decline was especially precipitous).[129] In a climactic party congress in January 1990, the Slovene wing of the League withdrew; the League never reconvened after the Slovene departure, and it effectively ceased to exist at the national level.[130]

The dissolution of the party structure left the Yugoslav National Army and the central government, led by the federal prime minister, Ante Marković, as the only truly national institutions of any importance.[131] Marković had been appointed prime minister in 1989 and assumed his duties amidst considerable optimism. An ethnic Croat by origin, Marković eschewed ethnic identifications. Instead, he projected the image of a pro-Yugoslav patriot and became the principal advocate of a united Yugoslavia. Though a nominal communist, he distanced himself from the party structure, declaring: "Yugoslavia will continue to function with or without the League of Communists."[132] To build popular support, he launched his own, noncommunist party, the Alliance of Reform Forces, which fielded candidates in four republics during the 1990 elections.[133] Marković had to govern through an institutional structure that was complicated to say the least, consisting of a Federal Executive Council as well as a Collective Presidency. Despite these pitfalls, the prime minister was able (for a brief period) to circumvent the bureaucracy to some extent, and to impose his own vision of how Yugoslavia should be governed.

Assisted by a team of prominent economists, including the Harvard professor Jeffrey Sachs, Marković launched a program of radical economic restructuring, which sought a full break with socialist economics.[134] Marković was convinced that through the introduction of a full market economy, Yugoslavia could overcome its economic difficulties, which in his view were the root causes of the political malaise. Marković achieved some initial success when his brand of shock therapy managed to end a bout of hyperinflation and (temporarily) restore confidence in the Yugoslav dinar.[135] He was greatly admired in the West for his promarket policies and his cooperativeness with the IMF; Western officials still view him in retrospect as something of a tragic hero, who "almost" saved Yugoslavia. The memoirs of US ambassador Warren Zimmermann describe Marković as follows: "He was one of the few admirable figures in a landscape of monsters and midgets; . . . his dynamism and supreme self-confidence impressed visiting Westerners. . . . George Soros, a shrewd judge of Eastern European politicians, told me after a visit to Belgrade that Marković was one of the most remarkable leaders he had met."[136]

In reality, Marković's economic success never quite lived up to its billing. The curbing of inflation had been achieved at great cost due to its emphasis on wage freezes. According to a Radio Free Europe report: "Most agree ... that the poorest segments of society will bear the greatest burden of the [Marković] government's attempt to overcome the economic crisis, as has happened in Poland and Hungary."[137] Nevertheless, the population was not only encouraged by the prime minister's sense of drive and purpose but also impressed by his positive relationship with the US ambassador and other Western interests, since this introduced the possibility of external financial support and debt relief.

Overall, the Marković government probably represented the last real opportunity for preventing war. A series of public opinion polls taken during the spring of 1990 found that Marković was the most popular political figure in the country; with the sole exception of Kosovo, a majority of respondents in every region expressed support for Marković's economic program. Also, a majority of Yugoslavs still favored preserving the country in some form, for 57 percent favored a federal or confederal system of government, while only 19 percent favored secession or national dissolution. Even in Slovenia and Croatia, most favored some form of a Yugoslav solution to the crisis.[138] The leaders of Slovenia and Croatia had probably already decided on a secessionist course, but their populations were not yet so sure. A significant level of economic aid by the United States, such as debt relief, could have been decisive at this point. Of course, an earlier infusion of economic aid—during the early 1980s—would have been even more effective. As late as 1990, debt relief was still a realistic alternative to war. However, as much as Western officials liked Marković's free-market policies, they failed to provide any significant aid. The United States declined even a request to postpone payment of part of the Yugoslav debt.[139]

By June 1990, inflation began to accelerate once again, despite the shock therapy, and "Marković's popularity began to plummet with the economy."[140] The prime minister's party, the Alliance of Reform Forces, fared poorly in all four republican elections where it participated. By December 1990, the Alliance was attracting only 5 percent support in public opinion polls.[141] As Marković declined, the locus of decision making gradually shifted away from the central government and toward the republics. Slovenia and Croatia increasingly refused to cooperate with IMF and central government–imposed austerity programs, and they also refused to contribute their required shares to the federal budget, beginning in the late 1980s. Both republics vetoed efforts to hold national elections; they insisted that elections should be held only in the individual republics. Had national elections been held at the time, Marković might have won, and his position would have been strengthened—but this possibility was blocked. The Republic of Serbia also contributed to the growing disorder. In 1990, the Milošević regime used federal funds for internal spending within Serbia (to augment the regime's popularity prior to elections), and it did so without central government authorization.[142] During 1990–1991, Slovenia and Croatia actively prepared for secession. Both republics restructured their Territorial Defense Forces into national armies, and they (quietly) began to purchase weapons from abroad.[143] Meanwhile, senior army officers warned the republics against secession.[144] The stage was set for civil war.

As tensions mounted, Slovenia and Croatia proposed a solution for the conflict: Yugoslavia should be restructured into a confederation. In October 1990, Slovene and Croat experts unveiled a detailed constitutional plan for confederation.[145] Officially, the plan was presented as a means of "saving" Yugoslavia and preventing a breakup; in reality, it was a cleverly disguised blueprint for achieving breakup through legal means. The proposed confederation was to be an "*international* organization modeled after the European Community" composed of the former Yugoslav republics. Each of the confederated republics would exist as "*independent, sovereign states*" (emphasis added).[146] And the member states were free to leave the confederation, if they wished to do so.[147] In his detailed assessment of the constitutional plan, Robert Hayden draws the following conclusions:

> [The confederation proposal] looks to have been a carefully constructed constitutional fraud, which seemed to promise the creation of a structure for a new Yugoslavia, but that instead took care to ensure that no viable institutions would in fact be created. Why would such a fraud be perpetrated? . . . Croatia and Slovenia were probably trying to overcome . . . resistance to the breakup of Yugoslavia by creating a structure that destroyed the country under the guise of restructuring it. As Susan Woodward notes: "Many outside observers and domestic liberals saw confederation as the best way out of the deadlock politically, paying almost no attention to its starting assumption that the republics were equivalent to [independent] states."[148]

The confederation plan was opposed by Serbia and Montenegro (as well as by the federal army), and it was not implemented. However, that Slovenia and Croatia proposed such a "reasonable" plan—and that they seceded only after the plan was rejected—went a long way toward convincing outside observers that the secessionists were in the right and their opponents were in the wrong.

With the collapse of their constitutional plan, Slovenia and Croatia resolved that secession was their best option.[149] During June 25–26, 1991, both republics officially declared their independence from Yugoslavia.[150] The army, as promised, intervened with military force in an effort to terminate the secessions. Yugoslavia was finished as an integral state, and nearly a decade of war, foreign intervention, and humanitarian disaster lay ahead.

Conclusion

Key issues that are often raised by the Yugoslav wars include the following: What historical lessons can be learned from this experience? In addition, what actions can world leaders take to prevent such wars from recurring in the future? Overwhelmingly, the answers to these questions involve the early use of military force. The United States and its allies, in this view, should have acted earlier and used force to restrain Serb aggression, to demonstrate Western resolve.[151] And inevitably, there are the familiar comparisons with World War II: At one point, Madeleine Albright adopted the view that "in dealing with Slobodan Milošević, the West must not repeat the appeasement at Munich in 1938 and other mistakes that initially allowed Hitler to move unimpeded against his neighbors and led him to conclude that Nazi policies would go unopposed."[152] Thus, the main historical lesson of the Yugoslav conflict has been the need for an early use of force against perceived aggressors.

There are two problems with this interpretation. First, it is based on the assumption that virtually all the Balkan conflicts had their origins in Serb aggression and that the other ethnic groups bore little or no responsibility for the breakup of the federation or for the wars that followed. As we have seen, this is not an accurate interpretation. While the racist and aggressive actions of Milošević undoubtedly were *one* set of factors, they were far from being the only factors. Franjo Tudjman was just as racist and aggressive as Milošević; the persecution of ethnic Serbs in Croatia was just as morally objectionable as the Serb-perpetrated atrocities in Kosovo. In addition, one also must consider the element of self-interest in the Croatian and also Slovenian secessionist efforts. The desire of Croatians and Slovenians to hold on to their hard currency reserves—rather than share them with the other republics—was a source of tension in the Yugoslav federation that went back at least to the 1970s. It is an issue that predated Milošević's rise to power. Interpretations that exclusively blame Milošević or the Serbs are inconsistent with the record of events.

A second problem with Albright's interpretation is its excessive emphasis on the purely *military* aspects of the Yugoslav wars, and the corresponding need for military solutions. What such analyses ignore is the economic deterioration that made the war possible in the first place, as well as the culpability of the Western financial community (especially the IMF) in contributing to this deterioration. The structural adjustment programs that were imposed upon Yugoslavia beginning in 1979 were not inevitable: They were the result of specific choices made by Western officials to pursue debt repayment and to disregard the social and political consequences of these policies. There were other policy options—such as debt relief—that were well within the means of the Western powers. Forgiving Yugoslavia's debt would surely have been less costly than the various efforts at military intervention during the period 1991–1999.[153] The insistence on imposing austerity measures must be considered one of the major causes of Yugoslavia's disintegration. Accordingly, the Western powers must bear a large part of the blame for the wars of 1991–1999 and the associated humanitarian disaster.

4

Germany Drops a Match

> Tribal conflicts, we are told, "flare up" unaccountably. I used
> to accept this, without much thought, but now when I hear
> of a tribal conflict "flaring up" I try to find out in whose
> interest it was to drop a match.
> —*Conor Cruise O'Brien*

The Yugoslav conflict began in 1991, a year when US policy makers were, to say the least, distracted. The year had begun with the Persian Gulf War—the largest use of US military force since Vietnam—and ended with the final breakup of the Soviet Union. Accordingly, Yugoslavia was one conflict that the United States was content at least initially to leave to the European powers, especially the dominant power in the region, Germany.[1] And thus, during the first six months of the Yugoslav wars, Germany was to play the leading role in "managing" the crisis. Only later would the United States find this German assertiveness embarrassing and seek to establish US authority in the Balkan conflict. Meanwhile, during 1991, German officials were effectively in charge, and Germany undertook its first major foreign policy adventure since the Third Reich.

Germany was clearly the main advocate within the European Community for supporting Slovenian and Croatian independence from Yugoslavia, while condemning actions by the Yugoslav National Army aimed at terminating the secessions through military force. German diplomatic activity reached a high point in December 1991 and January 1992, when Germany recognized Slovenia and Croatia and then successfully pressured the European Community to recognize them as well, thus terminating the existence of Yugoslavia. In retrospect, these German actions have been the source of much controversy, and some have criticized the allegedly "premature" nature of this recognition. Many key figures in the diplomacy of this period emphasize how German actions helped destabilize the political situation in the Balkans and helped spread the conflict. German officials have defended their actions as restrained and morally necessary. According to the memoirs of one diplomat, German policy sought to "direct the process of [Yugoslav] dissolution into orderly channels and to limit its destructive effects."[2]

It is interesting to note that both sides in this debate seem to accept that Germany intervened in the conflict only *after* the war had begun, and that Germany's actions were limited to diplomatic maneuvering. In this chapter, we will see that Germany's role was deeper—and far more significant—than has been recognized. We will see that Germany began encouraging Croatian nationalists and preparing them for independence months before the war began. Based on this new information, I argue that German officials did not simply *respond* to the war; they helped initiate it.[3] Germany was indeed the first major power to "drop a match" on the ethnic tensions of the Balkans—to use O'Brien's metaphor—and it thus played a key role in triggering the conflagration that followed. The European Community and the United States would prove active, if sometimes reluctant, partners with Germany.

German Intervention in the Yugoslav Conflict

Germany's covert intervention began in 1990, while Yugoslavia was still an integral state. In that year, German officials from the Federal Office for the Protection of the Constitution (BFV), a subdivision of the Interior Ministry, assisted in building up Croatia's intelligence service, the National Security Office (UNS).[4] In the course of this activity, German officials would openly collaborate with extreme nationalists in Franjo Tudjman's HDZ party.

This early German intervention, though little known, is nevertheless well documented. According to an article in *Jane's Intelligence Review*:

> Politically, the main external connection of Croatia's intelligence services has been with Germany. . . . It is an extremely controversial de facto alliance which has been regarded with considerable unease in some quarters in both the [European Community] and NATO. Domestically, Germany's alliance with Croatia in the areas of intelligence and internal security was made to order for the Serbian propagandists . . . who thus drew a direct analogy between this contemporary German-Croatian relationship and Nazi sponsorship of Ante Pavelić's Ustaša puppet state during the Second World War; . . . the German government was fully aware throughout that Ustaša elements were and remain prominent in the UNS and the HDZ governmental apparatus as a whole.[5]

The key point is *when* Germany began to provide intelligence support for Croatia. Here, the *Jane's* report is unequivocal:

> *Dating back to as early as 1990, when Croatia was still a constituent republic*
> *of an internationally recognized state* [emphasis added], German involve-
> ment with Croatia's intelligence services began with the UNS whose first
> name was a direct copy of Germany's BFV . . . Politically, however, the
> new UNS had little in common with the BFV which is the political intel-
> ligence service of a genuinely democratic state, a fact that made the links
> between the BFV and the UNS all the more controversial politically . . .
> staff training has reportedly been the most important input. Taking place
> in both Croatia and Germany, the provision of such operational training
> services was also reportedly later extended to [other Croatian agencies,
> beyond the UNS].[6]

The general picture is corroborated in a separate account in the US publication *Defense and Foreign Affairs Strategic Policy*, which confirms that "German intelligence officers provided significant support and training" to their
Croatian counterparts. They did so "at all stages, both in Croatia and in Germany." And *Strategic Policy* confirms that this German support commenced
before Croatia seceded from Yugoslavia.[7]

It is important to bear in mind that Germany was *not* helping Croatia
set up a postal service or an environmental protection agency; it was helping
build an intelligence and security service, and this was done in full secrecy.
These actions were not politically neutral: Many of the German-trained intelligence operatives were openly fascist, and they held positive views regarding the Ustaša regime during World War II. It thus appears that Germany
was actively preparing the Croatians for independence and giving them the
institutional wherewithal to achieve this. Croatian leaders were assured, well
in advance, that Germany, the dominant power in Europe, would support
their efforts to establish an independent state and to secede from Yugoslavia.
Germany also conveyed its assurances to Croatia's partner republic, Slovenia.[8] According to David Halberstam: "The Slovenians were already aware
[by February 1990] that the Germans . . . favored their independence."[9]

German support for the secessionists is noted by several other sources.
French Air Force general Pierre M. Gallois asserts that Germany began supplying arms to Croatia, including antitank and antiaircraft rockets, in early
1991—before the war began.[10] Off the record, US officials also acknowledged
German intervention. An investigative article in the *New Yorker* cites an
anonymous US diplomat who alleged that German foreign minister Hans-
Dietrich Genscher "was encouraging the Croats to leave the federation and
declare independence."[11] It is difficult to fully assess this allegation, given the
anonymity of the source. However, the *New Yorker* allegation is supported by
the memoirs of US ambassador Warren Zimmermann, which note "Gen-

scher's tenacious decision to *rush the independence of Slovenia and Croatia*" (emphasis added).[12] Genscher himself was openly sympathetic toward the secessionists. In his memoirs, he stated: "It was also important for us to establish that the Yugoslav peoples alone had the right to freely determine the future of their nation"—with the implication that the Yugoslav central government could not veto this right. Genscher also affirmed "an individual nation's 'right to secede' from the larger [Yugoslav] polity."[13] State Department official John Bolton later stated that Germany "induced the Slovenes and the Croats to jump ship," that is, to leave the federation.[14] German support for secession and for breaking up Yugoslavia is also noted by the former Canadian ambassador to Yugoslavia, James Bissett and by Croatian nationalist Stjepan Mesić.[15]

The full details of Germany's behind-the-scenes efforts to support Slovene and Croat nationalism must await the declassification of official documents and the opening of archives. However, the evidence available shows that Germany was taking specific measures to effect Yugoslavia's dissolution. In retrospect, Germany's actions contained a heavy element of miscalculation and showed a tendency to underestimate the destructive consequences that the intervention might have. In 1991, however, the prospective breakup of the Yugoslav federation seemed a triumph of a newly assertive German foreign policy.

Why did Germany support separatism? Clearly, part of Germany's interest was historically based. As we have seen, German foreign policy had a long record of activity in Eastern Europe and especially in the Balkans. The "eastern question" was of course, a major factor in German objectives in both world wars. During the post-1945 years, Germany had to resign itself to a period of political quiescence in light of widespread international distrust. This sense of restraint diminished, however, with the new circumstances that attended German reunification and the simultaneous end of the Cold War during 1990–1991. After reunification, Germany developed expansive ambitions, which aimed at reestablishing to some extent German dominance in eastern and southeastern Europe. In 1992, the *Washington Post* offered this assessment:

> German influence in the region—especially in Czechoslovakia, Hungary, and Poland—has become pervasive. . . . "It is our natural market," said Otto Wolff von Amerongen, for years the chairman of the Eastern Committee, an industrial group that helps German businesses make deals in Eastern Europe. "It will cost us more than anyone else but in the end, this market will perhaps bring us to the same position we were in before World War I. Why not?" . . . "It should be no surprise that Germany

would become the most important partner for Eastern Europe," said Heinrich Machowski, Eastern European analyst at the German Institute for Economic Research here. "Just look at the geography. Look at history. Look at language. The technical elite of the Eastern countries speak German."... "Germany is positioning itself to dominate not only eastern Germany and not only Eastern Europe but also the Soviet markets once they become viable," said Christian von Thun-Hohenstein, an investment banker.... "They'll have an automatic 'in' in the old Soviet Union and Eastern Europe because they will be the suppliers of the capital goods."[16]

True, Germany's trade with the former communist states was only a small percentage of its total trade.[17] However, trade with the East was increasing rapidly during the early 1990s, and there were expectations of much greater opportunities in the future.[18] Though it appears that the private sector was leading the way, German government officials too sought an expanded presence in the East.[19]

By early 1991, Germany was consolidating a sphere of influence in the Balkans.[20] The principal impediment to consolidating such a sphere was socialist Yugoslavia, which posed a potential brake on German ambitions in the region. Privatization of the economy was likely to be limited, given the considerable influence of Slobodan Milošević's Socialist Party, as well the communist-oriented Yugoslav National Army within the federation. Breaking the country apart was an obvious solution: The central government of Yugoslavia, still nominally communist, could be dissolved, while the most prosperous and procapitalist republics—Slovenia and Croatia—could be separated.

Clearly, anticommunism was an important motivation in the German attitude. A 1991 analysis from the German foreign ministry described the Yugoslav conflict as a "fight for the market economy against the centralized command economy, of democratic pluralism against one-party dominance, of constitutional statehood against military oppression."[21] This anticommunist policy was favored by Helmut Kohl's ruling Christian Democratic Union, and many on the Left agreed as well. Social Democratic leader Björn Engholm openly endorsed the Yugoslav secessions, noting: "The 'path to liberation' from the Stalinist hold on eastern and southern Europe now proceeds through the establishment of new countries"—and as a concomitant of this strategy, old countries such as Yugoslavia would be taken apart. Engholm added: "Similar developments can be expected in the whole region and in parts of the Soviet Union."[22] Thus, disassembling Yugoslavia and possibly other communist states into their constituent republics would finish communism and socialism once and for all, not only in the Balkans but also throughout Eastern Europe and Eurasia. Key impediments to German expansion would thus be removed, or at least greatly reduced. Germany's ideological objection to communism dovetailed with larger geostrategic interests in the region.[23]

The breakup of the Yugoslav federation initially created two new states, Slovenia and Croatia, and these were exceptionally friendly toward German objectives. Germany was especially eager to establish close relations with Croatia, which had after all been a puppet state of the Third Reich during the period 1941–1944. After Croatia declared independence, Chancellor Kohl coyly observed: "A very tight relationship exists between the Germans and the Croats, which has a lot to do with history."[24]

Finally, intervention in the Yugoslavia conflict was a way of announcing to the world and to Europe that Germany had truly arrived as a regional power, one willing and able to act unilaterally in certain circumstances. The timidity that had characterized German policy for so long was to be cast aside. A US social scientist, writing in *Der Spiegel*, noted that the breakup of Yugoslavia was a "step toward the creation of a new German sphere of influence in Middle and Eastern Europe." The article added that "it was not about peace in the Balkans, but the position of Germany in Europe."[25] The *Frankfurter Allgemeine Zeitung* took a similar view: "It can be taken for granted that Slovenia and Croatia—after achieving independence—will seek political, economic, and cultural ties . . . to Germany. If this were to happen, then the political balance, which has been tilted anyway after the collapse of the communist regimes in Eastern Europe, would shift even further from the West to Middle Europe"—that is, toward Germany.[26] And the new assertiveness was a way to advertise Germany's potential to act independently of the United States. In early 1992, an editor of Munich's *Süddeutsche Zeitung* declared: "The old days when Germany was tied to the US . . . are irretrievably gone."[27]

An additional factor was the influence of domestic pressure groups, notably the sizable Croatian emigré community in Germany. Expatriate Croats lobbied for an independent Croatia, and they influenced German policy toward Yugoslavia in much the same way that the Cuban emigré community in the United States influences policy toward Cuba.[28] From Bavaria, there was some religiously based support for Catholic Slovenia and Croatia, as opposed to the predominantly Orthodox republics of eastern Yugoslavia.[29] And as noted, the German business community was enthusiastic about the prospect of reestablishing commercial influence in the East.

Germany's efforts received strong support from the Vatican, which was eager to promote the two principal Catholic states in the Balkans, Slovenia and Croatia. According to Ambassador Bissett, "The Vatican was openly lobbying for [Slovenian and Croatian] independence," and this lobbying began as early as 1990.[30] The Vatican's prosecession policies also were influenced by ideological considerations: Support for anti-communist Slovenia and Croatia dovetailed nicely with the worldview of Pope John Paul II.[31] In addition, Austria was "pressing for the recognition of Slovene and Croatian independence," as noted by Bissett.[32] Austria had long-standing historical ties to the secessionist republics, which had both been part of the Austro-Hungarian Empire prior to World War I; they continued to have important economic and cultural ties to Austria.[33] Though Austria and the Vatican were not of course member states of the European Community, they nevertheless argued in favor of the secessionists.

This external support for secession was decisively important: As we saw in the preceding chapter, a majority of Yugoslavs in most republics opposed secession as late as 1990, according to a public opinion poll. This was even true for Slovenia and Croatia. If Germany had not offered encouragement, it seems doubtful that Slovenian and Croatian elites would have been willing to pursue secession and defy the federal authorities with such confidence. German intervention exacerbated the situation and pushed the crisis toward national disintegration and ethnic war.

The Yugoslav National Army and Secession

> [In 1861] all thoughts were anxiously directed to an
> impending civil war. . . . Both parties deprecated war, but
> one of them would *make* war rather than let the nation
> survive, and the other would *accept* war rather than let it
> perish, and the war came.
> —*Abraham Lincoln, 1865*

> Those who want this war are forcing it on all of us.
> —*Admiral Stane Brovet, Yugoslav
> deputy defense minister, 1991*

Let us now turn our attention to the internal aspects of Yugoslavia's dissolution.[34] The formal breakup of Yugoslavia began when Slovenia and Croatia announced their independence June 25–26, 1991. The secession crisis inevitably placed the Yugoslav National Army (JNA) center stage. The JNA had long enjoyed a position of considerable privilege in Yugoslavia. It was at the time one of the largest and best-equipped armies in Europe; expenditure on the military was by far the largest item in the federal budget. JNA officers (especially those of higher rank) enjoyed significant material advantages, including an array of high-quality vacation resorts reserved for the army.[35] But because the army was a bastion of socialist and Titoist tradition, its role also entailed an ideological dimension. In a January 1991 statement, the army's leaders declared: "Socialism is not finished and has not been brought to its knees. Yugoslavia . . . has managed to overcome the first strike of the anti-communist hysteria wave." The January statement emphasized the need to retain Yugoslavia "as a federative and socialist society."[36] In press accounts, the JNA has often been portrayed as Serb dominated, but this is not accurate.[37] It is true that ethnic Serbs constituted over 50 percent of the officer corps, due to the Serbs' traditional identification with the military; also many officers shared Milošević's endorsement of socialism.[38] However, the top JNA commanders had always been selected with the objective of maintaining an ethnic balance, and the Serbs did not dominate at that level.

As the war began, in June 1991, the minister of defense and the chief military officer was Gen. Veljko Kadijević, who was of mixed Serb and Croat descent and had been born in Croatia.[39] The deputy defense minister and chief naval officer, Adm. Stane Brovet (quoted earlier), was a Slovene; the army chief of staff, Gen. Blagoje Adžić, was a Serb; and the air force commander, Gen. Zvonko Jurjević was a Croat.[40] During the Slovenian secession crisis, the JNA dispatched Gen. Konrad Kolšek, another ethnic Slovene, to command federal task forces.[41] A combination of communism and Yugoslav nationalism—rather than Serb nationalism—remained the JNA's dominant ideology. On the eve of war, the army leadership was the principal force seeking to hold Yugoslavia together, by force if necessary. As Slovenia and Croatia declared their independence in late June, Gen. Kadijević warned: "Let no one delude themselves into believing that they will be able to do away with Yugoslavia and break its territorial integrity," a thinly veiled threat of military force.[42]

The Yugoslav central government under Prime Minister Ante Marković had been losing power and prestige during this period, but it continued to function. Though an ethnic Croat, Marković opposed the secessionists and sought to preserve Yugoslavia. By late June, Marković and his multiethnic government resolved to use the army as a last resort to prevent national collapse.[43] He signed an order authorizing the JNA to "protect the state border," with the implicit understanding that some degree of force might be necessary.[44] Slovenian nationalist Janez Janša later recalled that Marković had "ordered the armed intervention of [the JNA] in Slovenia."[45] And James Bissett, the Canadian ambassador, confirmed that "Marković . . . ordered the Army into Slovenia to restore order."[46] At this phase of the conflict, the prime minister and the army acted in concert. These actions led directly to war. On June 27, conflict commenced between the JNA and Slovene forces as federal troops sought to establish control of border crossings. The JNA, commanded by General Kolšek, faced the Slovene militia, which had been formed from elements of the republic-level Territorial Defense Forces, as well as local security units.[47]

The ten-day war that followed was militarily uneventful: The JNA was extremely reluctant to use its heavy weaponry and sought mainly to intimidate the Slovenes into calling off their secessionist efforts. Contrary to popular belief, the Slovenes did not in fact face a larger military force; it was the JNA that was outnumbered. Sixty-seven fatalities resulted from the war, and almost two-thirds of these were federal soldiers. Only twenty-three Slovenes were killed.[48]

The Slovenes in fact initiated most of the fighting.[49] According to the memoirs of Warren Zimmermann, the US ambassador at the time, the "not very heroic Slovenian (and later Croatian) tactic was not to take on the JNA directly but to lay siege to JNA barracks and try to starve the soldiers out." Ambassador Zimmermann also stated:

> It wasn't accurate to talk of a JNA "invasion." . . . Its troops were, quite normally, stationed in camps in every Yugoslav republic. . . . [The Slovene leadership, however,] won the support of the world's television viewers. . . . They made brilliant use of psychological warfare—blowing off air raid sirens even when there was no threat, shooting down an unarmed JNA helicopter, carrying only bread and then charging it with aggressive intent, comparing the JNA's limited actions (about which the Army had actually informed the Slovenes in advance) with the Soviet Union's 1968 invasion of Czechoslovakia. Unlike the JNA, paranoid about the West, the Slovenes welcomed foreign journalists, to whom they retailed the epic struggle of their tiny republic against the Yugoslav colossus. It was the most brilliant public relations coup in the history of Yugoslavia.[50]

Similarly, Secretary of State James Baker later noted: "The fact of the matter is that it was Slovenia and Croatia who unilaterally declared independence. . . . They used force to seize their border posts. And that, indeed, triggered the civil conflict."[51] These accounts are supported by Bissett: "The fighting started because Slovenia . . . declared unilateral independence and used force to seize customs posts along the Austrian border."[52]

Despite these considerations, newspaper coverage at the time was overwhelmingly favorable toward the secessionists, and hostile toward the JNA. The press presented the war as a simple morality tale featuring the courageous, westernized Slovenes—who sought only to defend themselves—

opposing a massive communist invasion force. The *Economist* provided this riveting account: "The air raid sirens went off.... An hour earlier jets had fired small rockets at Ljubljana castle.... Slovenia's nightmare was coming true: The Yugoslav Army was out of political control.... Hours later, tanks moved to take control of Yugoslavia's international frontier posts. The Slovene territorial forces resisted.... Now with the [federal] Army listening to no one, Slovenes are surer than ever that the old Yugoslavia must never return."[53] From the *Financial Times*: "Slovenes have learnt that the name 'Yugoslav' belongs to an army which sends bombs and tanks to crush them."[54] Retrospective analyses of the Slovenia war, written more recently, also assume that this was a war of aggression directed against the innocent Slovenes.[55]

Such accounts were off the mark—as Ambassador Zimmermann's account suggests—but they were presented in some of the world's leading publications and had considerable effect. Ambassador Bissett later noted: "The media coverage of the 'Slovene war' played a major role in shaping subsequent public opinion in the West. The federal troops were from the outset described as the 'Serb dominated' Yugoslav Army, and Western media soon depicted the struggle as one of David and Goliath, with the JNA playing the role of the giant Goliath."[56] The Slovenes themselves used anticommunist rhetoric in their propaganda, which fit in nicely with stereotyped preconceptions widespread among Western audiences at that time. From the United States, Slovenia's publicity office issued the following statement: "The communist Yugoslav Army has become a loose cannon—We plead for your help!!!"[57] Manipulation of the press by various parties would appear again and again as a staple feature of the various Balkan conflicts that followed the Slovenia affair.

Overall, the Slovene actions stunned the JNA, which had not expected that the crisis would lead to general combat. Caught off balance, the army declined to use anything close to the full firepower at its disposal, even to extricate its own besieged troops. General Adžić, the JNA chief of staff, later commented: "Having been brought up over decades in the Yugoslav spirit, we could not believe that so much evil and hatred could accumulate in one place and be expressed in such terrible forms."[58] There is no doubt that the army high command was out of touch with the national mood and greatly underestimated the Slovenes' determination to establish an independent state. Troop morale was low, especially among the large number of ethnic Serb conscripts; Serb nationalists had little interest in Slovenia, since in that republic there was no large group of ethnic Serb minorities that required external protection. The Serb soldiers were far more interested in secessionist Croatia, where their fellow Serbs were indeed threatened. As a result of these factors, the JNA efforts in Slovenia were marked by a high rate of desertion, which sapped the army's effectiveness. Large numbers of federal soldiers were forced to surrender to the Slovenes.[59] A final consideration was the overwhelming international hostility toward the JNA's early efforts to hold the federation together. This lack of external support served as an additional and probably decisive constraint on the army's initial efforts to resist the trend toward national disintegration.

The Slovenia war was the first step in a series of incidents that eroded the multiethnic character of the JNA itself and helped transform the army, over time, into a force for Serb nationalism. As we have seen, the middle and lower ranks of the officer corps had always contained a disproportionate number of ethnic Serbs. The desertion of most Slovene and Croat troops that preceded the war further increased the proportion of Serbs. An incipient power struggle emerged within the JNA between soldiers who sought to transform the army into a Serb force and those who wished to retain its multiethnic, Yugoslav character.[60] The pro-Yugoslav faction of the army—led by its senior commanders, who were predominantly non-Serb—would remain in charge for several more months. The army was not yet transformed into an instrument of Serb nationalism, but with the secession of Slovenia, the first steps in that direction had clearly been taken.

The JNA effectively abandoned Slovenia by mid-July and gradually withdrew its remaining troops from the republic. This action was to prove decisively important: It set a precedent not only that republics could secede from the federation but also that they could secede with relatively little effort and at low cost; or so it seemed at the time. And it was clear that the international press would provide extensive and positive coverage to secessionists, combined with negative coverage of even the mildest efforts by federal authorities to prevent secession.

The Origins of War in Croatia

The secession of ethnically homogeneous Slovenia was a relatively clean affair achieved with little bloodshed. The war in Croatia that followed was clearly not going to be so simple, owing to the sizable Serb minority in that republic; ethnic Serbs constituted some 12 percent of the population of Croatia.[61] The JNA intervention in Croatia, which began in the late summer of 1991, would mark the true start of the violent, destructive phase of Yugoslavia's dissolution. It was here that the JNA opted to use air raids, heavy artillery, and naval guns for the first time on a large scale, resulting in thousands of combat deaths. And it was in Croatia that the first substantial atrocities against noncombatants occurred.

The Croatian war had its origins with the nationalist forces that were unleashed during the election campaign of 1990, when Franjo Tudjman's HDZ party came to power. As we have seen, Tudjman's election campaign was marked by what Susan Woodward has termed "anti-Semitic and anti-Serb vitriol," which encouraged a wave of violent attacks against Serbs in urban areas of Croatia.[62] The anti-Serb violence had begun even before independence, and continued during and after the secessionist crisis of June–July 1991. Later, in 1993, an official from Helsinki Watch would comment: "Since 1991, the Croatian authorities have blown up or razed 10,000 houses, mostly of Serbs, but also houses of Croats [presumably those opposed to the HDZ regime]. . . . In some cases they dynamited homes with the families inside. Whole families were killed." By 1993, two-thirds of the Serbs living in Zagreb had been driven from their homes. These attacks were undertaken by Croat vigilantes, apparently with some degree of official encouragement.[63] Press accounts of the Yugoslav war have often emphasized the role of unremitting Serb aggression as virtually the sole cause of violence. Such accounts disregard Croat provocations against Serbs, which played a key role in triggering the conflict.

A second source of conflict can be traced to the rural areas of eastern Croatia, loosely known as the Krajina.[64] The Krajina had long been an area of ethnic conflict and, indeed, some of the worst massacres of World War II occurred in this area, as the Ustaša militias from the pro-Nazi Croatian puppet state sought to cleanse the region of Serbs and other despised ethnic groups. Krajina Serbs who managed to survive the Ustaša period had a strong sense of historically based grievance. These memories of mass killings were compounded by economic grievances: The Krajina region had always been one of the most economically backward regions of Croatia. This backwardness was intensified by the debt crisis and economic adjustment of the 1980s, which caused large-scale deindustrialization and hardships.[65]

During the period 1990–1991, as Croatia prepared for secession, the Serbs in Krajina once again feared persecution. The attacks against urban Serbs just described became well known among Serbs in the Krajina. Within the Krajina itself, there were petty acts of harassment and intimidation by the Croat authorities. A major point of contention concerned efforts by Croat authorities to "Croatianize" the language and suppress the use of the Cyrillic alphabet. According to a UN report: "Dual script road signs even in areas where Serbs were a majority were torn down, Serbian sounding words were purged from the official no longer Serbo-Croatian language, some Serbs were asked to sign loyalty oaths to the government and some lost their employment in government positions or were subjected to confiscatory taxation."[66] Many in the Krajina feared that worse was to come, and given the historical context, such fears are readily understandable.

While the urban Serbs were largely defenseless, those of the Krajina region, being more regionally concentrated, were able to resist. In addition, the Krajina Serbs received encouragement and support from Serb nationalists in neighboring republics, including the president of the Republic of Serbia—Milošević.[67] The Serbs of the Krajina established a de facto state structure by early 1991, with a "capital city," the town of Knin. The local leader, Milan Babić, a former communist, soon declared his intention to lead the Krajina region out of Croatia.[68]

A low level of fighting began in March 1991 between Croatian police and Serb militias in the border areas, and these clashes gradually escalated into full-scale war.[69] On June 26, 1991, acting in concert with Slovenia, Croatia formally declared its independence from Yugoslavia and seceded from the federation. The Serbs of the Krajina declared their independence from Croatia and formed the Republic of Serbian Krajina. The Krajina Serbs seemed intent on returning to what remained of the Yugoslav federation. The logic here was simple: If Croatia sought to secede from Yugoslavia, then the Krajina Serbs had the right to secede from Croatia and to return to Yugoslavia. This rationale was succinctly expressed by a Serb official in Krajina: "We respect the democratic will of the Croatian people to secede from Yugoslavia. . . . [We Serbs] too must have self determination."[70]

The decision to separate Krajina was the main trigger to war in Croatia. The local Serbs raised an army (supported by Milošević) and fought against the newly established Croatian National Guard, which sought to suppress the Serb rebellion. The Krajina war also saw the rise of private Serb armies, often led by criminal figures and soldiers of fortune such as the Tigers organized by Zeljko Ražnatović (more famously known by his nom de guerre, Arkan).[71] These private forces operated outside the normal military chain of command, and they would become notorious for their brutality and lack of discipline.

At first, General Kadijević and the JNA high command adopted an attitude of neutrality vis-à-vis the fighting in the Krajina, and in certain localities the army acted as conciliator. Once again, it is important to emphasize that the JNA was not yet an instrument of Serb aggression. According to Ambassador Zimmermann: "The Yugoslav Army was in a difficult position and in fact was probably split. [Even Croat officials] admitted that the JNA's record in Croatia since May [1991] hadn't been bad. . . . Kadijević was less extreme than [Chief of Staff] Adzić and certainly less extreme than the group of young colonels who were turning the JNA into a Serbian army. Even after the war had been raging for two months, Tudjman told me that

'Kadijević is still a communist but he's somebody I can deal with.' In July the JNA proclaimed the evenhanded mission of interposing itself between the combatants."[72] Similarly, a CIA report states that the "the JNA by and large did try to act as a neutral peacekeeping force [in Croatia]." The report also noted that the army leadership remained "devoted to the ideal of a federal Yugoslavia."[73]

This strategy soon proved untenable, and the army inexorably moved in a nationalist direction. The defections of the previous several weeks had left the JNA with a far higher proportion of ethnic Serbs among both the officers and enlisted men; many of these Serb soldiers openly supported the Krajina militias.[74] And the army commanders faced a delicate problem: A significant share of the Serb officers was originally from the Krajina, whose inhabitants had a tradition of military service dating back to the days of Tito's Partisans.[75] The JNA surely had the firepower to overcome the secessionists, at least initially; but this option was rendered problematic by low troop morale and rising desertions, combined with concern on the part of many officers with the fate of their fellow Serbs in the Krajina. The Serb troops were simply unwilling to fight for a multiethnic Yugoslavia. And finally, the lack of any international support for holding Yugoslavia together was surely an additional influence on the JNA commanders. Gradually, over time, the commanders gave in to the pressures.

By the late summer of 1991, the JNA became actively involved in the ethnic war—on the side of the Krajina Serbs.[76] With backing from the federal army, the Serbs now had the wherewithal to prevail on the battlefield, and they sought to press this new advantage. Accordingly, the Serbs expanded their territorial holdings beyond the remote border areas that had traditionally constituted the Krajina region. In September, joint JNA/Serb forces launched an offensive into the interior of Croatia, where Serbs and Croats were intermixed, and where Serbs did not constitute the clear majority.[77] This new strategy entailed a considerable augmentation in the fighting and constituted a new phase of the war. At a political level, the stepped-up fighting ended the army's role as an ethnically neutral institution. By December 1991, General Kadijević signed an order that established the following objectives for the army: "Protection of the Serbian population . . . and the creation of conditions in which Yugoslavia may be preserved for those people that wish to live in it."[78] The JNA commanders seemed to have virtually given up on their efforts to reintegrate Slovenia and Croatia, reconciling themselves to the possibility that the Krajina and its adjacent areas were all that could be salvaged for a socialist Yugoslavia.[79] Meanwhile, the central government in Belgrade, still nominally led by Prime Minister Marković, lost all semblance of control.[80] The most powerful civilian figure in what was left of Yugoslavia, Serbian president Milošević, assumed a higher profile, combined with augmented influence over the federal military. The JNA did not start off as a pro-Serb army, but in the course of the fighting it did gradually assume that role.

The JNA's entry into the ethnic war also entailed a considerable escalation in the scale of atrocities against civilians. Increasingly, Serb militias and JNA forces began to expel ethnic Croats from areas that they captured. Croats were "cleansed" from Ilok, Osijek, and other villages in the border region. In addition, the urban centers in Croatia came under fire.[81] The JNA bombarded historic Dubrovnik, using naval vessels in the Adriatic Sea, damaging famous buildings in the process. This siege was widely reported and played an important role in further demonizing the Serbs and the federal army. The *Economist* noted at the time of the siege: "The Army's shelling of refugee hotels and fine buildings in Dubrovnik has caused widespread revulsion."[82] The media-savvy Croatian defenders of Dubrovnik sought to make the most of the situation and located their guns inside churches, in order to draw JNA fire and further outrage world opinion.[83] The army also began a large-scale attack on Vukovar, a city that had been split between Croats and Serbs. The shelling of Vukovar over a three-month period demolished much of the downtown area; large numbers of Croat civilians had been killed in the course of the siege by the time Vukovar fell to the JNA/Serb forces in November 1991, or were subsequently massacred.[84]

The Croatian National Guard also engaged in atrocities, especially in ethnically mixed areas. Years after the fighting, the *New York Times* ran the following story on Croat atrocities in the town of Gospić:

> A former Croatian militiaman ... acknowledges that he killed 72 civilians, tortured prisoners with electric shocks, and ran a death camp. . . . The militiaman, Miro Bajramović, implicated senior Croatian officials in at least 400 executions of ethnic Serbian civilians by death squads six years ago [during the 1991 war], triggering impassioned denials of responsibility by senior government officials, . . . "I am responsible for the death of 86 people," Mr. Bajramović said; . . . he asserted that he and the comrades had executed at least 400 ethnic Serbs *on the orders of Croatia's Interior Minister Ivan Vekić*. . . . "The order for Gospić was to perform ethnic cleansing, so we killed directors of post offices and hospitals, restaurant owners, and many other Serbs," he said. . . . "The orders from our headquarters were to reduce the percentage of Serbs in Gospić." [emphasis added][85]

The militiaman's account was corroborated by other witnesses (one of whom was later murdered for his testimony).[86]

On balance, it seems likely that the Serb militias and the JNA initially were responsible for more atrocities than those committed by their adversaries, the Croat forces. A 1992 article in the *Washington Post* cited evidence that "Serb fighters and the Army have probably committed more numerous crimes."[87] This conclusion seems plausible in light of the greater firepower that was at the disposal of the JNA at this time, as well as their greater military success. Of the almost 730,000 refugees that were generated by the war, by November 1991, there were twice as many Croat refugees as Serbs.[88] The Croats would later seek to even the score. We will see in a later chapter that in 1995, when the Croats were able to establish military superiority, they expelled virtually all ethnic Serbs from the Krajina region. It seems fair to say that neither side conducted itself with much restraint.

Intervention by the European Community

The European Community saw the Yugoslav crisis as a major opportunity to prove its capacity to act in the international arena. As the Yugoslav war began, Luxemburg's foreign minister Jacques Poos noted: "This is the hour of Europe, not the hour of the Americans."[89] At least some European officials felt a proprietary interest in the Yugoslav conflict as one that fell within the European Community's sphere of influence. Accordingly, EC Commission president Jacques Delors warned the Americans not to intrude on Europe's handling of the Yugoslav matter, and he used blunt language to make his point: "We do not interfere in American affairs. We hope they will have enough respect not to interfere in ours."[90] The crisis was to serve as a test case for a new European foreign policy, one that was to be independent of the United States.

At a substantive level, European leaders made statements in favor of Yugoslav unity, and these statements were repeated up until the war commenced in June 1991.[91] Support for Yugoslav unity was especially strong in Great Britain, France, and Spain, where political figures worried about the broader effects of the Yugoslavia crisis: If Slovenia and Croatia could successfully secede, this would encourage separatists in Northern Ireland, Corsica, and the Basque regions.[92] And France had a historical legacy of friendship toward the largest republic in what remained of Yugoslavia, Serbia. On the other hand, the key EC state of Germany was clearly in favor of breaking up Yugoslavia, and was actively encouraging secession.

There was thus a split within the European Community between the dominant view, which generally supported Yugoslav unity, and the German view, which opposed it. However, one should not overstate the significance of these differences. In reality, the EC sentiment in favor of national unity was never very strong and, in some cases, the Community went on record as favoring the rights of the Yugoslav republics to secede. In March 1991, the European parliament adopted a resolution stating that the Yugoslav republics "must have the right freely to determine their own future in a peaceful and democratic manner and on the basis of recognized international and internal borders."[93] This resolution opened the door to possible future recognition of secessionist republics. The resolution also implied ("on the basis of international and *internal* borders") that the republics must remain intact, once they separated, and that secondary secessions by subunits such as Krajina would be inadmissible.

Once war began in late June 1991, the ambiguity in the European Community's policy ended. The Community condemned the Yugoslav central government and implicitly sided with the secessionist republics. The JNA's decision to use force to end secession—even the very minimal level of force that was used in Slovenia—was abhorred. British foreign minister Douglas Hurd stated: "The time has passed when you could keep a state together by shooting its citizens."[94] The British pointedly cut off exports of "dual use" equipment with potential military significance.[95] Even France refrained from supporting the JNA's efforts to terminate the secessions through military force.[96] And a significant element of elite opinion in France clearly favored the secessionist republics.[97] The same was true in Italy.[98] And of course, Germany led the prosecessionists. German foreign minister Genscher took the first step toward de facto recognition of Slovenia when he very publicly paid a visit to the country on July 2.[99] Genscher declared that the JNA troops "are closely linked to the old political order, the communist system."[100] On July 4, the London *Guardian* noted: "Over the past 48 hours there has been a pronounced shift away from the consensus that Yugoslavian unity still remained the top priority."[101]

The European public also became supportive of secession, and this was demonstrated by a December 1991 public opinion poll undertaken by the European Community's official Eurobarometer polling agency. Regarding what should be "the most important consideration" in the EC policy, respondents were asked to select from the following three options:

Option 1: Preserve Yugoslavia's territorial integrity
Option 2: Respect democracy and self-determination (including possible independence for republics)
Option 3: Don't know[102]

The survey found overwhelming support in favor of "respecting democracy and self-determination," including the right to independence, as a more important priority than preserving Yugoslavia's territorial integrity. In the European Community as a whole, the poll found 68 percent supported option 2—in favor of independence—against only 19 percent in favor of option 1. Prosecessionist sentiment was high across the continent, even in France.[103]

It is also interesting to note that the above survey—conducted by the European Community itself and published in an EC periodical—was remarkably tendentious. The nature of the question established the following: That supporting independence for Slovenia and Croatia was the same as respecting "democracy and self-determination"; selecting option 1, in favor of Yugoslavia's territorial integrity, implied opposition to the word "democracy." The very phrasing of this poll question underscores the strongly prosecessionist atmosphere that prevailed during this period.

Overall, there emerged a consensus in the European Community, early on, that the conflict was caused by aggressiveness and oppression by the Yugoslav central government and the army. The more negative features in the secessionist republics, especially Croatia, were passed over lightly. Even the openly fascist elements in the ruling HDZ party in Croatia—and the anti-Serb and anti-Jewish rhetoric that issued from the HDZ leader, Tudjman—received surprisingly little attention. One factor at play was the superior publicity tactics used by the Croats, which paralleled those used by the Slovenes. According to Glenny: "From the beginning, ordinary Croats seemed to understand instinctively that it was important to be open and friendly with the foreign press. Without doubt, this led to a positive presentation of the Croat cause in Western Europe and the United States. The Serb government, the JNA, and many ordinary Serbs close to the fronts were dismissive and hostile toward the foreign press."[104]

Efforts at Mediation

The European Community began an intensive diplomatic intervention aimed at resolving the crisis—but this proceeded from the assumption that the republics had a right to secede and that Yugoslavia's existence as an integral state was finished. The European Community appointed a troika of mediators consisting of three foreign ministers: Gianni de Michelis (Italy), Jacques Poos (Luxembourg), and Hans Van den Broek (the Netherlands). The troika managed to bring the various Yugoslav parties together to the Adriatic island of Brioni, where they established a tentative accord on July 7, 1991: The federal military would return to the barracks and cease their efforts to reintegrate Slovenia and Croatia through force. Slovenia and Croatia for their part were expected to suspend for a period of three months their seizure of Yugoslavia's border security posts. This three-month suspension was to serve as a cooling-off period of sorts, during which continued negotiations were to take place. It is important to note that the two republics were not expected to terminate their efforts to establish control of their international borders; but merely to suspend implementing these efforts for a fixed period. The accord also created the European Community Monitor Mission, the first of many peacekeeping forces in the Yugoslav conflict. The Monitor Mission was intended to supervise implementation of the Brioni accord in both Slovenia and Croatia and was staffed by a small number of EC personnel (who numbered about three hundred by the end of the summer of 1991).[105]

Perhaps the most important phrase of the Brioni agreement was the following: "It is up to *only the peoples* of Yugoslavia to decide upon their future" (emphasis added).[106] The implication was that the Slovenian and Croatian "peoples" could decide for themselves whether or not to secede, and that the federal government had no right to countermand their decisions. The document had effectively endorsed secession. Prime Minister Marković strongly objected; he "saw clearly that the [proposed Brioni accord] spelt the end of Yugoslavia and the death of his own efforts to hold it together." The EC negotiators (notably Van den Broek) effectively overruled Marković's objections, and the accord was finalized.[107] Several days later, EC Commission president Delors declared that the Yugoslav federation "is finished in its present form."[108]

The Brioni accord was largely ineffectual. Slovenia and Croatia had no intention of slowing their momentum toward permanent independence; it is doubtful that the EC negotiators seriously intended to delay the secessionists' efforts.[109] In Croatia, fighting continued and intensified in the Krajina region as the federal army became embroiled in the increasingly violent ethnic politics of that zone. There was no cease-fire.

The main effect of Brioni was to legitimate the secession of Slovenia and thus hasten the disintegration of the federation. German officials were clearly pleased at the outcome. Former diplomat Michael Libal notes in his memoirs that "on 18 July the decision was made in Belgrade to completely withdraw the JNA from Slovenia; . . . in Germany a sense of euphoria prevailed."[110] The Brioni accord had one more effect: It brought increased attention to the governments of individual republics, while it marginalized the federal prime minister Marković, whose efforts at preserving the federation appeared increasingly irrelevant and quixotic. After Brioni the Marković government in Belgrade was sidelined: "Thenceforth, he was rarely turned to and rarely included," according to Ambassador Zimmermann.[111] When

Marković officially resigned his post five months later, the event was barely noticed. With Brioni, the main institutions of national unity—the JNA high command and Prime Minister Marković—had been severely weakened. An incipient power vacuum was developing at the national level, which further accelerated the process of national disintegration. It also raised still further the influence of Serbian president Milošević, who rapidly moved to fill this power vacuum. European diplomacy had the peculiar effect of enhancing Milošević's status and his influence over future events.

During the three-month cooling-off period, EC diplomacy was to continue. Lord Peter Carrington, a former British foreign minister, was assigned the role of EC mediator. Carrington worked with Cyrus Vance, a US diplomat appointed by the UN Security Council.[112] Carrington convened the International Conference on Yugoslavia at The Hague; all Yugoslav factions were invited. Through this conference the European Community sought to manage Yugoslavia's dissolution in an orderly fashion. The European Community also established an Arbitration Commission under French jurist Robert Badinter to provide legal advice to the mediators.[113]

Lord Carrington's plan involved the following: The Yugoslav republics would be permitted independence and would then form a regional economic union. The regional union would maintain at least some of the economic ties of the former Yugoslav federation and, in doing so, would lay the groundwork for peaceful relations among the new states. The proposed union was to be established by "*sovereign and independent republics*, with international [legal] personality for those that wish it" (emphasis added).[114] The plan for regional union would ultimately fail and was never implemented. Serbia objected to schemes that would leave large numbers of ethnic Serbs outside its borders, in separate states; and it seems doubtful that Slovenia and Croatia had much interest in any further association with Serbia.

The most important feature of the Hague conference was that it reaffirmed Yugoslavia's permanent dissolution. According to an account by two BBC reporters, the Hague conference "began from the assumption that Yugoslavia had already broken apart."[115] In the view of Ambassador Zimmermann, Carrington "treated Yugoslavia as no longer existing."[116] And German diplomat Geert-Hinrich Ahrens stated that "no attempt was made to save the Yugoslav federation."[117] Formal recognition of the new states was only a matter of time.

Overall, a major feature of European policy during 1991 was its very weak support for Yugoslav unity. A second feature was the European Community's hostility toward the Krajina secession. The European Community took the view that Croatia and other republics could not be divided. In effect, this meant the following: Croatia had the right to secede from Yugoslavia but this same right would not be recognized for the Krajina Serbs, who wished to separate from Croatia. In the ensuing conflict in Krajina, the European Community supported the Croatian position and opposed that of the ethnic Serbs. At the Hague conference, Van den Broek, the Dutch foreign minister, affirmed that any changes in the republican borders "were not an option."[118]

This anti-Serb bent was evident at many levels. On the ground, the European Community favored the Croatian position and opposed that of the Serbs. The EC observers sent to the Krajina during the summer of 1991 were, according to US ambassador Zimmermann, acting with "pro-Croatian bias."[119] In the international press, the Serb leaders from the Krajina were generally described in the most negative terms.[120] By November, the *Economist* noted: "There is a growing feeling in Europe that the Serbs are in the wrong."[121] While Serbs were reviled, Slovenes and Croats were viewed quite positively. Much of the world press adopted this perspective, as have several academic studies that have appeared subsequently.[122]

Analysis of EC Policy

Let us pause to consider the reasonableness of the European Community position on Yugoslavia. As we have seen, the European Community condemned the JNA for using force against secessionist republics. In many respects this view is a surprising one. The JNA's actions against Slovenia and Croatia had strong support in international law and also in historical precedent. Central governments throughout modern history have used force to restrain secession and assert central authority. There are many examples: The US central government under Abraham Lincoln used force against southern secessionists, and this has been viewed positively by most historical accounts. No one expected Lincoln to solve the problem exclusively through pacific means. A century later, during 1967–1970, the Nigerian central government subdued the Biafra secession, and it did so with strong international support. In 1984, the Indian military used force to crush a Sikh separatist rebellion, again with international support. At the time, the *Economist* ran an article entitled, "India Does What It Had to Do," which recognized the right of central governments to use force against separatists.[123] When Spain, Turkey, and the UK faced armed separatist rebellions in recent years, they too used force to achieve their objectives.

Since 1945, the antisecessionist impulse has been overwhelming, with an important exception: During the decolonization in Africa, Asia, and the Caribbean region, the breakup of colonial empires was generally accepted.[124] The colonies, in effect, seceded from the empires, and this occurred with international approbation in most cases. This precedent offers few parallels to the Yugoslav case of 1991, however, since Yugoslavia could not reasonably be considered a colonial empire, and its breakup was not a case of decolonization. The secessionist republics of this period—Slovenia and Croatia—were not underprivileged colonies but were, in fact, the richest regions of the country.[125] To suggest that Slovenia and Croatia had a colonial relationship to the Yugoslav central government is surely a distortion.

Overall, international law has been fundamentally antisecession. In 1970, UN Secretary General U Thant stated the prevailing opinion: "So, as far as the question of secession of a particular section of a member state is concerned, the United Nations attitude is unequivocal; . . . the United Nations has never accepted and does not accept and I do not believe it will ever accept the principle of secession of a part of its member state."[126] There is no doubt that Slovenia and Croatia's secessions were illegal under Yugoslavia's constitution.[127] International support for secession in this case had no basis in historical precedent or in law.[128] The EC condemnation of the Yugoslav central government and the JNA seems difficult to understand.

It also may be argued that the EC policy was motivated by a concern for human rights. The salience of Serb and JNA atrocities has been widely and repeatedly emphasized as a cause for Yugoslavia's disintegration. Perhaps Slovenia and Croatia had to secede in order to escape oppressive conditions, and the European Community accepted these secessions out of a concern for human rights. Clearly, human rights considerations must override any legalistic objections regarding the danger of secessionism.[129] Under scrutiny, however, the human rights argument has little merit. In fact, there was no serious evidence of Serb oppression in Slovenia or Croatia prior to the secessionist actions. The main reasons for seceding, as we saw in the previous chapter, were economic in nature. The JNA's initial use of force in Slovenia was quite mild. And, it should be noted, the European states did not support human rights with any degree of consistency: Germany and to some extent the European Community had aligned itself with the very unsavory Tudjman regime, which had a poor human rights record and a taint of neo-Nazism. The European Community's stance on Yugoslavia's dissolution seems indefensible.

A second conundrum was the EC policy opposing the Krajina Serbs, who sought to separate from Croatia. It is important to note that this policy was clearly contradictory: On the one hand, the Community accepted the right of Croatia to separate from Yugoslavia, or at least viewed such separation with leniency. On the other hand, the European Community condemned efforts by the Krajina Serbs to separate from Croatia. Why the double standard?

The Badinter Commission provided a complicated legal rationale for the

European Community's position on the Krajina. The Commission invoked the doctrine of *uti possidetis*, which holds the following: When an empire breaks up, the new countries that result from the breakup must remain intact; no secondary secessions, after the initial secession, would be allowed. This doctrine emerged from the decolonization experiences of Latin America and Africa: When a colony became independent, the former colonial administrative boundaries formed the boundaries of the new state. In the case of Africa, for example, the boundaries established during the colonial era, no matter how problematic, were not to be changed. Thus, Nigeria was legally permitted to secede from the British Empire in 1960; once this occurred, however, the boundaries of Nigeria were considered permanent, and no part of Nigeria would be permitted to break away. The Badinter Commission declared that this doctrine, originally intended for a specific historical case, was of broader relevance. Accordingly, Croatia's boundaries would remain fixed, and Krajina could not secede. The Commission emphasized that the "principle of *uti possidetis*," which though "initially applied in settling decolonization issues in America and Africa, is today recognized as a general principle as stated by the International Court of Justice."[130]

The European Community's case was actually quite weak, as it involved a misrepresentation of the legal record. The only precedent cited by the Badinter Commission was the 1986 *Frontier Dispute* case before the International Court of Justice (ICJ), which involved Mali and Burkina Faso, two former French colonies. In this case, the ICJ cited *uti possidetis* in a restrictive manner, noting that it was "a principle which upgraded former administrative delimitations, *established during the colonial period* . . . [and] is therefore a principle of a general kind which is logically *connected with this form of decolonization* wherever it occurs" (emphasis added).[131] In short, the doctrine of *uti possidetis* was limited to matters arising from decolonization, a condition that had no relevance in the Yugoslav case. The Commission's citation of this doctrine went against historical and legal precedent. Overall, it seems difficult to explain the EC policy in this case as motivated by concerns of either human rights or legality.

Why then did the European Community act as it did? Clearly one motivation was anticommunism. Yugoslavia remained a nominally communist state, and the dominant institution that opposed secession, the Yugoslav National Army, was strongly communist in its core ideology. Thus the JNA and Yugoslavia itself were seen as communist anachronisms and unworthy of EC support. In an earlier period, Yugoslavia had symbolized a more humane, even partially democratic form of communism. By 1991, however, it was increasingly viewed as one more communist state. We have already seen the salience of anticommunism for German foreign policy; this attitude was evident throughout Europe.

Thus the London *Independent* stated in a July 4 editorial: "It is intolerable that, 18 months after the collapse of communism in Eastern Europe, two republics with democratically elected governments [Slovenia and Croatia] should be crushed by a communist-led army."[132] In France, *Le Monde* also used anticommunist rhetoric in its articles on Yugoslavia.[133] Catholic circles throughout the continent followed the lead of the Vatican in supporting Catholic separatists in Yugoslavia against the central government and federal army. Even much of the political Left regarded the remnants of communism as an embarrassment.[134] The anticommunist viewpoint was especially hostile toward the Republic of Serbia, which had voted for the former communist party in an election in 1990.

There was also a tendency to view Serbs in faintly racist terms. Typically, an article in the London *Daily Telegraph* noted: "There are fewer than two million Slovenes. . . . Unused to combat, their national heroes are poets who have kept the language alive. The republic attracts tourists for skiing and lakeside mountain holidays and is known for its wines. . . . Shaped by centuries in the Austro-Hungarian empire, they are Roman Catholics and use the Latin script. By contrast the Serbs, landlocked and eastward looking, still cling to neo-Communist centralism. Their religion is Orthodox Christianity, they use the Russian alphabet and suffer the influence of centuries of domination by the Ottoman Turks."[135] One has the impression of a primitive, Asiatic Serb people holding to an outmoded communist ideology, in contrast to the cultured Slovenes, who could appreciate fine wines, lakeside holidays, skiing, and poetry. Anticommunism was easily transformed into a more generalized "anti-Serbism." These ideological motivations were joined by narrower geopolitical ambitions on the part of central Europe's dominant power, Germany.

The European Community nevertheless saw the need to present its position on Yugoslavia in terms of legal and moral principles and to deemphasize, at least somewhat, the underlying ideological factors at play. As a result, the European Community position was riddled with inconsistencies; officials used rationalizations and dubious legal reasoning to obscure these inconsistencies. Jean Manas noted the Orwellian manner in which these issues have been discussed: " 'Yugoslavia' itself was relegated to the dustbin of history, while any efforts to change the republics' borders and to effectuate further secessions were pushed into the realm of illegality, if not immorality. Accordingly, Yugoslav troops trying to save the union and Serb troops trying to establish a rump Yugoslavia . . . were labeled as aggressors. Likewise

. . . Krajinin Serbs trying to create their own independent [republic] were dismissed as 'warlords' or 'thugs.'"[136]

The Role of the United States

US policy initially favored Yugoslav unity and opposed breakup. The Bush administration showed some awareness that breaking up countries— even communist ones—could be extremely destabilizing. In August 1991, President George Bush delivered a speech to the Ukrainian legislature in which he publicly opposed efforts by the Soviet republics to secede from the USSR. Bush warned the Ukrainians regarding the dangers of "suicidal nationalism."[137]

Bush's antisecessionist views clearly influenced his Yugoslav policy, at least initially. Some of the top figures in the Bush administration had professional experience in Yugoslavia, and they bolstered the antisecessionist impulse. Deputy Secretary of State Lawrence Eagleburger and National Security Advisor Brent Scowcroft had both served in Belgrade at various points in their respective careers (Eagleburger had served as ambassador, and Scowcroft as military attaché). Both spoke Serbo-Croatian. Eagleburger and Scowcroft exerted significant influence on US policy, initially in favor of maintaining Yugoslavia as an integral state.[138] The pro-Yugoslav proclivities of these two men affected the overall character of US policy during this period: Several days before the war began, Secretary of State James Baker traveled to Belgrade and stated that "neither the US nor any other country will recognize unilateral secession."[139] The statement was obviously aimed at Slovenia and Croatia. On June 27, at the start of the war, State Department spokesperson Margaret Tutwiler announced: "The United States continues to recognize and support the territorial integrity of Yugoslavia."[140] Within the Bush administration, there also was a sense of uneasiness about Germany's support for the secessionist republics; US officials viewed these actions negatively, as reckless adventurism.[141]

Yet there were important counterpressures. From Congress, prominent Republicans led by Sen. Bob Dole argued in favor of Slovenia and Croatia. In August, Dole sent out a letter to constituents that forcefully condemned both Milošević ("among the world's last hard-line communists") and the JNA.[142] James Jatras, a Republican congressional staffer in 1991, commented on the attitude that prevailed among his colleagues at the time: The Balkan conflict was considered a straightforward situation of "'democracy versus communism,' that Slovenia and Croatia were democratic, Serbia was communist, and that was what the struggle was about."[143] Within the State Department, a group of younger officials were sympathetic to the secessionists, and they privately criticized the official policy of support for Yugoslav unity.[144] Pro-Croatian lobbyists emphasized the ideological character of their struggles, and they too used anticommunist language to dramatize their points.[145] This rhetoric struck a chord with the Bush administration (including such figures as Eagleburger and Scowcroft, whose experiences were steeped in the Cold War). The Croat lobby's influence within the administration seemed to grow over time, and this influence was reflected in Bush's appointments. In 1992, Bush's nominee for the first US ambassador to Croatia was Mara Letica, who was "a founder of the Croatian-American Association." Croatian newspapers praised Letica as a "passionate lobbyist for Croatia."[146] The Croatia lobby gradually counteracted the pro-Yugoslav sentiments that initially existed within the Bush administration.

And in the final analysis, even the pro-Yugoslav figures in the administration, such as Eagleburger, never held their positions with much conviction. Eagleburger's lack of conviction on this issue was demonstrated early on during a 1990 trip to Yugoslavia. While meeting with Slovenian nationalists, Eagleburger stated that "the United States hoped Slovenia would not leave the federation, but in the end *we would not do anything to force the Slovenian government's policies*" (emphasis added).[147] This was the green light that the Slovenes were seeking—indicating that they had nothing to fear from the world's hegemonic power—and it may well have been crucial in Slovenia's (and also Croatia's) decision to seek independence. There is nothing in the record to suggest any *deliberate* effort by US officials to break up Yugoslavia. On the contrary, there appears to have been a mild preference (at least initially) for keeping the federation united. It is nevertheless clear in retrospect that Eagleburger's 1990 statement encouraged the secessionist forces and hastened the federation's demise.[148]

Once war actually commenced, the United States moved sharply against the Yugoslav central government. On June 30, 1991, the State Department criticized the JNA for threatening Slovenia.[149] Even Eagleburger stated that the JNA's use of force was "reprehensible" and "must be condemned."[150] That the Slovene militia was doing most of the fighting—as Ambassador Zimmermann would later acknowledge in his memoirs—escaped notice. And Eagleburger no longer noted the importance of Yugoslav unity. Instead, he emphasized that "the sovereignty of those republics [presumably Slovenia and Croatia] and their democratic, market-oriented process must continue; ... we are against the [JNA's] use of force to maintain the federation as it now exists. We're against the use of force period, but what we want is a new confederation."[151] The mention of confederation is significant, since several of the plans for confederation being discussed during this period entailed an association of fully *independent* states as a replacement for Yugoslavia.[152] The

Financial Times observed that Eagleburger's comments signaled a "US policy shift at the weekend, making clear that the status quo in Yugoslavia had become untenable."[153] A prosecession bandwagon was building and the United States, in effect, had climbed aboard.

It is important to emphasize that in all of these actions, the United States was not yet a key player.[154] Europe was to take the lead. Secretary of State Baker noted in his memoirs: "The Bush administration felt comfortable with the European Community's taking responsibility for handling the crisis in the Balkans. The conflict seemed to be one the European Community could manage. More critically, Yugoslavia was in the heart of Europe, and European interests were directly threatened; . . . unlike the Persian Gulf, our vital national interests were not at stake. The Yugoslav conflict had the potential to be intractable, but it was nonetheless a regional dispute."[155] During the first six months of the Yugoslav crisis, the United States was an influence of second-order importance. Nevertheless, America's policy contributed to an emerging international consensus that favored the secessionist republics and accelerated Yugoslavia's breakup.

Recognition

Through the fall of 1991, the EC and UN negotiators continued their mediation efforts, which aimed at an "orderly" dissolution of Yugoslavia. The United States, from the sidelines, supported these efforts.[156] It was generally understood that Slovenia and Croatia would in time obtain the international recognition that they sought. However, formal recognition would be delayed for a period of time, pending a regional settlement, which was being negotiated by Lord Carrington at The Hague.

Germany became impatient with this "go slow" approach. By mid-November, German officials hinted that they would break away from the EC position and recognize the independent republics. If necessary, Germany would do this unilaterally. There was thus an incipient conflict building between the dominant EC position led by France and Britain on the one hand, and Germany on the other. There were repeated entreaties from European and also US officials, who urged restraint by Germany. It was felt that Germany should not be allowed to scuttle the delicate negotiation processes then underway at The Hague. Alija Izetbegović, the president of Bosnia-Herzegovina, argued against premature recognition of Slovenia and Croatia, claiming that such action would force his republic into rapid secession that might in turn trigger civil war and thus widen the conflict.[157] UN Secretary General Javier Pérez de Cuéllar also weighed in against Germany's position.[158]

At a December 16–17 foreign ministers meeting in Brussels, the European Community reached a compromise. The recognition process would be accelerated. The Badinter Commission would issue a formal report on the extent to which Slovenia and Croatia met EC requirements for independence by January 15, 1992. If the two republics met the requirements, they would achieve immediate recognition. EC requirements for recognition included several points, the most important of which were "acceptance of the provisions laid down in the UN convention and the commitments entered into under the Paris Charter and the Helsinki agreements (rule of law, democracy, and respect for human rights)," and "protection of minorities in keeping with the Conference on Security and Cooperation in Europe."[159] The human rights issue was especially important. The persecution of ethnic Serbs in the Krajina had proven an embarrassment to the European Community, in light of the Community's embrace of Croatia's secession. Accordingly, the European states sought at least some semblance of protection for the Krajina Serbs. An impediment to the EC plan quickly appeared. Croatia did *not* have adequate protections for human rights, which the Badinter Commission had established as a prerequisite for recognition.[160] The implication was that EC recognition would be delayed until Croatia agreed to improve its record with regard to the Serb minorities. Germany balked at any delay.

There clearly was a rift within the European Community, but it is important not to overstate the extent of this rift. There was agreement on a broad range of issues. The European Community had already established that Yugoslavia was a thing of the past, and that Slovenia and Croatia would achieve recognition at some point. And there was general agreement that the Krajina Serbs should not be allowed to separate from Croatia. EC officials insisted that Croatia undertake constitutional changes to protect the Serb minority, and such changes had to occur before recognition would be possible. Still, these human rights requirements were not terribly demanding: We will see momentarily that the European Community expected only formal, *paper* protections for minority groups, without any mechanisms to ensure enforcement of these protections.

The major question was one of timing: When should the European Community formally recognize the independence of Slovenia and Croatia? On this point, there was a clear difference of opinion, with Germany insisting on immediate recognition, and other states objecting that recognition had to wait. In response, German officials announced that they would unilaterally recognize Slovenia and Croatia by January 15, no matter what the other EC states decided. They would simply dispense with the entire process of EC consensus building on this issue. This threat frightened Germany's neighbors, as such actions would have undercut the common European foreign policy that had been agreed to at Maastricht. The efforts at European political integration, built up so painstakingly over many years, would have been damaged. And there was the possibility that Germany might retaliate against nations that opposed its position regarding the Balkan crisis. All these factors argued in favor of accepting German leadership.[161] And events on the ground in Yugoslavia also weighed in Germany's favor: On January 2, 1992, a cease-fire was arranged in the Krajina region and UN peacekeeping forces were deployed.[162] It appeared (momentarily) that peace was breaking out. The settlement being negotiated at the International Conference on Yugoslavia no longer seemed necessary.[163]

The EC member states essentially capitulated and agreed to immediate recognition on Germany's terms. All twelve EC countries formally recognized Slovenia and Croatia as independent states on January 15, 1992. Full diplomatic relations were established. The objections regarding human rights of the Krajina Serbs were essentially brushed aside, through a diplomatic sleight of hand. Shortly before recognition occurred, the Croatian government made verbal assurances that "whatever the constitution said, Serbs in Croatia would not be mistreated." The assurances meant nothing in substantive terms, but they nevertheless satisfied the European Community. The *Economist* acidly noted: Croatia's "assurances, everyone knew, were as flimsy as the standards they were supposed to meet; most of the [EC member states] would almost certainly have gone ahead without them."[164] James B. Steinberg would later note that Croatia's concessions regarding minority rights were "cosmetic" in character.[165] Clearly, human rights considerations would not stand in the way of realpolitik.

Germany had in effect bullied the EC member states into recognizing Slovenia and Croatia, and this constituted its first independent foreign policy action of any consequence since 1945.[166] German officials publicly gloated over this achievement. Chancellor Kohl referred to the Balkan conflict as "a great victory for German foreign policy."[167] And in the streets of Zagreb, in January 1992, Croatian nationalists gathered to celebrate their international recognition; they sang a new song of thanks to Germany, with the refrain, "*Danke Deutschland.*"[168]

Conclusion

Overall, external intervention had a significant impact on the Yugoslav crisis. Germany played a key role in encouraging Slovenia and Croatia to secede, and surreptitiously assured them of external support for their secession efforts. Once the republics actually seceded, the European Community (backed by the United States) condemned the JNA's efforts to block secession. The widespread international hostility probably contributed to the JNA's decision to withdraw from Slovenia and allow the republic to secede.[169] The army's failure, in turn, guaranteed that the crisis would lead to full-scale war and mass destruction in Croatia (and later in Bosnia-Herzegovina and Kosovo as well). The European states must bear some responsibility for the breakup of Yugoslavia, and for the wars that resulted from that breakup.

A second effect of European and especially German intervention is that it stimulated the United States to augment its own role in the crisis. After the recognition debacle of January 1992, US officials began to regret their previous restraint, which had allowed the Europeans to take the lead. And there was a special concern regarding Germany. On January 7, right in the middle of the EC recognition controversy, the *New York Times* reported: "United States policymakers . . . say they have become disturbed during the last six months by what they regard as new assertiveness on the part of the German Government and its willingness to flex its muscles in international relations. . . . These officials are concerned that Germany, with its economic might and new tougher diplomatic tone, will become a dominant power in the new Europe, and perhaps beyond, that will not necessarily be in harmony with American policies."[170] The United States was becoming increasingly anxious regarding German unilateralism, which was viewed as a threat to American dominance in Europe.[171] US officials fundamentally reassessed their stance on Yugoslavia and determined that they would have to play a more assertive role.[172] The renewed US intervention was to come later, during the conflict over Bosnia-Herzegovina. In the next chapter, we see the effects of this US intervention, and how it inflamed the conflict still further.

5

The War Spreads
to Bosnia-Herzegovina

> Splitting up the admittedly imperfect but viable Yugoslav
> federation would be virtually impossible without drastic
> and brutal political and economic surgery. . . . Every
> conceivable divorce between Serbia and Croatia would of
> necessity involve not only a painful partition of Bosnia and
> Herzegovina but also the explosive question of the ethnic
> identity of Yugoslav Muslims and nightmarish exchanges
> of hundreds of thousands [of refugees]; . . . who in his right
> mind would want to open a Pandora's box?
> —*George B. Tomashevich, letter
> to the editor,* New York Times, *1980*

The breakup of the Yugoslav federation was a gradual event that occurred in
distinct phases. The secessions of Slovenia and Croatia in 1991 represented
the first phase of the breakup, which encouraged further acts of secession
by the remaining republics. The trend toward secession then established a
momentum of its own, which triggered a complete unraveling of national
unity. By December 1991, Yugoslavia's prime minister, Ante Marković, had
resigned, and shortly after this, the country officially ceased to exist.[1] For
the Republic of Bosnia and Herzegovina these events were to prove especially tragic: The federation's breakup destabilized Bosnia by disrupting the
delicate fabric of relations among its constituent ethnic groups. The Yugoslav
federation had long given a measure of security to the groups—the Muslims, Serbs, and Croats—which enabled them to function with a modicum
of interethnic cordiality. The federation's destruction ended Bosnia's atmosphere of security and set the stage for war. The breakup of Yugoslavia did
indeed entail "brutal political and economic surgery" and a "painful partition
of Bosnia and Herzegovina," just as Professor Tomashevich had predicted it
would in his April 1980 letter to the *New York Times.* The new circumstances
caused "nightmarish exchanges of hundreds of thousands" of refugees—
events that, once again, had been predicted.

In the previous chapter, we saw that foreign powers led by Germany played a key role in making possible Yugoslavia's breakup, and they therefore contributed to the larger tragedy of the wars that resulted. During the Bosnia war, there was a major shift in the character of the external influences. With Bosnia, the United States would for the first time play a leading role in managing the breakup of Yugoslavia. Previously, the United States had resisted major involvement in the Balkans, regarding the matter as a local, European concern of second-order importance. By early 1992, however, US officials initiated a policy change in favor of more direct involvement. With Bosnia's independence in 1992, the conflict thus began its "American phase."

The claim that the United States was active in the Bosnia war from its earliest phases will surprise some readers, given the widespread perception that US officials ignored Bosnia and were reluctant to intervene. Fairly typically, a 1992 editorial in the *Philadelphia Inquirer* condemned President Bush for an "obvious lack of leadership" with regard to Bosnia, and for "doing nothing except talk about sending food."[2] *New York Times* columnist Anthony Lewis compared Bush to Neville Chamberlain for his alleged unwillingness to take action in the Balkans.[3] Many academic studies adopt a similar view and criticize extended US "inaction" in Bosnia.[4] Such views constitute a basic misunderstanding of the historical record, as I argue in this chapter. In fact, the United States played a crucial role in the diplomacy of Bosnia's independence from the very beginning of the conflict; this intervention began even before Bosnia formally declared itself an independent state. In taking these steps, the United States would help spread and intensify the disorder that began in 1991.

US Support for Bosnian Independence

The main conduit for US influence was Bosnian president Alija Izetbegović and his government. Officially elected in late 1990, the Izetbegović government was staffed with pro-American figures. In memoirs, French general Philippe Morillon, who commanded UN peacekeeping forces in Bosnia, wrote: "The majority of the immediate advisors to President Izetbegović . . . had studied in the US and had many US contacts." General Morillon added that, among UN officials, "we would sometimes speak of the 'American mafia'" that surrounded Izetbegović.[5] A particularly important figure was Bosnia's UN ambassador and later foreign minister, Muhamed Sacirbey. Richard Holbrooke described Sacirbey as "one of the bright hopes for the fledgling Bosnian government. Married to an American, he was until 1992 as American as he was Bosnian; his enemies in Bosnia attacked him for speaking his native language with an American accent."[6] According to *New York Times* correspondent David Binder, US secretary of state James Baker "literally created … Bosnia-Herzegovina" as a formally independent state. Baker "did so with the blessing of President Bush and with considerable input from [Deputy Secretary] Larry Eagleburger and [ambassador to Yugoslavia] Warren Zimmermann."[7]

In international discussions, the United States became the Izetbegović government's main supporter. When that government considered taking Bosnia out of the Yugoslav federation and establishing an independent state, the United States encouraged these actions. Indeed, the Bush administration assumed a key role in arranging international recognition for an independent Bosnia. According to the State Department's Yugoslavia desk officer, George Kenney: "From mid-February [1992] on, we were pushing the Europeans hard to recognize Bosnia."[8] Ambassador Zimmermann stated similarly: "The [US] embassy was for recognition of Bosnia and Herzegovina." Zimmermann emphasized that he personally advocated recognition.[9] A National Security Council analysis noted that the "US *took the lead* in pressing for recognition of Bosnia-Herzegovina" (emphasis added).[10]

The United States gave crucial political and diplomatic support to the Izetbegović government. In the process of furnishing this support, the United States adopted an adversarial tone vis-à-vis the European powers. The Europeans, for their part, were skeptical about the merits of early recognition for Bosnia, fearing that this would trigger an ethnic conflagration. US diplomat Louis Sell, who worked in the US embassy in Belgrade, adds: "Observing what appeared to be the inevitable slide toward war, the EC began to get cold feet" and was reluctant to recognize Bosnia.[11] Even Germany now showed a measure of restraint and at first opposed early recognition. In an interview, Germany's foreign minister, Hans-Dietrich Genscher, later stated: "We did have some differences of opinion in early 1992 as the Americans supported the recognition of Bosnia, whereas we the Europeans believed we should first establish a framework for the whole region."[12] Despite these reservations, the United States continued to push the idea of an independent Bosnia. In short, the United States sought to sponsor Bosnia's independence in much the same way that Germany had sponsored Croatia and Slovenia in an earlier phase of the conflict. And we will see momentarily that the United States would play a decisive role in blocking measures that might have allowed Bosnia to achieve independence without war.

The Bush Administration Blocks a Negotiated Settlement

Despite increasing US influence, the European Community continued its efforts, begun in 1991, aimed at ending the Yugoslav federation through a negotiated secession of the various republics. The EC member states still sought to use the Balkan crisis to affirm the Community's potential as a global actor. The European Community's policy of international assertiveness had failed badly in Croatia during 1991, but the Europeans now sought to make up for this failure and to reestablish their diplomatic presence in Bosnia. The continued importance of the Balkan conflict was clear, and it was widely considered "the virility symbol of the Euro-federalists"[13]—a way of establishing the Community as a global player to be reckoned with.

The EC mediation activities were directed by José Cutileiro, a Portuguese diplomat. During February and March 1992, Cutileiro brought together the leaders of the three major ethnic groups from Bosnia (including President Izetbegović, who represented the Muslims) for a series of international conferences. The EC mediation was predicated on the assumption that Bosnian independence was inevitable, and Cutileiro sought a constitutional arrangement that might defuse ethnic tensions and thus preclude civil war. Cutileiro worked out a plan to divide Bosnia into three separate regions, each of which would possess a high level of autonomy. The central government in Sarajevo would be left with only limited powers as part of a confederalized state. Of the total area of Bosnia-Herzegovina, the Muslims were to be given effective rule in regions comprising 45 percent of the total, the Serbs would receive 42.5 percent, and the Croats (the smallest of the three groups) would receive 12.5 percent.[14]

The Lisbon agreement, as it became known, was hardly perfect, and it entailed a compromise among all three groups. For the Serbs, it represented some concession with regard to territory. Serbs accounted for less than half the population of Bosnia, and they owned a disproportionate share of the land; the 42.5 percent that they would receive under the Cutileiro plan constituted a reduction in territorial control.[15] From the Muslim side, the entire idea of confederation was a concession. The Muslims effectively controlled the central government, having won the parliamentary elections, and they favored a unified state; they viewed a confederation with a weak central government negatively.[16] From the Croat side, there was surely dissatisfaction that they would control far less territory than the other groups. Significant numbers of each ethnic group would have to live as minorities in areas dominated by another group.

Despite these flaws, the three ethnic groups all agreed to the plan on March 17, presumably because it was better than the alternative, which was war. Crucially, the Izetbegović government also agreed.[17] The possibility briefly emerged that war could be averted through a compromise settlement. The Bush administration, however, opposed the European efforts from the start, and this opposition contributed to the breakdown of the Lisbon agree-

ment. The administration's opposition flowed from a more basic rivalry between the United States and the European Community, which was growing during this period. With US encouragement, the Croats and Muslims
both withdrew from the agreement—effectively reneging on their commitments—March 25–26, 1992.[18] The Cutileiro plan was never implemented,
and full-scale war commenced within two weeks.

Let us look more closely at the role of US officials and their efforts to
undercut the Lisbon agreement. These efforts began with the US ambassador in Belgrade, Warren Zimmermann, who encouraged Izetbegović to
reject the peace plan. A *New York Times* article notes: "Immediately after
Mr. Izetbegović returned from Lisbon, Mr. Zimmermann called on him. . . .
'[Izetbegović] said he didn't like [the Lisbon agreement],' Mr. Zimmermann
recalled. 'I told him if he didn't like it, why sign it?'"[19] According to former
State Department official George Kenney: "Zimmermann told Izetbegović
. . . [the United States will] recognize you and help you out. So *don't go ahead
with the Lisbon agreement*" (emphasis added).[20] The former Canadian ambassador to Yugoslavia, James Bissett, confirms Kenney's account.[21] In other
words, Zimmermann offered Izetbegović a direct incentive—US recognition—in exchange for his rejection of the Lisbon agreement.

US efforts to undermine the plan extended well beyond the US embassy
in Belgrade. An official Dutch investigation offered this account: "[Secre-
tary of State] Baker's policy was now directed at *preventing* Izetbegović from
agreeing to the Cutileiro plan . . . and informing him [Izetbegović] that the
United States would support his government in the UN if any difficulties
should arise." In addition Baker "urged his European discussion partners to
halt their plans" for decentralizing authority in Bosnia.[22] It is interesting to
note that the section of the Dutch report that discusses this period is entitled, "The Cutileiro Plan and Its Thwarting by the Americans." Cutileiro
himself later claimed: "Izetbegović and his aides were encouraged to scupper
that deal [from Lisbon] by well meaning outsiders"—which was probably a
polite reference to the US activities.[23] According to EC mediator Peter Carrington, the "American administration made it quite clear that the proposals
of Cutileiro . . . were unacceptable."[24] Lord Carrington also claimed that US
officials "actually sent them [the Bosnians] a telegram telling them not to
agree" to Cutileiro's proposed settlement.[25] These facts strongly suggest that
the United States played a key role during this early period of the Bosnia
conflict; later claims of US inactivity in Bosnia are incorrect.[26]

The US strategy was successful in removing the possibility of an EC-
brokered agreement early in the conflict. Let us now consider a counterfac-
tual question: Could the Lisbon agreement have prevented war in Bosnia?
This must remain one of the key "what if" questions of the Yugoslav con-

flict that can never be answered definitively. The plan was accepted by the three parties only in preliminary form, with many details still to be worked out; whether or not a final agreement could have been achieved—even in the absence of US opposition—cannot be known for certain. Nevertheless, the Cutileiro plan clearly held considerable promise, a point acknowledged by former US diplomats. Zimmermann, for example, admitted in an interview with the *New York Times* that the Cutileiro plan "wasn't bad at all."[27] In his memoirs, Zimmermann goes further and states that the Cutileiro plan "would probably have worked out better for the Muslims than any subsequent plan, including the Dayton formula [that ended fighting in 1995]."[28] And according to Sell, who served in the US embassy in Belgrade, the "Cutileiro plan would have established a more effective Bosnian central government and probably resulted in less of an ethnically divided state than the accord agreed to at Dayton."[29] The Cutileiro plan had the added advantage that it sought to *prevent* war; this advantage was not shared by any of the subsequent peace proposals, including the Dayton accords.

Some observers doubt that the Lisbon agreement was viable; since, it is alleged, the Bosnian Serb leaders were not negotiating in good faith; they would never have accepted a compromise agreement.[30] There is no question that the Serb leadership contained several dubious figures, some of whom would later orchestrate serious war crimes. In March 1992, however, before full-scale war had begun, Serb leaders welcomed the Lisbon agreement, and they endorsed it in the strongest terms. Radovan Karadžić, who represented the Serbs at Lisbon, called the agreement "a great day for Bosnia and Herzegovina."[31] And it should be recalled that it was the *Muslims and the Croats*, not the Serbs, who actually reneged. There is no evidence that the Serbs were bent on war at this point. Even after Izetbegović reneged, the Serbs remained open to a compromise agreement similar to the Cutileiro plan. As late as April 1992, "the Serb leaders [in Bosnia] were probably still willing to accept a single state organized into a loose confederation divided into three ethnic 'cantons,'" according to an unclassified report by the Central Intelligence Agency.[32] A revival of the plan now proved impossible, and war was the result.

Overall, US policy—by pushing for early recognition of Bosnia while undercutting EC mediation—augmented the risks of a wider conflict. These risks were recognized in policy-making circles. Sell writes that in early 1992, "The United States . . . began to press for recognition of Bosnia, reducing the prospects—low as they might be—that continued negotiations could head off conflict."[33] Kenney states the matter more bluntly: "The [US] intelligence community was unanimous in saying that if you recognize, Bosnia is going to blow up."[34] The chronology of events supports the view that US policy helped precipitate violence: On March 27, the day after Izetbegović withdrew from the Lisbon accord—and did so at the urging of US officials—the Serbs declared their independence from Bosnia-Herzegovina, thus laying the groundwork for war. With US support, Bosnia-Herzegovina seceded from Yugoslavia and then achieved international recognition as an independent state on April 6. The Western European states set aside their reservations and went along with the US position on recognition.[35] Full scale ethnic war also commenced on April 6, thus coinciding exactly with the timing of international recognition. Viewed in retrospect, the US policy during this period must be viewed as a destabilizing force. Just as Germany had played a key role in destabilizing the region in 1991, the United States played the destabilizer in Bosnia in 1992.

Motivations for US Policy

We now pause to consider the larger international context during the period when Bosnia achieved independence. The early months of 1992 were marked by an upsurge of tensions between the United States and the major European powers, in the immediate aftermath of the Cold War. US concern about its influence in Europe was, of course, an issue of long standing (an issue discussed at length earlier this study). What I emphasize now is that these tensions intensified during the period when Bosnia was preparing for independence, and that US efforts to contain Europe and keep it under the wing of US hegemony had a major impact on the Bosnia conflict.

Shortly before the Bosnia war, at the 1991–1992 Maastricht conference, the EC member states approved the idea of a Common Foreign and Security Policy. For the Europeans, the idea of foreign policy collaboration was a major achievement, and it was the culmination of a process begun during the 1950s. The idea worried US officials, however, who feared that Europe was moving toward an independent foreign policy, one that was to function outside US and NATO influence. As a result, the United States might lose its dominant position in Europe, as well as the attendant political and economic benefits that had flowed from such dominance since 1945. These concerns were augmented by the more general anxiety that many US officials felt regarding the end of the Cold War and the disappearance of the familiar Soviet enemy.

Partly as a response to these concerns, a key group of neoconservative intellectuals within the Bush administration came together to craft a new post–Cold War strategy. The uniformed military had already developed a "base force" plan to preserve military spending at near Cold War levels on a permanent basis.[36] What was needed now was an overall strategic logic to justify the base force; this task was given to civilian officials at the Department of Defense. The new strategic logic was presented in the February 1992 draft of the Defense Planning Guidance (DPG) document. The new strategy sought to maintain the unilateral predominance that the United States possessed at the time, and to perpetuate that predominance as far into the future as possible. Any notions of multipolarity or shared global governance were brushed aside by the framers of the DPG; the United States alone would become the guarantor of the world's security. European efforts to forge an independent foreign policy, as implied in the Maastricht initiative, were viewed dimly. The Defense Planning Guidance pointedly called for the United States to oppose European efforts to achieve foreign policy independence. Overall, the document argued that US should reaffirm its leadership position as the world's unipolar power for a new post–Cold War order.

Bosnia would be the first major test case for the new strategy of predominance laid out in the Defense Planning Guidance. The Pentagon officials who were most responsible for crafting the DPG—Paul Wolfowitz and Zalmay Khalilzad—were among the most enthusiastic advocates of intervention in Bosnia.[37] And specific US actions during the Bosnia crisis corresponded closely with the objectives stated in the DPG: By supporting early independence for Bosnia, during March and April 1992, the United States asserted its predominance, thus correcting any perceptions that it might withdraw from Europe after the USSR's demise. This also helped correct for the earlier lack of US leadership in the Yugoslav crisis, which was now becoming an embarrassment.[38] While affirming its own power, the United States treated the European Community as an adversary. European efforts to resolve the crisis—and establish the EC as a diplomatic power—were undermined. Thus US officials scuttled the EC-brokered Lisbon agreement, which might have prevented war. In short, the administration's actions served to humiliate EC diplomatic efforts in Bosnia while they reaffirmed US primacy. These actions also destabilized the political situation in Bosnia and made war more likely; but stability per se was not in the US interest in this case. We will see that during the Clinton presidency, the Bosnia conflict would prove an ideal context for reaffirming the value of the NATO alliance for a new era, thus achieving yet another goal in the Defense Planning Guidance.

Thus US policy in Bosnia was motivated in part by considerations of geostrategic primacy. A second motive concerned US economic interests in Europe. During the early 1990s, there was a widespread perception that the European Community was developing into a "fortress Europe," with increased barriers to trade with the United States.[39] US economic interests would be damaged by the resulting loss of European markets. One argument in favor of intervention in Bosnia was that it would augment US influence on the EC member states, and this influence, in turn, could be used to block any further moves toward a fortress Europe. According to this view, intervention in Bosnia would serve to protect America's overseas markets and advance US interests; if the US *failed* to intervene, however, these interests would be harmed.

Former National Security Agency director William Odom emphasized these economic considerations: "Failure to act effectively in Yugoslavia will not only affect US national security interests, but also US economic interests. Our economic interdependency with Western Europe creates large numbers of American jobs."[40] Similarly, Sen. Richard Lugar, the ranking Republican on the Senate Foreign Relations Committee, noted that if the United States failed to intervene in Bosnia, it could cause a "loss of jobs and loss of income in this country" due to reduced export markets in Europe.[41] Thus a combination of US economic and geostrategic interests argued in favor of intervention. These realpolitik factors—not humanitarian sentiment—were the main motivations for US policy.

America's Allies: The Bosnian Muslims

Whatever the motivations, US policy in Bosnia was from the beginning closely allied with the Muslim ethnic group, as well as the Muslim-dominated Bosnian government under President Izetbegović.[42] Some readers will no doubt find this support quite natural, since the Muslim side was widely portrayed in positive terms throughout the war. Perhaps, it may be argued, the United States was favoring the morally better side, the one led by Izetbegović. This interpretation received considerable support from Western press coverage of the Bosnian war, which portrayed Izetbegović and his government favorably. Thomas Gjelton offers a typical account of the Bosnian president: "A short man with a grim wearied expression, bushy eyebrows, and sea blue eyes, he had an air of pain about him that may have come from the five years he spent in prison in the 1980s. Even critics conceded his basic decency, but his supporters worried that he was naïve.... Nevertheless, Izetbegović was determined to do whatever he could to avoid an armed confrontation.[43] But this portrayal of Izetbegović—as a benign and even pacifistic figure—is a myth, as we will see; in reality the Izetbegović government was just as intolerant and prone to violence as its Serb adversaries.

Throughout his life, Izetbegović had associated with Islamic political tendencies, often with an extremist bent. There is little in his background to suggest a commitment to pacifism, multiculturalism, or democracy. During World War II, Izetbegović lived in areas of Bosnia that were controlled by the pro-German Ustaša movement, essentially as a Nazi puppet state. During this period, Izetbegović helped found a group called the Young Muslims, which was openly profascist.[44] In 1970, Izetbegović published *The Islamic Declaration*, which set forth his political philosophy. In fairness, the *Declaration* contained some moderate language, including a call for the protection of non-Muslims within a Muslim polity. It also cautioned that Muslims should not seize political power before they constituted a majority. Nevertheless, the *Declaration* presented an extended argument for an Islamic state, including the "realization of Islam in all fields of personal life" and a "large Islamic federation stretching from Morocco to Indonesia and from tropical Africa to Central Asia."[45] In 1984, Izetbegović published another work, *Islam between East and West*.[46] This volume also had a strongly theocratic tone, as noted by the official Dutch investigation of the Bosnia war: "Reading this book [*Islam between East and West*] might well have revealed that Izetbegović had a somewhat fundamentalist streak."[47] We will see in the next chapter that the Islamic Republic of Iran would later become an important source of arms for Bosnia's Muslims.[48] Some sources deny that Izetbegović held fundamentalist views, and they disparage claims to the contrary as mere propaganda emanating from the Republic of Serbia and its leader, Slobodan Milošević.[49] Such views ignore the fact that this fundamentalism is well documented. Serb fears regarding Izetbegović's extremist proclivities were overstated, but they contained a measure of truth.

During the period of democratization, after 1989, Izetbegović helped create a new political party, the Party of Democratic Action (SDA). An inside view of the SDA is available from the memoirs of Adil Zulfikarpašić, an expatriate Bosnian Muslim businessman, who returned from the West in 1990 to help found the SDA. Zulfikarpašić is generally regarded as one of the most liberal-minded figures in Bosnia during this period.[50] Zulfikarpašić's memoirs describe how the SDA began as a moderate Muslim-based party—one that sought to avoid ethnically or religiously charged positions—but was gradually transformed in a more exclusionary direction, one openly hostile toward non-Muslim groups. Izetbegović played a key role in this transformation, according to Zulfikarpašić. His memoir describes one SDA rally held in 1990 attended by 300,000 people:

> I had been at Tito's rallies in Belgrade but I had never seen one like this. When people breathed it was like the roar of a tank, it was unbelievable. There were slogans, green flags, shouts, signs saying "We'll kill Vuk!" [Vuk Drašković, a Serb leader] and "Long Live Saddam Hussein!" Saddam Hussein? There were pictures of Saddam Hussein, people wearing Arab dress, hundreds of green [Islamic] flags. . . . Izetbegović's and the SDA's

main [press] organ published a text calling for the creation of a Muslim state and the strict implementation of *Sharia*, which is absolutely impossible in a multinational, multi-cultural, and multi-faith environment such as Bosnia.[51]

Overall, Zulfikarpašić described the party as having "fascist" tendencies, "with a personality cult" surrounding Izetbegović.[52] We will see momentarily that Zulfikarpašić's testimony is corroborated by other accounts.

Another worrying trend, from the Serb standpoint, was the increasing collaboration between the Muslim SDA and the Croat party, the Croatian Democratic Union (HDZ). The emergence of a Muslim/Croat political alliance, beginning in 1990, was basically a marriage of convenience, since the two groups were culturally distinct. The alliance was based on the suspicion that both groups felt toward the Serbs, who formed the largest ethnic bloc in the Yugoslav federation. In addition, the Muslim/Croat alliance of 1990–1991 recreated a similar alliance that had existed during World War II, when the two groups were the main supporters of the pro-Nazi Ustaša state, and both participated in the massacres of Serbs that occurred during this period.[53]

Given the historic associations, it is natural that Bosnia's Serbs viewed this ethnic collaboration with apprehension. Bosnian ethnic tensions were further exacerbated by the events taking place in neighboring Croatia, especially in the Krajina region. Ethnic Serbs in Croatia had been persecuted by the Tudjman government, and this persecution had preceded the onset of warfare, as we saw in earlier chapters. The Serbs of Bosnia feared that they too would suffer persecution at the hands of their ethnic enemies in much the same way as had their fellow Serbs in Croatia. The fears had at least some foundation: The Bosnian Croat party, the HDZ, had exactly the same name as Tudjman's party in Croatia, underscoring the close connections between ethnic Croats in the two republics. The Bosnian HDZ functioned as "a self-professed branch of Franjo Tudjman's ethnically based party" in Croatia, according to a CIA analysis.[54] In addition, the Muslim SDA party developed ties with the Croatian HDZ, and President Izetbegović spoke positively about Tudjman on a number of occasions, noting in 1990: "I know Mr. Tudjman, and respect him. . . . When I say he is a Croatian nationalist, one must not forget that one can be a nationalist in the positive sense."[55] Izetbegović made these remarks at a time when Tudjman was using openly anti-Serb rhetoric, while extolling the virtues of the former Ustaša regime during the period of Nazi collaboration.[56]

The ethnic chauvinism of the Muslim and Croat parties was, of course, hardly unique. The Bosnian Serbs too were moving in an intolerant direction.[57] During the period 1989–1990, there was a definite trend toward ethnic fragmentation—and away from multiculturalism—throughout Bosnia's population. This trend was confirmed during the elections of November 1990, when the overwhelming share of the votes went to the three main ethnically based parties: The Muslim SDA, the Croat HDZ, and the Serbian Democratic Party (SDS) (see Table 5.1). The three ethnic parties together received over 80 percent of the parliamentary seats. Several parties eschewed ethnic identification and sought to project a multiethnic message—including the remnants of the Bosnian League of Communists—but these failed to receive any significant support from the electorate. Basically this election was an "ethnic census" in which almost the whole population voted for parties that matched their respective ethnicities.[58] It was an ominous outcome.

The election was also a triumph for the SDA, since it received the most votes. Now overconfident from victory, the party reaffirmed its status as a strictly Muslim party. The Dutch investigation provides this account:

The election results had reinforced Muslim triumphalism. . . . Izetbegović remarked for example, he felt it was logical for Bosnia to become a state for Muslims as Croats and Serbs each already had a state of their own. . . . Rusmir Mahmutcehajić a prominent SDA member wrote that Serbs and Croats now had to adapt all aspects of their development to those of the Bosnian Muslims. . . . On state occasions, the SDA flag often flew alongside the Bosnian one. At party meetings, those present expressed their support for the Iraqi dictator Saddam Hussein and saw Arab clothing. The many green flags flying on such occasions, some with half moons, were a clear reference to Islam, not to any multi-cultural Bosnian identity;

Table 5.1. Legislative Election Results in Bosnia-Herzegovina, 1990

	Total seats won	Percentage of popular vote
SDA	86	36
SDS	72	30
HDZ	44	18
Others (8 parties)	38	16
Total	240	100

Source: Figures from Robert M. Hayden, *Blueprints for a House Divided: The Constitutional Logic of the Yugoslav Conflicts* (Ann Arbor: University of Michigan Press, 1999), 91–92; and Steven L. Burg and Paul S. Shoup, *The War in Bosnia-Herzegovina: Ethnic Conflict and International Intervention* (Armonk, N.Y.: M. E. Sharp, 1999), 54.

... the first three countries Izetbegović visited after being inaugurated as president were Libya, Iran, and Turkey. During a [later] trip to Pakistan, Saudi Arabia and Turkey in July 1991, he conveyed the impression that he was looking to conclude an Islamic alliance. He also requested that Bosnia-Herzegovina be granted observer status ... in the Organization of Islamic Countries.[59]

If Izetbegović was a believer in democracy and multiculturalism—as some accounts suggest—then he certainly had an odd way of expressing it.

The exclusionary politics that were practiced by Izetbegović and his SDA party contributed to the more general trend of ethnic polarization during this period.[60] In making this point, I do not imply that Izetbegović was solely or even primarily responsible for this polarization. Clearly, Serb leaders played equally important—and equally destabilizing—roles. And we will see momentarily that Serbian president Milošević helped promote Bosnia's ethnic polarization. I nevertheless have focused on the destabilizing actions of Izetbegović, since these have received so little attention in previous studies. There has been a tendency in most accounts to whitewash Izetbegović's role. According to British parliamentarian Paddy Ashdown, Izetbegović promoted "tolerance, restraint, and inclusiveness" among ethnic groups.[61] Bernard Kouchner claims that Izetbegović "gave the world a lesson in tolerance."[62] Wayne Burt describes the Bosnian president as "a moderate and well intentioned leader," while Roy Gutman claims that he "encouraged the pacifist strain" among Bosnians.[63] These accounts constitute serious misrepresentations of the historical record. Izetbegović was not the only villain in this story—but he was not a hero either.

Some feeble efforts were made by all parties to establish consensus, in an attempt to avert war. Shortly after the 1990 elections, an agreement was established to share out the key political positions among the three ethnic groups, creating what was in effect a coalition government: Thus, Izetbegović became the president; Jure Pelivan, a Croat, became the prime minister; and Momčilo Krajišnik, a Serb, became the speaker of the parliament.[64] Given the high level of ethnic polarization during this period, the coalition government had little prospect of success. Also, events within the Yugoslav federation served to increase tensions within Bosnia. During late 1991, it was increasingly obvious that Slovenia and Croatia had permanently seceded from the federation, and they would soon obtain international recognition. The Izetbegović government did not initially favor secession for Bosnia, but over time the prosecession bandwagon became irresistible.[65] By the fall of 1991, the Muslim and Croat leaders were both bent on joining this trend. The crisis reached a climax in October, when Muslim and Croat members of the legislature collaborated to sponsor a resolution in favor of leaving the Yugoslav federation and establishing an independent Bosnia.[66] The Serbs overwhelmingly opposed the plan. They feared that an independent Bosnia would be ruled by a Muslim/Croat government in which they would be relegated to permanent minority status as second-class citizens.

If the Muslims and the Croats were to establish an independent Bosnia, they would have to do so without Serb support. This proved a quandary, since achieving independence in this manner would have violated both the letter and the spirit of the Bosnian constitution, which was predicated on the assumption of consensus among the three ethnic groups.[67] However, the Muslims and Croats did not want to remain in a Yugoslav federation that was increasingly dominated by the Republic of Serbia and its unsavory president, Milošević; they were bent on achieving independence. During October 1991, the Muslim and Croat delegates forced a vote on the pro-independence motion, which achieved a majority vote and passed. The Serb delegates opposed it almost unanimously.[68] When the motion passed, it led to the effective breakdown of the multiethnic coalition government and set the stage for war. To gain further legitimacy for its efforts, the Izetbegović government proposed a referendum on the independence question, which was held during February 29–March 1, 1992. The Muslims and Croats voted overwhelmingly in favor. However, the Serb population boycotted the referendum and remained firmly opposed to any independence initiative.[69] Amidst the controversy on independence, armed clashes began in March 1992. Full-scale war commenced the following month, in April, at the same time that Bosnia was recognized as an independent state.

The Republic of Serbia: Its Role in Fomenting War

Another influence on the politics of Bosnian independence was, of course, the president of the Republic of Serbia, Slobodan Milošević. Contrary to widespread prejudice, Milošević was not the sole cause of the Bosnia war, just as he was not the sole cause of Yugoslavia's breakup. There is no doubt, however, that Serbia's president was one of the key factors that destabilized Bosnia and caused violence.

During early 1992, as Bosnia prepared for war, Milošević was consolidating his political power and eliminating remaining sources of opposition. This consolidation had a long genesis. Milošević's powers were constrained during the 1991 war in Slovenia, as we saw in Chapter 4, owing to the powers that still existed in segments of the Yugoslav central government in Belgrade and especially in the Yugoslav National Army (JNA). By early 1992, however, the civilian organs of the central government had largely ceased to function, while the JNA was in its death throes. The older, multiethnic commanders who had long dominated the army were losing influence to younger officers with a Serb nationalist bent. During January–February 1992, more than twenty JNA officers were forced to resign as part of a "purge designed to eliminate non-Serbs from the Yugoslav military leadership," according to the London *Times*.[70] The purged officers included the JNA's two top figures, Gen. Veljko Kadijević and Adm. Stane Brovet. Neither of these men was an ethnic Serb, and they were thus viewed with suspicion. According to one insider account, Milošević himself directly orchestrated these purges.[71] With the old officer corps now swept away, the JNA was reorganized more or less explicitly as a Serb army. Milošević had effective control of what remained of the army, and he would use it as his strike force in Bosnia.[72]

Now centralizing his authority, Milošević sought to reconstitute the political structure of Yugoslavia just as he had reconstituted the army. In April 1992, a new Yugoslav state was officially unveiled, centered on Serbia, along with the "autonomous provinces" of Kosovo and Vojvodina, which had always officially been part of Serbia. In addition, the Republic of Montenegro (traditionally a close ally of the Serbs) joined the new Federal Republic of Yugoslavia. This creation assumed the name "Yugoslavia," to appear to be a continuation of the old Titoist entity, though it comprised less than half its original population.[73] And unlike Titoist Yugoslavia, the new state clearly was based on the political dominance of a single ethnic group (the Serbs) and was run, de facto, by the Serb leader Milošević and his Socialist party.[74] Milošević's long-standing objective of political dominance was now largely achieved. He ruled his new Yugoslav creation in a semiauthoritarian manner (though not as a straight dictatorship).

Milošević was laying the groundwork for an aggressive policy, and the focus of this policy was the emerging crisis in Bosnia-Herzegovina. Milošević's plan for Bosnia involved two possible scenarios: The first scenario was that Bosnia would remain in the reconstituted Yugoslav federation—to be dominated by the Republic of Serbia and by Milošević himself. The Muslim and Croat groups within Bosnia would have to accommodate themselves to a newly subordinated status. Milošević thus encouraged Bosnia (and also Macedonia) to remain within Yugoslavia, and not to seek independence. According to Sell's memoir: "Milošević held out a public olive branch to the Muslims, suggesting that a 'common and equitable life' would be in the interests of both Serbs and Muslims. On January 21 [1992] the Serbian government issued an appeal to Bosnia and Macedonia" not to secede.[75] The second option Milošević foresaw was that Bosnia would in fact secede and this would lead to an ethnic war. In this event, the Serb president was determined to gain maximum advantage from the war by incorporating parts of Bosnia into a planned Greater Serbia.

The authorities in Bosnia-Herzegovina and Macedonia refused Milošević's entreaties to remain in a Serb-dominated Yugoslavia, and both republics moved toward full independence. Macedonia seceded with relatively few complications and little bloodshed.[76] Bosnia, of course, was not so fortunate, as it became the arena for the largest war of the whole Yugoslav conflict. Milošević and the Republic of Serbia would intervene extensively in this war.

To achieve his objectives of a Greater Serbia, Milošević cultivated a group of Bosnian Serb politicians associated with the SDS party, notably Radovan Karadžić, Nikola Koljević, and Biljana Plavšić. Though highly educated (all three held doctorates), these leaders would develop an international reputation for extremism, which was expressed most prominently by Plavšić. A professional biologist, Plavšić would later defend the persecution of non-Serbs in biological terms, as part of the Darwinian struggle for survival and therefore justifiable. Plavšić "termed Muslims 'genetically deformed' Serbs and ethnic cleansing a 'natural phenomenon'. Serbs had the 'biological right' to cleanse," in Plavšić's opinion.[77] And behind this group of local leaders stood Milošević himself. According to a CIA report, Milošević and his government provided direct "organizational support (and probably funds) for the SDS and some weapons for select SDS supporters."[78] This external support for the SDS, emanating from the Republic of Serbia, is widely recognized. Though never puppets of Milošević, the Bosnian Serb leadership was dependent on him for vital assistance.[79]

In addition, Milošević used the (increasingly docile) Yugoslav Army to help achieve his objectives. The army had in fact been building up the Bosnian Serb militias months before the fighting actually began. When full-scale war commenced in April 1992, federal troops supported the Bosnian Serbs, and this support was crucial in advancing the Serbs' position on the battlefield. Under international pressure, the Yugoslav Army began to withdraw from Bosnia in May 1992, but the withdrawal was largely a fiction. According to General Morillon, who commanded UN peacekeeping forces in Bosnia: "The army of the Serbs of Bosnia was the federal Army." Even after the official withdrawal, the federal army units were "repainted with new insignia and became officially the army of the Serbs of Bosnia, but they were the same forces, the same officers, the same equipment," according to General Morillon.[80]

The external support for the Bosnian Serbs placed the Muslim and Croat militias at a severe disadvantage.[81] An analysis by the US National Security

Council noted that the Serb forces gained access to some two-thirds of the stockpiled military equipment in Bosnia, thanks to support from the JNA. The Muslim forces, in contrast, had equipment that was "clearly inferior to that of the Serbian forces."[82] Among the three ethnic groups, the Bosnian Serbs were thus the best armed and best positioned to prevail on the battlefield. There is no evidence that the Serb people or Serb leadership were by nature more aggressive or bloodthirsty than their ethnic adversaries. What is clear, however, is that the Serbs were much better equipped to act offensively, and thus to commit atrocities.[83]

As war began, Serb forces launched a major offensive in northeast Bosnia, taking over a series of villages of mixed ethnicity, and then expelling most non-Serb inhabitants by force. By the end of 1992, Serb forces had overrun large portions of Bosnia-Herzegovina, and they controlled approximately 70 percent of the whole area of the country.[84] The process of ethnic cleansing, for which the war became famous, had begun.

The Politics of Atrocities

The Bosnia conflict quickly became notorious for the scale of its atrocities, especially those perpetrated by Serb forces against Muslim civilians. The widespread practice of ethnic cleansing was often associated with the killing of noncombatants, and also the raping of women and girls. The single massacre at Srebrenica in 1995 is believed to have killed some eight thousand unarmed Muslims.

The Bosnia war was the bloodiest Europe had witnessed for many decades, far worse than the earlier war in Croatia. It was surely the most destructive European conflict since the Greek civil war of the late 1940s, and possibly the most destructive since World War II.[85] To be sure, there were several conflicts during the 1990s (mostly in sub-Saharan Africa) that caused as many or more deaths than the Bosnia war.[86] Nevertheless, it was Bosnia that was the main focus of international human rights coverage during the period 1992–1995, and a vast atrocity literature was generated.[87] In the world's press, the subject of atrocities in Bosnia was one of the most extensively covered events of the entire post-1989 era, earning three Pulitzer Prizes.[88]

There can be no question that Muslims were the principal victims of the war, a fact borne out by two recent studies. One of these studies was conducted by the prosecution at the International Criminal Tribunal for the Former Yugoslavia (ICTY).[89] A second study was undertaken by the Sarajevo Research and Documentation Center (SRDC), funded by the

**Table 5.2. War Deaths in Bosnia-Herzegovina,
1992–1995, by Ethnic Group**

| | Estimated percentage of total deaths | |
	SRDC*	ICTY**
Muslims	70	69 (Muslims and Croats)
Croats	5	—
Serbs	25	31

Source: Statistics derived from Kjell Arild Nilson, "102,000 Drept i Bosnia," Norwegian
Press Service, November 14, 2004; and Nedim Dervisbegovic, "Bosnia War Death Toll Put
at Less Than 150,000," Reuters, December 10, 2004.

* Includes both military and civilian deaths.

** Includes civilian deaths only.

Norwegian Ministry of Foreign Affairs.[90] These two studies constitute the
best available estimates on deaths from the war. The two provide roughly
comparable estimates and leave little doubt that the Muslim group—which
was the least armed of the ethnic groups during most of the war—comprised the largest number of deaths (see Table 5.2). Given the context of the
war, it seems highly probable that a majority of the Muslims were killed by
Serb forces. However, a large number of Muslims were also killed in battles
with Croat forces, and an additional number of Muslims died during inter-
Muslim combat (especially in the Bihać region, in western Bosnia).

At the same time, it is clear that the atrocity stories have been considerably exaggerated. The number of deaths on all sides in the Bosnia conflict has widely been reported to total 200,000–250,000. These figures have
been repeated many times, in hundreds of newspaper and magazine articles,
both during the course of the war and after the war ended.[91] The recent
studies by the SRDC and the ICTY, however, suggest that these figures are
overstatements.

The ICTY study concluded that the death toll on all sides was approximately 110,000 (of whom slightly less than half were combatants and slightly
more than half noncombatants).[92] The study was described at length in the
Norwegian Press Service: "The most commonly used number for killed persons in the war in Bosnia-Herzegovina has been 200,000 [note that many
also give 250,000], and this number has been repeated [in] the international
media since 1994." The ICTY researchers "conclude that *this number is too
high*" (emphasis added).[93] The second study, by the SRDC, provides a similar
estimate. According to the SRDC study, the Bosnian death toll on all sides
was in the range of 97,000–107,000, which once again suggests that previous

reports had overstated Bosnian casualties.[94] The overstatement was noted in a 2006 interview with SRDC researcher Mirsad Tokača, published by the Bosnia Institute:

> Question: "Your research has destroyed the myth held by the Bosniaks which is that 200,000 of their co-nationals perished in this war. . . ."

> Tokača: "I have always thought that the earlier figure was too high. . . . The [reported] figure of 200,000 was not reached."[95]

In short, the death toll in the Bosnia war never attained the levels reported in the world's press.

It is clear that Serb forces were on the offensive during much of the war, and they conquered large areas of Bosnia-Herzegovina. But the extent of Serb aggression was once again exaggerated. Newspaper articles repeatedly noted that Serbs controlled some 70 percent of Bosnia's territory, despite the fact that they constituted only 31 percent the total population. Fairly typical is the following 1995 description from the *Toronto Star*, which noted that Bosnia's "population of 4.6 million is 44 per cent Muslim, 31 per cent Serbian . . . [and] 17 per cent Croatian. . . . *The Serbs now control more than 70 per cent of the land*" (emphasis added).[96] There was an insinuation that the Serbs must have *conquered* most of this 70 percent. Why, the reader might wonder, should the Serbs control so much land if they account for less than one-third of the population? What such reports omitted was that Serbs had always occupied most of Bosnia's land area, owing to their demographic dominance in rural regions. The Dutch government investigation estimates that ethnic Serbs controlled 56 percent of Bosnia's land prior to the war.[97] During the 1992–1995 period, Serbs extended their control of Bosnia's land area by approximately 14 percent above the amount of land that Serbs had held before the war. Clearly this 14 percent was gained through military conquest—but the extent of this conquest was nowhere near the levels implied in press reports. Such distortions appeared not only in newspaper articles, but also in US government reports.[98]

Yet another distortion related to Muslim prisoners held at Serb-run detention camps, notably Omarska, Keraterm, and Trnopolje. Atrocities in these camps were widely reported by journalists, who used forceful language to make their points. *Newsday* reporter Roy Gutman insisted that "Omarska was a death factory," implying that conditions there resembled Nazi death camps, such as Treblinka or Auschwitz.[99] The death camp allegations were circulated by the world's press and also by the Izetbegović government, generating widespread attention. Gutman himself won a Pulitzer Prize for his reporting on this issue. These reports, in turn, outraged international public opinion and led to increased demands for military intervention in Bosnia against Serb aggression.

Were these reports accurate? While there is no question that Serb guards at the camps committed killings, torture, and other atrocities, the claims of Nazi-style "extermination camps" or "death camps" were overstated. President Izetbegović himself admitted the overstatement, shortly before his death, in a remarkable 2003 interview with French political activist Bernard Kouchner. The interview was reported in Kouchner's published memoirs, as follows:

> Kouchner: "You claimed the existence in Bosnia of "extermination camps." You repeated this to journalists. This [claim] elicited concern all over the world. François Mitterrand sent me to Omarska [to investigate the claims]. . . . Conditions there were terrible, but *there was no systematic extermination*. Did you know this?"

> Izetbegović: "Yes, I thought that the claims [about extermination camps] would help trigger a bombing campaign [by the Western powers against the Serbs]. . . . I tried but *my claims were false. There were no extermination camps*, even though conditions [in the detention camps] were terrible." [emphasis added][100]

It appears that the earlier claims of Serb extermination camps contained an element of sensationalism.[101]

An additional focal point of press coverage throughout the Bosnia war was the suffering of civilians in Sarajevo due to sniper fire and artillery bombardment. In several cases, television cameras captured mass killings of pedestrians in real time, provoking widespread revulsion. Undoubtedly, the large majority of these incidents were perpetrated by Serb forces, who possessed more weapons than their adversaries and who besieged Sarajevo throughout most of the war.

There was an important dimension to these attacks, however, that received little coverage at the time: In several cases, Bosnian forces themselves bombarded Sarajevo and blamed the resulting deaths on the Serbs. David Owen, a European Community negotiator (and later a prosecution witness at the Milošević trial) notes that UN personnel had long suspected that at least some of the attacks were "being undertaken by Muslim units firing on their own people." Such suspicions were confirmed in August 1995, "when a French UN team pinpointed some of the sniping to a building which they knew was controlled by the Bosnian government forces."[102] Similarly, US general Charles Boyd writes that Bosnian "government soldiers . . . have shelled the Sarajevo airport, the city's primary lifeline for relief supplies; . . . *no seasoned observer in Sarajevo doubts for a moment that Muslim forces have found it in their interest to shell friendly targets*" (emphasis added).[103] In other incidents, the Bosnian Army intentionally provoked Serb shelling of civilian targets, according to Lieut. Gen. Michael Rose, a British officer who served with the UN peacekeeping forces. In his memoir, General Rose recounts a 1994 incident in which Bosnian Army soldiers fired their weapons from questionable locations, including a hospital. Rose concludes: "The Bosnians had evidently chosen this location [the hospital] with the intention of attracting Serb fire, in the hope that the resulting carnage would further tilt international support in their favor."[104]

It should also be noted that the government restricted the right of Sarajevo residents to flee the city, effectively blocking the exit for many besieged civilians.[105] This policy increased the potential for casualties and fit in nicely with the government's public relations strategy. In the world's media, the deaths from shelling and sniper fire were blamed exclusively on Serb forces, but in reality the Bosnian government bore some responsibility as well.

Such practices may seem paradoxical, since the Bosnian government was increasing the suffering of its own civilian population—but protecting civilians was not a high priority for the government. Indeed, at least some Bosnian officials viewed civilian casualties in a positive light, since they inflamed world opinion. Tim Ripley, who covered the war for *Jane's Defense Weekly*, described how the Bosnian government used civilian suffering strategically, to advance its objectives:

> The Bosnian government had long recognized that the public suffering of the citizens of Sarajevo was its most potent weapon in the battle to win international support . . . Veteran BBC correspondent Martin Bell spent many hours in discussions with Bosnia's "westernized" political leaders such as Deputy President Ejup Ganić. They were quite open about their war strategy of trying to force massive outside military intervention on their side. "They were driven by this strategy," said Bell. "It was their calculation that if [Bosnian] sacrifices were large enough they would force effective intervention." . . . To Western military men in Sarajevo, the Bosnian strategy of using children, old people, and other civilians as "staked goats" to generate international sympathy was abhorrent.[106]

These Machiavellian practices on the part of the Izetbegović government—which underscore the moral complexity of the war—elicited little notice at the time.

Public Relations and Propaganda

A significant factor in the Bosnia war was the role of professional public relations firms that represented warring parties. Although such firms were active during the Croatia war of 1991, it was in Bosnia that they became key players. The New York–based firm Ruder-Finn Global Communications played an especially central role. The *National Journal* offered this account:

> The Croatians and the Bosnians who have hired the high powered Ruder-Finn Inc. PR firm have out-organized and out-gunned the Serbs, who are making do with a small nonprofit PR operation in Chicago. The Croats and Bosnians have not only won this round, but they have also apparently acquired a powerful lobbying ally by winning the support of major Jewish organizations. . . . On August 5 [1992] three major Jewish organizations—the B'nai B'rith Anti-Defamation League, the American Jewish Committee, and the American Jewish Congress—ran a quarter page ad in the *New York Times* and held a rally in front of UN headquarters in New York City, recalling the Holocaust in World War II.[107]

Apparently, Ruder-Finn was effective in molding the public debate on Bosnia.

The significance of Ruder-Finn's efforts was dramatically demonstrated in an October 1993 interview of James Harff, who was president of the firm. The interview was conducted by French journalist Jacques Merlino, and it was translated into English in the Jewish magazine *Midstream*.[108]

> Merlino: What achievement are you most proud of?

> Harff: To have managed to put Jewish opinion on our side. This was
>   a sensitive matter. . . ; the Croatian and Bosnian past was marked
>   by a real and cruel anti-Semitism. . . . So there was every reason
>   for intellectuals and Jewish organizations to be hostile toward the
>   Croats and the Bosnians. Our challenge was to reverse this attitude.
>   And we have succeeded masterfully.
>   At the beginning of July 1992, New York *Newsday* came out with
>   the affair of [Serb] concentration camps [probably a reference to
>   Gutman's reports]. We jumped at the opportunity immediately.
>   We outwitted three big Jewish organizations—the B'nai B'rith
>   Anti-Defamation League, the American Jewish Committee, and
>   the American Jewish Congress. In August we suggested that they

publish an advertisement in the *New York Times* and organize
demonstrations outside the United Nations. . . .

When the Jewish organizations entered the game on the side of the
[Muslim] Bosnians, we could promptly equate the Serbs with the
Nazis in the public mind. Nobody understood what was happening
in Yugoslavia. . . . But in a single move, we were able to present a
simple story of good guys and bad guys, which would hereafter play
itself. . . . Almost immediately, there was a clear change of language
in the press, with the use of words with high emotional content
such as "ethnic cleansing," "concentration camps," etc., which evoked
images of Nazi Germany and the gas chambers of Auschwitz. The
emotional charge was so powerful nobody could go against it.

Some of the claims here must be treated with skepticism, since Harff's statements contain an element of self-promotion. At the same time, the picture he presents accords well with the available facts (especially in light of
Kouchner's revelations, noted earlier, regarding alleged Serb death camps).
And key points in the Harff interview are corroborated by the *National Journal* account.

In the context of this public relations campaign, journalists too became
partisans, and they did so openly. Reporters dispensed with the notion that
they were even-handed parties. According to Ed Vulliamy, who covered
Bosnia for the London *Guardian*, journalistic neutrality "is both dangerous
and morally reprehensible. By remaining neutral, we reward the bullies of
history and discard the peace and justice promised us by the generation that
defeated the Third Reich." In his disdain for neutrality, Vulliamy openly favored Western intervention in support of the Izetbegović regime.[109] CNN's
Christianne Amanpour also became a public advocate for Western intervention. Amanpour stated: "With this war [in Bosnia], it was not possible
for a human being to be neutral; . . . there was a clear aggressor and a clear
victim"; the implication was that the Serbs were playing the role of aggressor,
and the Muslims playing the victim.[110] In reference to his widely read book
Slaughterhouse: Bosnia and the Failure of the West, David Rieff acknowledges
that he "resolved to write as frankly incendiary a narrative as I could." Rieff's
book was an extended condemnation of the Western powers for their failure
to intervene in favor of the Muslim government.[111]

Partly because of these biases, the world's media overlooked the moral
shortcomings of the Izetbegović regime. Some of these shortcomings did,
however, come to light after the end of the war. I have already noted the issue of Bosnian forces shelling their own civilians. The Dutch investigation
notes further atrocities:

[At the start of the war in 1992,] the defense of Sarajevo still relied to an important extent on persons with a criminal background, such as the former pop singer Mušan Topalović ("Caco"), who had become a friend of Izetbegović during the latter's imprisonment in the 1980s. . . . *These criminals . . . had strong links with the government* in Sarajevo and the Bosnian government Army. . . . Topalović intimidated the non-Muslim population of Sarajevo: He had defenseless Serbs and Croats kidnapped, tortured, and murdered. *Hundreds were killed in this way.* . . . In fact Muslims also became victims of his actions. His followers kidnapped rich residents of Sarajevo in order to extract high ransoms, they participated in extortion, and they raped women. As time went on, Topalović accepted the authority of the Army headquarters less and less, and heeded only the links with the SDA [Izetbegović's party]. Izetbegović is said to have been a regular visitor to Caco's headquarters. [emphasis added][112]

In other areas of Bosnia, Muslim forces engaged in repeated acts of ethnic cleansing and other atrocities against both Serb and Croat civilians.[113] It is surely true that atrocities were more widely perpetrated by the *Serb* forces. But the greater Serb atrocities resulted from their superior firepower, which enabled offensive operations. When it was in their interest to do so, the Muslims too engaged in vicious behavior. President Izetbegović himself had some degree of complicity in these actions. The atrocities committed by Bosnian government forces do not seem consistent with the simplistic image of Muslim "victims" and Serb "aggressors" claimed by Amanpour—but they are nevertheless well documented.

Thus the activities of Ruder-Finn combined with journalistic bias established a climate of discussion that celebrated the Muslims and disparaged their Serb adversaries. In the context of such bias, important facts went unmentioned: The unsavory background of the SDA party and of its leader, Izetbegović; the Muslim/Croat roles in contributing to the breakdown of consensus in Bosnia and the initiation of violence; and atrocities perpetrated by the Izetbegović regime—all of these points received little or no attention.

The Bush Administration's Dilemma

By the time of Bosnia's independence, the United States was already deeply involved in the conflict. It had encouraged Izetbegović to secede from the Yugoslav federation—despite the risk of war—and then blocked European efforts to resolve ethnic tensions through negotiation. Once war actually began, however, the United States seemed powerless to protect its Muslim clients from the well-armed Serb militia. The war was thus becoming an embarrassment for the Bush administration, and the intense press coverage augmented the embarrassment still further.

Media commentators at this time argued for direct military action by the United States, which was viewed as the only way to stop the Serb onslaught. The problem was that the Joint Chiefs of Staff (JCS) opposed intervention, fearing that it might lead to a Vietnam-style quagmire. The principal source of this opposition was the JCS chair, Gen. Colin Powell, who had been a young infantry officer in Vietnam. In his memoirs, Powell frankly acknowledged his reluctance to support even limited military action in Bosnia. Powell scoffed at the idea of "limited" intervention, arguing that this was a recipe for escalation at a later date, with high risks and an uncertain outcome.[114] No doubt the Yugoslavs' reputation as fine guerrilla fighters, which was established during World War II, influenced the Joint Chiefs' thinking on this issue. The possibility of a guerrilla scenario elicited memories of the Vietnam debacle. Powell also felt uncomfortable about the prospect of fighting in the mountainous terrain of Bosnia, given that the US Army had just fought in the very different environment of the Persian Gulf. He noted succinctly: "We [in the army] do deserts, we don't do mountains."[115]

But the Joint Chiefs were not completely unified on the Bosnia issue. The air force chief of staff, Gen. Merrill McPeak, advocated military action, and (perhaps predictably) the general especially favored air strikes.[116] A tension thus emerged on the JCS between the pro-intervention air force and the anti-intervention army. David Halberstam provides an analysis of the way that memories of the Vietnam War influenced this tension:

> McPeak believed that he and others in the Air Force had been less damaged by Vietnam than the Army. Certainly, he and his peers who had flown there . . . had been frustrated. . . . [But] there had been no widespread smoking of dope or fragging of officers as he believed there had been in the Army. Morale had never deteriorated within his service . . . Many of the Army people, he felt, had returned from the war deeply hurt, almost emotionally wounded, as if there were an element of personal humiliation in what had happened that greatly affected the Army's view of succeeding crises.[117]

As a result of these considerations, General McPeak felt that Powell was overly cautious about using force in Bosnia. Nevertheless, the views of McPeak were overruled at meetings of the Joint Chiefs of Staff, where representatives of the other services sided with the army and accepted Powell's reservations.

Despite the caution prevailing in the JCS, there was growing pressure for some form of military intervention in support of the Muslim government. As previously noted, Wolfowitz and Khalilzad at Defense strongly supported intervention, as did Eagleburger at State.[118] The interventionists within the administration were backed by pundits and editorialists in the mass media. These writers often used dramatic prose to advance their case. In November 1992, Anthony Lewis wrote: "American action is crucial now, immediately, before cold and hunger complete the work of guns and knives in Bosnia. I still believe that President Bush can be moved to act. The alternative is to be remembered as are those who closed their eyes to Nazi persecution and murder."[119] There also was congressional pressure in favor of military intervention, and this pressure emanated from both Republicans and Democrats.[120]

In addition, there were demands that the North Atlantic Treaty Organization should help settle the war. The Center for Security Policy, a think tank with strong links to neoconservative figures at the Pentagon, advocated a NATO role: "Serbian-led forces occupying areas of Croatia and Bosnia-Herzegovina must be expelled—by force if necessary. . . . There is in fact only one organization capable of taking on and successfully executing this daunting task: NATO. Only the Alliance has the dedicated, highly trained, and rapidly deployable forces needed to thwart Milošević's hegemonic designs."[121] Deploying NATO forces to the Balkans would have meshed nicely with the overall thrust of US strategy during this period, as identified in the Defense Planning Guidance document. No doubt many US policy makers would have found it appealing to use NATO forces, since this would have made the organization appear relevant as its relevance was being questioned. There remained one problem with this strategy: A major NATO role in the Balkans would have required the United States to send troops and, in 1992, US policy makers were not willing to do this.[122]

In short, the arguments for intervention failed to overcome the basic caution that prevailed within the Bush administration. President Bush himself was against the idea of US military intervention in the Balkans, a view seconded by Secretary of Defense Dick Cheney.[123] In stating his objection to sending troops, Cheney emphasized the lack of clear objectives: "If I had 500,000 troops on the ground in Bosnia tomorrow, what would I tell them to do? Who is the adversary? What are the rules of engagement? How many Yugoslavs should we kill to keep Yugoslavs from killing other Yugoslavs? How do we get out? What do I define as victory?"[124] Cheney was otherwise a relatively hawkish figure, and he strongly supported the DPG strategy. On the specific issue of Bosnia, however, Cheney deferred to the more restrained views of the Joint Chiefs. Secretary of State James Baker too opposed military intervention. If the United States had intervened, Baker felt, "the casualties would have been staggering."[125] Whether or not this view was justified, it was widely shared.

Specific Policy Responses

The lack of US military action was damaging US credibility (especially since the United States had encouraged Bosnia to seek independence in the first place). The timing was especially bad, since this was considered a key period for the United States to reestablish the value of its leadership for a new, post-Soviet world. The rapid escalation of atrocities against Muslims, and the US inability to stop them, added to the credibility problem. Several measures were taken to address this problem.

First, the United States and Europe collaborated to field a UN peacekeeping mission in Bosnia. The UN Secretariat authorized a UN Protection Force (UNPROFOR) to undertake a series of actions in Bosnia beginning in April 1992. During the next several months, UNPROFOR soldiers facilitated humanitarian aid convoys, as well as relief flights into the Sarajevo airport. In time, the UNPROFOR operation would mushroom into the one of the largest peacekeeping operation in UN history, with a full strength of forty thousand troops from more than forty countries, all under a joint command.[126] UNPROFOR operated throughout Bosnia during the course of the war, 1992–1995.

The effects of the UN peacekeepers, however, were not great. The relief efforts helped alleviate the effects of the war on the civilian population, but only to a limited extent. And the UN troops could not act as peacekeepers in any meaningful sense, since there was no peace to keep. The basic problem was that UNPROFOR had nowhere near the authority or the resources that would have been necessary to stop the fighting. The main effect of UNPROFOR was political, in that it satisfied a widespread international pressure that the powers needed to "do something" in Bosnia. The key Security Council members, including the United States, were not yet willing to commit themselves to a combat presence in the Balkans, but at the same time they did not wish to seem unconcerned about the suffering caused by the war. The result was a weak UN peacekeeping presence. The peacekeepers were hardly a solution to the Bosnia problem—but they were perhaps better than nothing at all. And UN involvement had another advantage from the US standpoint: If the situation continued to deteriorate in Bosnia, the United Nations would make a useful scapegoat for any perceived failures. This aspect of UNPROFOR was especially prized by American officials, who were becoming estranged from a UN Security Council that was beginning to show signs of independence and even insubordination to the demands of US foreign policy.[127]

Second, the United States and Europe sought to isolate Yugoslavia in order to punish the Milošević regime for its role in aggravating the Bosnia war. In accord with this strategy, the UN Security Council imposed a series of economic sanctions against what remained of Yugoslavia beginning in May 1992.[128] According to one analysis, the sanctions "were heavier than those ever before imposed by the United Nations on a country. Import and export, together with transport to and from [Yugoslavia] were forbidden; financial transactions were almost totally forbidden; all scientific, cultural, and sporting contacts were broken off; and the level of diplomatic representation was drastically reduced."[129] The Security Council also maintained an arms embargo, which applied to all parties in the conflict.[130]

The United States and the European Community also sent a flotilla of naval vessels to the Adriatic Sea to establish a blockade of Yugoslavia and thus to enforce the sanctions.[131] This limited use of military force demonstrated Western resolve in the Balkans and addressed concerns that the powers were doing nothing about the war. There was a special effort to showcase US activity, and this was picked up in the press ("Washington Takes Leading Role in Seeking to Stem Yugoslav Strife," read a headline from the *Christian Science Monitor* from this period).[132] And the sanctions succeeded in imposing severe economic costs on the Milošević regime, and on the population of Yugoslavia more generally. But in a larger sense, these actions were ineffectual, in that they did not end the war.

Third, US officials sought to overthrow Milošević, whose policies had contributed to the Bosnia war. In November 1992, the *New York Times* reported: "Having failed to budge President Slobodan Milošević from his position as Serbia's strongman with economic and political sanctions, the United States is now trying to increase pressure for his ouster by supporting Serbian opposition to him, especially on Yugoslav television. . . . Senior State Department officials have said privately that the ousting of the Serbian president is a basic policy goal, although the administration has avoided saying this in public."[133] These covert operations failed; Milošević was able to remain in power, despite US efforts to remove him. And these covert moves did little to reduce violence in Bosnia.[134]

Fourth, US officials sought to blame Europe for the war. In May 1992, Secretary of State Baker launched "a barely disguised diatribe against the European Community," according to the London *Times*. "Mr. Baker listed Serbian atrocities and with uncharacteristic passion denounced those 'looking for reasons not to act'"—leaving little doubt that it was the Europeans, not the Americans, who were avoiding action, in Baker's view.[135] This was the opening salvo in what was to become an extended transatlantic conflict regarding the Bosnia war, which would continue throughout the period 1992–1995. Baker's statements are curious, given the US role in encouraging Bosnia to secede in the first place and then helping to scuttle EC mediation efforts that might have prevented war. Nevertheless, his criticisms deflected attention from America's own inability to resolve the fighting. And they also advanced a larger objective: The criticisms served to damage the credibility of the European Community, as well as EC efforts to forge a common foreign and military policy, thus helping to achieve a major goal of US post–Cold War strategy, as specified in the 1992 Defense Planning Guidance document. But blaming Europe was hardly an effective strategy for resolving the crisis. And Baker's anti-European speeches could not hide the fact that the United States too was unwilling to intervene with military force.

These various policy responses were, at best, palliatives and offered no real solution to the Balkan violence. And the international community seemed to be running out of alternatives: The United States had already blocked a diplomatic settlement. Yet military intervention was not possible, since the majority of the Joint Chiefs opposed it. Policy makers thus faced a dilemma in the Bosnia war, without any obvious solution.

The lack of any direct intervention in the Balkans was posing political problems for the US military itself, whose credibility was at stake. The timing was significant, as this was a period when the US armed services were seeking to justify their share of budgetary allocations. The services lacked any obvious mission, now that their longtime adversary, the USSR, had ceased to exist. As we have seen, the Joint Chiefs had developed a base force program to maintain near Cold War levels of military spending.[136] The quandary was how to justify this program without any major security threats. The basic problem was stated by Gen. Merrill McPeak, the air force chief of staff and an advocate of intervention in Bosnia. McPeak felt that "sooner or later the military would have to figure how to use the forces they were being paid so much for—a ticket of $275 billion a year."[137] Some new opportunity was needed, one where the United States could make up for its failure in the Balkans and could showcase its ability to project power in a decisive manner. The humanitarian crisis in Somalia would offer this opportunity.

Sideshow in Somalia

On December 8, 1992, more than twenty thousand US troops began landing in Somalia as the lead element of a multinational relief team, collectively termed Operation Restore Hope. Some nineteen other countries participated, although US troops formed the majority of the personnel. This operation, authorized by the UN Security Council, was officially intended to alleviate famine conditions in Somalia.[138] The famine had resulted from the collapse of the dictatorship of Mohammed Siad Barre, who had been overthrown by an insurgency in January 1991. After the overthrow, a series of warlords competed for control of the country; the resulting chaos was a major cause of the famine that led to Restore Hope. The operation itself was historically unique: It was by far the largest-ever deployment of US forces on the African continent, and one of the largest US interventions in any region since the Vietnam War. The Somalian case was also unique in that it was enthusiastically supported by General Powell and the JCS, making it the only purported humanitarian intervention widely favored within the military. Indeed, the Joint Chiefs appear to have been the main advocates for the intervention within the Bush administration.[139]

Restore Hope has long been a source of confusion to foreign policy analysts. The selection of Somalia seemed somewhat arbitrary: The humanitarian emergency in Somalia was not necessarily the most pressing in Africa. Other regions, such as southern Sudan, had similarly severe conditions. The timing of the operation too seemed strange. The troop landings took place after the Somali famine had peaked during the summer of 1992; by the time Restore Hope was launched in December, the crisis had begun to abate.[140] And Restore Hope was directed by a US president, George Bush, whose career had been steeped in realpolitik and who had not previously shown much interest, even publicly, in international relief efforts.

US conduct during the operation raises further questions about the mission's professed altruistic intent. The US forces initially supported Somali warlord Mohammed Farah Aideed as a favored intermediary. Yet Aideed had an appallingly violent reputation. French journalist Stephen Smith notes the irony of US support for the warlord: "To work out the conditions of the landings, [US officials] met with . . . General Aideed! The principal figure in the Somali war? The man who had used the orphanage of [aid organization] SOS as a human shield? Who . . . had shelled the capital during the 'second battle of Mogadishu' producing . . . thousands of casualties, nearly all civilians? It was him, General Aideed. It was with him that the American officials negotiated the arrival of forces, before they went to see in North Mogadishu Ali Mahdi [Aideed's rival]."[141] Throughout the first weeks of Restore Hope, US officials worked closely with Aideed and supported him in contests with rival warlords. During one battle in the city of Kismayu, US helicopter gunships directly aided Aideed's militia.[142] US support for Aideed weighs against the view that humanitarian sentiment or moral principle motivated Restore Hope.

Several theories have been suggested to explain the operation: One explanation argues that extensive press coverage of the famine ("the CNN effect") pressured a reluctant President Bush into undertaking the relief operation. But under scrutiny this explanation does not hold up. An empirical analysis shows that, in fact, the world's press only began to pay attention to the Somali famine *after* the US government had begun preparing to intervene. In other words, press interest in the famine followed government interest, and therefore it seems difficult to accept that press coverage could have caused the intervention.[143] Another interpretation argues that the outgoing Bush administration sought to create a quagmire in Somalia, a future embarrassment for Bush's newly elected replacement, Bill Clinton. However, this theory too seems doubtful: Clinton fully supported the troop landing.[144]

Operation Restore Hope can be understood only when viewed in the larger context of US anxieties with regard to Bosnia-Herzegovina. As noted, the Bush administration was seeking some way to demonstrate US leadership through the use of military force in a zone that General Powell and other military commanders would support. Somalia seemed a useful opportunity to undertake such an intervention, one that provided a distraction from US failures in Bosnia. Elizabeth Drew stated that the Bush administration sent troops to Somalia "in part because it had been attacked for its inaction in Bosnia."[145] Sidney Blumenthal quoted a former Bush administration official: "One looked at the two tragedies that were going on [Bosnia and Somalia]. Somalia was seen as an easier military proposition."[146] Former State Department official Robert Gallucci stated that Somalia was regarded as a "low risk, high payoff" operation—in contrast to Bosnia, which was considered high risk. And, he said, with "Somalia we could see a clear exit strategy," which once again offered a contrast with any prospective intervention in Bosnia.[147] Jon Western's academic study based on interviews with key figures also emphasized the importance of Bosnia in the decision-making process that led to Operation Restore Hope.[148]

One of the main features that recommended Somalia was that the country was mostly a desert zone, a terrain in which the US military felt especially comfortable after the success of Desert Storm, which had taken place the previous year.[149] Somalia had a large coastline and was accessible by sea; carrier-based aircraft could easily reach its interior. US troops could be readily landed, supplied, and protected from attack with few logistical complications. And Somalia had several additional advantages. It was an overwhelmingly Islamic country and intervention would propitiate critics who claimed the Bush administration did not care about Muslims in Bosnia. Somalia also had moderately large oil reserves, and the Continental Oil Company (Conoco) was undertaking exploration activities there at the time of Restore Hope. Conoco executives strongly supported the troop landing, which would serve to protect their investment.[150] This corporate enthusiasm no doubt made the whole operation seem more politically viable and, therefore, more attractive to the Joint Chiefs. And most importantly, a humanitarian operation in Somalia seemed less risky than the alternative, which was intervention in Bosnia.

The Joint Chiefs also sought to capitalize on the Somalia operation to advance their political agenda. General Powell bluntly referred to the troop landing as a "paid political advertisement on behalf of the base force" project.[151] The landing itself received extensive press coverage, which emphasized that US forces could still engage in overseas missions even after the collapse of the Soviet enemy. *Advertising Age* provided this account: "As US troops assist in the relief efforts in Somalia—and TV cameras cover their every move—the government hopes favorable publicity will boost military recruiting. While the coverage sparked complaints from the Pentagon and ridicule from TV critics, military officials believe the overall impression will help them. 'We hope its going to have a positive impact, *especially on the perception that the US military might not have missions in the world* or might not be recruiting,' said Col. Robert E. Wilson, Jr, head of the Marines' marketing branch" (emphasis added).[152]

Thus the public was reminded that the US military remained relevant when its relevance was open to question. Specific services, notably the navy, used the operation to showcase their own special capabilities. The aircraft carrier *USS Ranger* was dispatched to the Somali coast, where it played a key role in supporting the troop landing. Naval officers promptly used the resulting publicity as an argument "against mothballing any carriers," according to *Aviation Week*.[153] Restore Hope thus helped burnish the military's public image—which was an important advantage in an era of limited budgetary allocations.

The humanitarian mission provided additional advantages, in that it reaffirmed the importance of US dominance and helped cast this dominance in a benevolent light. In his national address on Somalia, President Bush reminded listeners: "Only the United States has the global reach to place a large security force on the ground in such a distant place quickly and efficiently and thus save thousands of innocents from death."[154] Restore Hope also reaffirmed the relevance of the Atlantic Alliance; NATO members Canada, Belgium, Italy, Germany, Turkey, and the United Kingdom all sent troops for the operation, and they did so under effective US direction. Even France, America's troublesome ally, sent a large troop contingent.[155] Restore Hope was not technically a NATO mission (since NATO did not yet have the authority to send forces "out of area"), but it was a reasonable substitute for one. The mission advertised the continued salience of the Cold War alliance system. Above all, Restore Hope demonstrated that the United States was still able to lead a multinational task force into remote corners of the globe—even after the demise of the USSR.

In the long run, of course, the Somalia operation would go badly. The planning that went into Operation Restore Hope appears, in retrospect, to have been remarkably superficial. It was based on the assumption that the operation would be a simple matter of distributing relief supplies to a starving population, without any major political ramifications. This assumption was proven wrong. US forces were inexorably drawn into the complex internal politics of Somalia—an activity for which the soldiers were ill prepared—which led to the mission's failure. The alliance with Aideed soon broke down, triggering open combat between Aideed's militia and the US military. After a series of armed engagements in 1993, the United States was forced to withdraw from Somalia, leaving the country in the same state of political disorder that had existed in the first place.[156] The Somalia intervention became one of the most important setbacks to US prestige since Vietnam.

And the Bosnia war still demanded attention. With a white-skinned population, Bosnia was assured of more sustained attention than was possible with an African crisis. The racialized nature of the world's press coverage clearly favored Bosnia. Thus the Somalia intervention was just a brief respite for policy makers, who still needed to address the unresolved problems associated with US policy in the Balkans.

Conclusion

The 1992–1995 war in Bosnia was, above all, a major human tragedy that cost tens of thousands of lives. The Western powers helped make this tragedy possible, and they did so over an extended period of time. A series of policy failures by the United States and Europe contributed to the breakup of Yugoslavia—and ultimately to the war in Bosnia-Herzegovina. In retrospect, it is clear that the preservation of Yugoslavia as an integral state was not a high priority for the Western powers, and little effort was made to preserve that state. The consequences for Bosnia were disastrous.

The Yugoslav federation was indeed a "Pandora's box," as Professor Tomashevich suggested in the epigraph that introduced this chapter. Any effort to open that box by breaking up the federation would entail unpleasant and irreversible consequences. Once Yugoslavia ceased to exist, Bosnia was especially vulnerable to political violence, given its multiethnic character. Surely it would have been better, from a humanitarian standpoint, if the Western powers had tried to maintain the Yugoslav federation, which might have prevented the Bosnia war and the resulting atrocities. That such efforts were not made, or at least not made with sufficient vigor, must be regarded as a historic failure, with tragic results.

In this chapter we saw that there were additional policy failures. The Bush administration aligned itself with the Muslim ethnic group and the Izetbegović government and encouraged that government to seek independence before a political settlement could be achieved. The United States also undermined the Lisbon agreement, which proposed a compromise among the ethnic groups that might have prevented the war. The Lisbon agreement was in fact the last realistic chance of preventing war in Bosnia, and the US role in undermining this agreement virtually guaranteed the onrush of violence that followed. The Lisbon agreement may be viewed as yet another in a long series of missed opportunities that might have prevented the Bosnia war.

Overall, it seems difficult to view US actions in Bosnia as anything other than an exercise in realpolitik: America's Muslim allies, despite their superior press coverage, were just as intolerant and chauvinistically inclined as were the other major factions. We have seen that the Muslim forces were perfectly willing to commit atrocities, and Izetbegović himself was complicit in some of these atrocities.[157] It is true that the Muslim soldiers engaged in significantly fewer atrocities than did their Serb counterparts, but this was because the Muslims had inferior weapons, not because of any basic moral difference between the two sides. John Deutch, then a Defense Department official, stated the matter this way: "One of the reasons it was so hard to have a good policy is how terrible all the sides were. . . . To whom would you give a Thomas Jefferson award? Not Milošević certainly. And not Tudjman, equally certainly. Izetbegović? Not a great candidate himself. . . . Probably Izetbegović would kill the fewest, *but perhaps only because he lacked the means*" (emphasis added).[158]

There is little to suggest an altruistic or humanitarian motivation for US actions. American policy is, however, quite comprehensible from the standpoint of power politics: The United States needed to raise its profile and reaffirm its dominant status at a key moment in history, several months after the end of the Soviet Union. The United States had gained major political and economic advantages from its hegemonic status during the Cold War, and it now sought to retain these advantages. The conflict in Bosnia offered an opportunity to achieve these objectives. By 1992, it was clear that the Balkan conflict was no longer a conflict of merely regional importance; on the contrary, it had become one of the most visible and important conflicts of the post-1945 era. It seemed unthinkable that the United States would remain on the sidelines. A closely related US objective was to weaken the European Community in a manner suggested by the 1992 Defense Planning Guidance document. During this period, the European Community was seeking to forge a common foreign policy—independent of NATO and the United States, to some extent—and the Europeans sought to use the Yugoslavia conflict to demonstrate this new foreign policy. The Bush administration, in contrast, wished to undercut these initiatives and to reduce Europe's sway in the Balkans. With the collapse of European mediation in March 1992, the United States had effectively achieved this objective. The United States was now well positioned to influence the outcome of the war.

This initial accomplishment soon presented a dilemma: The Bush administration was unable to end the fighting or offer military protection to its Muslim clients, who were being beaten militarily by the better-armed Serbs. US military intervention was blocked by the Joint Chiefs of Staff, who feared the political consequences of any casualties that might result from intervention. Yet if the United States failed to intervene, it risked appearing weak and would be viewed as a "pitiful, helpless giant," to use Richard Nixon's famous phrase.[159] The troop landing in Somalia was useful as a distraction from the Bosnia imbroglio, but this was only a temporary benefit. At some point, the United States would have to choose military intervention—despite the risks—or it would have to accept a major loss of credibility. In the next chapter, we see how the newly elected Clinton administration resolved this dilemma.

6

Only the Weak Rely on Diplomacy:
The Clinton Administration Faces Bosnia

It would be some time before I fully realized that the United States sees little need for diplomacy; power is enough. Only the weak rely on diplomacy.
—*UN Secretary-General Boutros Boutros-Ghali*

When the Democratic administration headed by President Bill Clinton was inaugurated in January 1993, the war in Bosnia-Herzegovina was immediately recognized as a major challenge. Shortly before the inauguration, an analysis by Richard Holbrooke set the tone: "Bosnia will be the key test of US policy in Europe. We must therefore succeed in whatever we attempt."[1] And President Clinton himself acknowledged that any perceived US failure in Bosnia would mean "to give up American leadership" more generally.[2] Despite these concerns, Clinton's first year in office produced few basic changes. The new president's Bosnia policy was initially similar to Bush's, and it was based on the same calculation of US interests. The Clinton administration embraced the Muslim government in Bosnia—just as its Republican predecessor had done—and provided the Muslims with political support. The Muslims' principal rivals for power, the Serbs, were accordingly reviled.[3]

Both administrations initially disdained diplomatic efforts to settle the war. The Bush administration undercut the European-brokered Lisbon agreement in 1992, and the Clinton administration would undercut a series of European and UN mediation activities. The effect in both cases was a substantial prolongation of the war. With regard to motive, both presidents sought to use the Bosnia conflict as an opportunity to reaffirm US hegemony over Europe, and to block efforts by the European Union states to challenge this hegemony. Another shared motive was to use the conflict as a means of finding a new, post–Cold War function for the North Atlantic Treaty Organization, which was considered a key extension of US hegemony. And both Bush and Clinton faced a policy dilemma in Bosnia: On the one hand, it was surely tempting (for both presidents) to act decisively by using America's overwhelming military power against the Serbs. On the other hand, both resisted military action, since this option presented the unacceptable risk of casualties. US policy in Bosnia thus entailed an element of deadlock.

Over time, as the Bosnia war dragged on and threatened to damage US credibility, the Clinton administration set aside its reluctance to use force, which led to a new policy that entailed the arming of Muslim and Croat militaries in 1994, and extensive NATO bombing raids against Serb targets in August–September 1995. Having achieved a military success, the Clinton administration was finally willing to accept a diplomatic settlement of the war, which resulted in the Dayton Accords of November–December 1995. The Accords constituted a US triumph, gave NATO a new raison d'être, and reaffirmed America's status as the world's only superpower.

Clinton Begins by Blocking a Negotiated Settlement

As Clinton entered office, the European Union was seeking, once again, to mediate the Yugoslav conflict and to use this mediation to showcase the Union's potential to act as a regional power. The United Nations supported these efforts. A joint mediation team was directed by David Owen, representing the European Union, and Cyrus Vance, representing the United Nations. In late 1992, these two men unveiled what became known as the Vance-Owen peace plan, which proposed the decentralization of power in Bosnia and the creation of a weak central government (in a manner that was reminiscent of the 1992 Lisbon agreement). The peace plan explicitly called for a return of all refugees. Persons who had been ethnically cleansed during the course of the fighting would have their land and property returned to them. To ensure effective implementation, the plan foresaw the extended occupation of the country by an international peacekeeping force. The various ethnic armies that had formed during the war were to be eliminated, and the country itself was to be gradually demilitarized. At the heart of the plan was the creation of ten new cantons. All cantons were to be ethnically mixed to some extent, though it of course was understood that one ethnic group would form a plurality or a majority in each. There was thus a tacit recognition that a specific ethnic group would be politically dominant in each canton. Overall, the plan called for 43 percent of the land area of Bosnia to be controlled by the Serbs; 32 percent would go to the Croats; and 25 percent to the Muslims.[4]

A major challenge for the negotiators was how to apportion the high-quality land areas. Traditionally, the Croats and Muslims had controlled the most productive areas of Bosnia, and the mediators made a special effort to ensure that most of these lands would be returned. The Serbs were to receive far less desirable tracts of land, as described by the *Washington Post*:

> Under the Vance-Owen boundaries, provinces controlled by the Muslim and Croat ethnic majorities would receive most of Bosnia's existing military and civilian factories, including those that generated the most wealth prior to the war, according to several analysts. Muslims and Croats also would receive most of the country's known natural resources.... "There is no question that, above all, the Muslims have the richest part of the country" under the plan mainly because the areas of Bosnia richest in resources and infrastructure happen to be where Muslims have traditionally lived, this [senior UN] official said, echoed by others. The basic numbers do appear to favor the Muslims.[5]

Restoring the demographic status quo as it existed prior to the onset of fighting—or at least an approximation of it—was a major objective of the peace plan. In European venues, the Vance-Owen peace plan was often viewed positively, as a reasonably fair solution to what seemed an intractable conflict. It also ensured that Europe would remain a key player in the international politics of the Balkans.

US officials, however, opposed the plan and sought to impede the negotiation process. Owen himself would later emphasize the US role in impeding negotiations. In 2003, for example, when Owen appeared as a prosecution witness at the Milošević trial, the cross-examination produced the following exchange:

> Milošević: "The Vance-Owen peace plan was abandoned in the first place by the Americans, or rather they didn't even support it. They didn't want to support it. Isn't that true?"...
>
> Owen: "There's a great deal of truth in that."[6]

Owen's basic position is confirmed by other sources. "The Clinton people were bad-mouthing the [peace] agreement in private," according to David Halberstam's account.[7] And this bad-mouthing did not occur only in private. In meetings of the UN Security Council, the US delegation refused to "'endorse,' 'welcome,' or 'support' the Vance-Owen plan."[8] Clinton's UN ambassador, Madeleine Albright, stated publicly: "I have watched with some amazement that the Europeans have not taken action," in Bosnia—a thinly veiled attack on Owen's negotiation efforts.[9] In memoirs, former British prime minister John Major observed: "The Americans were making it clear that they were opposed to the proposed Vance-Owen peace plan."[10] The US opposition to Vance-Owen "in some ways became more of a challenge to the prospects for the plan than the reactions of either Izetbegović or [Radovan] Karadžić," according to University of London researcher James Gow.[11] It seems fair to say that the United States did not play a supportive role with regard to the mediation efforts of early 1993.

US officials claimed that they opposed the peace plan because it favored the Serbs—that it rewarded aggression and ethnic cleansing. A special point of contention was the provision whereby 43 percent of Bosnia's land area would be placed under the political control of the Serbs, granting them more land than either of the other two ethnic groups. The 43 percent figure was considered far too high, given that Serbs were only 31 percent of the population. In the opinion of Clinton's secretary of state, Warren Christopher, the Vance-Owen plan "simply appeases Serbian aggression."[12] It may be argued that the Clinton administration was acting on the basis of moral principle, since the proposed peace plan favored the Serbs and was therefore unjust.

Under scrutiny, however, it is clear that this objection entails a basic misrepresentation of the record. In fact, the Vance-Owen plan was not especially favorable toward the Serbs, and for the most part it did not reward ethnic cleansing. The 43 percent that the Serbs were to receive under the plan was considerably *less* than the land area controlled by Serbs prior to the onset of fighting. Critics of the plan ignored the fact the Serbs had always controlled most of the land in Bosnia—since they were disproportionately agricultural—even before the war. When the war began in 1992, the Serbs owned or controlled some 56 percent of the total land, a proportion above what they were allocated by the Vance-Owen plan.[13] At the level of land quality, the Serbs were to receive some of the least valuable parts of Bosnia, which excluded most of the country's natural resources and industrial plants. The peace plan was not, in short, especially generous to the Serbs, and arguments to the contrary have little merit.

Vance and Owen sought to quell criticism of their plan. Realizing the importance of the United States in the negotiation process, they made special efforts to enlist its support. The negotiators activated their personal networks in America—which were considerable—and sought to use these networks to advance their peace plan. As a US citizen and former secretary of state, Vance consulted frequently with State Department figures in the Clinton administration (some of whom had served under Vance during the Carter presidency). And Owen was from Great Britain, long America's closest ally. As a British foreign minister during the 1970s, he had established a record that was strongly pro-US and pro-NATO; he also had an American wife. It would have been hard to find two men who were more pro-American in their backgrounds. Vance and Owen no doubt emphasized these credentials when conferring with their US counterparts. At a more substantive level, Vance and Owen recognized that NATO would play a key role in enforcing any agreement that emerged—an idea that dovetailed nicely with US efforts to find a new justification for NATO after the Cold War.[14] These bridge-building efforts were largely ineffectual, however, since Vance and Owen were now representatives of the United Nations and the European Union, respectively, and they were thus suspect in US eyes.[15] The records of these men were not sufficient to overcome their current affiliations. The Americans no doubt appreciated the efforts to carve out a role for NATO in the peace plan, but this too was insufficient to assuage the more basic US objection to the whole negotiation process.

The Clinton administration thus remained hostile toward the Vance-Owen plan. And the US hostility had an important impact on the negotiations: That the world's only superpower opposed the peace plan was well known to the various parties, and this surely reduced their willingness to make concessions or negotiate seriously. We will see that US opposition had an especially important impact on President Alija Izetbegović, who was America's main ally in Bosnia.

Overall, the chronology of events suggests that the Clinton team helped undermine the Vance-Owen peace plan. Initially, during late 1992, the plan appeared to have a reasonable chance of success. The Izetbegović government supported it, presumably because it aimed to reduce Serb gains. The peace plan was certainly better for the Muslims than the status quo. In memoirs, US diplomat Warren Zimmermann recalled that in the last weeks of 1992, the "Bosnian government's reaction to the [Vance-Owen] plan ... was not only positive, *it was enthusiastic*" (emphasis added).[16] And the Serbs too were receptive. According to an aide to Radovan Karadžić, "the Serbs ... considered the Vance-Owen plan a good basis 'not only for the present round of negotiations, but also as the basis for future rounds.'"[17] The outgoing Bush administration did not actively oppose the plan. As a lame-duck president, Bush showed little interest in any new initiatives in the Balkans.[18] A full settlement now seemed within reach.

The situation changed dramatically, however, once the incoming Clinton administration exerted itself, beginning in early January 1993. At this point, Izetbegović suddenly shifted his position and turned hostile toward the peace process. On January 7, Izetbegović stated that he "was not optimistic" about the peace talks.[19] Several days later, Bosnian government negotiators refused to sign a map proposed by Vance and Owen, which was an integral part of the peace plan. Why the change in attitude? The Dutch investigation emphasizes the importance of the Clinton team, and its role in influencing the Muslims against the peace plan: "An important contributing factor in the Bosnian government's negative response [to the peace plan] was the impending change of administration in Washington, where Bill Clinton was about to succeed George Bush as president; . . . immediately after the presentation of the Vance-Owen plan [in early January 1993] Izetbegović traveled to the United States to consult with the Clinton camp. . . . Izetbegović returned after holding talks with Vice President-elect Al Gore and other members of the Clinton camp under the impression that military intervention was imminent."[20] In light of these circumstances, the Muslims believed they were in a strong negotiating position vis-à-vis the Serbs. And if the negotiations failed, this would not necessarily be a negative outcome for the Muslims, who believed (inaccurately as it turned out) that they could count on their US connections to help them prevail on the battlefield. These US connections were strong indeed. The official US envoy to the Vance-Owen talks, Reginald Bartholomew, acted "primarily as a lobbyist for Izetbegović," according to the Dutch investigation.[21]

The US role was especially unfortunate, since a full peace accord might have been feasible at this point. In early February, Thomas Friedman wrote: "The Bosnian Serbs and the Bosnian Croats have signaled their willingness to accept the [Vance-Owen] plan."[22] Owen claimed he was "convinced [Karadžić] would have signed if Izetbegović had signed."[23] However, Izetbegović—confident that the United States supported him—was now unwilling to sign. An opportunity for an early settlement of the war may well have been lost.

The negotiations continued, but with increasingly negative results. The overconfident Izetbegović government adopted a hard-line negotiating stance. The Muslims insisted that they be granted additional territorial concessions, including a strip of land known as the Posavina Corridor, which lay in a northeastern part of Bosnia near the town of Brčko. The Posavina Corridor was only a minute portion of the total land area of Bosnia, but it was strategically placed between the two main portions of Serb territory. The negotiators were clearly hesitant to accept this demand, since doing so was virtually guaranteed to alienate the Serbs; it had been foreseen in advance that Karadžić would oppose any concessions regarding the Posavina Corridor.[24] Nevertheless, the EU negotiators reluctantly did agree to the map change in order to placate the Muslims and obtain their approval.

With the map altered in their favor, the Muslims signed all parts of the

Vance-Owen plan by the end of March 1993. The Muslims' ethnic allies, the Croats, signed as well. The Muslim signature at this point may have been a ploy rather than a serious negotiating position. An EU staffer who was close to the peace talks wrote that Izetbegović had signed "in all likelihood, because he felt certain Karadžić would reject the map."[25] Whatever Izetbegović's intentions, the change in the map with respect to the Posavina Corridor precluded any Serb support for the plan. The Dutch parliamentary investigation summed up the matter this way: "Owen and Vance thus felt themselves compelled to persuade the Bosnian government . . . by making a concession with regard to the Posavina Corridor." Once they had made this concession, however, "Vance and Owen's proposals to all intents and purposes became unacceptable to the Bosnian Serbs."[26]

As predicted, the Serb leadership refused to accept the plan in its amended form. Their hostility was partly because the peace plan denied them most of Bosnia's high-value territory. "You have left us with stones and rattlesnakes," was a common Serb objection.[27] This point alone would probably not have impeded Serb agreement. However, this compromise combined with the additional concessions that were made with regard to the Posavina Corridor rendered the plan completely unacceptable. Great efforts were made to pressure the Serbs into setting aside their reservations and accepting the plan. The services of the president of the Republic of Serbia, Slobodan Milošević, were enlisted. Milošević was seeking to improve his international reputation, which was severely tarnished at this point. More specifically, he hoped that by cooperating with Vance and Owen, he might be able to ease the international economic sanctions that were crippling Serbia's economy.[28] Milošević thus used his influence with the Bosnian Serb leaders and pressured them to accept Vance-Owen. The Bosnian Serbs resisted this pressure. Rather than reject it directly, however, Karadžić submitted the peace plan to a public referendum by the Bosnian Serb population. During May 15–16, the referendum was held, and the peace plan was overwhelmingly rejected.[29]

By late spring 1993, the Vance-Owen peace plan was dead. Upon first consideration, the plan would seem to have failed because of Serb intransigence. Under scrutiny, however, it is clear that US policy helped create the conditions that led to the intransigence—and that the policy played a key role in ending the peace plan. This was clearly Owen's view of the situation, as suggested in the following exchange during the Milošević trial:

> Milošević: "You described . . . that the new [Clinton] administration had already made up their minds and were *intent on killing off* the [Vance-Owen plan]."

Owen: "There is no doubt that was what they were doing." [emphasis added][30]

Just as the Bush administration acted to thwart the EU's first effort to settle the Bosnia conflict in 1992 (the Lisbon agreement), the Clinton administration thwarted yet another peace effort.

During the period 1993–1995, the Europeans and the United Nations continued to seek new plans for a negotiated end to the war. Several plans were presented to the warring parties, all of which entailed a division of territory along ethnic lines combined with a decentralization of power away from Sarajevo. These peace efforts were directed for the most part by Owen himself. Owen's partner, Vance, retired from the mediation process shortly after the failure of the Vance-Owen plan, and Norwegian diplomat Thorvald Stoltenberg replaced him as the UN representative. None of the peace plans advanced by the Owen-Stoltenberg team received strong support from the United States, which continued to disparage the negotiation process as an exercise in appeasement (just as it had done with regard to the Vance-Owen plan).[31]

The main impact of US policy was to prevent an early settlement of the Bosnia war. In his memoirs, Owen concludes: "From the spring of 1993 to the summer of 1995, in my judgment, the effect of US policy . . . was to prolong the war of the Bosnian Serbs in Bosnia-Herzegovina. Whether prolongation was recognized [by the US] as being the policy I do not know."[32] We have seen that there is a considerable body of evidence to support Owen's interpretation. The Bosnia war—which might have ended in 1993—would drag on for another two and a half years, with tens of thousands of additional casualties and horrendous atrocities against noncombatants.

Indecision in the Clinton Administration

Clinton was able to block the Vance-Owen plan, but there was now a danger that the United States might appear obstructionist. What was needed was a *US* plan to end the war, an alternative to Vance-Owen. The new president nevertheless began cautiously, without a clear sense of direction. There was considerable pressure for the United States to solve the problem by intervening with military force, but President Clinton was not yet ready to do this, given the risks involved.[33] As a reflection of his sense of caution with regard to the Bosnia issue, Clinton toned down the rhetoric that had characterized his campaign. At an April 1993 press conference, for example, the president refused to compare Serb atrocities in Bosnia with the Holocaust of World War II:

Question: "Do you see any parallel between the ethnic cleansing in Bosnia and the Holocaust?"

President Clinton: "I think the Holocaust [was] on a whole different level."[34]

Much later, when Clinton finally overcame his hesitation and resolved to intervene in the Balkans, he would freely make comparisons with the Holocaust.[35] In early 1993, however, Clinton was not sure how to proceed, and he avoided emotionally charged statements.

The president's indecision reflected, in part, a drifting administration divided between a series of hawkish, pro-interventionist civilian figures and a skeptical military. Within the executive branch, the main advocates of intervention were concentrated in the State Department, with Madeleine Albright and Richard Holbrooke playing the lead roles. The interventionists at State demanded direct military support for the Izetbegović government, against the Serbs. These hawkish views were shared by Vice President Al Gore and National Security Advisor Anthony Lake, as well as First Lady Hillary Clinton.[36] From Congress, there were impassioned calls for intervention from Democrats and Republicans in both houses. In April 1993, Sen. Bob Dole described the conflict in starkly moral terms and demanded action: "Mr. President, innocent men, women, and children are dying today in Bosnia. The human evil that murdered Jews, Armenians, and Cambodians lives. We must not stand by and invent excuses for inaction. We are the world's superpower. We must act."[37] Such views were also widely expressed by editorialists in the media (notably Anthony Lewis of the *New York Times*).[38]

But the idea of armed intervention elicited resistance from the Joint Chiefs of Staff. A key figure at this time was the JCS chair, Gen. Colin Powell, who was a holdover from the outgoing Bush administration. Powell firmly opposed intervention (which he felt might lead to a Vietnam-style quagmire, as we have seen), and his opinion carried weight with the new president. White House advisor Sidney Blumenthal offered the following assessment: "Until his departure in September 1993, Powell dominated Clinton's foreign policy councils. . . . At no other previous time in his career did Powell have as much influence as he had in 1993."[39]

Despite Powell's opposition, administration hawks made a feeble effort to forge an interventionist policy, which became known as "lift and strike." This concept entailed two components. First, the United States would seek Security Council authorization to lift the UN arms embargo for the Muslim and Croat soldiers in the Bosnian army (while maintaining the embargo against the Serbs). The US role was to use its influence at the United Nations in order to alter the terms of the embargo, and thus enable the creation of an arms pipeline. The second aspect of lift and strike entailed US and NATO air raids against Bosnian Serb positions. The basic idea was simple: A rearmed Bosnian army would serve as America's ground troops in the war, while NATO planes would furnish air cover.[40] A coordinated campaign would thus end the fighting on terms that were favorable to the Izetbegović government, while the whole operation would advertise America's leadership role.

The idea of lift and strike was widely debated within the administration, but it quickly ran into two sources of opposition. The first source was, once again, General Powell, who especially objected to the proposed US air strikes. Lift and strike also elicited criticism from the French and British governments, who both had large troop contingents in the UN peacekeeping mission, UNPROFOR. They feared that lift and strike would escalate the scale of violence and thus imperil the safety of their troops. Despite its martial rhetoric, the Clinton administration was unwilling to commit any ground forces. The Europeans viewed the US position—advocating military action without supplying any ground troops—as hypocritical and reckless. In his memoirs, British prime minister Major had this comment for the lift-and-strike proposal: "Gallingly, this approach [lift and strike] avoided committing American troops, yet maintained a high moral tone and a strident appearance of engagement with the [Bosnia] crisis."[41] And many European leaders doubted the wisdom of arming the Muslims, a move that risked intensifying the conflict and causing even more suffering for the Bosnians themselves.[42] And of course, the Europeans resented the US efforts to undermine the Vance-Owen peace plan.

When Secretary of State Christopher traveled to Europe in May 1993 to present the idea of lift and strike, he received a generally negative reaction, gaining little support from key allies.[43] The failure of Christopher's mission to Europe combined with the opposition from the US Army led to a major reconsideration. President Clinton himself developed doubts about the intervention strategy. By June, Clinton was increasingly viewing the Bosnia conflict as irresolvable, "a civil war going back centuries, literally centuries, based on ethnic and religious differences."[44] Lift and strike essentially died at this point.

The failure of the lift-and-strike policy led to a renewed period of drift and indecision in the Clinton administration, as the president turned his attention away from Bosnia to refocus on domestic issues. Overall, the first year of Clinton's Bosnia policy was well summed up by State Department official John Kornblum: "We went through the first year [1993] in a really

. . . depressed, almost disastrous state in the Balkans. We had essentially no policy. [The Clinton team] didn't seem able to put together a clear picture of what they wanted to do on Bosnia. And there was total disinterest or confusion."[45]

On the Ground: The Fighting Intensifies

While the major powers were unable to achieve consensus, the war intensified, as the Muslim-Croat coalition that had been the basis of the Izetbegović government began to fall apart. Large-scale fighting erupted between Muslim and Croat militias beginning in central Bosnia in January 1993. The fighting increased in April, when clashes broke out in the Lašva Valley region, and then spread widely.[46] A generalized political breakup between the two ethnic groups ensued. The Muslim-Croat alliance against the Serbs had always been a marriage of convenience, and now that alliance had collapsed altogether.[47]

The Muslim-Croat war—which lasted for almost a year—is one of the most confusing and least understood aspects of the whole Balkan drama. While the literature on the larger Bosnia war is voluminous, little has been written on this specific phase of the war. Observers at the time assumed that the fighting was sparked by Croat aggression directed against the Muslims. A recent work by military historian Charles Shrader (the only book-length study on this topic) challenges the conventional view of the Muslim-Croat war and presents evidence that it was, in fact, the Muslims who first attacked the Croats. His basic argument is that the Muslims had seen the ranks of their militias swell due to the earlier rounds of Serb-generated ethnic cleansing, which had increased their available manpower; this enabled the Muslims to begin offensive operations against their former allies, the Croats.[48] According to Shrader, the Croats "had neither the means nor the opportunity to engage in a planned program to attack, dispossess, and expel Muslims from the areas in which they lived" when this war began in early 1993.[49]

Whatever its origins, the Muslim-Croat war of 1993–1994 gradually assumed a gruesome character, and it generated new rounds of atrocities, as described in the official Dutch investigation: "Some of the most appalling acts in the Bosnian war took place in the battle between Croats and Muslims in Central Bosnia, such as the Croat mass slaughter of Muslims from Ahmici in [April] 1993, or the atrocities perpetrated by the [Muslim] forces against the Croatian inhabitants of the village of Uzdol, in the hills east of Gornji Vakuf in mid-September. Another mass murder took place in Stupni Do, where people and cattle were set on fire by the [Croat] Bobovac brigade."[50]

Both Muslim and Croat forces showed little restraint or mercy toward non-combatants. For the civilian population of Bosnia, the Muslim-Croat war added yet an additional source of terror and insecurity.

The various players in the war accommodated themselves to the change in alignment associated with the Muslim-Croat split. In July 1993, Croatian president Franjo Tudjman made a key decision to support the Bosnian Croats. The Republic of Croatia now appeared to be seeking a Greater Croatia (just as Serbia was seeking a Greater Serbia).[51] The Croatian Republic supplied the Bosnian Croats with thousands of soldiers and "volunteers," who assisted in the fight for a Greater Croatia.[52] The Bosnian Serbs for their part continued operations against Muslim areas (with continued support from Milošević), and in some cases, they coordinated with the Croat militias.[53] Facing a multifront war, the Muslim government seriously considered forging an alliance with the Serbs, which was to be directed against the new enemy, the Croats. Thus, by the summer of 1993, Bosnian vice president Ejup Ganić was telling the press that "the biggest mistake we made was at the beginning of the war when we concluded a military alliance with the Croats." In a later interview Ganić was even more specific: "We can only choose between two enemies. We will decide in favor of the Serbs. The English say: 'If you can't beat them, join them.' . . . We have already had secret talks with [the Serbs]."[54] Although such a Muslim-Serb alliance was never established, that it was considered demonstrates the extreme complexity of this war.

From the standpoint of Western observers, the Muslim-Croat split was bewildering. Until now, the Bosnia war had been portrayed as a straightforward case of Serb aggression against a multiethnic and democratic central government. The new phase of war complicated this image and made it more difficult than before to establish which side was the aggressor, and which the victim.[55] The progressive fracturing of the Bosnian state also complicated any prospective efforts by the Western powers to settle the war. At the same time, the new atrocities seemed to underscore the urgent need for a settlement. And yet the powers remained incapable of imposing a settlement at this phase, given the bureaucratic deadlock and interstate cleavages described earlier. In the absence of a definitive solution, there was widespread sentiment that the powers had to take some sort of action—they had to "do something"—to save face. The result was the creation of several "safe areas," Muslim enclaves that the international community committed itself to protecting from attack.

The Policy of Safe Areas

The safe-area plan was formalized with a series of UN Security Council resolutions during April–June 1993.[56] These resolutions designated Sarajevo and five other predominantly Muslim enclaves as special havens, which would be protected by UNPROFOR troops. In addition to Sarajevo, the enclaves included Srebrenica, Zepa, Goražde, Tuzla, and parts of the Bihać region. NATO aircraft were to provide cover for the UNPROFOR troops. Over time, these aircraft would engage in limited air strikes against Serb forces that threatened peacekeepers in the safe areas.[57] NATO planes also were used to enforce a no-fly zone that the Security Council had established over Bosnia, a circumstance that resulted in several instances of air-to-air combat between NATO and Serb aircraft.[58] These engagements marked the first time since NATO's creation in 1949 that its forces had engaged in direct combat.

There was a widespread perception in the press that the safe areas consisted entirely of vulnerable civilians under a relentless threat of attack, but the reality was more complicated. In fact, the safe areas were not demilitarized. Indeed, the militarization of the safe areas increased over time, and by 1995 the UN secretary-general noted:

> In recent months, [Bosnian] government forces have considerably increased their military activity in and around most safe areas and many of them, including Sarajevo, Tuzla, and Bihać, have been incorporated into the broader military campaigns of the government side. The headquarters and logistics installations of the Fifth Corps of the government Army are located in the town of Bihać and those of the Second Corps in the town of Tuzla. The government also maintains a substantial number of troops in Srebrenica (in this case in violation of a demilitarization agreement), Goražde, and Zepa, while Sarajevo is the location of the General Command of the government Army and other military installations. There is also an ammunition factory in Goražde.[59]

In practice, the policy of safe areas worked to the advantage of the Muslim militias and against their adversaries, especially the Serbs. The UN soldiers were protecting not only Muslim civilians, but also Muslim soldiers, who were themselves free to launch attacks. The situation obviously violated the concept of UN "impartiality," which is considered a central norm of peacekeeping.[60]

The Srebrenica safe area had an especially brutal history, and it was besieged by Serb forces virtually throughout the war. It is important to note, however, that Muslim troops also behaved brutally. Especially problematic was the Muslim commander Brigadier Naser Orić, who based his forces inside Srebrenica and conducted forays against Serb villages in the surrounding region. One UNPROFOR commander later described Orić's activities as follows: "Orić engaged in attacks during Orthodox holidays and destroyed [Serb] villages, massacring all the inhabitants. This created a degree of hatred that was quite extraordinary in the [Srebrenica] region. . . . [Orić] reigned by terror; . . . he could not allow himself to take prisoners. According to my recollections he didn't even look for an excuse. It was simply a statement: One can't be bothered with prisoners."[61] And once Srebrenica was declared a safe area, Brigadier Orić gained UN protection for his base of operations, from which he continued his attacks.

It was generally agreed that the safe-area plan was not a solution to the war, since the fighting continued and the peacekeepers could not provide adequate protection. The UNPROFOR soldiers were far too few in number, and too lacking in heavy weapons to accomplish their task. There also was a continual fear that the peacekeepers might themselves be attacked or taken hostage (this in fact happened repeatedly). All these deficiencies were clearly recognized at the time that the safe areas were created. It was widely acknowledged that the safe-area policy was "only a temporary measure" pending a final settlement of the war.[62] Yet the safe-area policy dragged on for more than two years. David Owen noted in his memoirs that the creation of safe areas was "the most irresponsible decision taken during my time" as a mediator in the Balkan conflict.[63] By the summer of 1995, these circumstances culminated in the collapse of the safe-area policy, and the horrific Srebrenica massacre.

It seems fair to conclude that the creation of safe areas was yet another instance of international realpolitik. The Dutch investigation later determined that the safe-area policy "was designed to ensure that the tense relations within the [NATO] alliance of America and Europe no longer persisted." The plan "had less to do with the reality of Bosnia than with the need to restore transatlantic relations."[64] Given the political deadlock that prevailed at the time, a policy of safe areas was all that could be achieved.

A Shift toward US Military Intervention

By the end of 1993, there were subtle but significant changes in the bureaucratic politics of the Clinton presidency. First, the main opponent of military intervention in Bosnia, General Powell, stepped down as chair of the Joint Chiefs of Staff in September 1993. His replacement, Gen. John Shalikashvili, was more open to intervention.[65] Second, the perception took hold that

NATO prestige already had been committed to Bosnia—since NATO aircraft now protected the safe areas and enforced the no-fly zone—and therefore it was essential to make a success of the operation. The importance of using Bosnia to prove NATO's relevance is a consistent theme during this period, repeatedly emphasized by key administration figures, including Warren Christopher, Richard Holbrooke, Strobe Talbot, and William Perry.[66] And it was recognized that any perceived US failure would have major consequences. In the view of State Department historian Derek Chollet: "The costs of a failed Bosnia policy would destroy the Clinton administration's ambitions for the NATO alliance."[67] These factors helped generate a new, more activist policy beginning in early 1994. While the 1994–1995 period would still entail numerous shifts and tergiversations, as well as renewed periods of indecision, one can discern movement toward direct US intervention.

The first objective of this new policy was to resolve the Muslim-Croat war within Bosnia. US officials worked behind the scenes to orchestrate such a resolution, and the Muslim-Croat war was officially ended. The two sides settled their differences in an agreement signed in Washington on March 1, 1994. A new constitution—which was "written primarily by Americans"—created a Federation of Bosnia and Herzegovina.[68] Political power in the Federation was decentralized to a considerable degree (though Izetbegović was to remain president).[69] No effort was made at this point to encourage Bosnian Serbs to join the Federation. Indeed, the whole idea of the Federation was to create a united Muslim-Croat front *against* the Serbs. The *Economist* later noted: "America had been working quietly to alter the balance of power on the ground by encouraging Muslims and Croats to stop quarreling and unite against the Serbs."[70] And the agreement facilitated the integration of the Muslim and Croat militias into a force that was at least nominally unified, thus increasing its military effectiveness. The Clinton administration was sufficiently interested in making a success of this project that it dispatched a US general to oversee the military integration.[71]

The Muslim-Croat agreement was brokered without any significant input from the United Nations or the European Union. European officials praised the agreement as a step toward peace, though in private some resented the US effort to dominate the negotiation process.[72] While the negotiations were still taking place, one diplomat objected that "the European view just will not be heard" by the Americans.[73] Despite these criticisms, the Federation was a political victory for the Clinton administration, which sought to recover some of the prestige it had lost from its previous indecision.

The creation of the Muslim-Croat Federation led to augmented US intervention in the Balkans, which now entailed arming the Federation. This strategy of arms shipments was favored by hawkish figures within the State

Department, including Charles Redman, Talbott, and Holbrooke. National Security Advisor Lake also was supportive.[74] The basic idea was to use US political influence to establish a covert arms pipeline for the reunited Muslim-Croat army. The arms themselves were to be delivered by Iran and other Islamic states, which were eager to help the beleaguered Bosnian Muslims. The United States (initially) would confine its role to *encouraging* these arms supplies. On April 27, President Clinton approved the plan.[75] The first phases of the plan required the support of Croatia's president Franjo Tudjman. President Tudjman's assent was crucial, since Croatia was to serve as the main transit point for the arms. The US action was quite simple: US officials discreetly met with Tudjman and urged that he allow Bosnia-bound arms shipments to pass through Croatian territory.

The most authoritative account of this phase of the war is by Dutch researcher Cees Wiebes, who obtained privileged access to Western intelligence archives and other official records. According to Wiebes, US encouragement "was all Tudjman needed to hear." In late April 1994, a joint Croatian/Bosnian delegation met with Iranian officials to work out the details of a three-way agreement whereby Iran would pass through Croatia to supply arms to Bosnia. The arms deliveries commenced almost immediately.[76]

The arms pipeline provided major advantages for US hegemony, which had now reestablished "leadership" in the Balkan crisis. The Bosnian army could function as America's ground forces in the conflict; this was especially useful in light of continuing US resistance to the idea of sending its own forces into combat. Through the arms supplies, the Clinton administration now had the best of both worlds: It could have a well-armed strike force in the Balkans, one that it could influence (if not altogether control). At the same time, Clinton could intervene with no risk of US casualties.

At first, the United States played no direct role in delivering the arms. The prospect of direct involvement was considered overly provocative, since it would have violated the UN arms embargo. The State Department's legal counsel advised against direct arms deliveries, although merely encouraging such deliveries seemed less problematic: "Suggesting to a foreign country that it might consider a covert action appeared perfectly legal; going one step further and encouraging a foreign country appeared legal but potentially risky from a political standpoint. Actually supporting the foreign action through direct participation . . . crosses the line into action"[77]—and was probably illegal. In addition, the French and British governments had long objected to any external arms shipments, as these threatened UNPROFOR peacekeeping troops in Bosnia, many of whom were French and British nationals. As a result of these considerations, US officials approached the issue with a measure of caution.

Over time, the United States became less cautious and very likely did play a direct role in the arms supply. In early 1995, UN officials reported a series of mysterious "black flights" that delivered arms into Bosnia and were believed to emanate from the United States. Wiebes provides the following information:

> [There were] secretive C-130 cargo aircraft flights and night time air drops on Tuzla. . . . When asked, a British general responded with great certainty to the question of the origin of the secret supplies . . . : "They were American arms deliveries. No doubt about that. And American private companies were involved in those deliveries." This was no surprising answer because this general had access to intelligence gathered by a unit of the British Special Air Services (SAS) in Tuzla. The aircraft had come within range of the unit's special night vision equipment, and the British saw them land. . . . [A] clandestine American operation had taken place in which arms, ammunition, and military communication equipment were supplied to the [Bosnian government army].[78]

Elsewhere in his study, however, Wiebes assumes a more cautious tone, and he qualifies his claims:

> The conclusion is that there are only suspicions but no hard evidence that American aircraft carried out the black flights. A British researcher put a question regarding American involvement [in the black flights] to various sources and most . . . answered him as follows: "Who else has the skill and expertise to carry out such a swift, delicate mission covertly? The Saudis? The Turks? The Iranians?" Specialized crews and types of aircraft for these night-time operations indeed appeared to point in only one direction: that of the United States.[79]

Overall, it seems reasonable to conclude that the United States probably was the source of these secretive flights, despite a lack of definitive evidence.[80]

It is interesting to note that the Central Intelligence Agency opposed the whole arms supply operation and does not appear to have played a major role in directing it. Instead, it was the State Department that was the main bureaucratic force behind the operation.[81] To make the deliveries, it appears that US officials used cargo aircraft associated with a front company, Southern Air Transport, and avoided using US Air Force planes. Using such privatized sources of transport reduced the risk of public exposure, and the overall technique fit in well with long-standing procedures for conducting covert operations.

Whatever the specifics of the mysterious black flights, Islamic states were the main source of arms for Bosnia. And these states were suppliers not only of weapons, but also of personnel. During the Bosnia war, there was a steady stream of Islamic extremists into Bosnia—and some of these were members of Al Qaeda. That Al Qaeda terrorists were present in Bosnia has been confirmed by Holbrooke, who notes that by late 1995: "Parts of Bosnia were becoming a sanctuary for Islamic terrorists, some of whom belonged to an organization whose name was still unknown in the West, Al Qaeda."[82] Whether the US government supported the presence of these foreign fighters in Bosnia is unclear. Certainly, the presence of Mujahideen added additional manpower to Bosnia's army, which meshed with the overall thrust of US policy.

The new policy benefited the Republic of Croatia, which was playing an increasingly central role in the US strategy. As we have seen, the arms supplies usually passed through Croatia, and the Croatian military seized many of the weapons for its own use. These seizures were part of a more general policy of augmenting Croatia's military capability. While the Bosnian arms buildup consisted mostly of light infantry weapons, the Croatian buildup was much more extensive, and it included the procurement of fighter planes, helicopters, missiles, and tanks.[83] In undertaking this rearmament, Tudjman had two basic objectives. First, he sought to regain control of the Krajina region in eastern Croatia. Local Serbs had seized control of the Krajina in 1991 immediately after the dissolution of Yugoslavia, as we have seen, and they had continued to occupy this region ever since as a (de facto) independent state. By 1995, however, Croatia was sufficiently powerful to contemplate an attack. Tudjman was eager to use his newly retrained army to subdue the Krajina rebellion and reintegrate it into Croatia. And second, Tudjman wished to use his military power as a means of influencing the war in Bosnia.

The United States raised no objection to Croatia's rearmament, including its acquisition of heavy weapons. And in November 1994, the Clinton administration furnished military personnel to help retrain the Croat armed forces. This training was undertaken by a private company, Military Professional Resources Inc. (MPRI), whose members were retired—not active duty—US military personnel. But the State Department had licensed the training mission, and there is little doubt that MPRI acted as an instrument of US policy. According to military correspondent Tim Ripley: "The significance of MPRI was more as a diplomatic signal of support [from the US], giving the Croats confidence to move to a military solution to the Krajina 'problem.'"[84] Most sources indicate that the MPRI training improved the

Croats' combat skills and helped prepare them for the technical demands of offensive warfare.[85]

The principal figure managing the relationship between the two countries was US ambassador to Croatia Peter Galbraith, who was playing a key role in the overall US policy toward the Balkans. The ambassador worked closely with Tudjman, and his ties to the Croatian president elicited criticism. According to Ripley: "One UN officer called [Galbraith] 'the Croatian ambassador to America,' and others referred to the US ambassador as 'the Prince of Darkness,' because of his close links with the authoritarian Tudjman regime."[86] The United States supported Tudjman, despite his long-standing policy of repression against ethnic Serbs who lived in Croatia and a very poor overall record on human rights. The strategy of supporting Tudjman was obviously a controversial one. And indeed, the whole strategy of orchestrating the arms supply was controversial, since it encouraged violations of the UN arms embargo. But Clinton had already made a decision to intervene in the conflict, and he was no longer enforcing the embargo.[87]

The US strategy of arming the Croat and Bosnian military forces antagonized the European states. The French and British governments remained concerned that the external arms flows would lead to upsurges in fighting, and these could endanger the French and British forces who served in the UNPROFOR peacekeeping mission. This was especially true of the French troops, who were exposed to the greatest risks and had suffered more than fifty fatalities.[88] Not surprisingly, French officials were highly critical of US policy.[89] And the French also adopted a cynical view of US motives with regard to Bosnia. According to a researcher with the Institute for International Relations in Paris, US policy was motivated by a desire to "enfeeble ... the long-term credibility of European defense plans," and thus to humiliate Europe.[90] British officials set aside their usual pro-Americanism and joined the French in attacking US policy. The intensity of the feud was such that it became "the most serious Anglo-American disagreement since the Suez Crisis," according to the memoirs of John Major.[91] The anti-American sentiment was expressed at all levels. Thus, British troops in Bosnia "flaunt their anti-Americanism whenever they can," according to UN official Phillip Corwin.[92] The Americans for their part expressed resentment about the perceived lack of British loyalty on the Bosnia issue. One US diplomat later claimed: "I learned to treat Britain as a hostile power. . . . I came to think of the British as like having the Russians around the State Department."[93]

The conflicts generated by the Bosnia war strained US-European unity at a more basic level and threatened to rupture the Atlantic alliance. When the Bosnia war was over, a series of accounts revealed the full extent of this transatlantic crisis. An article in *Jane's Intelligence Review* stated that the Balkan wars had "brought NATO within measurable distance of disintegration through disunity."[94] And the *Economist* later revealed that "America's role as leader of the [NATO] alliance was called into question during the transatlantic rows that erupted over the Bosnian war and, at their height, threatened to destroy NATO." The *Economist* added that when the war finally ended, "the alliance survived by the skin of its teeth."[95]

There was thus a real danger, by the middle of 1995, that the continuing fighting in Bosnia could cause a rupture of the Atlantic alliance. Rather than strengthening NATO, as President Clinton wished to do, his policies threatened to shatter it. However, a series of events within Bosnia led to a terrible massacre in the eastern enclave of Srebrenica, with major political ramifications. The results of this massacre served to generate a new international consensus on the Bosnian conflict, one that favored armed intervention. The Srebrenica massacre proved to be a turning point in the war.

The Srebrenica Massacre and Its Aftermath

The origin of the Srebrenica massacre lay in a series of Muslim attacks that began in the spring of 1995. These attacks were launched from UN-protected safe areas, including the one in Srebrenica. According to the Dutch investigation of the massacre: "The UN headquarters in Zagreb had . . . concluded that the Bosnian Muslims continually misused the safe areas to maintain their armed forces, while in some cases it looked as if they intended to provoke shelling by the Bosnian Serbs."[96] Such actions invited Serb reprisals, and this dynamic contributed to the fall of the safe area. Beginning on July 6, 1995, Serb forces assaulted Srebrenica and quickly overran it, despite the (nominal) UN protection.

The Bosnian government made no serious effort to defend the town and appeared unconcerned that it might be captured. EU negotiator Carl Bildt notes that Bosnian military forces assigned to protect Srebrenica were "not putting up any resistance. Later it was revealed that *they had been ordered by the Sarajevo commanders not to defend Srebrenica.*" And Bosnia's foreign minister, Muhamed Sacirbey, told Bildt that Srebrenica "had always been a problem for his government. They knew that a peace settlement would mean the loss of the enclave. So from this point of view, *what had happened* [the Serb capture of the town] *made things easier*" (emphases added). Bildt also noted that during his conversation with Sacirbey, "I was more upset about what had happened than he [Sacirbey] seemed to be. His calm reactions and controlled arguments still seem to me to be a mysterious piece of the Srebrenica puzzle."[97]

And military correspondent Ripley provides further evidence that the Bosnian government allowed Serb armies to seize the town:

> British, Dutch, and other UNPROFOR personnel and many veterans of the Sarajevo press corps, including [Martin] Bell of the BBC, and Nick Gowing of the Channel Four television network all came to the conclusion that *the Bosnian government decided to let Srebrenica fall to increase the pressure on the international community to intervene* against the Serbs. . . . A month before [the Serb attack], Sarajevo had ordered [Brigadier Orić, the local commander] . . . to leave for no apparent reason. He was then prevented from returning. As the situation worsened, the Sarajevo leadership made no effort to launch diversionary attacks. . . . Dutch peacekeepers near Tuzla told Gowing that they saw Bosnian troops escaping from Srebrenica . . . carrying brand new anti-tank weapons, still in their plastic wrappings. . . . [British UN peacekeeper Lieut. Col. Jim] Baxter said "they [the Bosnian government] knew what was happening in Srebrenica. I am certain they decided it was worth the sacrifice." [emphasis added][98]

The foregoing information raises the possibility that the Izetbegović government actually welcomed the conquest of Srebrenica and took specific measures to increase the likelihood that conquest would occur; and that in doing this, the government was acting on the basis of a larger strategy, which aimed at augmenting international sympathy for the Bosnian cause and thus drawing in NATO military intervention to be directed against the Serbs.

Whatever the Bosnian intentions, the capture of Srebrenica led to atrocities that were far larger in scale than anything that had occurred during three years of fighting. The lightly armed battalion of Dutch peacekeepers assigned to the safe area proved incapable of protecting the civilian population. With a free hand to act as they wished, the Serb armies began by expelling the town's women and children, producing yet another act of ethnic cleansing. And then the Serbs proceeded to murder some eight thousand military-age Muslim males.[99] According to the Dutch investigation of the massacre: "Muslims were slaughtered like beasts."[100]

The Srebrenica massacre was the worst war crime in Europe since the 1940s, and several international court rulings have defined it as a case of genocide.[101] As to the issue of responsibility, the massacre was directed by Gen. Ratko Mladić, the overall commander of the Serb armies in Bosnia, and Gen. Radislav Krstić, another Serb officer. There is no proof, however, that Milošević or his government played any direct role in the killings. According to a November 1995 State Department report: "The intelligence community for three years has looked for definitive evidence of President Milošević's personal involvement in managing ethnic cleansing and other war crimes, and has come up empty handed."[102] Yet Milošević had long supported the Bosnian Serb forces, and he was thus an indirect facilitator of the Srebrenica massacre.[103]

Word of the mass murder at Srebrenica spread quickly, and there was an international wave of revulsion against the new round of atrocities. The revulsion increased when, on July 25, Serb troops captured a second safe area, the enclave of Zepa.[104] And the fall of Zepa once again produced thousands of refugees (although fortunately, there was no large-scale massacre in this case). The Srebrenica atrocity combined with Zepa's capture transformed the international politics of the Bosnia war and led to a new campaign—supported by the United States—to defeat the Serbs.

Within the Clinton administration, the events of July 1995 strengthened the position of Galbraith, Albright, and other officials who favored direct intervention.[105] It appears that President Clinton had already resolved to seek a military solution to the Bosnia war, even before the Srebrenica massacre.[106] But the massacre made it easier for Clinton to justify a hawkish stance. As to the question of motive, there is no doubt that Clinton sought to reaffirm America's capacity for world leadership. The basic issue of maintaining US hegemony in the post–Cold War world is a key thread that runs through virtually all US policy discussions on Bosnia during this period. If the United States had failed to intervene at this point, its inaction would "undermine our credibility as leader of the [Atlantic] Alliance," according to Secretary of State Christopher.[107] Inaction risked making the president (and the country) look weak.[108] It was this fear that motivated a new level of US intervention in Bosnia.

An Offensive Strategy

> If Americans allow the arming of the [Bosnian] Muslims,
> they will soon find themselves complicit in ethnic cleansing,
> for that is what the Muslims are certain to do.
> —*Michael Ignatieff, 1993*

The Clinton administration finally opted for an offensive strategy, which played out during August–October 1995.[109] An important factor in this strategy was once again the Republic of Croatia, which was to team with the Bosnian army in order to defeat Serb forces in both Croatia and Bosnia. Croatian assistance was considered necessary, since by itself the Bosnian government military was insufficient to overcome Mladić's forces. The addition of Croatian military power, the decisive element, would lead to one victory after another. And this strategy would indeed make the United States complicit in ethnic cleansing, just as Ignatieff had predicted in his 1993 comment noted in the epigraph.

The first phase of the offensive began within the Republic of Croatia itself. On August 4, the Croats launched Operation Storm, which aimed to capture the Serb-controlled Krajina region.[110] The Tudjman regime was determined to quell the Serb rebellion in Krajina, prior to any direct intervention in Bosnia-Herzegovina. The attack on Krajina was substantial in scale, involving 100,000 Croat troops supported by artillery and aircraft.[111] The basic strategy entailed a heavy bombardment of Knin and other Serb towns ahead of infantry advances. The most detailed account is from the memoirs of Carl Bildt: "[UN observers] saw how the artillery salvoes seemed to move from one section of town [Knin] to another. They were not aiming for military targets—there were hardly any left. It seemed that the Croats were trying to spread fear.... We will probably never know how many died in the early hours of the morning. The UN observers reported that the number of innocent people killed was 'high'; ... they [UN observers] saw bodies of women and children lying, shot to ribbons along the streets."[112] It appears that the Tudjman regime sought to stun the Serbs into leaving immediately; many of those who remained would be killed or brutalized by successive waves of Croat ground troops.[113] From the Croatian standpoint, Operation Storm was a major success. Their armies captured most of the region in only four days, and they met very little resistance. Milošević made no effort to help the Krajina Serbs, who were now viewed as an unnecessary burden.[114]

Operation Storm also generated a humanitarian disaster. The attack forced from 150,000 to 200,000 Serbs to flee, producing what was probably the largest single act of ethnic expulsion of the entire war.[115] In addition, several hundred Serb civilians were killed. Many died during the shelling of towns, while others were killed at close range by infantry.[116] A full accounting of the atrocities will be difficult, since Tudjman's forces intimidated potential witnesses, as described by Bildt: "Croat authorities had immediately ordered all UN personnel [in Krajina] to remain in their quarters and not move, observe, or report. They meant business: A Danish soldier who tried to see too much was simply shot."[117] The Tudjman regime had been planning the expulsion for some time. As early as 1993, Tudjman stated in an official meeting: "There is a growing understanding that Croatia must resolve the [Krajina] problem by war, contrary to international norms, meaning by *ethnically cleansing the Serbs from Croatia*" (emphasis added).[118] Now, with Operation Storm, Croatian nationalists attained their long-sought objective of ridding the republic of undesirable ethnic groups.

The Croatian atrocities embarrassed the United States, and some figures sought to distance themselves from the whole operation, at least in public.[119] Despite this official distancing, the United States clearly *did* support Operation Storm, and such support was a decisive factor in Tudjman's decision to launch the attack in the first place.[120] Gen. Charles Boyd, who served as deputy commander of the US European Command, stated: "Croatia would not have taken the military offensives . . . without the explicit approval of the US government."[121] The Croatian foreign minister claimed that Operation Storm received "tacit approval" from US officials.[122] According to a *New York Times* article, Storm "was carried out with the tacit blessing of the United States."[123] The official Dutch investigation of the Bosnia war stated that Tudjman "had been assured of American support to sort out the situation in Krajina" as early as 1994.[124] President Clinton himself later acknowledged that, during the offensive, "I was rooting for the Croatians."[125] And after the operation had ended, the Americans quietly expressed satisfaction at the outcome. State Department official Robert Frasure wrote to a colleague: "We 'hired' these guys [the Croatian military] to be our junkyard dogs because we were desperate. We need to try to 'control' them. *But this is no time to get squeamish about things.* This is the first time the Serb wave has been reversed. That is essential for us to get stability, so we can get out" (emphasis added).[126] Several years later, in 1999, US officials obstructed international efforts to investigate Croat war crimes that had occurred in Krajina.[127] Overall, it seems fair to say that the United States had a measure of complicity in Operation Storm—including its unsavory aspects.

And when Operation Storm was complete, Croat forces crossed the border into Bosnia-Herzegovina. There, they linked up with the Bosnian Fifth Corps, the best unit in Izetbegović's army. These combined forces launched a new offensive code-named Operation Mistral. The Clinton administration was "encouraging the offensive," according to Holbrooke's memoirs.[128] And a British officer serving with UNPROFOR added: "The US was pulling the intelligence and information strings" for Mistral.[129] Over the next several weeks, during September through October, the Croat/Bosnian juggernaut attacked Serb positions throughout western Bosnia, with considerable success. The attacks also produced new waves of Serb refugees who feared reprisals.[130]

From the US standpoint, the outcome was once again positive. The Croat and Bosnian forces had after all, functioned as America's ground troops in the conflict, and it was a key aspect of US policy to ensure their success. The

Americans began to balk, however, when the Croat/Bosnian forces threatened Banja Luka, the principal Serb-controlled city in western Bosnia. On September 17, Holbrooke met with President Tudjman and stated: "Mr. President, I urge you to go as far as you can, but not to take Banja Luka." Because of this demand, Banja Luka was not attacked. Why the US restraint in this case? The reason appears to have been a fear that seizure of the town might have caused horrific atrocities. Holbrooke notes that "capturing Banja Luka would generate over two hundred thousand *additional* refugees. I did not think the United States should encourage an action that would create so many more refugees" (emphasis added).[131] And there was also the danger of a Srebrenica-style massacre. Given the increasingly vicious character of the war, the possibility of such mass killings could not be ruled out. Atrocities on this scale would have been too embarrassing for US officials to contemplate, and so they took steps to prevent them.

Despite the restraint shown in the case of Banja Luka, the offensives of August–October 1995 generated substantial atrocities. A correspondent for *Jane's Defense Weekly* estimates that several thousand Serb civilians were killed by the combined operations in the Krajina region of Croatia and in western Bosnia.[132] In addition, the offensives produced hundreds of thousands of Serb refugees (many of whom were ethnically cleansed from areas that had been predominantly Serb long before the war began). In addition, some thirty thousand anti-Izetbegović Muslims were expelled from the Bihać region of western Bosnia, since these were considered politically unreliable.[133]

Viewed from a strictly military standpoint, the Storm/Mistral operations were highly effective. When the attacks finally ended in late October 1995, the Izetbegović government controlled close to half of Bosnia's territory.[134] The Serbs lost most of the land that they had gained through conquest during the war's earlier phases. The balance of power in Bosnia was fundamentally altered, producing a solid achievement for both Izetbegović and Tudjman.

A Showcase for US Hegemony

The ground operations also constituted an achievement for US officials, who were able to intervene decisively in the Bosnia conflict, producing an outcome that could be classed a military victory. The problem was that US power was being projected for the most part indirectly, through proxy armies. What was needed was a *direct* display of US and NATO strength, through large-scale air strikes. Such strikes would support the Croat/Bosnian ground offensives, and (perhaps more importantly) they would advertise US military prowess. President Clinton was especially enthusiastic about the idea of strikes, since "the United States had to restore the credibility of NATO's air power."[135] The result was Operation Deliberate Force, a major air campaign against Serb-controlled areas of Bosnia, which took place during August and September 1995.

Deliberate Force was technically a multinational NATO campaign, but it was conceived and conducted largely by the United States. Shortly before the strikes were launched, US officials met with their European counterparts and, in essence, demanded their support. According to Chollet, who interviewed many key figures: "The Americans would go to explain what they were doing, not ask for permission. The message would be 'part invitation, part ultimatum.'"[136] Though European leaders resented this US diktat, they reluctantly went along with the plan. After the Srebrenica massacre, the Europeans were under pressure to take action, and they did not wish to appear obstructionist. NATO member states thus supported Operation Deliberate Force. Even France agreed to join the operation, despite reservations.[137] The United Nations might have been an impediment, since the Security Council had not issued any resolution in favor of large-scale attacks. However, the United States made no effort to bring the matter to the Security Council (where there was the danger of a Russian veto).[138] Instead, Secretary-General Boutros-Ghali simply made a statement endorsing the strikes, and UNPROFOR peacekeepers in Bosnia were withdrawn from front-line positions to prevent their being injured.[139] Overall, the United States sought to marginalize the United Nations as much as possible; Boutros-Ghali would later write that America "wanted no UN role whatsoever" in this phase of the Bosnia war.[140]

Operation Deliberate Force was launched on August 30 and continued for more than two weeks.[141] In contrast to previous NATO air strikes, Deliberate Force was large in scale, involving scores of planes flying from land bases in Europe and Turkey, as well as from aircraft carriers. More than 3,500 separate sorties were flown, and Serb military positions were attacked throughout Bosnia.[142] Although eight countries officially participated in the sorties, US aircraft flew 65 percent of them—leaving little doubt about who was really in charge of the bombing campaign.

The air operations received substantial press attention, far more than the Croat/Bosnian ground attacks during the same period. It was widely believed that the strikes played the decisive role in defeating Serb armies and ultimately ending the war. Several recent studies have cast doubt on this conclusion; they suggest that NATO aircraft did not greatly damage the Serbs' heavy weapons, nor did they break Serb morale.[143] In defeating the Serbs, it appears that the Croat/Bosnian offensives had a greater impact.[144] The main effect of Operation Deliberate Force was not military but political: It demonstrated the relevance of NATO, as well as the capacity of the United States to exercise leadership. An analysis of Deliberate Force in the *International Herald-Tribune* concluded: "The United States is today again Europe's leader; there is no other."[145] And a Swiss publication added: "One thing is clear: The US still makes the law in the Old Continent."[146]

The Dayton Accords

Having gained the upper hand on the battlefield through the bombings and (more importantly) the ground attacks, the United States proceeded to organize a peace conference, which took place in November 1995 at the Wright-Patterson Air Force Base in Dayton, Ohio. Key figures in the Balkan conflict, including Milošević, Tudjman, and Izetbegović, attended the conference in person; a team of US diplomats led by Assistant Secretary of State Holbrooke directed the peace talks. US officials made clear that they alone would be running the talks; UN personnel were accordingly excluded ("during the days of Dayton, the UN was a word that could not be uttered," noted Bildt).[147] Several European representatives, including Bildt, were permitted to attend, but they played no substantive role. According to one US official, the Europeans had "no negotiating power; they were there just to bear witness."[148] The London *Independent* noted that Dayton "was so much an American show that they do not even make a pretense of keeping European capitals informed. Europe remains as beholden to American power as it was in 1941."[149] US officials were determined to manage the conference and end this war, and they would do so without any help from the European Union or the United Nations.[150]

The location for the peace talks, a military base, seemed odd to many observers. A Bosnian official complained that accommodations were similar to the ones at "those cheap hotel chains, like 'Motel 6'"—not at all what one might expect for a major international conference.[151] From the standpoint of showcasing US power, however, the location was ideal. The following account, taken from a State Department document, conveys a sense of the martial ambience that pervaded the conference: "The US hosted a dinner for the senior delegation members at Wright-Patterson's Air Force Museum; . . . guests dined in the shadows of an enormous B-29, several Stealth F-117 fighters, and appropriately for some, a Tomahawk cruise missile that seemed to be pointed right at Milošević's table."[152] The participants were no doubt impressed by these unsubtle displays of US military strength.

In any case, the conference was successful in achieving a settlement of the war, officially signed on December 15, 1995.[153] The Dayton Accords entailed the creation of the Serb Republic, which would join the preexisting Muslim-

Croat Federation; the two units would constitute a new Bosnian state. Power in this new state would once again be decentralized, to afford the ethnic groups a high level of self-government. The authorities in Sarajevo (still led by Izetbegović) were to wield only limited powers. On the key issue of territory, the Serb Republic was granted 49 percent of the total area, while the Muslim-Croat Federation received 51 percent. A multinational Implementation Force (IFOR) was established, with sixty thousand troops to serve as peacekeepers and, essentially, to run Bosnia for a period of time.[154] The United States had seen to it that IFOR was placed under NATO (not UN) direction. And according to *Foreign Report*, IFOR was "dominated by the Americans."[155] The display of US power is a theme that runs through virtually every aspect of the Dayton settlement.

Overall, the Dayton Accords produced a mixed legacy.[156] On the one hand, they did succeed in ending the war, and there was no recurrence of active combat. As a means of reconciling the parties and unifying the country, however, the Accords were less effective. During early 1996, there was yet another round of ethnic attacks—this time with Serbs as victims. The attacks occurred in areas transferred from Serb authority to Muslim-Croat authority, as required under the peace agreement. Bildt describes one such attack, in the city of Ilidža: "Gangs of hooligans ran through the streets of Ilidža terrorizing the remaining three or four thousand Serbs, just minutes after the transfer of authority [to the Muslim-Croat Federation] took place. It was hard to believe this was not organized. When it was obvious that intervention by the Federation police was going to be kept to an absolute minimum, the pattern was clear. Just hours after the Federation had formally taken over Ilidža, all telephone links between the municipality and the [Serb Republic] were cut off."[157] A combination of violence and intimidation forced 100,000 Serbs to flee areas that came under Federation control in the months after the Dayton Accords. Neither IFOR nor the Izetbegović government made any sustained effort to protect the Serbs, or to dissuade the attackers.[158] Like all previous acts of ethnic cleansing that targeted Serbs, these attacks once again attracted no significant international condemnation and little notice.[159]

The ethnic expulsions surely made for an inauspicious beginning. Overall, the process of establishing Bosnia as a viable state has proven far more challenging than the framers of the Dayton Accords had anticipated. International peacekeepers still remained there in 2008, with no clear prospect of leaving.[160] In essence, the Dayton Accords recreated Bosnia as a de facto international protectorate, rather than as an independent state.

The Dayton Accords were nevertheless a triumph for US hegemony. According to Holbrooke: "After Dayton, American foreign policy seemed more assertive, more muscular."[161] Warren Christopher added that the Accords "reaffirmed the imperative of American leadership."[162] And the Accords also constituted a major personal accomplishment for President Clinton, whose reputation rose as a result. Retrospective accounts view the Accords as a turning point in the Clinton presidency.[163]

The Dayton Accords also humiliated the European Union and sabotaged EU efforts to forge an independent foreign policy. This point was widely recognized in the international press. The signing of the Accords marked "Europe's utter failure," according to a headline from the *World Press Review*. According to the *Sunday Times* of Sri Lanka, the Bosnia affair had cast "shame on European powers." This shameful image offered a sharp contrast with the United States, which "demonstrated in no uncertain terms that it has inherited global leadership after the collapse of the Soviet Union." *Le Monde* claimed that the Yugoslav conflict had entailed "a long series of frustrations and humiliations for the Europeans, dealt by the Americans, who wanted to be seen as running the show."[164] And this setback for European diplomacy was yet another achievement for the United States, which was only too happy to undercut a potential rival for power. Some Americans openly expressed pleasure on this point. Thus, former State Department official John Bolton gloated: "It's clear the Europeans failed and that United States leadership was required [to end the Bosnia war]. . . . I hope the Western Europeans have learned that lesson."[165]

And finally, the Bosnia conflict helped relegitimate the North Atlantic Treaty Organization and gave the organization a new purpose for the post–Cold War world. When the Bosnia war ended, "NATO's morale and international prestige soared sky high," according to the *Economist*.[166] NATO was not only preserved, but also expanded. In 1999, Poland, Hungary, and the Czech Republic officially joined NATO, accomplishing a long-sought US objective in Europe first discussed publicly in 1991.[167] The prestige that NATO had gained in Bosnia helped create the political conditions that made such expansion possible. According to Chollet, who served in the State Department at the time, "Without Dayton . . . 'NATO expansion would never have happened.'"[168]

Overall, the Bosnian intervention advanced America's position in the world. US policy had a less positive effect, however, from a humanitarian standpoint. As we have seen, the United States repeatedly blocked European and UN peace proposals throughout the war. The Vance-Owen plan might well have ended the war in 1993—but the US opposed the plan. It should be recalled that US officials criticized Vance-Owen because it allocated 43 percent of Bosnia's land to the Serbs. This percentage was considered too high and was condemned as a form of appeasement and a reward for ethnic cleansing. Yet, two and a half years later, with the Dayton Accords, the United States allocated 49 percent of Bosnia to the Serbs; the earlier criticisms of Vance-Owen were conveniently forgotten.[169] US diplomacy was instrumental in preventing an early settlement of the war and probably prolonged the fighting for several additional years.

Conclusion

With the Dayton Accords, the United States advanced a key set of interests set forth by the 1992 Defense Planning Guidance document: to affirm America's position as the continent's only superpower; to undercut challenges to US hegemony that emanated from the European Union; and to establish a new function for NATO, which was to serve as the key instrument of US power in Europe.[170] Through intervention in Bosnia, President Clinton achieved all three objectives. US hegemony was thus reestablished on a much stronger foundation than previously, while a challenge to that hegemony from the European Union was undercut, at least for the moment. And NATO received a new function. US hegemony was thus more secure than before, and the advantages that flowed from hegemony—for both the US state and private sector—were better protected. To be sure, these accomplishments had been achieved at a high human cost, since US policy helped prolong the Bosnia war. And the accomplishments were made possible, in part, by the cleansing of Serbs from large areas of Croatia and Bosnia-Herzegovina. But it is a basic theme of this chapter that US intervention was not an act of idealism but, on the contrary, a classic act of power politics.

The European Union would make one final attempt, during the late 1990s, to overcome its setbacks and establish an independent foreign policy. Europe would yet again challenge US hegemony, leading to a new round of transatlantic conflict. It would take another war—this time over Kosovo—to settle the issue once and for all, and subordinate Europe.

7

Kosovo and the Reaffirmation of American Power

> We believe that no lasting solution [in the Balkans]
> can be reached through violence.
> —*Brent Scowcroft, 1992*

> Let's at least have a real air war. . . . The stakes have to be
> very clear: Every week you [the Serbs] ravage Kosovo is
> another decade we will set your country back by pulverizing
> you. You want 1950? We can do 1950. You want 1389?
> We can do 1389 too. . . . Give war a chance.
> —*Thomas Friedman, 1999*

From 1991 to 1999, the international response to the Yugoslavia case evolved considerably. In the early phases, during 1991–1992, the world community opposed the use of violence to resolve conflict and condemned the Yugoslav military for its very modest use of force to stop secession in Slovenia. Both Serb and Yugoslav forces were condemned again during the wars in Croatia and Bosnia-Herzegovina. With the 1999 conflict over Kosovo, however, the NATO powers agreed that force was a perfectly legitimate way to achieve their objectives. And had Belgrade not capitulated when it did, NATO officials were prepared to intensify their use of force. The international attitude toward the acceptability of violence had been transformed. Another transformation related to the role of the United Nations in mediating the conflict. In the early phases of the Yugoslav war, the United Nations played a prominent role, at least formally, in authorizing international activities in the Balkans; by 1999, the United Nations was marginalized, as the war was initiated without authorization from the Security Council or any other UN organ.

Above all, the 1999 Kosovo war marked the decline of Europe's political sway, combined with a reassertion by the United States. In 1991, the United States had initially been reluctant to become involved in the conflict; by 1999, it was unquestionably playing the lead role. The Kosovo war definitively established US primacy on the European continent and ensured that the United States would remain the dominant power for years to come. The European effort to assert its independence at US expense was effectively checked, accomplishing a long-standing US objective.

The Kosovo Conflict in Context

The 1999 war in Kosovo has been widely remembered as a humanitarian war motivated by altruistic considerations.[1] We will consider the merits of this argument at greater length later in the chapter. For now, we will note that there were other, more concrete motivations for US policy. We will see that the principal motivations for the war were to establish a new basis for US hegemony in Europe and a new rationale for the primary institutional embodiment of that hegemony—the North Atlantic Treaty Organization.

But first let us consider the larger context: The late 1990s was a period of increasing tensions among the advanced industrialized countries and especially between the United States and the European Union. Such tensions threatened to disrupt the system of multilateral trade and investment, undergirded by US hegemony, that had been the hallmark of the post-1945 economic system. The EU tendencies toward monetary unification throughout the 1990s were viewed as serious threats to US financial power, and especially to the role of the US dollar as the world's reserve currency, as we saw in Chapter 2. This specific threat came to a climax on January 1, 1999, when the euro was officially established as the currency of eleven members of the European Union. The *Financial Times* termed the euro "a seismic challenge to the dollar."[2] In the view of Germany's Helmut Schmidt, the launching of the euro "could set up a monumental conflict; . . . it will change the whole world situation so that the United States can no longer call all the shots."[3] The advent of the euro coincided with a gradual upsurge of contention between the United States and Europe regarding trade in aircraft, genetically modified foods, telecommunications, and fruit products.[4] These conflicts seem to have been peaking during March 1999—which was the month that the Kosovo war began. What was needed was a new military crusade, one that could serve as a substitute for the Cold War, to give the United States and Europe a new sense of common purpose. Kosovo was to provide this crusade.

Another factor that affected official thinking during this period was a renewed European effort to establish an independent foreign and military policy. This was of course a major European ambition throughout the post–Cold War period. However, this ambition became more intense during the late 1990s, due to the perception that the Americans had been overly domineering during the Bosnia-Herzegovina conflict. A British military analyst writing in *Jane's Intelligence Review* in 1999 noted: "The wars of Yugoslav succession have already brought NATO within measurable distance of disintegration; . . . had the Bosnian war not been brought to termination in 1995 by the Dayton agreement . . . there would surely have been a transatlantic rift."[5]

American conduct during the Bosnia war thus left a legacy of bitterness. The negative perception of the United States extended even to Great Britain, which now became more receptive to the Franco-German view that the Europeans should distance themselves from NATO. In December 1998, French and British officials met in the town of St. Malo and declared their intention that the European Union should have a military capability to act "autonomously" from NATO and, by implication, from the United States as well.[6] The St. Malo declaration was made with the usual caveats that it was not a threat to NATO; important figures in the US foreign policy establishment were nevertheless apprehensive. It seemed that the St. Malo declaration, combined with the launch of the euro, was part of a generalized European challenge. That even Great Britain might participate in this challenge was viewed with special concern.[7]

The US response to all these perceived threats was to reinvigorate the NATO alliance. As always, the basic problem was finding a plausible purpose for such an alliance after the fall of communism. To overcome this obstacle, US officials proposed a "New Strategic Concept," which advanced a fundamental alteration in the alliance's function. The basic idea was that NATO should protect Western interests in virtually any part of the world. NATO was to be reconfigured from a military alliance with purely regional responsibilities—its function during the Cold War—to an alliance with global responsibilities. US officials had long sought to endow NATO with an offensive out-of-area function; with the adoption of the New Strategic Concept, the out-of-area objective would be effectively achieved.[8]

From the US standpoint, the New Strategic Concept offered clear advantages. A strengthened NATO represented an institutional alternative to the unreliable European Union, thus undercutting European efforts aimed at foreign policy and financial independence. And a strong NATO would reduce interallied economic tensions—which were very much on the minds of US policy makers, including those involved in transforming NATO. These concerns were frankly noted by Gen. Wesley Clark in a 1999 article on NATO's future:

The figures speak volumes. US trade with Europe, amounting to over $250 billion annually, produces over three million domestic jobs. US companies employ three million people in Europe. One in 12 factory workers in the United States is employed by a European Union (EU) firm operating in this country, of which there are some 4,000. Half of the world's goods are produced by the United States and the EU. . . . Companies from the EU form the largest investment block in 41 US states. Fifty-six percent of US foreign investment occurs in Europe. Europe buys 30 percent of US exports.

After discussing US economic interests, General Clark concluded: "*As a result of those* [economic] *interests*, we have continued to maintain a strong military presence in Europe" (emphasis added).[9] The New Strategic Concept was thus viewed as a means of preserving the system of multilateral trade and investment, described by Clark, along with the economic advantages that this system offered to the United States.

In achieving US objectives, an important consideration was timing. The war in Kosovo coincided with NATO's fiftieth anniversary celebrations, which were held in April 1999. Clearly, the celebrations were important for symbolic reasons. In addition, US officials were planning to use the occasion to inaugurate the New Strategic Concept.[10] And US corporations too sought to make a success of NATO's anniversary celebrations.[11] A broad range of interest groups in the US government and the private sector thus sought to use the fiftieth anniversary of NATO as an occasion to give the alliance a new mission and a new raison d'être. The difficulty was to sell this project to a reluctant Europe, which remained unpersuaded with regard to the need for the New Strategic Concept and with regard to US plans for NATO more generally.[12] Clearly, a justification was needed to ensure that US objectives would be implemented. The conflict in Kosovo provided that justification. According to an article in *Le Monde*, one of the main US motivations in Kosovo was to "legitimate NATO as a new world-wide police force."[13]

US analysts regarded the war in much the same way, that is, as a means to cement US hegemony in Europe through a revived NATO. In arguing his case for war, President Clinton noted the salience of US relations with Europe, especially the economic aspects of these relations. In a March 1999 speech, Clinton stated: "We need a Europe that is safe, secure, free, united, a good partner with us for trading; . . . if we're going to have a strong economic relationship that includes our ability to sell around the world, Europe has got to be a key. . . . *Now that's what this Kosovo thing is all about*" (emphasis added).[14]

Background to Conflict in Kosovo

In most public discussions, the human rights aspect was the main justification for the NATO war; the NATO powers, it is argued, sought to restrain Serb oppression in Kosovo. But ultimately, Serb misconduct served mainly as a *pretext* to justify NATO actions, rather than as a genuine motivation.[15] Nevertheless, there can be no question that Serb oppression in Kosovo did exist, and that this oppression had a long history. Let us briefly consider the factors internal to Kosovo that led to the upsurge in fighting and, ultimately, to the war with NATO.

The Albanians had clear grievances. Of all the major constituent groups in the Yugoslav federation, the Kosovo Albanians were by far the poorest. As a result, they were only weakly integrated into the Yugoslav system. Within the province, there was considerable tension between the Albanian ethnic group—which constituted the majority in the province—and the Serbs. The Serbs in Kosovo were better educated and more affluent than the Albanians, and they held a disproportionate share of the public sector jobs. During the early period of communist Yugoslavia, the central government tended to side with the Serbs against the Albanians. The federal interior minister, Aleksander Ranković, a relatively hard-line figure and an ethnic Serb, dealt harshly with any assertion of Albanian nationalism.[16]

After a 1966 political shake-up, Ranković fell from power, and there was a considerable change in the government's attitude with regard to the "Kosovo problem."[17] Tito now made concerted efforts to address local grievances. Kosovo was granted increasing measures of self-government and, after a constitutional revision in 1974, the Kosovo Autonomous Province became a "republic in all but name."[18] In addition, the federal government provided substantial development funds to upgrade Kosovo's infrastructure.[19] A program of affirmative action for ethnic Albanians was established, which implicitly penalized Serbs. From 1966 to 1985, the proportion of Serbs in public sector jobs declined from over 50 percent to only 22.5 percent. The level of Albanian participation in public sector jobs rose.[20] The federal government invested heavily in Kosovar education, especially higher education, and again there was a special emphasis on the Albanian ethnic group. The University of Priština, which had originally been a regional section of the University of Belgrade, in Serbia, was given separate status and considerable funds. Throughout the educational system, the teaching of the Albanian language, initially discouraged, was now given full federal government support.[21]

Journalistic accounts from this period emphasize a general easing of repression. Dan Morgan offers this observation: "Traveling through Kosovo in 1970, I found an 'Albanian spring' in full swing, nurtured by Tito. The

Albanian language was being used alongside Serbian at the University . . . and Shakespeare's plays could be read in Albanian. Years of Serbian police control were being relaxed. Albanians and Serbs were sharing power in the towns and provincial governments."[22]

These reforms, though perhaps laudable in principle, intensified political tension in Kosovo. Despite the infusion of development funds from Belgrade, Kosovo remained exceptionally underdeveloped in comparison with all other regions of Yugoslavia.[23] And the increased use of the Albanian language during the 1970s ensured that most Kosovars lacked fluency in Serbo-Croatian, the dominant language in the federation. The province's integration in the federation—which had never been strong—was probably weakened by the increased use of Albanian. The University of Priština augmented the number of university-educated Kosovars, but due to lagging economic development, these graduates often faced frustrating job prospects. Students thus became a major source of dissatisfaction and political agitation.[24]

A basic fact of life in Kosovo during the post–World War II period was a tendency toward increasing Albanian demographic dominance (see Table 7.1). Serbs were gradually declining as a percentage of the total population and, by 1981, they comprised a small minority of what had become an overwhelmingly Albanian region. There is no doubt that Serbs were fleeing the province in large numbers, and fear of oppression accounts for part of this flight. Morgan notes that as "an Albanian communist political machine flexed its muscles in the 1970s and 1980s, Serbs felt threatened, and many thousands left for Serbia proper."[25] While precise figures for the later period are not available, it is generally believed that ethnic Serbs comprised only 10 percent of Kosovo's total population by 1991 (a percentage that remained fairly stable until 1999).[26]

Ethnic tensions in Kosovo festered and intensified during the 1980s, owing to the increasingly austere economic conditions of this period (see Chapter 3). In the trough of the economic downturn, between 1986 and 1988, the unemployment rate reached almost 60 percent—by far the highest in the federation.[27] This situation helped bring out the worst in the local population, as the search for scapegoats naturally led to augmented ethnic turmoil. In the context of such conditions, a tyranny of the majority was exerted by the dominant Albanian group against ethnic Serbs, as well as other rival groups. The idea of an ethnically pure Kosovo, free of non-Albanians, became popular during this period.

In the 1980s, there was indeed talk of ethnic cleansing in Kosovo, but at this point it was the ethnic *Serbs* who were in danger. In 1986, the *Christian Science Monitor* quoted a resident who stated that many of his fellow Albanians "want to drive Serbs and Montenegrins from Kosovo. They talk

**Table 7.1. Ethnic Composition of Kosovo:
Percentage of Total Population, by Year**

	1961	1971	1981
Albanians	67.0	73.7	77.5
Serbs	23.5	18.4	13.3
Yugoslavs	0.5	0.1	0.2
Others*	9.0	7.8	9.0

Source: Data from Susan Woodward, *Balkan Tragedy: Chaos and Dissolution after the
Cold War* (Washington, D.C.: Brookings, 1995), 34.

* Includes non-Albanian Muslims, Croats, Montenegrins, and Macedonians, as well as
unspecified "others."

of an 'ethnically clean' Kosovo."[28] An analysis of Western press reporting
on Kosovo found that during the 1980s the terms "ethnically clean" or "ethnic cleansing" were first used with Serbs as potential victims and Albanians
as potential perpetrators.[29] A 1989 survey, later published in the *American
Journal of Sociology*, indicated that ethnic Albanians had "the greatest intolerance toward other groups of any national group in the former Yugoslavia."[30] Though outbreaks of interethnic violence remained infrequent during
this phrase of the conflict, the Albanians engaged in systematic harassment
of the Serb minority.[31] What was going on during the 1970s and 1980s, in
short, was an Albanian backlash against decades of mistreatment by Serbs;
this backlash triggered a gradual Serb exodus from the region, as Serbs could
no longer tolerate the tensions.

Amidst the increasingly desperate conditions, the local Serbs naturally
welcomed the external protection offered by Serbia's president Slobodan
Milošević. President Milošević in turn was looking for some issue to assert
his popularity over that of his rivals, and conveniently found it in the province. After extensive manipulation by operatives from Milošević's Socialist
party and various Serb nationalist groups, the autonomous status of Kosovo
was effectively ended in 1989.[32] Thereafter, Kosovo was ruled through martial
law directed by the Republic of Serbia. A generalized atmosphere of political
and social repression was established. Now the situation was reversed, and it
was the Serbs who dominated the province, with the Albanians as victims. A
UN General Assembly resolution in February 1994 summarized conditions
in Kosovo:

Large-scale repression committed by the Serbian authorities.... Police
brutality against ethnic Albanians, [including] arbitrary searches, seizures

and arrests, torture and ill-treatment during detention and discrimination in the administration of justice, which leads to a climate of lawlessness in which criminal acts, particularly against ethnic Albanians, take place with impunity; ... discriminatory removal of ethnic Albanians officials, especially from the police and judiciary, the mass dismissal of ethnic Albanians from professional, administrative, and other skilled positions in state-owned enterprises and public institutions ... the closure of Albanian high schools and universities [and] ... the closure of Albanian-language mass media.[33]

Kosovo was reduced to colonial status, and the Albanian majority was repressed. In addition, Serbia engaged in cultural imperialism in Kosovo, especially with regard to education. School "reforms" were introduced from 1990 to 1992 that limited the teaching of classes in Albanian. Serbo-Croatian (later Serbian) became the dominant language of instruction in Kosovar schools from the elementary to the university level.[34] Openly racist statutes restricted ethnic Albanians from buying or selling property without special permission.[35]

In sum, the Kosovo question contained an element of moral complexity. It is tempting to emphasize Albanian victimization at the hands of the Serbs; there is considerable evidence to support this view, especially after 1989. The problem is that such perspectives ignore the history of Albanian provocations against Serbs that preceded the repression of 1989. The imposition of martial law followed years of oppression orchestrated primarily by the Albanians, with Serbs as victims. Both ethnic groups clearly had major historical grievances and reasons for fear; neither group was prepared to show much tolerance or sympathy for the other. During the 1999 war, the NATO powers sided with the Albanians—and enabled the Albanians to ethnically cleanse the province of most Serbs during the months that followed the war. The long-standing objective of an Albanian-dominated Kosovo, free of troublesome Serbs, was achieved in most of the province.

Albanian Resistance and the Rise of the Kosovo Liberation Army

The imposition of repression in June 1989 served Milošević's political interests, as the move made him quite popular among Serb nationalists throughout the federation. From the Albanians' standpoint, of course, the repression was a disaster, as they lost their administrative autonomy, and all that they had gained politically since 1966. Albanian support for remaining in Yugoslavia disappeared altogether. The first specific Albanian response to the loss of autonomy was a movement of nonviolent resistance led by Ibrahim Rugova, an ethnic Albanian academic, and his League for Democracy in Kosovo (LDK).[36] The Serb security forces appear to have tolerated its activities to some degree, presumably out of fear that an outright ban would have been politically inflammatory and would have led to more threatening movements. The LDK called for general noncooperation with all aspects of the Serb rule, with the ultimate objective of full independence from Yugoslavia; later, after communist Yugoslavia ceased to exist, it sought independence from Serbia. Rugova's group was remarkably well organized, and set up a parallel administration with a network of underground schools, health clinics, and social service agencies. These services enabled Albanians to avoid official (Serb-run) facilities.[37]

During 1991–1992, the LDK announced plans for a full-scale underground government, with a president and 130-seat parliament. An election of sorts was held; the Serb security forces reluctantly allowed the event to proceed, and voting occurred in private homes and LDK administrative centers. Given the circumstances, the election results were hardly perfect, but it was generally acknowledged that the LDK at least at this phase had overwhelming popular support. Nearly all Albanians agreed with the LDK's call for secession.[38] Rugova was officially declared president of what was effectively a shadow government in Kosovo.[39]

The LDK clearly had significant faults. According to Tim Judah, the LDK "brooks little dissent and those that challenge it are howled down in the LDK publications and can even be ostracized in the tight-knit Albanian community."[40] Its methods contained a measure of intolerance for dissenting opinions. And Rugova's organization sought to augment the ethnic polarization and segregation in the province.[41] Despite these faults, the LDK was sincerely committed to nonviolent methods and at least some degree of democracy. Opposed to the LDK was a series of small groups that rejected nonviolence. During the early 1990s, however, Rugova's personal prestige ensured that the LDK remained the principal resistance group, and that the LDK's more extreme rivals initially were reduced to the margins.

Rugova's strategy depended, above all, on support from the Western powers and the United Nations.[42] In theory, the United States was sympathetic to Rugova's position, to the extent that US policy during this period was becoming hostile toward the Serbs and was supporting Serb adversaries, including the Kosovar Albanians. In December 1992, the United States issued a threat to the Milošević government: "In the event of conflict in Kosovo caused by Serbian action, the US will be prepared to employ military force against Serbians in Kosovo and Serbia proper."[43] In addition, international human rights organizations and the mass media covered repression in Kosovo from time to time. There was also an "Albanian lobby" on Capitol Hill (closely associated with Sen. Bob Dole), which urged greater official involvement in Kosovo.[44] As early as 1993, the New York public relations firm Ruder-Finn advised the Kosovar Albanians and, in the words of Ruder-Finn's president, "helped formulate the [Albanian] message in a way that Americans could identify with."[45]

Despite all this, Western interest was not high. The Bush administration's warning was mostly bluster, as the United States was not yet willing to use military force in the Balkan region. And of all the conflicts generated by the breakup of Yugoslavia, Kosovo was not a priority. The province was simply too underdeveloped and too remote to elicit significant support from the major powers. This lack of external interest in Kosovo was dramatically demonstrated during the Dayton peace talks in 1995. At Dayton, the Kosovo issue was never explicitly addressed, and it was mentioned nowhere in the final version of the Accords.[46]

The US decision to exclude Kosovo from the Dayton talks was an embarrassment to Rugova, and it called into question his entire strategy of nonviolence.[47] Rivals to the LDK gained popularity as a result.[48] The decline in Rugova's popularity after Dayton led directly to the rise of the Kosovo Liberation Army. The KLA was formed by a series of smaller groups that emerged after the traumatic events of 1989. With increasing support and an infusion of arms, the KLA gradually eclipsed the authority of Rugova's LDK. For funding, the KLA had an effective network of supporters among the Albanian diaspora in the United States and Western Europe, which collectively established a support fund, Homeland Calling.[49] Their first major action, with the first use of the term "Kosovo Liberation Army," occurred in February 1996, when KLA forces attacked Serb refugees in northern Kosovo.[50]

Clearly, the KLA contained some disturbing features, including ties to international heroin trafficking networks.[51] And there also is evidence of Al Qaeda activity, according to the *Wall Street Journal*:

> The most senior leaders of al Qaeda have visited the Balkans, including Bin Laden himself on three occasions between 1994 and 1996. The Egyptian surgeon turned terrorist leader Ayman Al-Zawahiri has operated terrorist training camps [and other facilities] . . . throughout Albania, Kosovo, Macedonia, Bulgaria, Turkey, and Bosnia. This has gone on for a decade. Many recruits to the Balkan wars came originally from Chechnya, a jihad in which Al Qaeda has also played a part. . . . Bin Laden . . . recruited some Albanians to fight with the KLA in Kosovo, according to the Paris-based Observatoire Géopolitique des Drogues.[52]

We have already seen that Al Qaeda supported Muslims in Bosnia-Herze-govina, and it should come as no surprise that they did the same in Kosovo.

Apart from its international ties, there is no doubt that the KLA itself used terrorist tactics.[53] As a basic facet of their strategy, the Albanian guerrillas repeatedly attacked Serb civilians.[54] Indeed, their first major military action was an attack on Serb refugees in 1996. The terrorist character of these tactics was apparent to Western officials, including British parliamentarian Paddy Ashdown, who later testified as a prosecution witness during the Milošević trial. The following exchange occurred during the cross-examination of Lord Ashdown:

Milošević: "It was a well-known fact that these [KLA] were terrorists, that this was a terrorist organization."

Ashdown: "Mr. Milošević, I never denied that it was a terrorist organization."[55]

State Department officials also viewed the KLA as a terrorist group until a few months before the March 1999 war (when US policy shifted in favor of the KLA). According to journalist Stacy Sullivan, who interviewed many KLA figures, the guerrillas "hit the Serb housing settlements, and they claimed responsibility for downing a civilian aircraft and planting a car bomb that injured the rector of the university. By definition, these were terrorist acts."[56] And at least initially, the KLA that acted with greater violence than had Milošević's forces, a point conceded by British defense secretary George Robertson during parliamentary testimony: "Up until [January 1999], *the KLA were responsible for more deaths in Kosovo than the Yugoslav authorities had been*" (emphasis added).[57]

To a large extent, the KLA military strategy was one of provocation. Albanian guerrilla units attacked Serb police and civilians, knowing that such actions invited Serb counterattacks, including attacks against Albanian civilians. Hashim Thaçi, a KLA commander, stated: "Any armed action we undertook would bring retaliation against civilians. We knew we were endangering a great number of civilian lives."[58] Such tactics were viewed as necessary to outrage world public opinion and to bring increased attention from the world's press (which had long neglected coverage of Kosovo while emphasizing the conflicts in Croatia and Bosnia-Herzegovina). The increased press attention, it was expected, would lead to military intervention from the Western powers in favor of the Albanians.[59] According to David Halberstam: "The Albanians or at least the KLA *wanted* [violence] so they would look like victims of Serb reprisals" (emphasis in original).[60] Even

Madeleine Albright, whose memoirs focus almost exclusively on Serb savagery, briefly concedes that the KLA "seemed intent on provoking a massive Serb response so that international intervention would be unavoidable."[61] This strategy—baiting the Serbs into attacking Albanian civilians, and thus increasing pressure for external intervention—worked quite well. This is precisely the scenario that played out during 1998–1999, leading to NATO intervention and a KLA victory.

The International Community Responds

By the late 1990s, it was clear that the United States, rather than the European Union, would assume primary responsibility for managing the crisis in Kosovo. The Dayton Accords had firmly established US—and not European—primacy in the area. The United States was nevertheless slow to respond. Part of the reason was simply fatigue from the intense level of US involvement in earlier conflicts in the former Yugoslavia, which were settled (more or less) by 1995. And when the Kosovo problem began to intensify during early 1998, world attention was elsewhere. Policy makers were preoccupied with international economic turmoil in the aftermath of the 1997 Asian financial crisis, which by 1998 was spreading to other regions. A major US hedge fund collapsed in 1998, and there was brief though widespread fear that this was a harbinger of even greater instability.[62] In the *Financial Times*, a banking executive exhorted international elites to resolve the crisis quickly, or "their children may read in their history books that the triumph of capitalism over communism lasted only for a brief period in the last decade of the 20th century."[63] Also in 1998, the Clinton administration had to contend with increasing tensions with Iraq, Al Qaeda terrorist attacks in East Africa, a congressional election, and the Monica Lewinsky sex scandal.

In this context, the Kosovo problem emerged on the scene fairly suddenly, with growing insurgent activity by the KLA combined with retaliation by Serb forces. At first, US officials viewed this conflict as an unwelcome distraction. In her memoirs, Secretary of State Madeleine Albright compared the world scene to a chess game and noted: "The game room was already crowded to overflowing early in 1998 when yet another familiar adversary—Slobodan Milošević—came crashing through the door."[64] The pace of US and Western diplomatic activity increased somewhat beginning in February 1998, when President Clinton dispatched Robert Gelbard, his special envoy to the Balkans, for a meeting with Milošević. Gelbard condemned both KLA violence and the vicious crackdown by Serb security forces.[65] The Contact Group of six key nations—the United States, United Kingdom, France, Italy, Germany, and Russia—began intensive rounds of diplomacy.

Working with the Contact Group, the Security Council adopted a resolution on March 31, 1998, that echoed Gelbard's statements, condemning both Serb and KLA actions.[66]

The initial US and international responses reflected an instinctive hostility toward Milošević, as well as his Socialist government, and also toward the Serbs more generally.[67] This hostility was a carryover from years of previous policy. However, there was also some degree of evenhandedness. Gelbard for example acknowledged that the KLA was "without any question a terrorist group."[68] Some observers later criticized Gelbard's statements, which purportedly encouraged Serb reprisals against the KLA.[69] At a factual level, it seems difficult to dispute the point that the KLA used terrorist tactics. A March 1998 statement by the Contact Group included the following clarification: "Our condemnation of the actions of the Serbian police should not in any way be mistaken for an endorsement of terrorism. . . . We wholly condemn terrorist actions by the Kosovo Liberation Army or any other group or individual."[70] The United States took a number of actions to reduce the KLA's sway. US officials promoted Rugova's more moderate LDK as an alternative to the KLA. In May 1998, the Americans arranged a meeting between Milošević and Rugova aimed at negotiating a de-escalation of violence.[71] As late as July 1998, General Clark even threatened to use force to disrupt international arms shipments to the KLA.[72] This threat was never implemented, but that it was presented at all is significant. In addition, the United States rejected any possibility of independence for Kosovo (and thus stood in opposition to the key objectives of the KLA and also Rugova's LDK, both of which demanded independence).[73]

The most notable feature of US policy in Kosovo during this early phase was its unfocused and ad hoc character, a reflection of the conflict's initially low priority.[74] It would appear that the evenhandedness was a result of this lack of focus. And the diplomacy was largely unsuccessful in stemming the crisis. Efforts to promote direct negotiations between Rugova and Milošević failed, as the LDK was firmly committed to secession and the Serbs were equally firmly opposed; the two positions were essentially irreconcilable, rendering the negotiations pointless. And the meeting itself served to weaken Rugova's position among the Albanian population, who were suspicious of any negotiations with the hated Serbs. The extremists in the KLA were accordingly strengthened. International calls for an end to external support for the Albanian guerrillas went largely unheeded.

During the summer and fall of 1998, US policy began to harden somewhat. Albright now advocated air strikes against the Serbs, and her position was supported by several top air force generals (who were eager to demonstrate the effectiveness of their weapons), as well as NATO commander

Wesley Clark. The president's influential spouse, Hillary Clinton, also appears to have favored strikes. A key factor influencing official thinking was the realization that a NATO war over Kosovo could strengthen the Atlantic alliance and thus contribute to one of the central US policy objectives of this period. On the other hand, some policy makers still opposed using force. Defense Secretary William Cohen and National Security Advisor Samuel Berger both remained skeptical that air power alone would defeat the Serbs; they also feared that a failed air campaign could lead to demands for sending US troops to the Balkans, and this could produce a Vietnam-style quagmire. And, apart from the air force, most of the senior military commanders also opposed intervention.[75] There thus was no consensus within the administration on how to respond to the new Balkan crisis.

The result of this deadlock was a half-hearted effort to resolve the crisis through diplomacy, rather than force. In October 1998, President Clinton dispatched Richard Holbrooke to seek a cease-fire in Kosovo. While the details of Holbrooke's demands were complicated, the most important feature was that they required Milošević to cease offensive activities in Kosovo and to pull back his troops from all areas of the province that had been occupied since the upsurge in fighting in early 1998. In addition, the Yugoslav authorities had to allow an international mission to supervise the troop pullback.[76]

At the outset, it must be emphasized that the US position was asymmetrical, since it placed all the blame on the Serbs for the upsurge in fighting. Any pretense that the United States was an evenhanded mediator now disappeared. And there was little in the US effort that could even be called mediation. Instead, Holbrooke offered Milošević an ultimatum: He must accept terms or the United States would bomb Serbia. To emphasize the point, the US dispatched the NATO commander, General Clark, along with a German officer, Gen. Klaus Naumann, who both met with Milošević.[77] The generals sought to underscore NATO's seriousness of intent. In memoirs, Clark described his statement to Milošević: "Mr. President, you are going to have to withdraw all your excess forces [from Kosovo]. . . . If you don't withdraw, Washington is going to tell me to bomb you, and I'm going to bomb you good."[78]

The Serb Pullback

The terms put before Milošević were certainly humiliating, but the Serb leader accepted them, and the pullback plan was announced during late October.[79] The KLA publicly condemned the Holbrooke agreement, since it made no offer of independence; but the agreement was to prove quite beneficial to the Albanian guerrillas.[80] After signing, Milošević withdrew most of his forces from Kosovo and permitted international monitoring, as required. The Organization for Security and Cooperation in Europe (OSCE), a Cold War–era international organization, fielded a multinational force of two thousand unarmed personnel, directed by a US diplomat with extensive experience in combat zones, William Walker. The OSCE Kosovo Verification Mission proceeded to monitor compliance with the Holbrooke agreement.[81]

Though Western officials would later accuse Milošević of undermining the agreement, these accusations were not accurate.[82] In fact, Milošević did initially comply. This compliance is confirmed by General Naumann, who was a central figure in the diplomacy of this period. Appearing as a prosecution witness at the International Criminal Tribunal for the Former Yugoslavia in 2002, General Naumann stated that *the Yugoslav authorities honored the [Holbrooke] agreement. . . .* I think one has to really pay tribute to what the Yugoslav authorities did. This was not an easy thing to bring 6,000 police officers back within 24 hours, but they managed" (emphasis added).[83] Naumann's views are supported by the Independent International Commission on Kosovo, which noted: "Serbia initially implemented the [Holbrooke] agreement and withdrew its forces accordingly."[84]

Two problems emerged with the agreement. First, the Kosovo Liberation Army used the Serb restraint as an opportunity to launch a new offensive. A key limitation of the Holbrooke agreement was that it made explicit demands only on the Serbs, while the KLA guerrillas, who rejected the accord, met no demands at all. This loophole worked to the advantage of the KLA. And once again, the guerrillas engaged their long-standing practice of attacking isolated Serb outposts as a strategy of provocation. This strategy is noted in the following exchange between a BBC interviewer and General Naumann:

> BBC: We've obtained confidential minutes of the North Atlantic Council or NAC, NATO's governing body. The talk was of *the KLA as the "main initiator of the violence. . . .* It launched what appears to be a *deliberate campaign of provocation* [against the Serbs]." This is how William Walker [head of the OSCE Verification Mission] himself reported the situation then, in private.

> Gen. Naumann: Ambassador Walker stated in the NAC that the majority of violations [of the Holbrooke agreement] was caused by the KLA. [emphases added][85]

Similarly, the *Washington Post* noted that after the Serb pullback, the "KLA intended to draw NATO into its fight . . . by provoking Serb forces into further atrocities."[86] Henry Kissinger estimated that "80 percent of the cease-fire violations [between October 1998 and February 1999] were committed by the KLA."[87] An Albanian military commander later conceded that "the cease fire was very useful for us."[88]

In short, it was the KLA, not the Serbs, who were undermining the Holbrooke agreement. On November 1, Serb officials urged the West "to put pressure on ethnic Albanian rebels" in order to force the guerrillas to cease their attacks.[89] Such entreaties had little effect. The KLA offensive continued, and it soon goaded the Serb/Yugoslav forces into launching a counter-offensive. This period involved an intensification of the war, as the Serbs were now determined to pursue a military solution. The effect was brutal, leading to several mass killings in insurgent-controlled regions of Kosovo; and these atrocities, in turn, drove large numbers of Albanian civilians from their homes. The Holbrooke agreement became irrelevant at this point, as the fighting intensified.

A second problem with regard to the agreement was that the OSCE mission was highly politicized. In theory this mission was to consist of "neutral observers" who monitored the extent of compliance or noncompliance with the agreement.[90] In reality, some of the observers were covert CIA officers, who quietly advanced the agenda of the KLA (and in doing so, compromised the impartiality of the verification mission). According to the London *Sunday Times*: "American intelligence agents [associated with the OSCE mission] have admitted they helped to train the Kosovo Liberation Army," which included offering "field advice" on how best to fight the Serbs. One CIA officer with the OSCE mission commented: "I'd tell them [the KLA fighters] which hill to avoid, which wood to go behind, that sort of thing."[91] And the *Wall Street Journal* reported that the KLA received "official NATO/US arms and training support."[92] Secretary of State Albright strongly implied US support for the Albanian guerrillas in an interview with the BBC:

> BBC: "There was no clear mechanism to punish them [the KLA] if they failed to behave in what you call a reasonable way?"
>
> Albright: "Well I think the punishment was that they would *lose* completely the backing of the United States and the Contact Group." [emphasis added][93]

When the OSCE left Kosovo in March 1999, the intelligence operatives gave the KLA their "satellite telephones and global positioning systems" so that the "guerrilla commanders could stay in touch with NATO and Washington," according to the *Sunday Times*; this tactic would aid coordination between US and KLA forces once the war began, shortly after the OSCE departure. It is also interesting to note that "several KLA leaders had the mobile phone number of Gen. Wesley Clark, the NATO commander."[94] The United States now became a direct ally of the Kosovo Liberation Army, whose guerrillas would function, in effect, as NATO ground forces once the air strikes commenced.

The upsurge in fighting was undoubtedly a disaster for the Albanian population of Kosovo, and tens of thousands of refugees were generated by the Serbs' counterinsurgency sweeps through large areas of Kosovo. In guerrilla campaigns throughout history, civilian populations are often integrated to some extent into combat activities, when they provide food and shelter to the combatants. This was clearly true of the Kosovo war, where the Albanian population was overwhelmingly supportive of the insurgency. In other cases "Albanian civilians were press ganged into service" by the KLA, according to the British Broadcasting Corporation.[95] The Serbs, for their part, used classic counterinsurgency techniques, which included attacks against civilians that supported the KLA.[96] A series of massacres resulted. The most famous massacre, which was to play an important role in the lead-up to war, occurred in the village of Račak, where Serb security forces killed forty-eight Albanians in January 1999.[97] A report by Human Rights Watch noted: "It is possible that some of these men were defending their village" earlier in the day, prior to the massacre. "However, they clearly did not resist the [Serb] police at the time of capture or execution." The report concluded that the Račak victims had been "arbitrarily killed."[98]

The Rambouillet Peace Conference

US officials gave considerable attention to the Račak massacre and demanded international action to end the fighting. The result was a Contact Group–directed peace conference at Rambouillet, outside Paris, during February 1999.[99] This conference involved negotiations between an Albanian delegation led by Hashim Thaçi, a KLA military commander, and a Yugoslav government delegation led by Milan Milutinović, a Serb politician. The agenda for the conference was preestablished by a series of draft settlement plans that called for a restoration of Kosovo's autonomy (revoked by Serbia in 1989), combined with an armed peacekeeping force to police the accord. Kosovar autonomy was to exist within the Federal Republic of Yugoslavia. No secession was initially contemplated.[100]

The conference cochairs were British foreign minister Robin Cook and

French foreign minister Hubert Védrine. It was necessary to give European nations prominent roles in directing the conference; at least for public purposes, the United States was relegated to a secondary role. This strategy sought to assuage European governments, which had been so offended by US dominance at the 1995 Dayton conference. In his remarks officially opening the talks, Foreign Minister Cook went out of his way to emphasize the international and European—rather than American—component of the conference:

> We meet with the authority of the Security Council, the support of the European Union and the OSCE, and the backing of NATO. We are here as representatives of the Contact Group, and of the two sides in the conflict in Kosovo; ... today Britain and France preside jointly over these talks—a symbol of the strong partnership which we have forged. ... Throughout the talks Hubert Védrine and I will be reporting to our colleagues [of the Contact Group] in Italy, the United States, and Russia, as well as Germany, which has a particularly important role as presidency of the European Union.[101]

Pretenses aside, there is little doubt that the Europeans' high profile at Rambouillet was mostly for show. Behind the scenes, the United States dominated the conference. A retrospective account by James Rubin, the State Department spokesperson, left little doubt that US officials, led by Albright, molded the conference agenda and the ultimate outcome, while they sidelined European objections.[102] The proposed agreement that was initially pushed on both the Serb and the Albanian delegations was "largely a product of US envoy Christopher Hill," according to the *Boston Globe*.[103] While speaking with the press, US officials at the conference criticized the ability of European mediators (particularly Cook) and undercut their effectiveness.[104]

It is also important to note that the conference organizers, especially the United States, began with a strong predilection in favor of the Albanian perspective and against the Serbs.[105] US negotiators made it clear to the Serbs that they would be bombed if they declined what the Americans believed to be an acceptable agreement. On February 14, in her first press briefing on the Rambouillet talks, Secretary Albright warned: "The threat of NATO air strikes remains real."[106] If the KLA refused an agreement, the only danger to them was that the United States might undercut their international support; there was no threat of military action.[107]

The Serb delegation for their part negotiated with some degree of seriousness. Toward the end of the conference, the Serbs "seemed to have embraced the political elements of the settlement, at least in principle," according to Marc Weller, who served as an advisor to the Albanian delegation.[108] State Department official Rubin claims that the Serbs had agreed to "nearly every aspect of the political agreement."[109] Even Albright, though hyper-critical of the Serb delegation, acknowledged that they had accepted most of the proposals for a political settlement.[110] These political elements included regional autonomy for Kosovo and an end to repression. With regard to the more contentious implementation aspects, Milošević himself implied that he would accept a peacekeeping force in Kosovo to supervise the agreement, led by either the United Nations or the OSCE (though he continued to resist the idea of a NATO-led force, which the United States demanded).[111] Over-all, the Serb delegation adopted a flexible negotiating stance at Rambouillet. Later claims that the Serbs were intransigent—and that they "refused even to entertain" the possibility of a negotiated settlement[112]—are inconsistent with the record of events.

A key point of contention emerged on February 23, however, when the Contact Group mediators presented the full text of the proposed agree-ment. This text contained a Military Annex ("Annex B"), which introduced a fundamentally new demand on the Yugoslav government—and which ulti-mately doomed the peace talks. It called for the following: "NATO person-nel [in the proposed Kosovo peacekeeping force] shall enjoy, together with their vehicles, vessels, aircraft, and equipment, free and unrestricted passage and unimpeded access throughout the FRY [Federal Republic of Yugosla-via]."[113] This section was highly significant, since it meant that a NATO peacekeeping force would occupy not only Kosovo, but also potentially all of Serbia and all that remained of Yugoslavia. Milošević and other FRY of-ficials repeatedly objected to the Military Annex.[114] Many non-Serbs also found fault with the Annex. A British parliamentary investigation later con-cluded that the Military Annex "would never have been acceptable to the Yugoslav side, since it was a significant infringement on its sovereignty."[115] MIT analyst Barry Posen, writing in *International Security,* noted: "The clause [contained in the Military Annex] is to say the least undiplomatic, and its introduction into the accords raises questions about either the wis-dom or the motives of whoever introduced it."[116] Kissinger observed that the proposed Rambouillet accord was "not a document that even an angelic Serb could have accepted. It was a terrible diplomatic document that should never have been presented in that form."[117]

An obvious question is raised: Why did the Military Annex contain the offending clause, which sought to open the whole of Yugoslavia to NATO occupation? One interpretation is that the wording was simply an act of in-competence by some of the Western negotiators (or in the words of the Brit-ish parliamentary investigation, "a serious blunder").[118] This interpretation seems doubtful. In his memoirs, General Clark reveals that he personally assisted in writing the Annex. By all accounts, Clark has a reputation for meticulous staff work and attention to detail.[119] He was not the type to engage in obvious blunders. A more likely interpretation is that the Military Annex was part of a larger strategy orchestrated by the United States to block any possibility of a diplomatic settlement, and thus to create a pretext for war. Kissinger noted that the Rambouillet conference was "an excuse to start bombing."[120]

New Evidence That the Peace Talks Were Sabotaged

We now have confirmation from a key participant that elements in the Contact Group intentionally "forced Slobodan Milošević into a war."[121] Former UK defense minister of state John Gilbert made this point in a parliamentary hearing in 2000; Gilbert was the chief of intelligence in the Ministry of Defense during the Kosovo war, and a supporter of that war. His comments have not been challenged or contradicted by any other official. With regard to the motives of the Contact Group negotiators, he offered this observation: "I think certain people were spoiling for a fight in NATO at that time; . . . we were at a point when some people felt that something had to be done [against Serbia], so *you just provoked a fight.*" With regard to the peace terms themselves, Gilbert was unequivocal: "I think the terms put to Milošević at Rambouillet were absolutely intolerable: How could he possibly accept them[?] *It was quite deliberate*" (emphases added).[122]

Lord Gilbert did not specifically mention the Military Annex (and its clause about NATO access to all of Yugoslavia); but it is easy to see that the Annex fit in well with the overall picture of provocation that Gilbert described. In any case, the Military Annex effectively undermined the peace talks. Until its advent, the negotiators had made significant progress toward an agreement. When the Military Annex appeared, however, the Serbs seemed to lose all interest in the negotiations.[123] In Weller's view, "the Belgrade government had changed its initially moderately positive assessment" of the negotiations after the Annex was put forth.[124] The general atmosphere is nicely captured by an incident during follow-up negotiations in Paris, which took place in mid-March. When the Contact Group mediators approached the Serb delegation, the Serbs responded: "Have you come to fuck us again?"[125] No real progress could be made at that point. It was clear that negotiations had irretrievably broken down, leading to the NATO war of March–June 1999.

The chronology of events suggests that the United States was eager for military action. Why this emphasis on force instead of diplomacy? A "humanitarian" war in Kosovo had the advantage of drawing the NATO allies together, thus reducing the tensions over trade and financial issues, which threatened to rupture the alliance. Government officials and commentators repeatedly mentioned these motives during the lead-up to war. In arguing the case for war, National Security Advisor Samuel Berger acknowledged that one of the main motivations for war was "to demonstrate that NATO is serious."[126] The need to reaffirm NATO's importance, combined with the collapse of peace talks, set the stage for an air war against Serbia.

Humanitarianism and US Policy

Let us now consider at greater length the argument that US and NATO policy was motivated primarily by humanitarian considerations. Milošević, according to this view, was an aggressive and exceptionally warlike leader, a threat to the whole Balkan region. With regard to Kosovo, "we're talking about the fourth war which Mr. Milošević ordered his forces to unleash," according to General Naumann.[127] It was also widely believed that Milošević was an irrational figure, "detached from reality," possibly due to psychiatric disturbances.[128] This interpretation argues that the United States was morally obligated to protect the Kosovar Albanians from violence and persecution, which were being directed by the Serb leader. The problem with such views is that they overstate Milošević's uglier characteristics; they exaggerate to an almost cartoonish extent. Milošević did not single-handedly trigger the previous wars in Slovenia, Croatia, and Bosnia-Herzegovina, as we have seen. Other leaders, such as Franjo Tudjman, played major roles in causing Yugoslavia's dissolution and the wars that followed. And we have no serious evidence that Milošević was acting irrationally.

In the case of Kosovo, both sides must bear responsibility for the upsurge in fighting. Even Tony Blair acknowledged (in private) that "the KLA ... were not much better than the Serbs."[129] To argue that the Serbs alone were responsible is surely a distortion. And it is also a distortion to argue that Milošević was incapable of negotiating in good faith: He was perfectly capable of reaching agreements—and enforcing those agreements—when it was in his interest to do so.[130] In Kosovo for example, he initially implemented the terms of the Holbrooke agreement in the fall of 1998. The agreement broke down primarily because of *Albanian* attacks against Serbs, and this point is widely recognized. Overall, the allegation that Milošević was the sole cause of the fighting appears inconsistent with the record of events.

Yet another allegation was that Milošević had a long-standing scheme to expel virtually the entire Albanian population, and that NATO intervention was thus needed to protect the Albanians. The main support for these claims was a revelation by German Defense Ministry officials that they had discovered a secret Serb plan, code-named Operation Horseshoe. This plan, supposedly crafted by the Serb military in 1998, called for the general removal of ethnic Albanians from Kosovo. The existence of this Serb plan was first widely reported in early April 1999 during the NATO air war, and it elicited extensive interest.[131] Critically, it was emphasized that Horseshoe was not a contingency plan, but a firm intention to expel the Albanians; it was to be implemented whether or not NATO commenced bombing.

In fact, the Horseshoe allegations were based on very thin evidence, and it now seems doubtful that such a plan ever existed. After the war was over, German brigadier general Heinz Loquai revealed that the whole operation was "fabricated from run-of-the-mill Bulgarian intelligence reports." General Loquai claimed that German officials "turned a vague report from Sofia into a 'plan,' and even coined the name Horseshoe."[132] Loquai also noted that German officials had misrepresented the contents of the Bulgarian reports, which actually emphasized Serb plans to destroy the KLA, not the Albanian population more generally. When considered in retrospect, Operation Horseshoe looks like fairly standard wartime propaganda.[133]

And finally, it was widely alleged that the Serbs had committed genocide in Kosovo. In a public speech on March 23, 1999, President Clinton cited the genocide argument as one of his main justifications for the 1999 NATO war.[134] Since the end of the war, however, this claim also has lost credibility. In fact, international tribunals (quietly) determined that the Kosovo atrocities did *not* qualify as genocide. At the International Criminal Tribunal for the Former Yugoslavia, for example, none of the three separate indictments against Milošević mentioned the crime of genocide with respect to Kosovo. In each of the three documents of indictment, Milošević was accused of committing various crimes in Kosovo—but the word "genocide" appeared nowhere.[135] Apparently, the case for genocide was sufficiently weak that not even the prosecution wished to pursue the matter. And in a separate 2001 case, the UN-directed Supreme Court of Kosovo concluded that Serb atrocities "were not genocide."[136]

Serb Atrocities in Perspective

It is of course indisputable that Serb forces committed atrocious acts in Kosovo—including systematic attacks against civilians who sympathized with the KLA—and that these attacks occurred both before and after the NATO bombing. Even if we leave aside the provocative accusation that Serb crimes amounted to genocide, the crimes that *did* occur were terrible enough. At the Milošević trial, Lord Ashdown emphasized the Serbs' "excessive, outrageous" use of force during counterinsurgency sweeps.[137] There is no doubt that the Serbs used excessive force in Kosovo, and such actions deserve condemnation.[138]

As a justification for Western intervention, however, the "excessive force" argument seems questionable. Compared with other counterinsurgency wars, the Serb actions in Kosovo were relatively mild. During the period up to the start of the NATO air war, the total number of deaths on both sides (both military and civilian) was two thousand.[139] The number of Albanian civilians killed by Serb forces has never been estimated precisely, but it was probably in the range of several hundred. This surely is a ghastly figure, but it is *not* large for a counterinsurgency war. Charges of mass murder, at least during this phase, were greatly overstated. In Kosovo, there also was a substantial number of refugees generated by the fighting, which totaled about 200,000 by March 1999.[140] But refugee flows are common during counterinsurgencies, including several conducted by members of the Contact Group that organized the Rambouillet conference. If one considers the US war in Vietnam, the French in Algeria, the British in Kenya, the Russians in Afghanistan—or even the recent US-led counterinsurgency in Iraq—the Kosovo case does not stand out for its atrocities. When compared with other wars, the Serb methods of counterinsurgency do not seem unusually cruel or extreme.

To gain some historical perspective, let us consider a more detailed comparison. The case I have chosen for comparison is a counterinsurgency campaign conducted on Cheju Island in South Korea during 1948–1949. The Cheju case involved an uprising by a left-wing People's Army that was repressed by central government security forces and their associated militias. Cheju Island had some features in common with Kosovo and is thus a useful comparison case. As in Kosovo, in the Cheju rebellion the insurgents had overwhelming support from the local inhabitants, who opposed the central government. The duration of the fighting in Cheju—more than a year at its peak—was comparable to that of the war in Kosovo. Cheju was a small and geographically isolated area; with only about 250,000 people, it was much less populated than Kosovo. Regarding the extent of killings in Cheju during the counterinsurgency, Bruce Cumings provides this account: "American sources estimate that 15,000 to 20,000 islanders died, but the ROK [South Korean government] official figure was 27,719. The North said that more than 30,000 islanders had been 'butchered' in the suppression. The governor of Cheju, however, privately told American intelligence that 60,000 had died. . . . In other words, one in every five or six islanders had perished."[141] This description of the Cheju case gives some sense of what a truly unrestrained counterinsurgency against a relatively small population looks like. The brutality in Kosovo did not reach this level, or anything close to it. The exceptional attention paid to the atrocities in Kosovo must be considered, at least in part, a result of media sensationalism and governmental exaggeration.

Overall, the argument in favor of a humanitarian motivation for US policy is unpersuasive. As we have seen, the United States supported the Kosovo Liberation Army, despite its unsavory record. And when the KLA sought to undermine the Holbrooke agreement, and did so with success, the United States declined to restrain the guerrillas. Indeed, the United States began providing direct military aid to the KLA, thus rewarding the guerrillas for triggering an upsurge in fighting. At Rambouillet, the United States took actions that virtually guaranteed a collapse of the peace talks and made war inevitable. According to Lord Gilbert, such actions were taken deliberately, with the intent of scuttling the peace talks. The US insistence on using war as a solution to ethnic conflict in Kosovo—well before it had exhausted possible diplomatic solutions—seems inconsistent with a humanitarian intent. And we shall see that US actions during and after the NATO air war, which greatly increased civilian suffering, seem even less comprehensible from a humanitarian perspective.

The Politics of War

> There was a series of strained telephone calls between
> Albright and [UK foreign minister] Cook, in which [Cook]
> cited problems "with our lawyers" over using force in
> the absence of UN endorsement. "Get new lawyers," she
> suggested.
>
> —*James Rubin, State Department spokesperson*

After the collapse of peace talks, in mid-March, the United States prepared for war.[142] Within the Clinton administration, a near consensus gradually emerged that a war was essential to preserve US and NATO credibility. It also was recognized that the Kosovo crisis offered an important opportunity: A successful NATO war against Serbia would prove an ideal context in which to sell Europe on the New Strategic Concept. And from a negative standpoint, if the United States failed to impose its will in Kosovo, the results would damage US credibility in Europe and thus weaken the alliance.[143] Albright would emphasize the issue of NATO credibility in inter-bureaucratic arguments, and this had considerable effect.[144] Even Defense Secretary Cohen, who was a skeptic about using force, was worried about the NATO factor.[145] From Congress, longtime supporters of the Albanian lobby generated backing for the administration, even among the Republican majorities in each house. There was still significant opposition to war from the uniformed military, which distrusted the Democratic president and feared the possibility of a quagmire. But the military was no longer able, by itself, to prevent war.

Outside the United States, there existed a widespread perception that the United States was excessively eager to resolve the Kosovo problem through military as opposed to diplomatic means. There was considerable tension between the United States and the other five members of the Contact Group. Even the normally loyal British were skeptical of America's Kosovo policy (although the Blair government would later shift to a hawkish position on this issue).[146] In a memoir, State Department spokesperson Rubin writes:

> Nearly all our allies including the British, put roadblocks in the way of decisive action prior to the Rambouillet peace conference in 1999. . . . [During 1998] the Russians blamed the Albanian "terrorists" for stirring up trouble and called on us to punish the rebels. Some ministers, especially the German foreign minister Klaus Kinkel argued for unity with the Russians, the equivalent of no action at all. Italy did not want to give up its lucrative business dealings with neighboring Serbia. . . . [Later, during the Rambouillet talks] the Europeans were still riddled with doubts about the Albanians. . . . The Italians were now collaborating with the Serbs to end the conference on Belgrade's terms; . . . the French were sabotaging our efforts to bring the Albanians on board.[147]

Other sources have corroborated the general picture that Rubin presents of friction among the NATO allies.[148] In dealing with its allies, the United States thus faced a dilemma. On the one hand, it sought to project the image of a strong America, ready to furnish disinterested leadership to Europe and the world with regard to the Balkan crisis. On the other hand, the methods that the United States used to achieve this goal—which involved belittling European diplomatic efforts—risked irreparable damage to its relations with key allies. There was the associated risk that such incidents might cause the Europeans to break with the United States and reject its leadership.

There was thus a real danger that the Kosovo crisis might result in public recriminations among the NATO members (as had occurred during the Bosnia war and had nearly torn NATO apart). Several fortuitous events prevented this from happening: First, a series of financial scandals weakened the central decision-making body of the European Union, the European Commission, and, on March 16, 1999, EU Commission president Jacques Santer was forced to resign, along with all of the other Commission members.[149] The EU executive was thus immobilized during a key period in the diplomacy over Kosovo. Second, there was a temporary rift between France and Germany. In March 1999, the *Economist* noted: "The corridors of power were abuzz with French complaints of German incompetence and arrogance; the Germans were bemoaning France's habitual intransigence."[150] Since Franco-German cooperation had long been the political motor of the European Union, the tensions between the two countries further weakened the overall European position.

Thus, the European Union was sidelined, and it played no significant independent role in the Balkan diplomacy of this period. With regard to Kosovo itself, not a single EU member state publicly opposed the US position. Even the French agreed to participate in the planned air war. The Europeans did not wish to be blamed for any upsurge in fighting (as had occurred during the Bosnia war), and they were unable to craft a unified alternative to the US policy of waging war against Yugoslavia. NATO, in contrast, emerged even stronger than before.

The only difficulty was that, outside Western Europe, active opposition remained. Both China and Russia threatened to use their vetoes against any effort to gain Security Council support for military action. The United States responded by simply going forward without UN approval. The principal argument in favor of such action was that the humanitarian emergency in Kosovo was "overwhelming in character and required an emergency response," and that such considerations must outweigh any legalistic concerns about UN approval.[151] The difficulty with this interpretation was that it depended on a definition of the Kosovo case as an "overwhelming" emergency; this was a very elastic category, to say the least. Some two thousand people had died in the Kosovo war; by this standard, almost any military conflict could be considered an overwhelming case that required immediate action.

From the US standpoint, the decision to go to war without UN approval was quite useful: It established a precedent which said, in effect, that any time the United States and its allies *believed* a severe humanitarian emergency existed, they could bypass the UN Security Council. And since there would always be conflicts that presented humanitarian crises as bad as or worse than the one in Kosovo, NATO could invoke this precedent and go to war—without UN approbation—whenever it wished. The Kosovo precedent thus removed a significant constraint on US hegemony, one that was increasingly viewed as a nuisance.[152]

The war, now called Operation Allied Force, officially commenced on March 24, when NATO planes began bombing targets in Kosovo and Serbia. The operation was directed by General Clark, the NATO military commander. In directing the war, General Clark worked closely with Javier Solana, a Spanish diplomat who was secretary-general of NATO.[153] The collaboration between these two men nicely symbolized the multinational character of the operation, though no one could doubt that the United States was really in charge: Some 70 percent of the aircraft that participated in the bombing were from the United States.[154]

The initial results of the war were disappointing to NATO planners. Most Western officials expected Serb capitulation within days.[155] Their adversaries, however, responded with a degree of ingenuity that frustrated this objective. The Serbs had consulted extensively with the Iraqi military, which had gained much experience fighting the United States during the 1991 Gulf War. Based on these consultations, the Serbs made effective use of their antiaircraft weapons, and these posed a threat to low-flying NATO planes. The Serb army also camouflaged its armored vehicles and ground equipment, which protected them from the air strikes. In addition, NATO was hampered by having opted for a conservative strategy: No casualties among the NATO forces would be acceptable. Given the declared unwillingness to risk the lives of its flyers and an effective Serb defense, NATO abandoned low-altitude bombing runs shortly after the war began. Thereafter, most air strikes were conducted at an altitude of about fifteen thousand feet, too high to inflict much damage to Serb positions.[156] Inside Kosovo, the KLA continued their ground attacks to support the air strikes, but these combined operations failed to achieve a Serb capitulation. There was no quick victory.

Another problem was that the NATO air strikes could not protect Albanian civilians on the ground in Kosovo. Indeed, the NATO war triggered new Serb attacks, which were directed against virtually the entire Albanian population. The result was a massive wave of ethnic cleansing—much larger than any previous wave—which the Serbs orchestrated as a form of ethnic revenge. According to the *Economist*: "Reports from the war zone . . . suggested *a close correlation between the intensity of NATO's air strikes and the brutality of the Serbs' repression*—but not of the kind NATO intended. On May 3rd, for example, NATO claimed its 'most successful' day of bombing so far, with attacks on tanks and artillery in Kosovo and about 40 fixed targets elsewhere in Serbia. On the same day, an exceptionally brutal round of ethnic cleansing was carried out by the Serbs, with sickening atrocities reported" (emphasis added).[157]

There can be little doubt that NATO's air campaign worsened the ethnic cleansing. And the effects were considerable: During the course of the war,

March–June 1999, some 850,000 ethnic Albanians, approximately half the population, were forced out of Kosovo. This was a level of expulsion four times higher than that caused by the ethnic cleansing that had preceded the bombing. If one also considers expulsions that occurred within Kosovo's borders, the figure is even more substantial. All told, some 90 percent of the Albanian population had been displaced by the end of the war.[158]

The Serb forces must, of course, bear the primary moral responsibility for orchestrating this calamity.[159] However, NATO must bear some of the blame, for creating a situation that virtually guaranteed ethnic cleansing. Indeed, the US military had foreseen that the air war might cause augmented atrocities. During the lead-up to war, Gen. Hugh Shelton, chair of the Joint Chiefs of Staff, briefed President Clinton and his cabinet about possible atrocities, and this briefing was paraphrased in the London *Sunday Times*: "There was a danger, he [General Shelton] told them, that far from helping to contain the savagery of the Serbs in Kosovo . . . air strikes might provoke Serb soldiers into greater acts of butchery. Air strikes alone . . . could not stop Serb forces from executing Kosovars."[160]

The continued NATO failures, and the sense that the war was taking interminably long, generated political tensions within the alliance by the end of April 1999. That the atrocities were *increasing*, not decreasing, obviously made matters worse for NATO planners. The prospect of a short war followed by a Serb capitulation now looked like wishful thinking and miscalculation. To be sure, none of the NATO states openly opposed the war effort, as this would have been excessively provocative toward the United States. The NATO fiftieth-anniversary celebrations went ahead as planned during late April, and the New Strategic Concept was formally approved.[161] But the event was "extraordinarily somber," according to the *Financial Times*, given the lack of success in Kosovo.[162] If the war continued much longer there was the risk of an open breach within NATO.

Important elements of the European establishment began to openly express hostility toward US policy. Former chancellor Helmut Schmidt stated that Germans were held "on a leash by the Americans," and that Germany had "violated international law and the Charter of the United Nations" with its participation in Operation Allied Force. From France, former interior minister Charles Pasqua objected that NATO "has become the de facto department of diplomacy, defense, and security in Europe."[163] From Italy, Left-leaning parliamentarians threatened to withdraw from the coalition government in protest against the bombing.[164] Interallied tensions also began to reappear with regard to economic issues, and to do so with an unpleasant tone. On May 8, the *Economist* noted:

Trade relations between America and Europe have rarely been so bad. Even as they fight side-by-side against Serbia, they are taking aim at each other across the Atlantic. They are embroiled in a battle over hormone-treated beef. They are at loggerheads over genetically modified crops. They have fallen out over noisy aircraft, mobile telephones and data privacy. They are coming to blows over aerospace subsidies and champagne. And they have yet to patch up their split over bananas; . . . transatlantic trade tiffs are nothing new. . . . But this is different. The mood in both Washington and Brussels is resentful and uncompromising. Events could easily get out of hand.[165]

The prospect of failure in Kosovo risked not only embarrassment for NATO, but also an intensification of more basic interallied feuds over a wide range of areas. In addition, Russia and China gradually increased their criticism of NATO conduct; in the Russian press, there was talk of "a new Cold War."[166]

The NATO response to these problems was twofold. One strategy was to step up the campaign to publicize Serb atrocities and to exaggerate them. We have already noted the effects of the alleged Operation Horseshoe. According to the London *Times* account of Horseshoe, the ethnic cleansings that occurred after March 23 "were premeditated and *not a reaction to the air strikes*" (emphasis added). The *Times* added: "The Horseshoe Plan appears to have dispelled any lingering pacifist doubts among Western leaders" regarding the soundness of the bombing campaign.[167] The publicity about Horseshoe helped ease Western concern that the bombing itself might have triggered the expulsions. The only problem was that the whole Horseshoe story was "a fake"[168]—but this was not revealed until the war was over.

In addition, US defense secretary Cohen claimed that 100,000 Albanians were "missing" and "may have been murdered." This was quickly picked up by the world's press, which reported that 100,000 had in fact been murdered.[169] Not to be outdone, another US official, David Scheffer, stated that 225,000 Albanians were missing, again with the insinuation that they might have been murdered. Scheffer dramatically compared Serb atrocities in Kosovo with the mass killings perpetrated by the Khmer Rouge in Cambodia and the Hutu militias in Rwanda.[170] After the war was over, these casualty figures were generally regarded as substantial overstatements. Recent forensic investigations of mass graves have turned up little to substantiate the higher death tolls implied by Cohen and others. Current estimates of Albanian deaths are in the range of 10,000.[171] At the time of the bombing, however, exaggerated atrocity stories silenced criticisms of Operation Allied Force.

A second and more important NATO response to criticism was to inten-sify the bombing campaign. In May, the number of allied aircraft committed to the war effort more than doubled, while the list of potential targets was lengthened. The bombing during this phase "involved hitting [Serb] civil-ian infrastructure," according to Gen. Rupert Smith, deputy NATO com-mander.[172] Over the next weeks, power plants, bridges, and factories were hit. A Zastava automobile plant was bombed, as was a Serb government television station and the Chinese embassy.[173] The air raids involved both high explosives and antipersonnel cluster bombs.[174] While the sorties did remarkably little damage to the Serb military, there can be no question that they increased the number of civilian casualties.[175] And the casualties from this phase of the air war included Albanians in Kosovo.[176]

There was also discussion of further escalation of the war effort, if the Serbs failed to come to terms. While NATO officials remained skittish about committing ground troops, serious consideration was given to waging an unrestricted air war, with the intention of demolishing Serbia's cities.[177] The extent of the planned bombing escalation was implied in the columns of Thomas Friedman, with his normally excellent official contacts. It seems likely that Friedman was speaking for elements of the Clinton administra-tion when he wrote with enthusiasm about the need to bomb Serbia back to the Middle Ages.[178] According to Posen: "Serbia faced . . . the possi-bility that its economic infrastructure would be systematically destroyed."[179] NATO had committed too much of its prestige to the war to contemplate losing, and it would go to considerable lengths to avoid this possibility.

To gain some historical perspective on what the planned escalation might have looked like, consider the Korean War, which entailed one of the most destructive bombardments in the history of warfare. Gen. Curtis LeMay later recalled that "we eventually burned down every town in North Korea . . . and some in South Korea too."[180] Another US general added: "Everything [in Korea] is destroyed. There is nothing left standing worthy of the name."[181] Clearly, the NATO bombing during the 1999 Kosovo war involved far more restraint than had existed in Korea. By the end of May, however, NATO planners seemed ready to forgo restraint and devastate Serbia.

In early June, the Milošević government agreed to a peace plan, and the war officially ended on June 10.[182] The reasons for the Serb willingness to end the war can be traced to three factors. First, there was the fear of fur-ther bombing escalations already noted.[183] Second, Russia ceased its diplo-matic support for Serbia and pressed its ally to end the stance of defiance. And third, NATO (quietly) agreed to compromise. The final agreement that ended the war differed from the one offered at Rambouillet with regard to a key point: US officials no longer insisted that all of Yugoslavia had to be occupied. The final agreement also provided for an end to repression in Kosovo, internal self-government, and a NATO-led occupation force.[184] Despite the compromised character of the final agreement, the war was widely viewed at the time—and is remembered—as a triumph for the Atlantic alliance.

The NATO occupation was to be implemented by a multinational Kosovo Force (KFOR), which was modeled to some extent on the peacekeeping force in charge of Bosnia-Herzegovina.[185] The UN Secretariat agreed to provide assistance to KFOR, especially in the areas of policing and civil administration.[186] It would appear that the United Nations sought accommodation with a newly victorious United States to make amends for its earlier defiance. In any case, the UN personnel surely added legitimacy of the Kosovo occupation, and thus deflected criticism.

The occupation forces granted special privileges to the Kosovo Liberation Army. According to the *Economist*: "NATO has struck a fairly generous deal with the KLA. Whereas Serbia was given 11 days to pull its large garrison and hundreds of pieces of heavy equipment out of Kosovo, the KLA has been granted at least 90 days to hand over its weapons. KLA fighters are given 'special consideration' by the UN when drawing up Kosovo's new police force." By September, "in most of Kosovo's towns and villages it is the KLA and its nominees in the 'parallel government' . . . who call the shots. In larger towns they are supposedly subject to the UN; in smaller ones not even that fiction is maintained."[187] It seemed that the United States—the real power behind the occupation—was rewarding the group that had served as its ground troops during the bombing. Having now placed the KLA in power in large parts of Kosovo, the occupation forces must bear some responsibility for the atrocities that followed.

The KLA used its newly privileged position to persecute the Serbs, as well as other minorities (notably the Roma) considered suspect by the Albanians. The resulting atrocities were tracked by the Organization for Security and Cooperation in Europe, and they are described as follows:

> The summer of 1999 was a season of vengeance and raw predatory violence. The OSCE collected dozens of horror stories. A deaf and mute Roma man was abducted from his home, because his family had allegedly cooperated with the former [Serb] authorities. A 44-year old Serb man was "beaten to death with metal sticks by a Kosovo Albanian mob." . . . Serbs were shot and killed while working in their fields. These attacks and dozens of others like them were reported by field staff working with the OSCE. *All these attacks occurred when NATO-led KFOR was responsible for security in Kosovo.* [emphasis added][188]

By February 2000, between four hundred and seven hundred Serbs were murdered, presumably by Albanian vigilantes.[189] These murders were effective in driving out most of the remaining Serbs.[190] These expulsions entailed a particularly distasteful aspect: Some of the fleeing Serbs had once inhabited the Krajina region of Croatia but had been ethnically cleansed during and after the Croat offensives of 1995; following their expulsion, these Krajina Serbs had resettled in Kosovo. Now they were being ethnically cleansed for a second time.[191] All told, almost a quarter of a million people—including Serbs, Roma, and other disfavored groups—fled Kosovo during the period after the war ended.[192] The KLA's long-sought objective of an ethnically "clean" Kosovo was achieved in at least some municipalities, especially in the central and southern regions. Such tactics helped ameliorate the long-standing problem of ethnic conflict in the province by creating new facts on the ground—albeit in a brutal way.

Conclusion

As a purported humanitarian war, Operation Allied Force had major limitations. NATO attacks killed between five hundred and two thousand civilians (and injured some six thousand).[193] Even if one accepts the lower estimate, the bombing killed approximately as many civilians as all the Serb-perpetrated attacks that preceded the bombing.[194] The level of Serb atrocities against Albanians increased on a vast scale after the NATO bombing began. Far from restraining Serb atrocities, the NATO bombing campaign appears to have intensified them. When the war ended, the scale of the disaster increased still further, due to the mass ethnic cleansings of Serbs and Roma, this time with the Albanians as perpetrators. If Operation Allied Force sought to establish the principle that ethnic cleansing is inadmissible as a means of settling conflicts, then the operation was a conspicuous failure.

On the more "positive" side, if there can be said to be a positive side, the war achieved some notable successes in its reaffirmation of US hegemony. The United States set a precedent that NATO could go to war virtually whenever it wished, without Security Council authorization. The Kosovo war also helped establish US dominance over Europe. The war showcased the military capabilities of the United States, which remained the most impressive feature of its power; this was a capability that Europe could not match. General Naumann commented that, in the future: "Europeans and Americans may no longer be able to fight alongside each other on the same battlefield."[195] The United States thus looked like a pillar of strength in contrast to European weakness. According to *Le Monde*, the Kosovo war was widely considered "a European—and a UN—humiliation, as well as a success for NATO."[196]

The subordination of European ambitions to US hegemony was symbolized by a shift of personnel. Shortly after the war ended, Javier Solana left his position as secretary-general of NATO to become the chief EU spokesperson for foreign and military policy. Solana's appointment to such a sensitive post showed that Europe would now "work closely with NATO," according to the London *Independent*.[197] Later, in November 1999, Solana was appointed secretary-general of the Western European Union (WEU), which now effectively became the European Union's military wing.[198]

The Kosovo victory offered additional benefits to US power. International tensions over trade issues—which had been so acute before and even during the war—receded in the wake of the military success.[199] President Clinton saw his international prestige soar after the war ended. And US forces gained a large and apparently permanent base in Kosovo, Camp Bondsteel, thus adding to America's "empire of bases" and satisfying the military's quest for bureaucratic expansion.[200] The US generals may not have wanted this war, but they gained from it nonetheless. Camp Bondsteel enhanced the already substantial US presence in southeastern Europe, providing augmented protection for planned pipelines into the region (which promised to open up resource-rich zones in the Caspian Sea area).[201] The Kosovo war also benefited corporate interests associated with the military-industrial complex, for the US victory created a much more favorable environment for lucrative weapons procurements. A May 1999 *New York Times* article provided this account: "America's weapons makers are already anticipating that Kosovo may help secure a strategic victory for them—not on the battlefield, but in Congress . . . Washington now seems inclined to increase outlays for weapons. . . . 'Kosovo has definitely changed things here on defense spending issues,' said Representative Duncan Hunter. . . . 'Kosovo underscores what the [military procurement] industry has been saying—that we need to get a sustainable rate of spending,' said Daniel T. Burnham, chief executive of the Raytheon Company."[202] When the war ended, *Business Week* noted that the weapons procurement budget was scheduled to increase "thanks partly to Kosovo."[203]

A range of interests in the US private sector thus benefited from the war. The war also generated benefits for the US state. During the course of the war, the value of the dollar rose significantly, while the dollar's principal adversary currency, the euro, declined. The image of a "strong" America and a "weak" Europe, which the war had helped to foster, probably contributed to the euro's drop. On May 31, *Barron's* financial weekly offered this assessment: "While the strength of the US economy relative to that of Europe is a major reason for the euro's weakness, *the war in Kosovo also is being blamed*" (emphasis added).[204] America's position as financial hegemon was bolstered.

But the main benefit of the Kosovo war was the reestablishment of the key institution of US hegemony in Europe, NATO. An *Irish Times* article noted: "For neutral countries in Europe, the conclusion is inescapable: NATO is the only military structure in the near future."[205] Even neutrals had to recognize that the European Union could no longer offer an alternative to American power. Thus, with its victory in Kosovo, the United States had beaten back a long-standing challenge. The future of US hegemony—with its myriad benefits for both the US state and private sector—was now assured.

8

Conclusion

War is a racket. It always has been.
—*Maj. Gen. Smedley Butler, US Marine Corps*

The concept of humanitarian interventionism has recently endured new challenges as a result of the 2003 US invasion of Iraq. Presented as a straightforward case of humanitarian intervention, the invasion was intended to "liberate the people of Iraq from a cruel and violent dictator," in the words of President George W. Bush.[1] Indeed, Bush's speeches during the lead-up to war contain numerous claims of America's humanitarian intent. True, the humanitarian justifications for war were not the only justifications; many security-based arguments also were advanced (such as the need to protect the United States against Saddam's weapons of mass destruction and terrorist connections, which later proved nonexistent). But overall, the war was presented as an idealistic action that advanced moral principles as well as US national interests; and it was supported as such by a wide range of liberal intellectuals.[2]

But the Iraq war has gone badly indeed, and the humanitarian effects of this particular intervention must be regarded as negative. In this context, some recall the earlier interventions in Yugoslavia with nostalgia. To state the matter simply, Yugoslavia is remembered as the "good war"—which achieved genuinely humanitarian outcomes—and it thus offers a welcome contrast with the Iraq fiasco. The Balkan nostalgia also results from electoral politics: Democratic politicians are drawing attention to the "successful" US bombing campaigns in Kosovo and Bosnia-Herzegovina as examples of how intervention should be undertaken. By emphasizing the positive aspects of these campaigns, Democrats are trying to show that they too are capable of using military force (with the implied additional claim that they can do so more effectively, more competently, and more humanely than their Republican opponents). But the benign image of the Balkan interventions extends well beyond Democratic circles, and it is bipartisan to a significant degree. The main purpose of this book has been to debunk this benign image, and to argue that it relies on a series of myths. In this conclusion, I briefly reconsider some of these myths.

The Effects of Intervention

When judging the merits of any humanitarian intervention, the main consideration must be the effects of intervention, that is, whether the intervention improved or worsened living conditions in the target country.[3] In Iraq, of course, the results have been disconcerting, as the US invasion of that country clearly worsened conditions, by any reasonable standard. There are many indicators of this failure, but the most salient is the annual death rate for Iraqis, which has increased significantly since the invasion.[4]

I have argued at length here that external intervention in Yugoslavia also produced negative effects, especially from a humanitarian standpoint. One important finding is that intervention helped create the conditions that led to war: In Chapter 3, we saw that the International Monetary Fund imposed draconian structural adjustment programs on Yugoslavia after 1979, which lowered living standards to depression levels. These conditions, in turn, generated political conflict, as citizens from various ethnic groups sought to blame scapegoats from rival groups for the country's problems; opportunistic politicians such as Slobodan Milošević sought to advance themselves by playing the ethnic card and thus exacerbated latent conflicts. The communal violence that resulted from structural adjustment produced tragic results.

Western governments were complicit in imposing these IMF programs. The US government seems to have played an especially important role in guiding the Fund's actions with regard to the Yugoslav federation and also more generally. US and IMF officials disregarded evidence that structural adjustment was producing destructive results.

In several instances, Western decision makers missed important opportunities to alleviate Yugoslavia's economic crisis and refused to ease up on their demands for austerity. In 1990, for example, Yugoslav prime minister Ante Marković urged the Bush administration to provide financial relief to his country, including a possible postponement of debt payments. External financial support at this crucial point could have reduced some of the worst effects of the economic crisis, and thus bolstered Marković and his multiethnic government. At the same time, debt relief would have undercut such demagogues as Milošević, who were taking advantage of the desperate conditions. It should be recalled that in 1990, Prime Minister Marković was the most popular politician in Yugoslavia, and he received high public opinion ratings throughout the federation. With outside financial support, he might have prevented the federation from breaking apart. Despite this, no debt relief was provided—and war was the result. The West's failure was noted by economist Jeffrey Sachs, who served as an economic advisor to Yugoslavia during this period. According to Sachs, the international community "made no effort of any sophistication to help hold the country [Yugoslavia] together."[5]

In addition to structural adjustment, there were more direct forms of Western intervention. Germany secretly helped Croatian nationalists establish an intelligence service, presumably as a prelude to secession. Serb propaganda would later emphasize Germany's role, but in this case the propaganda contained a large element of truth. The covert German role has been confirmed by accounts in British and US military publications (see Chapter 4). In taking these actions, Germany sought to advance its economic and political standing in Eastern Europe. And we saw that State Department official Lawrence Eagleburger, for his part, quietly informed Slovene nationalists that the United States would take no action to oppose secession. These actions contributed directly to Slovenia's and Croatia's later decisions to separate from the federation, which triggered open combat.

As the war began, the Yugoslav National Army sought to use force to stop the secession of Slovenia (and the force used was minimal, with twenty-three Slovenes killed). We saw that the Yugoslav Army still retained its multiethnic identity during this phase of the war, and it was not yet Serb dominated. In taking military action, the army initially worked in concert with Prime Minister Marković and sought to preserve national unity. And we saw that, with regard to secession, international precedent and law had long endorsed the right of central governments to use force, as a last resort, to preserve national unity. The army was acting in accord with accepted practice for dealing with matters of secession. This body of precedent was disregarded, however, as the United States and the major states of Europe condemned the Yugoslav Army for using force. Partly because of these condemnations, federal troops withdrew from Slovenia—which guaranteed the full disintegration of Yugoslavia and the beginning of a wider war.

It is easy to see that the Western states could have had a very different policy that might have produced more humane results. If the United States and the European states had refrained from giving moral support to secessionists in Yugoslavia and insisted that any breakaway republic would be internationally isolated, it seems unlikely that Croatia and Slovenia would have separated from the federation. That the Western powers did not act in this way contributed still further to Yugoslavia's breakup, and to the humanitarian disaster that resulted.

External intervention, now led by the United States, helped spread the fighting to Bosnia-Herzegovina, as we saw in Chapters 5 and 6. US officials encouraged the Muslim-led government under Alija Izetbegović to board the secessionist bandwagon and declare independence. An especially tragic feature of US policy was its opposition to European efforts to prevent the war. In March 1992 EU mediators brokered the Lisbon Agreement, which called for a decentralized Bosnia, a weak central government, and a high degree of regional autonomy. Representatives of all three of Bosnia's ethnic groups supported the initial drafts of the agreement, which raised the possibility that war could be averted. US officials disapproved of the plan, however, and they urged Muslim negotiators to withdraw from the agreement. When the Muslims complied and withdrew, the result was the collapse of the Lisbon Agreement and the commencement of a three-and-a-half-year war.

During the war, the European Union (and also the United Nations) made repeated efforts to mediate the conflict and end the fighting. The US, once again, sought to undermine these mediation efforts and thus scuttled one peace settlement after another. In the end, of course, it was the United States that settled the Bosnia War, with the Dayton Accords of November 1995. It was also the United States—not Europe or the UN—that received credit for ending the war. The Dayton Accords were nevertheless similar to several peace plans that the US had previously opposed.

Overall, the main effect of US policy was to prevent an early settlement of the Bosnia war, and to prolong the fighting for several additional years. And the military aspects of US policy in Bosnia raised the human costs of the war. During the summer of 1995, American officials helped orchestrate a series of ground offensives by Muslim/Croat forces in Croatia and western Bosnia—which were coordinated with an intensive NATO bombing campaign—all directed against the Serbs. These combined operations produced repeated instances of ethnic cleansing, and hundreds of thousands of refugees.

US intervention in Kosovo had similarly tragic consequences, as we saw in Chapter 7. The Milošević government seemed open to a diplomatic settlement of its ongoing war with the Kosovo Liberation Army. Milošević initially honored the Holbrooke agreement of October 1998 and withdrew most of his troops from Kosovo in accord with that agreement. NATO officials later admitted that the agreement broke down due to Albanian (not Serb) provocations. And at the Rambouillet peace talks in early 1999, the Serbs accepted the need to withdraw most of their troops from Kosovo, to restore Kosovo's autonomous status, and to allow an international peacekeeping force to police the accord. The main unresolved issue at this point was the precise composition of the peacekeeping force. A full settlement may well have been in reach, but this possibility was never seriously tested. Instead, the United States sought to provoke the Serbs into rejecting the Rambouillet agreement, by making its peace terms as humiliating as possible. The provocation went as follows: Late in the negotiation process, the Serbs were presented with a new demand—that NATO forces were to occupy *all* of Serbia and what remained of Yugoslavia, as well as Kosovo. Western officials knew that this demand was unreasonable, and that the Serbs had no option but to reject it. According to a senior British official, John Gilbert: "The terms put to Milošević at Rambouillet were absolutely intolerable."[6] We saw that the United States took the lead in sabotaging these peace talks, and that the European states went along (albeit reluctantly) with the US strategy. The collapse of the Rambouillet talks that resulted from these actions was followed by a two-month NATO bombing campaign against Serbia. It is widely believed that NATO's decision to wage war in this case was taken "essentially as a last resort," after all diplomatic options had been exhausted.[7] But this perception has little to do with reality. And we saw that the NATO bombing campaign itself escalated the scale of Serb atrocities. The main effect of intervention in the Kosovo case was, once again, to heighten the level of human suffering.

Some instances of international action in Yugoslavia look more positive. The European and UN efforts to broker a peaceful settlement of the Bosnia conflict, though ultimately unsuccessful, were nevertheless laudable. Had they been allowed to succeed—in the absence of US opposition—they might well have saved many lives. On balance, however, the record of activity by both the United States and the European Union was strongly negative from a humanitarian standpoint.

In light of the foregoing, it is difficult to accept the view that Yugoslavia was a successful intervention, or that it offers a sharp contrast with intervention in Iraq. Indeed, there were significant parallels between US interventions in Iraq and the Balkans. The most important parallel is that in both cases, intervention worsened the humanitarian problems. Another parallel concerns the role of neoconservative intellectuals in the policy process, including such figures as Paul Wolfowitz, Zalmay Khalilzad, and Richard Perle. These men were early and enthusiastic supporters of military intervention in the Balkans, and they also advocated for the invasion of Iraq.[8] Wolfowitz appears to have played an especially important role as one of the strongest advocates of US intervention in Bosnia during the first Bush presidency; and he became a key figure in the lead-up to the Iraq war during the second Bush presidency. There are yet additional parallels. With regard to Kosovo, the United States and NATO went to war, despite the absence of UN Security Council approval. Then in the Iraq case, the United States once again waged war without Council approval. And in general, the US proclivity toward emphasizing military action and disparaging diplomacy—which has been a hallmark of recent adventures in the Middle East—also was evident during the Balkan interventions.

Of course, there are important differences in the interventionist styles of the Clinton and Bush administrations, notably Clinton's greater sense of caution and technical competence and Bush's greater willingness to commit US ground forces in combat. Also, the Bush doctrine of preemptive warfare (as explicated in the administration's 2002 National Security Strategy) represents an aggressive shift in the US military posture.[9] Nevertheless, the differences between the two presidencies appear less striking under scrutiny. A key conclusion of this study is that there were major similarities between Clinton's interventions in the Balkans, on the one hand, and Bush's intervention in Iraq, on the other.

The Motives for Intervention

Another perceived difference between the Balkan and Iraq interventions concerns the question of motives. In the Iraq case, few doubt that US action was motivated at least to some extent by self-interest and realpolitik. Even viewed in the most charitable light, the decision to invade was surely affected by the presence of huge oil reserves, both in Iraq itself and in the surrounding region. Even supporters of the war acknowledged the salience of the oil factor. In early 2003, Thomas Friedman noted: "Any war we launch in Iraq will certainly be—in part—about oil. To deny this is laughable."[10] Most now accept that selfish motives played some role in the US invasion of Iraq.

The Yugoslav interventions, however, appear to have had a completely different set of motives: It is widely believed that US and NATO interventions were undertaken even though Yugoslavia offered no obvious benefits to the intervening powers. There was no significant supply of oil or any other vital resource in the Balkan region, and the Western powers (so the argument goes) had nothing to gain by intervening there. NATO members intervened in the Balkans *despite* the fact that such intervention went against their interests. The perceived lack of self-interest in this case is comforting to many, and this perception goes a long way toward explaining the retrospectively positive image of the US/NATO role in the Balkan wars.

I have argued that this view is yet another myth. While it is true that Yugoslavia itself was of little intrinsic value, it nevertheless was important as an arena in which various powers sought to demonstrate their power positions for the post–Cold War world. There were three main actors in the Yugoslav conflict, each of which sought to use the conflict to advance its own agenda. First, the European Union sought to establish a common foreign and military policy, beginning in 1991, that would function with some degree of independence from the United States and NATO. Yugoslavia was to be the first test case of this independent foreign policy, to demonstrate the European Union's capability. Second, a newly reunified Germany was acting unilaterally, outside the EU framework for the most part, and it also sought to use the Balkan crisis to demonstrate its potential as a regional force.

Third, of course, was the United States—a power that ultimately dominated the diplomacy of the Balkan wars. The US objective was to establish a new function for the North Atlantic Treaty Organization, which was the main institutional expression of US power in Europe. Accordingly, NATO was given a prominent role in managing the Yugoslav conflict: It was NATO that officially directed the bombing campaigns in Bosnia in 1995 and Kosovo in 1999. When the bombing ended, NATO-led peacekeeping forces were given the task of governing postwar Bosnia, and later Kosovo. Through these activities, US officials were able to reinvigorate the Atlantic alliance, thus achieving a key objective. An editorial in the *Financial Times* summed up the matter this way: "The Kosovo crisis has confirmed the relevance of NATO—just as criminals confirm the relevance of policemen. Ten years ago, when the Berlin wall came down, it [NATO] seemed destined to join its Warsaw Pact adversary in the dustbin of history. But the [Kosovo] crisis and Mr. Milošević's brutal ethnic cleansing of Albanians, have helped to confirm the continuing relevance of an international military force."[11] Chapters 2–7 of this study presented extensive evidence to support the *Financial Times* contention regarding the central importance of NATO for US policy in the Balkans.

Despite all their differences and jealousies, the Western powers nevertheless agreed on key aspects of the Yugoslav crisis. Specifically, the policies of the United States, Germany, and the European Union were all guided in part by anticommunist ideology, as was noted by Hubert Védrine, a close advisor to French president François Mitterrand: "[There was a tendency] to simplify this conflict, which was exceptionally complex, through an unsophisticated and Manichean ideology inherited from the Cold War. . . . [For Western audiences] the 'enemy' . . . was the Yugoslav federation, held responsible for the survival of a hated communism, which had to be destroyed."[12] Anticommunist views were widely expressed at the time of Yugoslavia's 1991 demise, and to some extent during the various conflicts that emerged afterward. This ideological dimension accounts for the lack of any serious international effort to preserve the Yugoslav federation, which was considered a Cold War anachronism. And as we have seen, Germany actively supported anticommunist Croatia. In general, the Yugoslav conflict was marked by intense and often acrimonious contestation among the Western powers, but there were some issues on which there was broad consensus, among them anticommunism.

It is therefore incorrect to view Western intervention in Yugoslavia as devoid of self-interest. Both Europe and the United States acted in ways that were consistent with stated policy objectives. And this intervention did not begin late in the war, as is commonly believed. If we define intervention as direct and deliberate meddling by one state in the internal affairs of another state, then intervention began from the very earliest phases of the Yugoslav conflict. Writers such as Samantha Power, who emphasize the lateness of intervention and the reluctance to intervene, are mistaken.[13]

In some sense, the external interventions seem surprising, given Yugoslavia's limited importance in terms of either economic resources or geostrategic location. But states have often intervened in relatively marginal areas simply to demonstrate their power and their potential for leadership. During the Cold War, for example, some of the largest US interventions, such as those in Korea and Vietnam, occurred in countries that had not initially been considered central to US interests. The 1983 invasion of Grenada was undertaken despite the minute importance of that island. During the post–Cold War era, the United States became even more anxious about the credibility of its leadership—in the absence of any major threat—and more eager than before to use military force.[14] Military analyst Andrew Bacevich describes the contrast between the Cold War and post–Cold War eras: "During the Cold War . . . large-scale US military actions totaled a scant six. Since the fall of the Berlin Wall, however, they have become almost annual events. . . . [For the Clinton and Bush II administrations], bombing something—at times almost anything—became a convenient way of keeping up appearances."[15] The use of force in the Balkans fit in nicely with this perceived need to keep up appearances. US interventions in the Yugoslavia case thus maintain a long (if inglorious) tradition whereby great powers intervene in an opportunistic manner to affirm their credibility and showcase their power.[16]

The Role of the Military-Industrial Complex

> The military and the monetary,
> They get together whenever they think it's necessary.
> —*Gil Scott-Heron, "Work for Peace"*

Another important influence on US policy was an entity that Dwight D. Eisenhower termed the military-industrial complex.[17] It is difficult to discuss this issue dispassionately, since the very term conjures up images of dark, conspiratorial forces for some readers, and it has thus received little attention from academics or journalists in recent years (though it was widely discussed during the 1960s and 1970s). Despite these cautions, the military-industrial complex remains a perfectly valid concept, in my opinion, and the recent lack of interest appears unwarranted. It seems intuitively plausible that the uniformed services and weapons procurement companies might in some cases act as an interest group, or a cluster of intertwined interest groups. The existence of the military-industrial complex has been endorsed by high-level military officers—who were well placed to know its workings—beginning of course with Eisenhower himself.[18] The concept is in fact gradually being revived by such well-informed figures as Chalmers Johnson, a former CIA consultant.[19]

And there can be little doubt that the military-industrial complex had an interest in the Yugoslav drama. US arms manufacturers appear to have favored military action in the Balkans (a point discussed in the preceding chapter); and they benefited from these interventions, especially the 1999 Kosovo war. Indeed, a broad range of US interests supported intervention, according to *Barron's* financial weekly in a March 1999 article:

> Wall Street is nothing if not patriotic. Hardly had the rain of missiles and bombs begun to fall on Kosovo than the stock market struck the colors with a blazing rally. The spirited response was all the more stirring because the market had been sagging like a weary old nag under the weight of a myriad of real and imagined aches. But once it heard the music and saw the flag, it tossed aside those petty cares with alacrity and sent up its own inspiring barrage of flares and rockets. . . . Street people rushed to participate in the rally even though like most of us ordinary civilians, they were far from sure where Serbia is or why NATO is so mad at it. We must confess that we're still a tad hazy on the location part, even after following the president's urging and getting down our atlas.

The *Barron's* article added that wars typically produce stock market rallies and conceded that "war is undeniably hell, but it can provide a shot in the arm for share prices."[20] Business enthusiasm for war in Kosovo was not dampened by the likelihood that investors were unable to locate the region on a map, and that they had only a foggy idea of what the war was supposed to accomplish.

No doubt business interests are gratified by successful displays of US power—in the Balkans or elsewhere—which serve to protect investments worldwide and to intimidate anyone who might threaten them. In addition, business interests favored the reinvigoration of NATO, which the Kosovo war was helping to facilitate.[21] It is difficult to know, however, what influence (if any) these interests may have had on official policy. At a minimum, investors did not oppose US action in the former Yugoslavia, and this lack of business opposition surely made it easier for the Clinton administration to pursue an interventionist policy.

For the uniformed military, the Balkan wars posed a political dilemma. On the one hand, the services strongly favored high levels of military spending. During the early 1990s, Colin Powell and other generals lobbied for a base force program and other projects that aimed to keep military spending at near–Cold War levels, despite the demise of the Soviet Union. On the other hand, the generals were reluctant to use their expensive weapons in risky combat situations. In the specific cases of Bosnia and Kosovo, the US military for the most part opposed the use of force. The services were afraid that any bombing campaign might prove ineffective, and that this could lead to demands for US ground troops; such a prospect raised the danger of combat casualties and a Vietnam-style quagmire, an unsettling scenario from the standpoint of the Joint Chiefs of Staff.

In essence, the Joint Chiefs wanted to have it both ways: They wanted a military of vast size and scope; but they also sought to avoid using these forces in combat. This stance proved politically untenable. Madeleine Albright's famous lament—"What are you saving this superb military for . . . if we can't use it?"[22]—offered a telling criticism. And the generals had no effective response. Stated simply, the US military needed overseas interventions to persuade the public that military spending remained necessary after the Cold War—and that it was not just a gift to the military-industrial complex. It was insufficient for the services to procure expensive equipment and then engage in endless preparations, training exercises, and war games. As Bacevich viewed the matter: "With Pentagon expenditures holding steady at approximately $300 billion per year throughout the 1990s, it was incumbent upon the military to demonstrate some tangible return on the nation's investment."[23] At some point, the equipment had to be used in combat. All these factors constituted the political backdrop to the Clinton administration's decisions to use force in Bosnia and Kosovo.

Human Rights and Intervention

Most studies overlook the self-interested characteristics of external interventions in the various Balkan wars and assume that such interventions must have resulted from the Serb-perpetrated killings, rapes, and acts of ethnic cleansing, as well as the international revulsion against such acts. My study affirms that these atrocities were grave and extensive, and that Serb forces committed a disproportionate share of them. And Milošević certainly stands out as one of the major causes of these atrocities.

As a general explanation for Western policy, however, the human rights perspective is unsatisfactory. It ignores the fact that the Western states helped *provoke* the war in 1991. And the US role in repeatedly blocking peace agreements that might have ended atrocities without military intervention seems inconsistent with any humanitarian motivation. These actions were certainly helpful in affirming the hegemonic role of the United States, and thus in advancing US interests. But they cannot be defended on moral grounds.

Furthermore, international condemnations applied almost exclusively to *Serb* atrocities. The numerous atrocities committed by other ethnic groups (typically against the Serbs) were ignored. This inconsistency was especially evident with regard to Croatia, where both the United States and European states established close relations with President Franjo Tudjman, whose regime had a taint of pro-Nazi sentiment and had engaged in extensive human rights violations. Beginning in 1991, Croatian nationalists launched armed attacks against ethnic Serbs who lived in Zagreb and other Croatian cities, forcing many to flee. The Tudjman regime bore at least some responsibility for encouraging these attacks. These pogroms started several weeks before the war, and they constitute some of the first major instances of ethnic cleansing. Yet these Croatian atrocities elicited no international condemnation, and virtually no notice.[24] And in some cases, US officials became accomplices to ethnic cleansing. Such complicity was evident in 1995, when Croatian forces launched an offensive against Serb residents of the Krajina region. In the end, the Serbs were forced out of Krajina, resulting in one of the largest acts of ethnic cleansing of the war. US advisors helped the Croatians prepare their offensives and made no serious efforts to stop the resulting atrocities.[25] And the European states, for their part, failed to offer any more than pro forma objections regarding either the atrocities themselves or the US support for Croatia. The overall hypocrisy of Western policy was well expressed at the time by Charles Krauthammer:

> This week in four days of blitzkrieg by the Croatian army, 150,000 Serbs living in the Krajina region of Croatia were ethnically cleansed; . . . where were the moralists who for years have been so loudly decrying the ethnic cleansing of Bosnia's Muslims? Where were the cries for blood, the demand for arms, the call to action on behalf of today's pitiful victims? Where were the columnists, the senators, the other posturers who excoriate the West for standing by when Bosnian Muslims are victimized and are silent when the victim of the day is Serb?[26]

There was a tendency for Western writers and officials to whitewash these Croat atrocities, or to ignore them altogether. More recent accounts perpetuate this whitewash.[27]

There was thus a moral double standard: Serb atrocities were condemned, while crimes by other ethnic groups were regarded leniently. And there are additional examples of double standards. In Bosnia, the regime of Alija Izetbegović committed numerous atrocities throughout the 1992–1995 war—and these too elicited no significant protests from foreign governments or the world's press. After the 1999 bombing campaign in Kosovo, Albanian vigilantes assassinated hundreds of ethnic Serbs, and they effectively drove out tens of thousands of Serbs (and also members of other ethnic groups). Yet, NATO and UN occupation forces made no serious effort to protect the Serbs or restrain the repression. These moral double standards seem difficult to reconcile with a humanitarian explanation for Western policy.

The Exaggeration of Serb Atrocities

Another feature of the Balkan conflict was the tendency of Western media needlessly to exaggerate the atrocities committed by Serb armies. If one wished to condemn Serb forces, one needed to describe only what those forces actually did in places like Vukovar, Srebrenica, and Račak, as well as the many other locations where atrocious behavior took place. The reality was damning enough, and there was no need to exaggerate anything.

And yet there was plenty of exaggeration, misrepresentation, and propaganda dissemination. We have seen several examples here. Atrocities committed at Serb-run detention camps were presented in sensationalist fashion, for example, and they became "extermination camps" comparable to Auschwitz. President Izetbegović himself encouraged these interpretations. Yet, in 2003, shortly before his death, Izetbegović conceded that "there were no extermination camps" in Bosnia.[28] He also conceded that his previous claims to the contrary had been deliberate misrepresentations, intended to outrage Western public opinion and thus trigger Western military intervention against the Serbs. The number of people killed during the Bosnia war also was exaggerated. During the war, the death toll on all sides was often claimed to be in the range of 250,000; but the actual toll is now believed to be about half this figure. And the Ruder-Finn public relations firm assisted the Bosnian government in presenting its case to the media, as we saw, emphasizing Serb atrocities as much as possible. In an interview, Ruder-Finn's president, James Harff, was quite open about his role.[29] Exaggeration also emerged during the Kosovo conflict: At one point, NATO officials claimed that the Serbs had a secret plan, code-named Operation Horseshoe, to expel virtually the entire Albanian population from Kosovo, and that the NATO bombing came just in time to prevent this. Such claims were widely reported in the world's press. After the war, it emerged that NATO had no serious evidence that Horseshoe ever existed.[30] At another point, officials at the US Defense Department implied that Serb forces had murdered at least 100,000 Albanians. And again, these claims were widely reported. Yet it was later revealed that the 100,000 figure was inaccurate, and that Serb killings were one-tenth this number.[31] In some respects, these factual distortions are readily comprehensible: It seems natural enough that writers covering the Balkans would wish to honor the dead—but misreporting the facts seems a poor way of achieving this.

And the repeated use of terms like "genocide" and "holocaust" to describe Serb atrocities in general must be considered a systematic distortion. Serb atrocities were never inflicted on a scale that justified the frequent analogies with Nazi atrocities. Even the terrible massacre at Srebrenica, where 8,000 Muslim males perished in 1995, was significantly less terrible than the mass murders of World War II. When viewed in historical perspective, the Yugoslav wars do not appear unusually brutal or destructive: The Bosnia conflict, with approximately 100,000 deaths, may be classed a medium-sized war, while Kosovo and Croatia were relatively small in scope.[32] If we wish to consider these wars genocides, then virtually all wars must be reclassified as genocides. And to emphasize so heavily the atrocities that took place in the Balkans and call them genocide, and then to ignore the numerous other world conflicts where atrocities were just as severe—or more severe—seems unacceptably arbitrary.[33]

It is a basic principle of human communication that words and phrases must have restrictive definitions to prevent overuse, which can cause language to lose meaning. This is in fact what has happened with the word "genocide," which has lost much of its meaning in recent years. If we wish to argue that wars must be considered genocidal whenever a group is intentionally destroyed "in whole or in part," and that numbers of victims are unimportant, then wars automatically become genocides by definition. In nearly all wars, groups of people are targeted and killed, "in whole or in part," under circumstances that cannot be justified by combat.

It is important to note that the entire concept of genocide was redefined by the Yugoslav drama. Until 1991, "genocide" always implied a mass killing of exceptional magnitude. The term was almost never used unless the number of victims ranged in the hundreds of thousands or (more typically) in the millions. With the beginning of the Yugoslav conflict, however, the situation changed. In that conflict, virtually all Serb atrocities were considered genocidal, similar to Hitler's Final Solution against the Jews. In 1999, Claude

Lanzmann, the director of the documentary *Shoah*, objected to the overuse of World War II comparisons:

> Intellectuals didn't use this reference to the Holocaust even in the worst period of the Algerian war, when FLN combatants were being murdered in large numbers and tortured, and huge areas of the country were entirely emptied of their inhabitants. Same thing with the Vietnam War, when hundreds of villages were being flattened by napalm along with forests, rice paddies, and so on. Even during the Biafra war, which saw the birth of humanitarian ideology and practice, people did without the comparisons with Nazism.... These perpetual references to the Holocaust [with regard to the Yugoslavia wars] are a way of muzzling all discussion. Talking forbidden! Argument over![34]

The equation of the atrocities committed by Serb forces during the 1990s with those committed by the Nazis grotesquely misrepresents the former, while it trivializes the latter.

It must be emphasized, once again, that the atrocities that the Serbs really did commit were terrible enough. But none of this can justify the exaggerations that so often appeared in Western newspapers and government statements, throughout the various wars. Nor does it justify the reckless use of terms like "genocide" or "holocaust."

The Balkan wars must be remembered as yet another case where exaggerated atrocity stories helped generate public outrage, and thus justified military intervention. In this respect, the Yugoslavia case bears comparison with the 1991 Gulf War, where propaganda played an important role in galvanizing world opinion behind the US-led intervention. At one point, it was widely claimed that Iraqi troops had looted incubators from a Kuwaiti hospital and allowed infants to die on the floor. This lurid story was widely circulated, and it even appeared in an Amnesty International report. When the war was over, however, it was revealed that the entire incubator incident never happened; it was the creation of a New York public relations firm, Hill & Knowlton.[35] Atrocity propaganda has been effective in many other instances throughout history: During World War I, for example, exaggerated reports of German atrocities in Belgium inflamed public opinion in the United States, justifying later US intervention in that war. The 1898 Spanish-American war was influenced by inaccurate reports of Spanish atrocities in Cuba.[36] And the present analysis of Yugoslavia also should remind us that propaganda retains its ability to shape public perceptions and distort reality.

The Yugoslavia Case in Perspective

A striking feature of the Balkan conflict was the level of international attention that it received. I have undertaken a survey of *New York Times* coverage and found the following: During calendar years 1991 through 1999, 1,020 front-page articles focused primarily on the conflict in Yugoslavia—in other words, Yugoslavia was on the first page of the *Times* every third day, on average, for nearly a decade.[37] And this reporting elicited a more general interest in the issue of humanitarian emergencies and the associated idea of humanitarian intervention as a solution to these emergencies. The fascination with humanitarian intervention became intense, and it has shaped public discourse ever since.

In the context of this new discourse, there has been an asymmetrical focus on specific conflicts, such as Bosnia, Kosovo, Rwanda, or most recently, Darfur. An obvious problem with this focus is that it diverts attention from more systemic issues, such as Third World underdevelopment or infectious disease. Suffice it to say, systemic problems fail to elicit the level of interest and emotionalism that wars evoke. Consider the issue of AIDS: This disease has killed tens of millions of people and has shattered entire countries, especially in sub-Saharan Africa. In the most severely affected states, life expectancy has dropped precipitously. AIDS has orphaned vast numbers of children, many of whom are themselves infected. The severity of this problem is difficult to overstate. Yet there has been relatively little international response in terms of either funding or press coverage. The AIDS crisis in Africa in fact received only 1 percent of the front-page coverage accorded to the Balkan wars.[38] Such inattention seems odd, since AIDS has produced a far larger number of victims than have the Balkan wars. This lack of newspaper coverage applies not only to AIDS, but to a range of other infectious diseases, including such long familiar threats as malaria, tuberculosis, schistosomiasis, and sleeping sickness, as well as newer ones such as avian influenza. It appears that only wars are taken seriously, while other issues are neglected.

And let us also consider the problem of Third World economic crises, and the IMF-directed structural adjustment programs that are associated with such crises. These are major sources of world poverty and have contributed to reduced medical services and premature death. But once again, efforts to correct these problems suffer from a lack of press coverage and little official interest. There are many reasons for this lack of interest, but one reason is that attention has been diverted by the all-consuming issues of ethnic war and humanitarian intervention.

The overemphasis on war combined with the neglect of economic crises seems unjustified—especially since economic crises often *cause* wars.[39] In the case of Yugoslavia, for example, we saw that a debt repayment crisis during the 1980s was a major factor in triggering that country's disintegration and the fighting that followed. Another illustration is Rwanda, which suffered an economic shock in 1989 when the international price of its principal export, coffee, turned downward. Rwanda was then forced into a structural adjustment program, which lowered living standards and set the stage for heightened levels of ethnic violence. The 1994 massacres of Rwandan Tutsis stemmed directly from these conditions.[40]

The Rwanda case has generated extensive discussion among academics, and much of this discussion has been critical of international responses to the anti-Tutsi killings. Specifically, it is argued that the United States should have intervened with military force to stop the killings, and that America's failure to use force was a tragedy.[41] But there is another way to view the matter: Perhaps the real tragedy of Rwanda is that no international effort was made to support the price of coffee in 1989, and that so little was done to address the economic crisis that resulted from the price drop. Developing a strategy to prevent ethnic wars should surely be our highest priority. Yet some readers will feel dissatisfied with such "technical" methods of addressing the problem. Working out the details of an economic aid program is surely less exciting than sending in the 82nd Airborne Division for a moral crusade. Nevertheless, a strategy aimed at preventing ethnic conflicts before they explode—by alleviating the economic stresses that can cause such conflicts—may well prove more effective than intervening after fighting begins.

And a prevention strategy has one additional advantage: Even if the strategy fails, it is at least unlikely to *worsen* the crisis. The same cannot be said for military intervention. Some will insist on a dual strategy: We must address systemic problems such as Third World poverty, but at the same time the international community should be prepared to use force where prevention efforts fail and ethnic fighting erupts. This view is unrealistic, however, given limited resources. We cannot fund everything, and the need for budgetary trade-offs must be explicitly acknowledged. President Eisenhower described the basic problem in 1953:

> Every gun that is made, every warship launched, every rocket fired signifies, in the final sense, a theft from those who hunger and are not fed, those who are cold and are not clothed. . . . The cost of one modern heavy bomber is this: a modern brick school in more than 30 cities. It is two electric power plants, each serving a town of 60,000 population. It is two fine, fully-equipped hospitals. It is some 50 miles of concrete highway. We pay for a single fighter plane with a half million bushels of wheat.

We pay for a single destroyer with new homes that could have housed more than 8,000 people.[42]

Eisenhower's speech is often quoted to emphasize the futility of war, but I use it here to make a different point: Humanitarian interventions and other forms of military action are extremely expensive. Funds that are used for intervention will preclude spending for more pressing needs, such as disease eradication, debt relief, or efforts to combat global climate change. Surely, the tens of billions of dollars that were allocated for intervention in Yugoslavia, or the hundreds of billions that are now being spent in Iraq, could have been put to better use.[43] The overcommitment of funds for intervention seems difficult to justify, a point that was well stated by Jeffrey Sachs in 2003: "The world is out of kilter when President Bush asks for $87 billion for Iraq and only $200 million [less than one quarter of 1 percent of the Iraq total] for the global fund to fight AIDS, tuberculosis, and malaria."[44] There is obviously a problem of skewed priorities, one that extends well beyond the Bush administration.

And despite the prodigious allocation of funds, intervention has *not* proven very effective in alleviating human suffering. The record is indeed a poor one: Of the most recent interventions, Iraq has been a catastrophic failure, while Afghanistan may well be moving in the same direction.[45] The Somalia operation was terminated in 1995, having accomplished little. And we saw that multiple interventions in Yugoslavia exacerbated atrocities and increased suffering. Among the major post–Cold War interventions, only the 1994 Haiti operation appears to have had a positive effect. These cases underscore the obvious point that military interventions can produce unpredictable results, and run the risk of worsening rather than improving conditions. Experience has not borne out the assumption that intervening will inevitably be better than doing nothing.

In the future, we should expect advocates of humanitarian intervention to answer at least three questions. First, how much will we have to spend on the called-for intervention, and are we willing to spend that amount? Second, what programs should we defund, or dispense with altogether, to cover costs? And third, on what grounds should we assume that intervention will improve humanitarian conditions in the target country, rather than exacerbate them? These seem like reasonable questions, and they should be asked with greater frequency. At the very least, asking such questions will place the whole discussion on a more rational basis.

I close this discussion of humanitarian intervention with an analogy from the practice of medicine. It is a basic principle of medical ethics that doctors must avoid harming their patients. One performs a surgical procedure only if there is good reason to assume that surgery will produce better results than less extreme forms of treatment. That a patient is suffering is, of itself, insufficient reason to operate, since operating runs the risk of augmenting the suffering. And sometimes, the best course of action is to take no action at all, to do nothing. Perhaps the same cautions should apply with regard to humanitarian crises. Certainly, we should avoid risky practices that are likely to make the crisis even worse than before. First, we should do no harm.

Notes

Preface

1. "Cold Warrior in a Strange Land," March 22, 2006, *www.antiwar.com/ engelhardt/?articleid=8739*.
2. Senator Robert Byrd, "We Stand Passively Mute," February 12, 2003, *www.guardian. co.uk/world/2003/feb/18/usa.iraq*.

Chapter 1

Epigraphs: Blair quoted in *Moral Combat: NATO at War*, BBC documentary, March 12, 2000, *news.bbc.co.uk/hi/english/static/events/panorama/transcripts/transcript_12_03_00.txt*; David Rieff, "A Nation of Pre-Emptors?" *New York Times Magazine*, January 15, 2006. Rieff had previously been a supporter of humanitarian intervention, though he now appears more skeptical.

1. Samantha Power, *"A Problem from Hell": America and the Age of Genocide* (New York: HarperCollins, 2002), 504.
2. The academic literature on this topic has become quite vast. A few of the more prominent analyses are: J. Holzgrefe and Robert Keohane, eds., *Humanitarian Intervention: Ethical, Legal, and Political Dilemmas* (Cambridge: Cambridge University Press, 2003); Georg Meggle, ed., *Ethics of Humanitarian Intervention* (Frankfort: Ontos, 2004); Fernando R. Tesón, *Humanitarian Intervention: An Inquiry into Law and Morality* (Ardsley-on-Hudson, N.Y.: Transnational Publishers, 1988); Jennifer Welsh, ed., *Humanitarian Intervention and International Relations* (Oxford: Oxford University Press, 2006); Oliver Ramsbotham and Tom Woodhouse, *Humanitarian Intervention in Contemporary Conflict: A Re-Conceptualization* (Cambridge: Polity Press, 1996); Robert Phillips and Duane L. Cady, *Humanitarian Intervention: Just War versus Pacifism* (Lanham, Md.: Rowman and Littlefield, 1996); Robert DiPrizio, *Armed Humanitarians: U.S. Interventions from Northern Iraq to Kosovo* (Baltimore: Johns Hopkins University Press, 2002); Arne Johan Vetlesen, "Genocide: A Case for the Responsibility of the Bystander," *Journal of Peace Research* 37, no. 4, 2000; Albrecht Schnabel and Ramesh Thakur, eds., *Kosovo and the Challenge of Humanitarian Intervention: Selective Indignation, Collective Action, and International Citizenship* (Tokyo: United Nations University Press, 2000); Richard Falk, "The Complexities of Humanitarian Intervention: A New World Order Challenge," *Michigan Journal of*

International Law 17, no. 2, 1996; Nicholas Wheeler, *Saving Strangers: Humanitarian Intervention in International Society* (New York: Oxford University Press, 2000); and Adam Lebor, *"Complicity with Evil": The United Nations in the Age of Modern Genocide* (New Haven: Yale University Press, 2006).

3.   Todd Gitlin, "Bosnia Isn't Vietnam, It's Spain, 1936," *Los Angeles Times*, September 14, 1993; Mary Kaldor, "A Response [to David Rieff]," *Journal of Human Rights* 1, no. 1, 2002; Bernard-Henri Lévy, "The Spirit of Europe Lives or Dies in Sarajevo," *Independent*, July 31, 1995; Václav Havel, *To the Castle and Back* (New York: Knopf, 2007); Richard Burt and Richard Perle, "The Next Act in Bosnia," *New York Times*, February 11, 1994; Susan Sontag, "A Lament for Bosnia," *Nation*, December 25, 1995; "Deputy Secretary Wolfowitz: Interview with Sam Tannenhaus, *Vanity Fair*," US Department of Defense, *DOD News*, May 9, 2003; Joshua Muravchik, *The Imperative of American Leadership* (Washington, D.C.: AEI Press, 1996); Anne-Marie Slaughter, *The Idea That Is America: Keeping Faith with Our Values in a Dangerous World* (New York: Basic Books, 2007); Stanley Hoffmann, "Yugoslavia: Implications for Europe and for European Institutions," in Richard Ullman, ed., *The World and Yugoslavia's Wars* (New York: Council on Foreign Relations, 1998); William Shawcross, *Allies: The US, Britain, Europe, and the War in Iraq* (New York: Public Affairs, 2004); Elie Wiesel, "The Perils of Indifference," speech given in Washington, D.C., April 12, 1999, *clinton4.nara.gov/WH/EOP/First_Lady/html/generalspeeches/1999/19990412.html*; Bernard Kouchner, "The Right to Intervention: Codified in Kosovo," *New Perspectives Quarterly* 16, no. 4, 1999; Jean Bethke Elshtain, "Just War and Humanitarian Intervention," *American University International Law Review* 17, no. 1, 2001; Christopher Hitchens, "Never Trust Imperialists (Especially When They Turn Pacifist)," *Boston Review*, December 1993–January 1994; Michael Ignatieff, *Virtual War: Kosovo and Beyond* (London: Chatto and Windus, 2000); Michael Walzer, "The Triumph of Just War Theory (and the Dangers of Success)," *Social Research* 69, no. 4, 2002; and Paul Berman, *Power and the Idealists: The Passion of Joschka Fischer and Its Aftermath* (Brooklyn: Soft Skull Press, 2005).

4.   A useful critique of this general point is in David Chandler, *From Kosovo to Kabul: Human Rights and International Intervention* (London: Pluto, 2002).

5.   UN General Assembly, "Convention on the Prevention and Punishment of the Crime of Genocide, Adopted by Resolution 260 (III) A of the United Nations General Assembly on 9 December 1948," art. 2, *www.un.org/millennium/law/iv-1.htm*.

6.   Quoted in David Alonzo-Maizlish, "In Whole or in Part: Group Rights, the Intent Element of Genocide, and the 'Quantitative Criterion,'" *New York University Law Review* 77, no. 5, 2002, 1392. Emphasis in original.

7.   See interview with Mirsad Tokača in "Genocide Is Not a Matter of Numbers," *Bosnia Report*, December–March 2006, *www.bosnia.org.uk/bosrep/report_format.cfm?articleid=3 055&reportid=170*. Similarly, a published study claims that ethnic cleansing is "basically a 1990s synonym for genocide." Peter Ronayne, "Genocide in Kosovo," *Human Rights Review* 5, no. 4, 2004, 61.

8.   In addition, some have argued that "genocidal rape" is a specific form of genocide. See Adam Jones, "Gender and Genocide in Rwanda," *Journal of Genocide Research* 4, no. 1, 2002; and R. Charli Carpenter, "Surfacing Children: Limitations of Genocidal Rape Discourse," *Human Rights Quarterly* 22, no. 2, 2000. On women and war, see also Julie Mertus, *War's Offensive on Women* (Bloomfield, Conn.: Kumarian Press, 2000).

9. This view is succinctly expressed in David Rieff, "Denying Moral Equivalence," *Foreign Affairs* 74, no. 6, 1995.

10. Elshtain, "Just War and Humanitarian Intervention," 14–15.

11. For a recent effort to draw parallels between Western actions in Bosnia and British appeasement during the 1930s, see Ed Vulliamy, "Bosnia: The Crime of Appeasement," *International Affairs* 74, no. 1, 1998. See also Roy Gutman, "The Collapse of Serbia?" *World Policy Journal* 16, no. 1, 1999.

12. Milošević himself "caused three wars," according to "Milošević in His Own Stew," an editorial in the *Christian Science Monitor*, September 22, 2000. See also Noel Malcolm, *Kosovo: A Short History* (New York: New York University Press, 1999), x.

13. Franklin Foer quoted in Michelle Norris, "Darfur, Front and Center, in *The New Republic*," National Public Radio, May 12, 2006.

14. The UN Charter (chap. 1, art. 2, sec. 4) states: "All Members shall refrain in their international relations from the threat or use of force against the territorial integrity or political independence of any state." Note that Section 7 makes an exception for "enforcement measures" that derive from Security Council authorization. Also chap. 7, art. 51, allows states to defend themselves against armed attack. From the Charter of the United Nations, *www.un.org/aboutun/charter/*.

15. UN General Assembly, "Declaration on the Inadmissibility of Intervention and Interference in the Internal Affairs of States," A/RES/36/103, December 9, 1981, *www.un.org/documents/ga/res/36/a36r103.htm*. This resolution reaffirmed a series of anti-interventionist resolutions passed by the General Assembly beginning in 1965. Anti-interventionist language also appears in the Charter of the Organization of American States: "No State or group of States has the right to intervene, directly or indirectly, for any reason whatever, in the internal or external affairs of any other State." OAS Charter, as amended, 1997, chap. 4, art. 19, *www.oas.org/juridico/english/charter.html*. The recent tendency of the United States to use threats of military attack as a way of forcing countries into signing agreements—a technique repeatedly used during the Kosovo war—is legally problematic. The Vienna Convention on the Law of Treaties states: "The expression of a state's consent to be bound by a treaty which has been *procured by the coercion of its representative through acts or threats* directed against him shall be without any legal effect" (emphasis added). Article 51, "Vienna Convention on the Law of Treaties, Done at Vienna on 23 May 1969, Entered into force on 27 January 1980," *untreaty.un.org/ilc/texts/instruments/english/conventions/1_1_1969.pdf*.

16. See discussion in Hans J. Morgenthau, "To Intervene or Not to Intervene," *Foreign Affairs* 45, no. 3, 1967.

17. The need to "reform" international law in order to facilitate future interventions and to legalize the process is discussed in Allen Buchanan, "Reforming the International Law of Humanitarian Intervention," in Holzgrefe and Keohane, eds., *Humanitarian Intervention*.

18. For claims that the 1999 Kosovo war was illegal but nevertheless justified, see Independent International Commission on Kosovo, *Kosovo Report: Conflict, International Response, Lessons Learned* (Oxford: Oxford University Press, 2000), 4. For a similar view, see also UK House of Commons, "Foreign Affairs, Fourth Report: Kosovo," May 23, 2000, secs. 128 and 132, *www.publications.parliament.uk/pa/cm199900/cmselect/cmfaff/28/2802.htm*. This illegality has nevertheless been a source of awkwardness for some defenders of the Kosovo intervention. Consider the following self-contradictory statement by Jamie Shea, who served as NATO's press spokesperson

during the Kosovo war: "The UN must never be circumvented deliberately, [but] in exceptional cases military action that is supported freely and in coalition by democratic governments can be legitimate without explicit UN Security Council endorsement." Shea first argues against circumventing the UN, but then he endorses practices that involve circumventing the UN. From Jamie Shea, "NATO—Upholding Ethics in International Security Policy," *Cambridge Review of International Affairs* 15, no. 1, 2002, 78.

19. For a discussion of impartiality, see David Gibbs, "The United Nations, International Peacekeeping, and the Question of 'Impartiality': Revisiting the Congo Operation," *Journal of Modern African Studies* 38, no. 3, 2000. On peacekeeping in general, see also Alan James, *Peacekeeping in International Politics* (New York: St. Martin's, 1990); and Michael Pugh, "Peacekeeping and IR Theory: Phantom of the Opera?" *International Peacekeeping* 10, no. 4, 2003.

20. Some analysts advocated a shift in UN peacekeeping doctrine, with a greater emphasis on armed force, sometimes referred to as "wider peacekeeping": See John Ruggie, "The United Nations and the Collective Use of Force: Whither or Whether?" *International Peacekeeping* 3, no. 4, 1996, 9–10; and Richard Betts, "The Delusion of Impartial Intervention," *Foreign Affairs* 73, no. 6, 1994.

21. I discuss hostile reactions toward the United Nations and European efforts to achieve a compromise settlement in Chapter 6.

22. "Again," *New Republic*, May 15, 2006.

23. Michael Reisman quoted in Ann Orford, *Reading Humanitarian Intervention: Human Rights and the Use of Force in International Law* (Cambridge: Cambridge University Press, 2004), 167–68.

24. See Thomas G. Weiss, "Triage: Humanitarian Interventions in a New Era," *World Policy Journal* 11, no. 1, 1994, 67.

25. "Again."

26. Walzer, "The Triumph of Just War Theory," 931–38. See also Fernando R. Tesón, "Ending Tyranny in Iraq," *Ethics and International Affairs* 19, no. 2, 2005, 3. Walzer's recent interest in humanitarian intervention represents a transformation of his position. In an earlier study, he adopted a skeptical stance: "Clear examples of what is called 'humanitarian intervention' are very rare. Indeed, I have not found any, but only mixed cases where the humanitarian motive is one among several." Walzer, *Just and Unjust Wars: A Moral Argument with Historical Illustrations* (New York: Basic Books, 1977), 101.

27. In general, the potential risks of intervention are downplayed in Power, *"A Problem from Hell."*

28. E. H. Carr cynically noted in his classic study of international relations: "Theories of international morality are . . . the product of dominant nations or groups of nations," and thus reflect the interests of those nations. Carr, *The Twenty Years' Crisis, 1919–1939: An Introduction to the Study of International Relations* (New York: Harper and Row, 1964), 64, 79. In reading these statements, it is important to bear in mind that Carr is not advocating moral relativism (a position he explicitly rejects); he argues only that what is widely *considered* morality is the product of power. For an application of this general principle to humanitarian intervention see Jean Bricmont, *Humanitarian Imperialism: Using Human Rights to Sell War* (New York: Monthly Review Press, 2006).

29. Martha Finnemore, *The Purpose of Intervention* (Ithaca: Cornell University Press, 2003), 52–53. Note that US officials have often staged interventions in remote areas without any obvious strategic or economic value simply to demonstrate "credibility." In 1975,

for example, Henry Kissinger stated that the United States "must carry out some act, somewhere in the world, which shows its determination to be a world power." This remark was made at the time of the US defeat in Vietnam, but it could easily be generalized. Kissinger quoted in David Schmitz, *The United States and Right-Wing Dictatorships* (New York: Cambridge University Press, 2006), 124–25.

30. Berman, *Power and the Idealists*, 84.

31. This possibility is explored in Charles Kegley, "The Neo-Idealist Moment in International Studies? Realist Myths and the New International Realities," *International Studies Quarterly* 37, no. 2, 1993.

32. Power, *"A Problem from Hell,"* 514–15.

33. Ignatieff, *Virtual War*, 178.

34. And during the Cold War, many US officials viewed their own actions in predatory terms. Thus a 1954 report on covert action stated bluntly: "There are no rules. . . . Hitherto acceptable norms do not apply. If the United States is to survive, long-standing American concepts of 'fair play' must be reconsidered. We must develop effective espionage and counterespionage services and must learn to subvert, sabotage, and destroy our enemies. . . . It may become necessary that the American people be made acquainted with, understand, and support this fundamentally repugnant philosophy." Report by Gen. James Doolittle to President Eisenhower, quoted in Schmitz, *The United States and Right-Wing Dictatorships*, 132.

35. Hitchens, "Never Trust Imperialists." For another leftist argument in favor of intervention (which appeared in a Marxist publication), see Rabia Ali and Lawrence Lifschultz, "Why Bosnia?" *Monthly Review* 45, no. 10, 1994.

36. The most prominent example is once again Christopher Hitchens, *A Long Short War: The Postponed Liberation of Iraq* (New York: Plume Books, 2003).

37. Curiously, one of the intellectuals who opposed the Iraq invasion was Samantha Power herself. In 2008, while looking back on the Iraq fiasco, Power downplayed her previous emphasis on the need for military force. However, I agree with Thomas Cushman, who noted: "The implication of [Power's book] *A Problem from Hell* is that, in the end, the only way to really stop genocide is through armed intervention." From Evan Goldstein, "Scholar Who Stepped Down as Obama Advisor Expressed Complex Views on Human Rights," *Chronicle of Higher Education*, March 12, 2008.

38. With regard to the intellectual dilemmas that Iraq has posed for interventionist liberals, see George Packer, "The Liberal Quandary over Iraq," *New York Times Magazine*, December 8, 2002.

39. Bruce Cumings, *The Origins of the Korean War*, vol. 2, *The Roaring of the Cataract, 1947–1950* (Princeton: Princeton University Press, 1990).

40. US Department of Defense, *United States–Vietnam Relations, 1945–1967* (Washington, D.C.: US Government Printing Office, 1971).

41. For an overview of these and other covert operations, see William Blum, *Killing Hope: US Military and CIA Interventions since World War II* (Monroe, Me.: Common Courage Press, 2003). On Lebanon, see Irene Gendzier, *Notes from the Minefield: United States Intervention in Lebanon and the Middle East, 1945–1958* (New York: Columbia University Press, 1997).

42. Discussed in David Gibbs, "Reassessing Soviet Motives for Invading Afghanistan: A Declassified History," *Critical Asian Studies* 38, no. 2, 2006.

43. See, for example, Ilan Pappé, *The Ethnic Cleansing of Palestine* (Oxford: OneWorld Press, 2006); and Benny Morris, *The Birth of the Palestinian Refugee Problem Revisited*

(Cambridge: Cambridge University Press, 2004). Though these two authors hold very different political perspectives, their views regarding the circumstances that led to the Palestinian refugee crisis are not that far apart.

44. The public testimony and cross-examination at the Milošević trial is fully available online at *www.icty.org* (under "Milošević (IT-02-54)").

45. I have largely avoided the legal aspects of the Hague tribunal, though I will note that the tribunal has been politicized to a significant degree. The politicization of the Milošević trial was nicely captured in the following exchange, which preceded the 2003 testimony of Gen. Wesley Clark:

> Milošević: "I don't quite understand the position of this witness [Gen. Clark], since . . . representatives of [the US government] may be able to review the transcript, to approve some of it, to redact some of it possibly, and only then to release it to the public. *I am not aware of any legal court in the world delegating its authority of this kind to any government. This would be the first time for any such thing to happen*" [emphasis added].

> Judge Richard May: "We are not going to argue this point. We have made our order. The reason that the [US] government [has] any rights in the matter at all is . . . that in order to provide information to this Court, it is occasionally—and I stress occasionally—necessary for governments to do so [to review and redact the record], and they are allowed to do so [to review and redact] under our Rules on certain terms, and these are one of the terms which has been followed in this case."

Shortly after this exchange, General Clark was sworn in as a witness, and the procedural issue raised by Milošević was closed. Judge May did not dispute the contention that the US government was allowed to redact the records of Clark's testimony prior to public release, and that such action had no precedent in the history of law. The interests of US hegemony apparently outweighed considerations of legal precedent. On the other hand, there is no doubt that Milošević directed war crimes, and the idea of an international trial for him seems appropriate, at least in principle. These quotes are from preliminary discussion prior to the testimony of Wesley Clark, International Criminal Tribunal for the Former Yugoslavia, December 15, 2003, 30368–69, *www.icty.org*. For detailed analyses of the Milošević trial, see Gary Jonathan Bass, *Stay the Hand of Vengeance: The Politics of War Crimes Tribunals* (Princeton: Princeton University Press, 2000); and Laura Bingham, "Strategy or Process? Closing the International Criminal Tribunals for the Former Yugoslavia and Rwanda," *Berkeley Journal of International Law* 24, no. 3, 2006. For more critical perspectives, see Michael Mandel, *How America Gets Away with Murder: Illegal Wars, Collateral Damage, and Crimes against Humanity* (London: Pluto, 2004), chap. 5; John Laughland, *Travesty: The Trial of Slobodan Milošević and the Corruption of International Justice* (London: Pluto, 2006); and Kate Hudson, *Breaking the South Slav Dream: The Rise and Fall of Yugoslavia* (London: Pluto, 2003), chap. 10.

46. Orwell begins a classic essay: "Autobiography is only to be trusted when it reveals something disgraceful. A man who gives a good account of himself is probably lying." This is an overstatement, but the basic point—about the need to read autobiographies and memoirs with a suspicious eye—certainly holds true. See George Orwell, "Benefit

of Clergy: Some Notes on Salvador Dali," 1944, *www.orwell.ru/library/reviews/dali/english/e_dali*.

47. The popular view of the press as a reasonably impartial record of events is *not* widely held by academic specialists in the field of communications. Thus: "It is an article of faith among virtually all scholars of communication that media in Western democracies speak with one, narrow voice and that they restrict rather than enhance political debate. It would be hard to find a paper presented at the meetings of the International Communication Association challenging this premise." Robert Stevenson, professor of journalism and mass communication, University of North Carolina, Chapel Hill, letter to the editor, *Chronicle of Higher Education*, October 3, 1997. Also see Daniel Hallin, "The Media, the War in Vietnam, and Political Support: A Critique of the Thesis of an Oppositional Media," *Journal of Politics* 46, no. 1, 1984. The potential for systematic bias in press sources is often overlooked in statistically based political science research, which thus may produce unreliable results. See, for example, the following study, which relies on thousands of Reuters dispatches: Joshua S. Goldstein and Jon C. Pevehouse, "Reciprocity, Bullying, and International Cooperation: Time-Series Analysis of the Bosnia Conflict," *American Political Science Review* 91, no. 3, 1997.

48. Netherlands Institute for War Documentation, "Srebrenica—A 'Safe' Area: Reconstruction, Background, Consequences, and Analyses of the Fall of a Safe Area," 2003, *srebrenica.brightside.nl/srebrenica/*.

Chapter 2

Epigraph: Colin Powell quoted in Joseph Romm, "Laid Waste by Weapons Lust: Military Spending Policies," *Bulletin of the Atomic Scientists*, October 1992, 121.

1. Geir Lundestad, " 'Empire by Invitation' in the American Century," *Diplomatic History* 23, no. 2, 1999. See also: Charles Kupchan, "After Pax Americana: Benign Power, Regional Integration, and the Sources of a Stable Multipolarity," *International Security* 23, no. 2, 1998. In a similar vein, John Lewis Gaddis writes that US policy makers during the Cold War possessed "little imperial consciousness or design." Quoted in Robert Buzzanco, "What Happened to the New Left? Toward a Radical Reading of American Foreign Relations," *Diplomatic History* 23, no. 4, 1999, 584.

2. Irving Kristol, "The Emerging American Imperium," *Wall Street Journal*, August 18, 1997. See also Michael Mandelbaum, *The Case for Goliath: How America Acts as the World's Government in the Twenty-First Century* (New York: Public Affairs, 2005).

3. David Calleo, "Restarting the Marxist Clock? The Economic Fragility of the West," *World Policy Journal* 13, no. 2, 1996, 64.

4. Joyce Kolko and Gabriel Kolko, *The Limits of Power: The World and United States Foreign Policy, 1945–1954* (New York: Harper and Row, 1972).

5. Thus in 1993, Bruce Cumings wrote: "Today, you need an electron microscope to find 'imperialism' used to describe the US role in the world." "Global Realm with No Limit, Global Realm with No Name," *Radical History Review*, no. 57, 1993, 47.

6. Christopher Layne and Benjamin Schwarz, "American Hegemony—Without an Enemy," *Foreign Policy*, no. 92, 1993, 5, 7–8. These themes are elaborated more fully in Layne, *The Peace of Illusions: American Grand Strategy from 1940 to the Present* (Ithaca: Cornell University Press, 2006), and "Rethinking American Grand Strategy," *World Policy Journal* 15, no. 2, 1998.

7. Kees Van Der Pijl, *Global Rivalries from the Cold War to Iraq* (London: Pluto, 2006);

and Ted Galen Carpenter, *A Search for Enemies: America's Alliances after the Cold War* (Washington, D.C.: Cato Institute, 2002). For similar arguments, see also: James Petras and Steven Vieux, "Bosnia and the Revival of US Hegemony," *New Left Review*, no. 218, 1996; Petras and Morris Morley, "Contesting Hegemons: US-French Relations in the 'New World Order,'" *Review of International Studies* 26, no. 1, 2000; and Ted Galen Carpenter, "Foreign Policy Masochism: The Campaign for US Intervention in Yugoslavia," Cato Foreign Policy Briefing Paper 19 (Washington, D.C.: Cato Institute, 1992).

8.   George Orwell, "Toward European Unity," *Partisan Review* 14, no. 4, 1947.

9.   Samuel Huntington, "The Erosion of American National Interests," *Foreign Affairs* 76, no. 5, 1997, 45.

10. See for example, Trevor Barnes, "The Secret Cold War: The CIA and American Foreign Policy in Europe, 1946–1956, Part I," *Historical Journal* 24, no. 2, 1981, and "The Secret Cold War: The CIA and American Foreign Policy in Europe, 1946–1956, Part II," *Historical Journal* 25, no. 3, 1982; and Alfred W. McCoy Jr., *The Politics of Heroin in Southeast Asia* (Harper and Row, 1972), chaps. 1, 2. Regarding the CIA's "culture war" in Europe, see Frances Stoner Saunders, *Who Paid the Piper? The CIA and the Cultural Cold War* (London: Granta Books, 1999).

11. Quoted in Michael Hudson, *Super Imperialism: The Economic Strategy of American Empire* (New York: Holt, Rinehart, and Winston, 1972), 189–90. Regarding the issue of US-British tensions during the early Cold War, see also Jeffrey A. Engel, *Cold War at 30,000 Feet: The Anglo-American Fight for Aviation Supremacy* (Cambridge, Mass.: Harvard University Press, 2007).

12. P. N. Jester quoted in David Gibbs, "Political Parties and International Relations: The United States and the Decolonization of Sub-Saharan Africa," *International History Review* 17, no. 2, 1995, 310–11.

13. Quoted in John Palmer, *Europe without America?* (Oxford: Oxford University Press, 1987), 30.

14. Russell Warren Howe, *Along the Afric Shore* (New York: Barnes and Noble, 1975), 152. Another arena of US-European rivalry was in Latin America, where French arms exports, especially the Mirage series of fighter planes, offered stiff competition for the United States. See analysis in Eric Stewart, "The Political Economy of United States Arms Transfers to Latin America during the Cold War," MA thesis, Department of Latin American Studies, University of Arizona, 1999.

15. Palmer, *Europe without America?* 62.

16. See David Halberstam, *The Best and the Brightest* (New York: Fawcett-Crest, 1972), 772.

17. See discussion in Michael Moffitt, *The World's Money: International Banking from Bretton Woods to the Brink of Insolvency* (New York: Simon and Schuster, 1983), 34–40; and Robert Solomon, *The International Monetary System, 1945–1976: An Insider's View* (New York: Harper and Row, 1977), chaps 11, 12.

18. This was explored in depth in David Spiro, *The Hidden Hand of American Hegemony: Petrodollar Recycling and International Markets* (Ithaca: Cornell University Press, 1999).

19. This is openly conceded by Melvyn Leffler, who writes that in 1947, during the height of Cold War tension, "no one feared Soviet military aggression." *A Preponderance of Power: The Truman Administration and the Cold War* (Stanford: Stanford University Press, 1992), 163.

20. Whether these purely *numerical* advantages offset qualitative NATO advantages in terms of superior training and equipment is a separate matter, which we will not

assess here. For an argument that the Warsaw Pact military advantages in Europe were overrated, see the analysis by former NSC staffer Robert Johnson in *Improbable Dangers: US Conceptions of Threat in the Cold War and After* (New York: St. Martin's, 1997), chaps. 3, 4; Malcolm Chalmers and Lutz Unterseher, "Is There a Tank Gap? Comparing NATO and Warsaw Pact Tank Fleets," *International Security* 13, no. 1, 1988; John A. Thompson, "The Exaggeration of American Vulnerability: The Anatomy of a Tradition," *Diplomatic History* 16, no. 1, 1992; and Mathew Evangelista, "Second Guessing the Experts: Citizens' Group Criticism of the Central Intelligence Agency's Soviet Military Estimates," *International History Review* 19, no. 3, 1997.

21. See Calleo, "Restarting the Marxist Clock?" 60.
22. This is the basic theme of Palmer, *Europe without America?* which was published in 1987.
23. David Harvey, *A Brief History of Neo-Liberalism* (Oxford: Oxford University Press, 2005).
24. Denis Lacorne, Jacques Rupnik, and Marie-France Toinet, *The Rise and Fall of Anti-Americanism: A Century of French Perception* (Basingstoke: Macmillan, 1990).
25. Joseph Nye Jr., "Soft Power," *Foreign Policy*, no. 80, 1990.
26. Steven Greenhouse, "Clamor in the East: Czechs Fault Policies of Hard-line Communists as Cause of Industrial Lag," *New York Times*, December 1, 1989.
27. Peter Gowan, "Western Economic Diplomacy and the New Eastern Europe," *New Left Review*, no. 182, 1990.
28. Gowan, "Western Economic Diplomacy," 79.
29. Quoted in Frederick Kempe, "German Giant: Helmut Kohl Takes Europe's Center Stage, Surprising His Critics," *Wall Street Journal*, November 30, 1990.
30. From "Les Français Jugent les Etats-Unis de Plus en Plus Négativement," *Le Monde*, October 31, 1996. Also "Les Lepénistes Pro-Américains," *Le Monde*, October 31, 1996. The quotes appear in translation from the French.
31. Also reported in "Les Français Jugent les Etats-Unis."
32. Susan Strange, "The Defective State," *Daedalus* 124, no. 2, 1995, 71.
33. Quoted in Fareed Zakaria, "Loves Me, Loves Me Not," *Newsweek*, October 5, 1998. The British diplomat is not named.
34. "World Law and World Power," *Economist*, December 5, 1998, 16.
35. Yekaterina Karsanova and Dimitry Epshtein, "The Fall of America," *Moskovskiye Novosti* (Moscow), January 31–February 7, 1999. Presented in English translation in *World Press Review*, May 1999.
36. Samuel Huntington, "The Lonely Superpower," *Foreign Affairs* 78, no. 2, 1999," 37–38.
37. Huntington, "Lonely Superpower," 38.
38. Quoted in Ann Devroy and Jeffrey Smith, "Clinton Reexamines a Foreign Policy under Siege," *Washington Post*, October 17, 1993. The tendency of Americans to miss the Cold War was a basic theme in H. W. Brands, *The Devil We Knew: Americans and the Cold War* (New York: Oxford University Press, 1993).
39. Henry Kissinger, *Diplomacy* (New York: Simon and Schuster, 1994), 819–20. Similarly, a book coauthored by Condoleezza Rice stated that the US troop presence in Europe "served as the ante to ensure a central place for the United States as a player in European politics. The Bush administration placed a high value on retaining such influence, underscored by Bush's flat statement that the United States was and would remain 'a European power.'" Philip Zelikow and Condoleezza Rice, *Germany Unified and Europe Transformed: A Study in Statecraft* (Cambridge, Mass.: Harvard University

Press, 1995), 169. A similar view appears in Hubert Védrine, *Les Mondes de François Mitterrand: A l'Elysée, 1981–1995* (Paris: Fayard, 1996), 657.

40. Gabriel Robin, "A Quoi Sert l'OTAN?" *Politique Etrangère* 60, no. 1, 1995, 179. Translated from the French. See also Dominique David, "La Communauté entre la Paix et la Guerre," *Politique Etrangère* 58, no. 2, 1993, 81, 84–85.

41. Quoted in Marc Fisher, "Germany's New Role Stirs Some Concern in US," *Washington Post*, January 23, 1992.

42. See Marc Fisher, "Germans Caught in US-French Rift: Army Corps Dispute Complicates New Foreign Minister's Visit," *Washington Post*, June 27, 1992.

43. See statement in "Success at Maastricht: A Landmark Summit," *PR Newswire*, December 11, 1991.

44. On the WEU, see Philip Gordon, "The Western European Union and NATO's 'Europeanisation,'" in Gordon, ed., *NATO's Transformation: The Changing Shape of the Atlantic Alliance* (Lanham, Md.: Rowman and Littlefield, 1997). See also Robert Hutchings, *American Diplomacy and the End of the Cold War: An Insider's Account of US Policy in Europe, 1989–1992* (Baltimore: Johns Hopkins University Press, 1997), 275–77; and Edward Mortimer, *European Security after the Cold War: An Assessment of the Dangers to Peace in Europe since the Soviet Collapse, and of the Western Responses They Require* (London: Brassey's/IISS, 1992), 55–61.

45. See William Johnsen and Thomas-Durell Young, "France's Evolving Policy toward NATO," *Strategic Review*, Summer 1995, 19, and "Franco-German Security Accommodation: Agreeing to Disagree," *Strategic Review*, Winter 1993, 12.

46. Jacques Delors, "European Integration and Security," *Survival* 33, no. 2, 1991, 105.

47. Bartholomew is paraphrased in Edward Mortimer, "Europe's Teetering Pillar: The French Are Resisting NATO Leaders' Efforts to Modify the Continent's Defence Arrangements," *Financial Times*, May 1, 1991. Casper Weinberger quoted in Lawrence Kaplan, *NATO and the United States: The Enduring Alliance* (New York: Twayne Publishers, 1994), 175.

48. Quoted in Jacques Amalric, "L'Europe Vue du Potomac," *Le Monde*, June 6, 1992. Translated from the French.

49. Julius W. Friend, "US Policy toward Franco-German Cooperation," in Patrick McCarthy, ed., *France-Germany, 1983–1993: The Struggle to Cooperate* (New York: St. Martin's, 1993), 172–73.

50. Fisher, "Germans Caught in US-French Rift." On US criticism, see also "Franco-German Corps Strains NATO's Post-Cold War Strategic Relations," *Aviation Week and Space Technology*, June 1, 1992.

51. C. Fred Bergsten, "America and Europe: Clash of the Titans?" *Foreign Affairs* 78, no. 2, 1999, 20.

52. "The Editors: Continental Divide," *New Republic*, January 25, 1999, 7–8.

53. The leaders in question were Raymond Barre, Pierre Bérégovoy, and Helmut Kohl. Mark Nelson expressed doubt regarding the charges of orchestration; but he acknowledged that some US officials viewed European monetary integration dimly. See Nelson, "Transatlantic Travails: Europe and America," *Foreign Policy*, no. 92, 1993, 81–82; and John Holmes, *The United States and Europe after the Cold War: A New Alliance?* (Columbia: University of South Carolina Press, 1997), 195.

54. John Updike epigraph quote from Huntington, "Erosion of American National Interests," 29.

55. See James Mann, *The Rise of the Vulcans: The History of Bush's War Cabinet* (New York:

Viking, 2004), chap. 13. According to Mann, the actual writing was done primarily by Khalilzad. Others involved in drafting the document included I. Lewis Libby and J. D. Crouch II. See Jim Lobe, "Hardliner's Hard-Liner Led Bush's Iraq Review," InterPress Service, January 9, 2007.

56. See Patrick Tyler, "US Strategy Plan Calls for Insuring No Rivals Develop," *New York Times*, March 8, 1992; and "Excerpts from Pentagon's Plan: 'Prevent the Re-Emergence of a New Rival,'" *New York Times*, March 8, 1992.

57. "Excerpts from Pentagon's Plan." The full text of the draft DPG has recently become declassified and publicly available (though the document is heavily redacted). See US Department of Defense, "Defense Planning Guidance, FY 1994–1999," February 18, 1992, *www.gwu.edu/~nsarchiv/nukevault/ebb245/doc03_full.pdf*.

58. Tyler, "US Strategy Plan Calls for Insuring No Rivals Develop." This quote is from the Tyler article, which paraphrases the document.

59. "Excerpts from Pentagon's Plan."

60. Even as late as 2004, public opinion polls affirmed strong European support for NATO. This is true despite the generally negative view of US foreign policy during this period. See Polly Toynbee, "A Degree of Bullying and Self-Interest? No Thanks: The Decline of American Studies Reveals Our Increasing Dislike of the US," *Guardian*, August 25, 2004.

61. This has been especially true with regard to European cooperation in the US policy of "extraordinary rendition." See European Parliament, "Draft Report: On the Alleged Use of European Countries by the CIA for the Transportation and Illegal Detention of Prisoners," November 24, 2006, *abcnews.go.com/images/International/european_report2_clean.pdf*.

62. Gaddis quoted in Peter Grier, "Hot Debate over US Strategic Role," *Christian Science Monitor*, March 16, 1992; and Barry Posen and Andrew Ross, "Competing US Grand Strategies," in Robert Lieber, ed., *Eagle Adrift: American Foreign Policy at the End of the Century* (New York: Longman, 1997), 133.

63. The Pentagon later redrafted the DPG and released the new version in May 1992. The emphasis in this new document was on cooperative rather than controlling relationships between the United States and its allies. See Barton Gellman, "Pentagon Abandons Goal of Thwarting US Rivals," *Washington Post*, May 24, 1992.

64. Mann, *Rise of the Vulcans*, 214–15.

65. Efforts by elements of the US establishment to disrupt European unity are also noted in Stanley Sloan, "US-West European Relations and Europe's Future," in Glennon J. Harrison, ed, *Europe and the United States: Competition and Cooperation in the 1990s* (Armonk, N.Y.: M. E. Sharpe, 1994), 171.

66. We will see in Chapter 6, however, that British officials intermittently flirted with the idea of moving away from the United States and toward the German-French position, which aimed at foreign policy independence.

67. Regarding latent pro-US sentiment that remains present in European society, see Leo Panitch, "The New Imperial State," *New Left Review*, no. 2, 2000, 17.

68. See Robert Grant, "France's New Relationship with NATO," in Philip H. Gordon, ed., *NATO's Transformation: The Changing Shape of the Atlantic Alliance* (Lanham, Md.: Rowman and Littlefield, 1997), 53–54; Charles Barry, "Combined Joint Task Forces in Theory and Practice," in Gordon, ed., *NATO's Transformation*; and Ronald Asmus, *Opening NATO's Door: How the Alliance Remade Itself for the New Era* (New York: Columbia University Press, 2002), 35.

69. Edward Foster, "Eurocorps' Quest for Identity," *International Defense Review*, November 1, 1994, 29. See also J. Lewis, "Pegasus 95 Launches Eurocorps' Operations," *Jane's Defence Weekly*, January 1, 1996.

70. Brigitte Sauerwein, "Eurocorps 'Condemned to Success,'" *International Defense Review*, February 1, 1995, 5 (electronic version from Lexis-Nexis).

71. "Count your NATOs," *Economist*, April 24, 1999.

72. Jeffrey Sachs strongly implies that in 1992, Cheney and other figures in the Defense Department blocked efforts to furnish large-scale financial assistance to Russia, which was still viewed as a military adversary. Sachs, *The End of Poverty: Economic Possibilities for Our Time* (New York: Penguin, 2005), 139–40.

73. "NATO Seeks Significance in a Post–Cold War Climate," *Jane's Defence Weekly*, May 16, 1992, 840. See also Thomas-Durell Young, "Preparing the Western Alliance for the Next Out-of-Area Campaign," *Naval War College Review* 45, no. 3, 1992, 37; Paul R. S. Gebhard, *The United States and European Security* (London: IISS/Brassey's, 1994); and James Kurth, "First War of the Global Era: Kosovo and US Grand Strategy," in Andrew J. Bacevich and Eliot A. Cohen, eds., *War over Kosovo: Politics and Strategy in a Global Age* (New York: Columbia University Press, 2001), 75.

74. Robin, "A Quoi Sert l'OTAN?" 173. Translated from the French.

75. Christopher is paraphrased in Stewart Powell, "NATO's Eastern Question," *Air Force Magazine*, January 1996, 57.

76. Powell, "NATO's Eastern Question," 57–58.

77. Katherine Seelye, "Arms Contractors Spend to Promote an Expanded NATO," *New York Times*, March 30, 1998.

78. Tim Smart, "Count Corporate America among NATO's Staunchest Allies," *Washington Post*, April 13, 1999.

79. Corporations noted in Smart, "Count Corporate America."

80. Retired Rear Adm. Eugene Carroll, on "NATO, Dead or Alive?" show transcript, April 25, 1993, America's Defense Monitor video, Center for Defense Information Web site, *www.cdi.org/adm/632*. Carroll noted that European officers benefited from NATO as well.

81. See the classic study, Anthony Downs, *Inside Bureaucracy* (Boston: Little, Brown, 1967), 200.

82. From Marc Fisher, "Eastern Europe Swept by German Influence," *Washington Post*, February 16, 1992; and David Binder, "As Bonn Talks Louder, Some in the U.S. Wince," *New York Times*, January 7, 1992.

83. Even Tony Blair took the view that "the way NATO worked was the US basically ran it." Blair paraphrased in Alastair Campbell, *The Blair Years: The Alastair Campbell Diaries* (New York: Knopf, 2007), 404.

84. See Craig Whitney, "At Odds with US, France Says No to NATO Role," *New York Times*, October 2, 1997; and Jean-Maire Colombani, "Arrogances Américaines," *Le Monde*, February 26, 1998.

85. "The EU Turns Its Attention from Ploughshares to Swords," *Economist*, November 20, 1999, 51–52.

86. Bergsten, "America and Europe," 20.

87. In general, macroeconomic trends have not always conformed with the more positive views of globalization. See Roberto Patricio Korzeniewicz and Timothy Patrick Moran, "World Economic Trends in the Distribution of Income, 1965–1992," *American Journal of Sociology* 102, no. 4, 1997; and Branko Milanovic, "The Two Faces

of Globalization: Against Globalization as We Know It," *World Development* 31, no. 4, 2003.

88. The role of the "internationalist" business bloc is a basic theme in Ronald W. Cox and Daniel Skidmore-Hess, *U.S. Politics and the Global Economy: Corporate Power, Conservative Shift* (Boulder, Colo.: Lynne Rienner, 1999).

89. From testimony by James Ortega, president of Saenz Hofmann Financial, in US Congress, *Quota Increase of the International Monetary Fund* (Washington, D.C.: US Government Printing Office, 1991), 31. I thank Jerri-Lynn Scofield for bringing this source to my attention.

90. Quoted in Kevin Phillips, *Wealth and Democracy: A Political History of the American Rich* (New York: Broadway Books, 2002), 230.

91. This benefit is emphasized in Peter Gowan, *The Global Gamble: Washington's Faustian Bid for World Dominance* (London: Verso, 1999).

92. Regarding US anxiety that it might lose its dominant position in international financial policy making, see Martin Feldstein, "EMU and International Conflict," *Foreign Affairs* 76, no. 6, 1997.

93. Melvyn Westlake, "Welcome to a Tri-Polar World," *The Banker*, July 1991, 22. A tripartite economic division of the world was already viewed as a possibility during the 1980s. See comments by Charles Meismer of Chemical Bank, quoted in Jeffrey Frieden, *Banking on the World* (New York: Harper and Row, 1987), 178–79.

94. David Owen, "Atlantic Partnership or Rivalry?" in Henry Brandon, ed., *In Search of a New World Order: The Future of US-European Relations* (Washington, D.C.: Brookings, 1992), 15.

95. C. Michael Aho, " 'Fortress Europe': Will the EU Isolate Itself from North America and Asia?" *Columbia Journal of World Business* 29, no. 3, 1994, 32.

96. "Maastricht as Seen from Afar," *Economist*, November 30, 1991, 49. See also Alain Frachon, "Washington: Une Appréciation Globalement Positive, Mais des Inquiétudes pour l'OTAN," *Le Monde*, December 9, 1991; Paul Johnson, "Arguing for Free Trade," *Commentary*, August 1995; and "Learning to Live with Super-Europe," *Business Week*, December 23, 1991.

97. See Ronald Cox, "Corporate Coalitions and Industrial Restructuring: Explaining Regional Trade Agreements," *Competition and Change* 1, no. 1, 1995.

98. Jagdish Bhagwati, "Fast Track to Nowhere," *Economist*, October 18, 1997, 21.

99. Chalmers Johnson quoted in Teresa Watanabe, "Japan Looks Homeward—Toward Asia," *Los Angeles Times*, October 25, 1994. Van Der Pijl situates Japanese moves toward foreign policy independence in the context of an anti-Japanese thrust by the Clinton administration. See Van Der Pijl, *Global Rivalries*, 311, 317, 320–29.

100. Robert Wade and Frank Veneroso, "The Asian Crisis: The High Debt Model Versus the Wall Street-Treasury-IMF Complex," *New Left Review*, no. 228, 1998.

101. Regarding US unpopularity in Asia, see Nicholas Kristof, "Asians Worry That US Aid Is a New Colonialism," *New York Times*, February 17, 1998.

102. Sakakibara is paraphrased in "Mr. Yen Sees Light at the End of the Tunnel," *Japan Times*, February 7, 1999.

103. On Eastern Europe, see Katherine Seelye, "Arms Contractors Spend to Promote an Expanded NATO," *New York Times*, March 30, 1998. On US-French competition in Africa, see "En Afrique, les Etats-Unis se Heurtent à la France et à Plusieurs Pays du Continent," *Le Monde*, October 15, 1996; and Peter Schraeder, *African Politics and Society: A Mosaic in Transformation* (Boston: Bedford/St. Martin's, 2000), 326–28.

104. "AIOC Continues to Juggle Export Pipeline Options," *East European Energy Report*, March 31, 1997.

105. Ian Katz and John Templeman, "Is Europe Elbowing the US out of Latin America?" *Business Week*, August 4, 1997, 56. See also Laurence Whitehead, "The European Union and the Americas," in Victor Bulmer-Thomas and James Dunkerley, eds., *The United States and Latin America: The New Agenda* (Cambridge, Mass.: Harvard University Press, 1999), 63–64.

106. Officially APEC was created in 1989, but it achieved a prominent role only during the Clinton presidency, beginning in 1993.

107. Jean-Pierre Langellier, "Les Non-dits du Dialogue Euro-Asiatique," *Le Monde*, March 2, 1996. Translated from the French.

108. Amy Borrus, "Why Pinstripes Don't Suit the Cloak and Dagger Crowd," *Business Week*, May 17, 1993; and Peter Schweizer, "The Growth of Economic Espionage: America Is Target Number One," *Foreign Affairs* 75, no. 1, 1996.

109. Janet Bush, "World Government Is Not Imminent," *Times* (London), January 27, 1999. And C. Fred Bergsten noted that recent trends could lead to "the tripartite world that has been expected, or feared, for some time." Bergsten, "Towards a Tripartite World," *Economist*, July 15, 2000, 23–26.

110. For the best general analysis of the economic basis of political rivalry during this period, see Kees Van Der Pijl, "From Gorbachev to Kosovo: Atlantic Rivalries and the Re-Incorporation of Eastern Europe," *Review of International Political Economy* 8, no. 2, 2001.

111. Hutchings, *American Diplomacy and the End of the Cold War*, 159.

112. Haig quoted in Arnaud de Bourchgrave, "Haig: Syria Should Be Next Target," UPI, January 7, 2002.

113. Michael Lind, "A Plea for a New Global Strategy: Looking Past NATO," *New Leader*, June 30, 1997. See also Holmes, *The United States and Europe after the Cold War*, 113.

114. John S. Duffield, "NATO's Function after the Cold War," *Political Science Quarterly* 109, no. 5, 1994–1995, 785–86.

115. Jonathan Clarke, "Replacing NATO," *Foreign Policy*, no. 93, 1993–1994, 31.

116. It also has been argued that NATO had an important economic function from the beginning of its existence in 1949. See Benjamin Fordham, *Building the Cold War Consensus: The Political Economy of U.S. National Security Policy, 1949–51* (Ann Arbor: University of Michigan Press, 1998).

117. Mohammed A. Bamyeh, "The New Imperialism: Six Theses," *Social Text* 18, no. 1, 2000; William Robinson, *A Theory of Global Capitalism: Production, Class, and State in a Transnational World* (Baltimore: Johns Hopkins University Press, 2004); and Michael Hardt and Antonio Negri, *Empire* (Cambridge: Harvard University Press, 2000).

118. Layne and Schwarz, "American Hegemony," 15.

119. For multinational corporations, another way to cope with instability is to hire mercenary forces, which have become increasingly important. See Steven Brayton, "Outsourcing War: Mercenaries and the Privatization of Peacekeeping," *Journal of International Affairs* 55, no. 2, 2002; and Jeremy Scahill, *Blackwater: The Rise of the World's Most Powerful Mercenary Army* (New York: Nation Books, 2007).

120. Thomas Friedman, "A Manifesto for the Fast World," *New York Times Magazine*, March 28, 1999, 65.

121. Robert Nozick epigraph quoted in Franco Marcoaldi, "A Nation in Search of an

Enemy," *La Repubblica* (Rome), English translation in *World Press Review*, February 1992, 41.

122. See William Greider, *Fortress America: The American Military and the Consequences of Peace* (New York: Public Affairs Press, 1998).

123. Irving Kristol, "A Post-Wilsonian Foreign Policy," *Wall Street Journal*, August 2, 1996.

124. Regarding US efforts to find new threats, see Michael Klare, *Rogue States and Nuclear Outlaws: America's Search for a New Foreign Policy* (New York: Hill and Wang, 1995).

125. During the early 1990s, US military strategy was based on a two-war scenario, i.e., that the United States should be able to fight two medium-sized rogue states simultaneously. This strategy elicited ridicule. In 1991, a Defense Department analyst commented that the two-war strategy was "just a marketing device to justify a high [military] budget." Ronald Steel observes that "it is hard to refute the conclusions of one analyst that the Pentagon's 'planning requirements have been invented to justify the forces and structures we have rather than to cope with the world we face.'" Quotes from Buzzanco, "What Happened to the New Left?" 599; and Ronald Steel, *Temptations of a Superpower* (Cambridge, Mass.: Harvard University Press, 1995), 54.

126. The use of the September 11, 2001, terrorist attacks as a justification for US expansion is discussed in David Gibbs, "Pretexts and U.S. Foreign Policy: The War on Terrorism in Historical Perspective," *New Political Science* 26, no. 3, 2004, *www.gened.arizona.edu/dgibbs/pretexts.pdf*

127. George Packer, "The Liberal Quandary over Iraq," *New York Times Magazine*, December 8, 2002.

128. David Halberstam, *War in a Time of Peace: Bush, Clinton, and the Generals* (New York: Simon and Schuster, 2002); and Andrew J. Bacevich, *The New American Militarism: How Americans Are Seduced by War* (New York: Oxford University Press, 2005).

Chapter 3

Epigraph: Ruth E. Gruber, "Serb Says Money Counts More Than Ethnicity," *San Diego Union Tribune*, December 11, 1988.

1. Regarding Serbian aggressiveness, Ivo Banac states: "Serbia unleashed a war of conquest against its western neighbors." See Banac's foreword in Sabrina Petra Ramet, *Balkan Babel: The Disintegration of Yugoslavia from the Death of Tito to Ethnic War*, 2d ed. (Boulder, Colo.: Westview, 1996), xvii. For similar views regarding the Serbs' guilt, see Branimir Anzulovic, *Heavenly Serbia: From Myth to Genocide* (New York: New York University Press, 1999).

2. Aryeh Neier, "Inconvenient Facts: Review of Noam Chomsky's *The New Military Humanism*," *Dissent* 47, no. 2, 2000, 111–12.

3. Noel Malcolm, *Kosovo: A Short History* (New York: New York University Press, 1999), x.

4. Madeleine Albright, *Madam Secretary* (New York: Miramax Books, 2003), chap. 23.

5. Quoted in "US Envoy Recalls 'Monster' Milošević," BBC News, March 13, 2006, *news. bbc.co.uk/2/hi/europe/4802380.stm*.

6. Doug Henwood, " 'I am a Fighting Atheist': Interview with Slavoj Žižek," February 2002, *bad.eserver.org/issues/2002/59/zizek.html*.

7. On the interwar period, see Joseph Rothschild, *East Central Europe between the Two World Wars* (Seattle: University of Washington Press, 1983), 278–79; Dennison I. Rusinow, *The Yugoslav Experiment, 1948–1974* (Berkeley: University of California Press, 1977), xvii; and Ivo Banac, *The National Question in Yugoslavia: Origins, History,*

Politics (Ithaca: Cornell University Press, 1988). Alex Dragnich argues that there was no systematic discrimination against non-Serbs during this period, in "The Anatomy of a Myth: Serbian Hegemony," *Slavic Review* 50, no. 3, 1991.

8. Kate Hudson, *Breaking the South Slav Dream: The Rise and Fall of Yugoslavia* (London: Pluto, 2003), 14; and Robert Hayden, "Yugoslavia's Collapse: National Suicide with Foreign Assistance," *Economic and Political Weekly*, July 4, 1992, 1378. On the interwar period in general, see also Aleksa Djilas, *The Contested Country: Yugoslav Unity and Communist Revolution, 1919–1953* (Cambridge, Mass.: Harvard University Press, 1991), chaps. 1, 2.

9. Hervé Joly, "Les lnvestissements Directs des Groupes Industriels Allemands en Europe du Centre-Est entre 1919 et 1945," in François Bafoil, ed., *Les Stratégies Allemandes en Europe Central et Orientale: Une Géopolitiques des Investissements* (Paris: Harmattan, 1997), 28, 49. Foreign investment is calculated in terms of foreign stock ownership of companies in Yugoslavia.

10. See the classic study of German economic diplomacy, Albert O. Hirschman, *National Power and the Structure of Foreign Trade* (Berkeley: University of California Press, 1980).

11. Fred Singleton, *A Short History of the Yugoslav Peoples* (Cambridge: Cambridge University Press, 1985), 175.

12. Singleton, *Short History*, 177–78.

13. This estimate is from Singleton, *Short History*, 177–78. For further discussion of Ustaša atrocities, see Lisa Adeli, "From Jasenovac to Yugoslavism: Ethnic Persecution in Croatia during World War II," PhD thesis, Department of History, University of Arizona, 2004; Jozo Tomasevich, *War and Revolution in Yugoslavia* (Stanford: Stanford University Press, 2001); Jonathan Gumz, "German Counterinsurgency Policy in Independent Croatia, 1941–1944," *Historian* 61, no. 1, 1998; David Bruce MacDonald, *Balkan Holocausts? Serbian and Croatian Victim-Centred Propaganda and the War in Yugoslavia* (Manchester: Manchester University Press, 2002); and Djilas, *Contested Country*, chap. 4.

14. On the mass killing of Jews in Yugoslavia, see Lucy W. Dawidowicz, *The War against the Jews* (New York: Holt, Rinehart, and Winston, 1975), 391–92.

15. Noel Malcolm, *Bosnia: A Short History* (New York: New York University Press, 1994), 188–89; Malcolm, *Kosovo*, 309–11; Yves-Marc Ajchenbaum, "Il y a Cinquante Ans: Une Division SS Islamiste en Bosnia," *Le Monde*, November 15, 1993; and Bogdan Denitch, *Ethnic Nationalism: The Tragic Death of Yugoslavia* (Minneapolis: University of Minnesota Press, 1996), 118.

16. United Nations, "Report on the Historical Background of the Civil War in the Former Yugoslavia: United Nations Commission of Experts, Security Council Resolution 780 (1992), Professor M. Cherif Bassiouni, Chairman," March 1994, 23; and Susan Woodward, *Balkan Tragedy: Chaos and Dissolution after the Cold War* (Washington, D.C.: Brookings, 1995), 241.

17. Diana Johnstone, *Fool's Crusade: Yugoslavia, NATO, and Western Delusions* (New York: Monthly Review Press, 2002), 186.

18. Regarding the lively culture of debate in Titoist Yugoslavia, see Rusinow, *Yugoslav Experiment*, 142–43.

19. "Eastern Europe: Striking Innovation," *Economist*, December 3, 1977, 67.

20. There has been some tendency to extol the multiculturalism of Bosnia-Herzegovina, but this seems overstated, according to anthropologist Xavier Bougarel: "During the 1980s, the percentage of mixed marriages in Bosnia-Herzegovina (about 12 percent of

the total) was equivalent to Yugoslavia as a whole. . . . Sarajevo contained fewer mixed marriages (28 percent) than some Croat cities." *Bosnie: Anatomie d'un Conflit* (Paris: La Découverte, 1996), 87. Translated from the French.

21. See "Constitution of the Socialist Federal Republic of Yugoslavia," in William Simons, ed., *Constitutions of the Communist World* (Alphen ann den Rijn, Netherlands: Sijthoff and Noordhoff, 1980).

22. S. Woodward, *Balkan Tragedy*, 31, 37.

23. For a general description of the military structure, see US Central Intelligence Agency [USCIA], *Balkan Battlegrounds: A Military History of the Yugoslav Conflict* (Washington, D.C.: CIA Office of Russian and European Analysis, 2002), vol. 1, 46–48.

24. Slavenka Drakulić, *How We Survived Communism and Even Laughed* (London: Hutchinson, 1992).

25. Figures for growth of net factor productivity were also strongly positive during the period 1953–1965. See Bela Balassa and Trent Bertrand, "Growth Performance of Eastern European Economies and Comparable Western European Countries," *American Economic Review* 60, no. 2, 1970, 316.

26. Basil Davidson, "Misunderstanding Yugoslavia," *London Review of Books*, May 23, 1996, 20.

27. Rusinow, *Yugoslav Experiment*, 140. For a sympathetic account of Yugoslavia's accomplishments see Michael Barratt Brown, *From Tito to Milošević: Yugoslavia, the Lost Country* (London: Merlin, 2005), especially chaps. 2–9.

28. Robert Alan Dahl, *After the Revolution: Authority in a Good Society* (New Haven: Yale University Press, 1970), chap. 3, and *A Preface to Economic Democracy* (Berkeley: University of California Press, 1985), chap. 5; Charles A. Lindblom, *Politics and Markets: The World's Political-Economic Systems* (New York: Basic Books, 1977), chap. 24; and Carole Pateman, *Participation and Democratic Theory* (Cambridge: Cambridge University Press, 1970), chap. 5. Some academic specialists continued to give respectful treatment to the Yugoslav system as late as 1989. See Steven Burg and Michael Berbaum, "Community, Integration, and Stability in Multinational Yugoslavia," *American Political Science Review* 83, no. 2, 1989.

29. Denitch, *Ethnic Nationalism*, 28.

30. Nearly 50 percent of ethnic Serbs lived outside the Republic of Serbia, which diluted the Serbs' overall influence in the federation. See United Nations, "Report on the Historical Background of the Civil War," 31.

31. See his Department of State biography, "Biographical Sketch of Josip Broz Tito, President and Marshal of Yugoslavia," no date. Available through Declassified Documents Reference System (Thomson-Gale databases).

32. Denitch, *Ethnic Nationalism*, 105.

33. Ivo Banac, "Yugoslavia," in Joel Krieger, ed., *Oxford Companion to Politics of the World* (New York: Oxford University Press, 1993).

34. Nikolai Botev, "Where East Meets West: Ethnic Intermarriage in the Former Yugoslavia, 1962 to 1989," *American Sociological Review* 59, no. 3, 1994, 463. Output is measured in gross social product. See also John Allcock, *Explaining Yugoslavia* (London: Hurst, 2000), 83–86.

35. This is discussed at length in Evan Kraft, "Evaluating Regional Policy in Yugoslavia, 1966–1990," *Comparative Economic Studies* 34, no. 3–4, 1992.

36. Warren Zimmermann, *Origins of a Catastrophe: Yugoslavia and Its Destroyers—America's*

Last Ambassador Tells What Happened and Why (New York: Times Books, 1996), 29; and Sliva Mežnaric, "Sociology of Migration in Yugoslavia," *Current Sociology* 32, no. 2, 1984.

37.   Botev, "Where East Meets West," 463.

38.   See Renéo Lukic, *L'Agonie Yougoslave (1986–2003): Les Etats-Unis et l'Europe Face aux Guerres Balkaniques* (Québec: Presse de l'Université de Laval, 2003), 73; Richard F. Nyrop, ed., *Yugoslavia: A Country Study* (Washington, D.C.: US Government Printing Office, 1982), 184; and Allcock, *Explaining Yugoslavia*, 90–91.

39.   Andrew Borowiec, "Money Makes, Breaks Yugoslavia," *Washington Times,* July 1, 1991. See also Ilija Todorovic, "Regional Economic Nationalism in the Former Yugoslavia," in Raju Thomas and H. Richard Friman, eds., *The South Slav Conflict* (New York: Garland, 1996), 171–72; and Denitch, *Ethnic Nationalism*, 53. The general picture of Croat nationalism as motivated substantially by economic grievances is confirmed in an analysis by a pro-Croat lobby group. See letter from Senator Robert Taft Jr. to Henry Kissinger, January 24, 1972. Available from Declassified Documents Reference System (Thomson-Gale databases).

40.   David Dyker, *Yugoslavia: Socialism, Development, and Debt* (London: Routledge, 1990), 102.

41.   Regarding the economics of energy, see Allcock, *Explaining Yugoslavia*, 93–94.

42.   The number of overseas Yugoslav guest workers in Western Europe was equivalent to 22 percent of Yugoslavia's domestically employed workforce. See Rusinow, *Yugoslav Experiment*, 44, 65, 251; and Allcock, *Explaining Yugoslavia*, 88–89.

43.   John E. Roemer, *A Future for Socialism* (Cambridge, Mass.: Harvard University Press, 1994), 85–89.

44.   Quoted in Pateman, *Participation and Democratic Theory*, 90.

45.   The epigraph quotes are from Allcock, *Explaining Yugoslavia*, 98; and from Jude Wanniski, Memorandum to A. M. Rosenthal, April 15, 1999, *www.polyconomics.com/memos/mm-990415.htm*. Allcock's question gave the respondents three choices: "the economy, the constitution, or Kosovo."

46.   Dyker, *Yugoslavia*, 96.

47.   David Spiro, *The Hidden Hand of American Hegemony: Petrodollar Recycling and International Markets* (Ithaca: Cornell University Press, 1999).

48.   Dyker, *Yugoslavia*, 95. Imported crude oil accounted for 28 percent of Yugoslavia's total energy needs by 1975. Nyrop, *Yugoslavia*, 133.

49.   "Jugoslavia: Economic Earthquakes," *Economist*, March 1, 1980, 65.

50.   Susan Woodward, "Orthodoxy and Solidarity: Competing Claims and International Adjustment in Yugoslavia," *International Organization* 40, no. 2, 1986, 534–35.

51.   Dyker, *Yugoslavia*, 131–32. On the general role of debt in triggering the later ethnic war, see also Michael Barratt Brown, "The Role of Economic Factors in Social Crisis: The Case of Yugoslavia," *New Political Economy* 2, no. 2, 1997.

52.   S. Woodward, "Orthodoxy and Solidarity," 536.

53.   John Lampe, *Yugoslavia as History: Twice There Was a Country* (Cambridge: Cambridge University Press, 1996), 326–27.

54.   Glenn Curtis, ed., *Yugoslavia: A Country Study* (Washington D.C., US Government Printing Office, 1992), chap. 3 ("Unemployment and Living Standards" subsection), *lcweb2.loc.gov/frd/cs/yutoc.html*.

55.   Dyker, *Yugoslavia*, 169. Emphasis in original.

56.   "Advantage None: Yugoslavia's Volatile Federation Is Reforming Its Banks from the

Bottom Up," *Banker,* September 1990; and "Yugoslavia," *Keesing's Record of World Events* 37, 9 (Supplement), September 1991. Some studies exaggerate the Titoist regime's responsibility for Yugoslavia's economic problems, while they downplay or ignore completely the international character of the 1980s debt crisis. See, for example, Robert J. Donia and John V. A. Fine Jr., *Bosnia and Herzegovina: A Tradition Betrayed* (New York: Columbia University Press, 1994), 198.

57. Joseph Stiglitz, "The Insider: What I Learned at the World Economic Crisis," *New Republic,* April 17, 2000; and Jeffrey Sachs, "The IMF and the Asian Flu," *American Prospect,* March–April, 1998.

58. Jerome Levinson quoted in Doug Henwood, "Impeccable Logic: Trade, Development, and Free Markets in the Clinton Era," *NACLA Report on the Americas* 26, no. 5, 1993, 3 (electronic version available through Academic OneFile).

59. William Ryrie of the International Finance Corporation, an arm of the World Bank, quoted in Henwood, "Impeccable Logic," 3.

60. Wanniski memorandum. It is clear that US officials strongly supported externally imposed economic programs and repeatedly coaxed Yugoslav officials to cooperate. See US National Security Council, "US Position on Yugoslav Paris Club Debt Rescheduling," June 10, 1987; and US National Security Council, "Summary of Deputy Secretary Whitehead's Meeting with Yugoslav Prime Minister Branko Mikulić regarding Yugoslavia's Plans to Deal with Its Economic Crisis," November 12, 1987. Both documents from Declassified Documents Reference System (Thomson-Gale databases).

61. US Department of State [USDOS], "Yugoslavia: Prospects for the Federation," IRR No. 145, January 22, 1988, 3. Available from Declassified Documents Reference System (Thomson-Gale databases).

62. Regarding US influence in the workings of the IMF, see Kevin Phillips, *Wealth and Democracy: A Political History of the American Rich* (New York: Broadway Books, 2002), 230; and US Congress, *Quota Increase of the International Monetary Fund* (Washington, D.C.: US Government Printing Office, 1991), 31.

63. For further discussion of the effects of structural adjustment on Yugoslavia, see Ann Orford, *Reading Humanitarian Intervention: Human Rights and the Use of Force in International Law* (Cambridge: Cambridge University Press, 2004), 87–96; K. Hudson, *Breaking the South Slav Dream,* chap. 4; and Netherlands Institute for War Documentation [NIOD], "Srebrenica—A 'Safe' Area: Reconstruction, Background, Consequences, and Analyses of the Fall of a Safe Area," 2003, prologue, chap. 3, sec. 3; and part 2, chap. 2, sec. 1, both at *srebrenica.brightside.nl/srebrenica/.*

64. USDOS, "Yugoslavia: Prospects for the Federation," 8.

65. S. Woodward, *Balkan Tragedy,* 63–64.

66. Botev, "Where East Meets West," 463.

67. Botev, "Where East Meets West," 463.

68. Randy Hodson, Dusko Sekulic, and Garth Massey, "National Tolerance in the Former Yugoslavia," *American Journal of Sociology* 99, no. 6, 1994, 1548, 1551.

69. On the relationship between ethnic conflict and regional economic inequality, see Michael Hechter, *Internal Colonialism: The Celtic Fringe in British National Development* (New Brunswick, N.J.: Transaction Publishers, 1999); Amy Chua, *World on Fire: How Exporting Free Market Democracy Breeds Ethnic Hatred and Global Instability* (New York: Doubleday, 2003); and David Harvey, *A Brief History of Neo-Liberalism* (Oxford: Oxford University Press, 2005), 83–86.

70. The memoirs of Bosnian president Alija Izetbegović emphasize the decline in living standards during the late 1980s. Izetbegović, *Inescapable Questions: Autobiographical Notes* (Leicester, UK: Islamic Foundation, 2003), 9.

71. Tim Judah, *Kosovo: War and Revenge* (New Haven: Yale University Press, 2002), 38–42.

72. S. Woodward, *Balkan Tragedy*, 56, 75; Jasna Dragović-Soso, *Saviours of the Nation: Serbia's Intellectual Opposition and the Revival of Nationalism* (Montreal: McGill-Queen's University Press, 2002).

73. S. Woodward, *Balkan Tragedy*, 77. Emphasis in original.

74. Residents of Kosovo and Vojvodina voted as part of the Republic of Serbia. A majority of Albanians in Kosovo, however, boycotted the vote in protest against Serb repression. See Blaine Harden, "Ethnic Albanians Boycott Key Election in Yugoslav Province," *Washington Post*, December 10, 1990.

75. Appearing as a prosecution witness at the Milošević trial in 2003, David Owen made the following statement: "Mr. Milošević you see now is not fundamentally racist. I think he is a nationalist, but even that he wears very lightly. I think he's a pragmatist." Nevertheless, Milošević certainly pursued policies that were racist in their effects, his personal feelings notwithstanding. Owen testimony, International Criminal Tribunal for the Former Yugoslavia [ICTY], November 3, 2003, 28404, *www.icty.org*. The widespread fascination with Milošević has generated a series of biographies, including: Vidosav Stevanovic, *Milošević: The People's Tyrant* (New York: St. Martin's, 2004); Dusko Doder and Louise Branson, *Milošević: Portrait of a Tyrant* (New York: Free Press, 1999); Slavoljub Dukic, *Milošević and Marković: A Lust for Power* (Montreal: McGill-Queen's University Press, 2001); Adam Lebor, *Milošević: A Biography* (London: Bloomsbury, 2002); and Lenard J. Cohen, *Serpent in the Bosom: The Rise and Fall of Slobodan Milošević* (Boulder, Colo.: Westview, 2001).

76. Louis Sell, *Slobodan Milošević and the Destruction of Yugoslavia* (Durham, N.C.: Duke University Press, 2002), 25; and S. Woodward, *Balkan Tragedy*, 107. Regarding Milošević's ties to the Western financial establishment, a biography notes: "During 1979 . . . Milošević attended the annual meeting of the International Monetary Fund and World Bank, held in Belgrade, where he met David Rockefeller; . . . in March 1980, Milošević visited New York . . . where he met a number of leading American bankers, including David Rockefeller once again, Leland Prussia, Chairman of the Board of Bank of America, and John F. McGillicuddy, Chairman of the Board of Manufacturers Hanover Trust. When McGillicuddy visited Yugoslavia the following year, Milošević was his host." Cohen, *Serpent in the Bosom*, 50–51.

77. State Department official Lawrence Eagleburger would later comment on his initially positive image of Milošević, who was viewed as a reformer. See Eagleburger, "NATO in a Corner," *New York Times*, April 4, 1999.

78. An anonymous American quoted in David Halberstam, *War in a Time of Peace* (New York: Simon and Schuster, 2002), 27. Despite the generally favorable impression, some officials expressed concern about Milošević's unscrupulous methods. See USDOS, "Yugoslavia: The Serb National Question," August 14, 1988. Available through Declassified Documents Reference System (Thomson-Gale databases).

79. Regarding Milošević's populist style, see Dragović-Soso, *Saviours of the Nation*, chap. 5.

80. Quoted in Lenard J. Cohen, *Broken Bonds: Yugoslavia's Disintegration and Balkan Politics in Transition* (Boulder, Colo.: Westview, 1995), 74–75. Ellipsis in original.

81. In 1986 the Serbian Academy of Sciences and Arts issued a key memorandum that presented a series of alleged grievances, along with a litany of complaints against other

ethnic groups. From the full text of the memorandum, it is clear that this document is a call to Serbian nationalism, and it sensationalized Serb grievances. However, the document contained no direct advocacy of violence or ethnic cleansing to achieve Serb objectives. Recent interpretations that present the memorandum as an organized plan for ethnic cleansing and mass murder seem overstated when compared with the document itself. For the English full text, see "Memorandum of the Serbian Academy of Sciences and Arts, 1986," in Snežana Trifunovska, ed., *Former Yugoslavia through Documents: From Its Dissolution to the Peace Settlement* (The Hague: Martinus Nijhoff, 1999), 4–44. See also Ivo Banac, "Historiography of the Countries of Eastern Europe: Yugoslavia," *American Historical Review* 97, no. 4, 1992, 1099–2004; and Dragović-Soso, *Saviours of the Nation*, 177–88, 220–21. One academic writes: "Had the Serbs formulated a genocidal program of Great Serbianism with the infamous 1986 [Serbian Academy] memorandum?"—the implication being that the document did in fact propose such a program. This is a substantial exaggeration. Quote from Nicholas Miller, "Search for a Serbian Havel," *Problems of Post-Communism* 44, no. 4, 1997, 5 (electronic version available through EBSCOhost).

82. "Profile: Vojislav Šešelj," BBC News, November 7, 2007, *news.bbc.co.uk/2/hi/ europe/2317765.stm*.

83. On Milošević's use of the Kosovo issue as a means of generating support, see Dragović-Soso, *Saviours of the Nation*, 208.

84. The speech did, in passing, make one specific hint at violence: "Now, we are again engaged in battles and are facing battles. They are not armed battles, *although such things cannot be excluded yet*" (emphasis added). "Speech by Slobodan Milošević at the Central Celebration Marking the 600th Anniversary of the Battle of Kosovo, Gazimestan, 28 June, 1989," in Heike Krieger, ed., *The Kosovo Conflict and International Law: An Analytical Documentation* (Cambridge: Cambridge University Press, 2001), 11. See also excerpts of the speech in Franke Wilmer, *The Social Construction of Man, the State, and War: Identity, Conflict, and Violence in Former Yugoslavia* (New York: Routledge, 2002), 136–37.

85. Malcolm, *Kosovo*, 344–45. See also Cathérine Samary, *Yugoslavia Dismembered* (New York: Monthly Review Press, 1995), 79.

86. S. Woodward, *Balkan Tragedy*, 96–97.

87. Misha Glenny, *The Fall of Yugoslavia: The Third Balkan War* (New York: Penguin, 1996), 34.

88. When Slovene authorities barred the demonstration, Serbia responded by initiating a boycott of goods from Slovenia. Yet the Slovene authorities were preparing for secession even before the confrontation with Serbia. In May 1989, the Slovene political party Demos declared its "firm intention to prepare the ground for . . . the possibility of a unilateral declaration of independence." This statement is especially important, since Demos would later win national elections, and it formed the new government. And in September 1989, "the Slovenian parliament adopted a series of constitutional amendments paving the way for eventual secession." Quotes from Dragović-Soso, *Saviours of the Nation*, 232. The first quote is directly from Demos, and the second quote is Dragović-Soso's description of the Slovenian parliament's actions. For Slovenian perspectives on the breakup, see Janez Drnovšek, "Riding the Tiger," *World Policy Journal* 17, no. 1, 2000; and Janez Janša, *The Making of the Slovenian State, 1988–1992: The Collapse of Yugoslavia* (Ljubljana: Založba Mladinska Knjiga, 1994). For background, see NIOD, "Srebrenica," prologue, chap. 4, sec. 3.

89. Cohen, *Broken Bonds,* 157.

90. Cohen, *Broken Bonds,* 155.

91. "25,000 Rally in Belgrade, Protesting Serbian Leadership," *Washington Post,* March 28, 1991.

92. "Former Communists in Serbia Win Majority in Parliamentary Vote," *New York Times,* December 26, 1990.

93. Peter Millonig, "A Case for Yugoslavia's Breakup," *Christian Science Monitor,* January 29, 1991.

94. Glenny, *Fall of Yugoslavia,* 45.

95. Mark Thompson and Philipp Kuntz, "Stolen Elections: The Case of the Serbian October," *Journal of Democracy* 15, no. 4, 2004.

96. Freedom House, "Country Reports: Yugoslavia (Serbia and Montenegro)," in *Freedom in the World: The Annual Survey of Political Rights and Civil Liberties, 1998–1999* (New Brunswick, N.J.: Transaction Publishers, 1999).

97. Or perhaps it was an "illiberal democracy" of the sort described in Fareed Zakaria, "When Switching Channels Isn't Enough: The Rise of Illiberal Democracy," *Foreign Affairs* 76, no. 6, 1997.

98. Milošević quoted in Cohen, *Broken Bonds,* 79.

99. Quote from Glenny, *Fall of Yugoslavia,* 40.

100. "Marković Comments on Kadijević and Economic Reforms," Tanjug in BBC Summary of World Broadcasts, December 6, 1990. In memoirs, Marković would later express regret about the collapse of socialist Yugoslavia, as well as the ethnic violence that resulted. She is coyly silent, however, about her husband's role in helping create the conditions that led to violence. See Mira [Mirjana] Marković, *Night and Day: A Diary* (Kingston, Ont.: Quarry Press, 1996).

101. Regarding the corruption issue, see Kees Van Der Pijl, *Global Rivalries from the Cold War to Iraq* (London: Pluto, 2006), 270.

102. The portrayal of Milošević as opportunist is a recurring theme in Dragović-Soso, *Saviours of the Nation,* especially chap. 5.

103. Quoted in NIOD, "Srebrenica," prologue, chap. 4, sec. 4.

104. Blaine Harden, "3 Yugoslav Republics Fear Crackdown," *Washington Post,* August 19, 1991; "Sliding toward Civil War in Yugoslavia," *Los Angeles Times,* March 22, 1991; and "Serbians Reelect Socialist Party," *Toronto Star,* December 26, 1990.

105. "A Dinosaur Down but Not Out: Slobodan Milošević, Serbia's President," *Independent,* March 23, 1991.

106. Johann Reissmueller, "Worum es in Jugoslawien Geht," *Frankfurter Allgemeine Zeitung,* February 4, 1991. Translated from the German.

107. Daniel Vemet, "La Poudrière Yougoslave: Les Pays Européens Ont Tort de ne pas Assez se Preoccuper des Risques d'Eclatement de la Fédération," *Le Monde,* May 24, 1991. Translated from the French.

108. Similarly, Slovenia and Croatia were viewed positively as Balkan outposts of market "reform." See US Department of State, Bureau of Public Affairs, letter from Joan Colbert to Hal Zimmermann, April 9, 1991, Bush Presidential Records, WHORM Subject File, General Scanned Records, CO176 [219365], George H. W. Bush Presidential Library.

109. Paul Hockenos, *Homeland Calling: Exile Patriotism and the Balkan Wars* (Ithaca: Cornell University Press, 2003), part 1; and Brown, "The Role of Economic Factors." Regarding the background of Croatian nationalism, see also Christopher Cviić,

"Croatia," in David A. Dyker and Ivan Vejvoda, eds., *Yugoslavia and After: A Study in Fragmentation, Despair, and Rebirth* (New York: Longman, 1996).

110. Jill Irvine, "Ultranationalist Ideology and State Building in Croatia, 1990–1996," *Problems of Post-Communism* 44, no. 4, 1997, 8 (electronic version available through EBSCOhost).

111. The first and third quotes appear in David Martin, "Croatia's Borders: Over the Edge," *New York Times*, November 22, 1991; the second quote is from Cohen, *Broken Bonds*, 112.

112. Stephen Kinzer, "Pro-Nazi Rulers' Legacy Still Lingers for Croatia," *New York Times*, October 31, 1993.

113. Denitch, *Ethnic Nationalism*, 41.

114. Glenny, *Fall of Yugoslavia*, 121–23; and also David Binder, "Croatia Forced Thousands from Homes, Rights Group Says," *New York Times*, December 8, 1993. Some studies downplay or ignore these anti-Serb attacks. See for example, Branka Magaš, *The Destruction of Yugoslavia: Tracing the Break-Up, 1980–92* (London: Verso, 1993); Shale Horowitz, "War after Communism: Effects on Political and Economic Reform in the Former Soviet Union and Yugoslavia," *Journal of Peace Research* 40, no. 1, 2003, 41–42; and James Gow, *The Serbian Project and Its Adversaries: A Strategy of War Crimes* (Montreal: McGill-Queen's University Press, 2003), 43–47, 159.

115. David C. Gompert, "How to Defeat Serbia," *Foreign Affairs* 73, no. 4, 1994, 43.

116. Misha Glenny, "Yes, He Was a Monster, but He Was Our Monster," *Sunday Telegraph* (London), December 12, 1999.

117. Franjo Tudjman, "All We Croatians Want Is Democracy," *New York Times*, June 30, 1990. Similarly, a Slovene government representative was given space in the *Christian Science Monitor*. See Peter Millonig, "A Case for Yugoslavia's Breakup," *Christian Science Monitor*, January 29, 1991.

118. Franjo Tudjman, "Our Liberty Is Our Life," *Washington Post*, July 4, 1991.

119. Some academics have whitewashed Tudjman's role. Thus, Sabrina Ramet characterizes Tudjman as one of several "noncommunist liberals" while she downplays the regime's repressiveness. . She also writes that Serbian politicians "spread stories of a 'Vatican-Comintern conspiracy' (supposedly designed in part to benefit Croatia) *and accused Croatian politicians of genocidal tendencies*" (emphasis added). Ramet neglects to mention comments made by Tudjman that praised the Ustaša regime and its genocidal actions. See Ramet, *Balkan Babel*, 42.

120. Jeri Laber and Kenneth Anderson, "Why Keep Yugoslavia One Country?" *New York Times*, November 10, 1990. At the Milošević trial, Laber testified as a prosecution witness and awkwardly tried to defend the article. See Laber testimony, ICTY, December 11, 2002, 14383–385, *www.icty.org*.

121. Robert Hayden, *Blueprints for a House Divided: The Constitutional Logic of the Yugoslav Conflicts* (Ann Arbor: University of Michigan Press, 1999), 71, 78.

122. Hayden, "Yugoslavia's Collapse," 1377, 1381.

123. Dirk Kurbjuweit, "Yugoslavia's Other War," *World Press Review*, November 1991, 45. Translation of article from *Die Zeit*.

124. Jens Schneider, "Slovenia Searches for Europe," *World Press Review*, January 1993, 42. Translation of article from *Süddeutsche Zeitung*.

125. Testimony of Stjepan Mesić, prosecution witness, ICTY, October 2, 2002, 10669, *www.icty.org*. Mesić specifically said that Croatia favored a confederation plan;

this was essentially the same as saying that Croatia sought independence, since the confederation plan being considered at that time entailed independence.

126. Janez Prasnikar and Zivko Pregl, "Economic Development in Yugoslavia in 1990 and Prospects for the Future," *American Economic Review* 81, no. 2, 1991, 195. Regarding Slovenia's proclivity toward market economics, see also "Une Economie en Crise," *Le Monde,* April 6, 1990.

127. Paraphrased in Glenny, *Fall of Yugoslavia,* 63. According to Glenny, Tudjman did not actually undertake much market reform of the Croatian economy.

128. Shortly before the beginning of war, Harvard economist Jeffrey Sachs shifted his position and began advising the Republic of Slovenia. Given Sachs's influence in financial circles, this move suggests that important segments of finance were rethinking the strategy of keeping Yugoslavia united. Regarding Sachs's role, see Martin Kettle, "New Cash for Old Country," *Guardian,* April 26, 1991; Janša, *The Making of the Slovenian State,* 99; and Daniel Vernet and Jean-Marc Gonin, *La Rêve Sacrifié: Chroniques des Guerres Yougoslaves* (Paris: Editions Odile Jacob, 1994), 70. Once the secession crisis actually began, the world's financial press, including the *Financial Times* and the *Economist,* favored Slovenia (see discussion in the next chapter).

129. Cohen, *Broken Bonds,* 48.

130. USCIA, *Balkan Battlegrounds,* vol. 1, 45. The Federal Constitutional Court was another Yugoslav institution that was losing power during this period. In January 1991, the court invalidated declarations of autonomy by the Slovene legislature; the inability of the court to enforce its ruling caused it to lose authority.

131. See Marković's testimony as a prosecution witness during the Milošević trial, ICTY, October 23, 2003, *www.icty.org.* Ante Marković was not related to Milošević's wife, Mirjina Marković.

132. Quoted in Cohen, *Broken Bonds,* 79.

133. Described in Cohen, *Broken Bonds,* 103–4.

134. Sachs's memoirs briefly mention his work for the Yugoslav central government (though they do not mention his later role as advisor to Slovenia). See Jeffrey Sachs, *The End of Poverty: Economic Possibilities for Our Time* (New York: Penguin, 2005), 127.

135. For an official description, see "Yugoslavia: How to Stop Inflation?" *Yugoslav Survey,* December 5, 1989.

136. Zimmermann, *Origins of a Catastrophe,* 43–44.

137. Milan Andrejevich, "Yugoslavia: The Government's Economic Reform Program," *Report on Eastern Europe,* February 9, 1990 (Radio Free Europe publication).

138. Hayden, *Blueprints for a House Divided,* 28, 64.

139. See Sachs, *End of Poverty,* 127; Zimmermann, *Origins of a Catastrophe,* 50–51; Todorovic, "Regional Economic Nationalism in the Former Yugoslavia," 181; and Robert Hutchings, *American Diplomacy and the End of the Cold War: An Insider's Account of US Policy in Europe, 1989–1992* (Baltimore: Johns Hopkins University Press, 1997), 304–5.

140. S. Woodward, *Balkan Tragedy,* 129.

141. Lampe, *Yugoslavia as History,* 351. On the Alliance's failure, see also Sell, *Slobodan Milošević,* 105–6.

142. S. Woodward, *Balkan Tragedy,* 74, 78, 87, 110, 118, 131, 132. Regarding noncooperation with the federal government, see also Susan Woodward, "Costly Disinterest: Missed Opportunities for Preventive Diplomacy in Croatia and Bosnia and Herzegovina, 1985–1991," in Bruce Jentleson, ed., *Opportunities Missed, Opportunities Seized:*

Preventive Diplomacy in the Post–Cold War World (Lanham, Md.: Rowman and Littlefield, 2000), 137; Dirk Kurbjuweit, "Yugoslavia's Other War," *World Press Review,* November 1991 (translation of article from *Die Zeit*); and NIOD, "Srebrenica," prologue, chap. 4, sec. 5.

143. USCIA, *Balkan Battlegrounds,* vol. 1, chaps. 3, 7.

144. "Yugoslav Military Warns Would-Be Breakaway Republics," Xinhua Press Service, June 21, 1991.

145. See "Slovenian Assembly Calls for Confederal Structure for Yugoslavia," BBC Summary of World Broadcasts, March 12, 1990. See full text of proposals in "A Confederate Model among the South Slavic States," *Review of International Affairs* (Belgrade), October 20, 1990.

146. Quotes from original documents in "A Confederate Model among the South Slavic States," 11–12.

147. The right of republics to leave the proposed confederation is strongly implied throughout the text of the proposal. See "A Confederate Model among the South Slavic States," 12, 16.

148. Hayden, *Blueprints for a House Divided,* 63–64.

149. The breakdown in interrepublic amity led to a major controversy in May 1991 regarding the post of chair of the federal Collective Presidency. Croat representative Stjepan Mesić was scheduled to assume the presidency, but Serbia used its influence to block Mesić's appointment. In retrospect, it seems very likely that Mesić was working behind the scenes to break up Yugoslavia and to advance Croatian nationalism. He was a member of Tudjman's HDZ party and later chaired the HDZ's executive committee. Western pressure nevertheless enabled Mesić to assume the presidency of Yugoslavia in early July, and he held the post for several months. He subsequently resigned and returned to Croatia, where he stated pointedly: "*I have fulfilled my duty—Yugoslavia no longer exists*" (emphasis added). The president of the Croatian parliament congratulated Mesić, noting that Mesić had "kept his promise that he would be the last president of Yugoslavia." Sources: "Mesić Declared SFRY President," Tanjug in BBC Summary of World Broadcasts, July 2, 1991; Oliver Daube, "Croatians Hold Up EC as Model for Yugoslav Republics," Agence France Presse, July 9, 1991; "Stipe Mesić Elected Chairman of the HDZ Executive Committee," Croatian Radio, Zagreb, in BBC Summary of World Broadcasts, December 29, 1991; and "Croatian Assembly Recalls Stipe Mesić from Post of President of SFRY Presidency," Tanjug in BBC Summary of World Broadcasts, December 7, 1991. In his memoir, Mesić frankly presents himself as a Croat nationalist. See Stipe [Stjepan] Mesić, *The Demise of Yugoslavia: A Political Memoir* (Budapest: Central European University Press, 2004). See also Mesić's testimony as a prosecution witness before the ICTY, October 2, 2002, 10636–637, *www.icty.org.*

150. The full text of the secessionist declarations can be found in "Acts of the Republics of Slovenia and Croatia on Sovereignty and Independence," *Yugoslav Survey* 32, no. 3, 1991.

151. This is implied by James Gow's title, *The Triumph of the Lack of Will: International Diplomacy and the Yugoslav War* (New York: Columbia University Press, 1997).

152. Albright is paraphrased in "Editorial: War and Analogy," *New York Times,* April 18, 1999.

153. On the cost of intervention in Bosnia, former State Department official George Kenney wrote in 1997: "The international community has spent about $20 billion on

Bosnia, much of that from the United States." Note that the full cost would have to include peacekeeping after 1997, as well as additional costs for Western actions in Kosovo, Croatia, and Macedonia. From Kenny, "Look at Bosnia before Leaping into Albania," *Los Angeles Times*, April 14, 1997. For additional cost estimates of Western intervention in the Balkans, see: Center for Strategic and Budgetary Assessments, "Total Cost Of Allied Force Air Campaign: Preliminary Estimate," June 10, 1999, *www.csbaonline.org*; Center for Strategic and Budgetary Assessments, "After the War: Kosovo Peacekeeping Costs," June 7, 1999; Tim Butcher, "The Balkans—Legacy of War," *Daily Telegraph*, February 9, 2000; and US General Accounting Office, "Bosnia: Operational Decisions Needed before Estimating DOD's Costs," February 1998, *www.fas.org/man/gao/nsiad98077.htm*. It seems reasonable to conclude that the total cost of Western intervention would certainly have exceeded the $16.5 billion total value for Yugoslavia's 1990 debt (even after accounting for inflation).

Chapter 4

Epigraph: Conor Cruise O'Brien, *To Katanga and Back: A UN Case History* (New York: Universal Library, 1962), 238. O'Brien made this comment with regard to the Congo Crisis of 1960–1961.

1. The general sense that US officials were too distracted in 1991 to pay much attention to Yugoslavia is emphasized by Robert Hutchings, *American Diplomacy and the End of the Cold War: An Insider's Account of US Policy in Europe, 1989–1992* (Baltimore: Johns Hopkins University Press, 1997), 307; and David Halberstam, *War in a Time of Peace* (New York: Simon and Schuster, 2002), 86. The (coauthored) memoir by Bush provides no significant discussion of Yugoslavia; see George H. W. Bush and Brent Scowcroft, *A World Transformed* (New York: Knopf, 1998).

2. Michael Libal, *Limits of Persuasion: Germany and the Yugoslav Crisis, 1991–1992* (Westport, Conn.: Praeger, 1997), 160–61. For additional defenders of German policy, see Sabrina Petra Ramet and Letty Coffin, "German Foreign Policy toward the Yugoslav Successor States, 1991–1999," *Problems of Post-Communism* 48, no. 1, 2001; Jean-François Juneau, "La Politique de l'Allemagne à l'Egard de la Croatie, 1991–2006," in Renéo Lukic, ed., *La Politique Etrangère de la Croatie: De son Indépendence à nos Jours* (Quebec: Les Presses de l'Université de Laval, 2006), 49–51; Hans-Dietrich Genscher, *Rebuilding a House Divided: A Memoir by the Architect of Germany's Reunification* (New York: Broadway Books, 1998), chap. 13; and Geert-Hinrich Ahrens, *Diplomacy on the Edge: Containment of Ethnic Conflict and the Minorities Working Group of the Conferences on Yugoslavia* (Baltimore: Johns Hopkins University Press, 2007). For critics of Germany's role, see Marrack Goulding, *Peacemonger* (Baltimore: Johns Hopkins University Press, 2003), chap. 17; and Javier Pérez de Cuéllar, *Pilgrimage for Peace: A Secretary-General's Memoir* (New York: St. Martin's, 1997), chap. 17.

3. Serb and Yugoslav officials exaggerated the extent of German intervention. However, this was an exaggeration that had a large measure of truth. For Yugoslav views of Germany see Marie Subtil, "Yougoslavie sus à l'Expansionism Germanique," *Le Monde*, July 13, 1991.

4. In German, Bundesamt für Verfassungsschutz. See description of the BFV provided by the Federation of American Scientists, *www.fas.org/irp/world/germany/bfv/index.html*. See also the BFV's official Web site, *www.verfassungsschutz.de/*.

5. Marko Milivojević, "Croatia's Intelligence Services," *Jane's Intelligence Review*, September 1994, 409.

6. Milivojević, "Croatia's Intelligence Services," 409.

7. Gregory Copley, "FRG Helps Develop Croatian Security," *Defense and Foreign Affairs Strategic Policy*, February–March 1994. Journalist Erich Schmidt-Eenboom alleges that German intelligence officers were making contact with Croat nationalists as early as 1971. Schmidt-Eenboom, *Der Schattenkrieger: Klaus Kinkel und der BND* (Düsseldorf: ECON, 1995), chap. 9.

8. The two republics were coordinating their activities during this phase, according to a senior Croat official. Zdravko Tomac, *The Struggle for the Croatian State: Through Hell to Democracy* (Zagreb: Prokifon, 1993), 126.

9. Halberstam, *War in a Time of Peace*, 29.

10. Gen. Pierre M. Gallois, "Balkans: La Faute Allemande," *Le Quotidien de Paris*, January 28, 1993.

11. Quoted in John Newhouse, "The Diplomatic Round: Dodging the Problem," *New Yorker*, August 24, 1992, 64. Newhouse expresses doubt that Germany was encouraging Croat nationalism and thus "playing a double game," but he offers no evidence.

12. Warren Zimmermann, *Origins of a Catastrophe: Yugoslavia and Its Destroyers—America's Last Ambassador Tells What Happened and Why* (New York: Times Books, 1996), 146. Note that Zimmermann does not say that Genscher rushed the international *recognition* of Slovenia and Croatia's independence; he makes the much more provocative statement that Genscher rushed independence. In memoirs, the Slovene defense minister Janez Janša downplays the role of foreign support, but he concedes that by July 1, "Genscher strongly supported our cause." See Janša, *The Making of the Slovenian State, 1988–1992: The Collapse of Yugoslavia* (Ljubljana: Založba Mladinska Knjiga, 1994), 189.

13. Genscher claimed that the 1974 Yugoslav constitution gave the republics the right to secede, but this is a serious misrepresentation of the facts. For a discussion of the 1974 constitution and the issue of secession, see note 127 of this chapter. Elsewhere in his memoirs, Genscher blandly claimed that Germany and other European states supported a united Yugoslavia and opposed the country's breakup; but these claims too seem implausible in light of his quote here and other evidence of German intervention presented in this chapter. See Genscher, *Rebuilding a House Divided*, 491, 493. The memoirs of another German diplomat, Geert-Hinrich Ahrens, also acknowledge that German policy emphasized "self-determination" as a higher priority than the preservation of Yugoslavia's territorial integrity—in other words, Germany favored the secessionists. See Ahrens, *Diplomacy on the Edge*, 40–41.

14. US Congress, "Prepared Statement of John R. Bolton, Senior Vice President, American Enterprise Institute, before the House Committee on International Relations," Federal News Service, November 10, 1999, 3 (electronic version available through Lexis-Nexis). Bolton served as assistant secretary of state for international organization affairs during the time of Yugoslavia's breakup.

15. James Bissett states: "Germany and Austria were pressing for the recognition of Slovene and Croatian independence. It is now known that as early as 1990 Croatian and Slovene leaders held meetings with senior politicians from both of these countries urging support for independence." Bissett, "Balkan War, Balkan Peace, Balkan Future?" ("Slovenian Independence" section), no date, *www.deltax.net/bissett/western/slovenia*.

htm. Mesić's views were revealed in the following exchange between Milošević and Slovenian leader Milan Kučan, which took place during Kučan's cross-examination at the Milošević trial:

> Milošević: "Do you remember . . . on the NTV private TV station in which you participated together with Stipe [Stjepan] Mesić [?] . . . Now, do you remember that . . . Mesić declared that the former Minister of Foreign Affairs of Germany Hans-Dietrich Genscher and the Pope John Paul II, by the direct agreement and support designed to break up the former Yugoslavia [and] had practically contributed most to that [Yugoslavia's breakup] actually happening?"

> Kučan: "*Those were the stance of Mr. Mesič.*" [emphasis added]

Kučan thus confirms Milošević's account regarding the statements of Mesić. From testimony by Kučan, prosecution witness at the Milošević trial, International Criminal Tribunal for the Former Yugoslavia, May 21, 2003, 20918–20, *www.icty.org.*

16. Marc Fisher, "Eastern Europe Swept by German Influence," *Washington Post,* February 16, 1992.

17. Trade with Yugoslavia accounted for 1 percent of West Germany's 1989 total. Peter J. Katzenstein, "The Smaller European States, Germany, and Europe," in Katzenstein, ed., *Tamed Power: Germany in Europe* (Ithaca: Cornell University Press 1998), 289.

18. See statistics in Andrei S. Markovits, Simon Reich, and Frank Westermann, "Germany: Hegemonic Power and Economic Gain?" *Review of International Political Economy* 3, no. 4, 1996, 717.

19. Jonathan Kaufman, "Amid East's Balkanization, Germany Reasserts Itself," *Boston Globe,* August 28, 1991.

20. For mention of this emerging sphere of influence, see Viktor Meier, "Im Hintergrund Amerika," *Frankfurter Allgemeine Zeitung,* January 7, 1991; and Robert Livingston quoted in Ralph Hartmann, *"Die Ehrlichen Makler": Die Deutsche Aussenpolitik und der Bürgerkrieg in Jugoslawien* (Berlin: Dietz, 1998), 186.

21. Quoted in Hartmann, *"Die Ehrlichen Makler,* 188. Translated from the German.

22. "Engholm Verlangt Entschlosseneres Vorgehen der Bundesregierung," *Frankfurter Allgemeine Zeitung,* August 7, 1991. Translated from the German. I quote directly from the newspaper text, which paraphrased Engholm.

23. On the anticommunist motivation of German policy, see Daniel Vernet, "Le Retour de la 'Question Allemande,'" *Le Monde,* December 23, 1991.

24. Kohl quoted in Hartmann, *"Die Ehrlichen Makler,"* 188. Translated from the German.

25. Robert Livingston quoted in Hartmann, *"Die Ehrlichen Makler,"* 186. Translated from the German.

26. Quoted in Hartmann, *"Die Ehrlichen Makler,"* 187. Translated from the German.

27. Quoted in Marc Fisher, "Germany's New Role Stirs Some Concern in US," *Washington Post,* January 23, 1992.

28. For discussion of the Croatian diaspora in the conflict, see Tomac, *The Struggle for the Croatian State,* 513; and Paul Hockenos, *Homeland Calling: Exile Patriotism and the Balkan Wars* (Ithaca: Cornell University Press, 2003), Part I.

29. Hans Stark, "Dissonances Franco-Allemendes sur Fond de Guerre Serbo-Croate," *Politique Etrangère* 57, no. 2, 1992, 341; Marcus Tanner, *Croatia: A Nation Forged in*

War (New Haven: Yale University Press, 2001), 254; and Daniel Vernet and Jean-Marc Gonin, *La Rêve Sacrifié: Chroniques des Guerres Yougoslaves* (Paris: Editions Odile Jacob, 1994), 79.

30. In addition to Ambassador Bissett, Stjepan Mesić also claimed that the Vatican played a key role in fomenting Yugoslavia's breakup. See Bissett, "Balkan War" ("Slovenian Independence" section). On Vatican support for Croatia, see also Tomac, *The Struggle for the Croatian State*, 146–48. On Mesić, see note 15.

31. The politics of the Catholic Church vis-à-vis Croatia, both during World War II and during the events leading to war in 1991, are discussed in Jacques Merlino, *Les Vérités Yougoslaves Ne Sont Pas Toutes Bonnes à Dire* (Paris: Albin Michel, 1993), 158–75.

32. Bissett, "Balkan War" ("Slovenian Independence" section).

33. Regarding Austrian interests in Slovenia and Croatia, see "Zwischenprüfung für die Gemeinschaft," *Frankfurter Allgemeine Zeitung*, August 15, 1991; " 'Slowenien Wechselt nach Osterreich,'" *Frankfurter Allgemeine Zeitung*, February 8, 1991; Waltraud Baryli, "Inquiétude en Autriche," *Le Monde*, July 4, 1991, and "Prête à Reconnaître l'Indépendence de la Slovénie et la Croatie, L'Autriche Critique la Trop Longue Passivité des Douze," *Le Monde*, September 7, 1991; and Vernet and Gonin, *La Rêve Sacrifié*, 80–81.

34. The first epigraph is from Abraham Lincoln, Second Inaugural Address, March 4, 1865, *www.bartleby.com/124/pres32.html*. Adm. Stane Brovet quoted in the second epigraph is from Lenard J. Cohen, *Broken Bonds: Yugoslavia's Disintegration and Balkan Politics in Transition* (Boulder, Colo.: Westview, 1995), 232.

35. Susan Woodward, *Balkan Tragedy* (Washington, D.C.: Brookings, 1995), 39; and Zimmermann, *Origins of a Catastrophe*, 85–87.

36. Judy Dempsey and Anthony Robinson, "Crisis in Yugoslavia: Hardline Generals in Federal Army Fail to Force Slovenia into Submission," *Financial Times*, July 1, 1991. The ideological character of the army was also noted during the Milošević trial by Slovenian leader Milan Kučan, a prosecution witness. Kučan stated that "the Army had a very strong ideological and political stamp, and that its ideological homeland was the League of Communists of Yugoslavia." See Kučan testimony at the ICTY, May 21, 2003, 20980, *www.icty.org*.

37. See "Yougoslavie: Armée Fédérale ou Serbe?" *Le Monde*, July 4, 1991.

38. Zimmermann, *Origins of a Catastrophe*, 89–91.

39. Though Kadijević did not testify before the Milošević trial or any of the other post-Yugoslav trials in The Hague, his role was discussed on several occasions. Prosecution witnesses generally described him as a Yugoslav nationalist who acted independently of Milošević Thus, a former JNA general, Aleksander Vasiljević, made the following remark during questioning:

Question: Your superior Kadijević, was he technically subordinated to the accused [Milošević] or not? . . .

Vasiljević: No [Kadijević was not subordinated to Milošević], neither in technical terms nor in any other way.

Similarly, prosecution witness Borisav Jović noted Kadijević's independence. In addition, James Bissett—the former Canadian ambassador—stated that Milošević "had no control over the federal Army" at the time of the Slovenia war. A CIA study refers to Kadijević as "one of the tragic actors in the Yugoslav drama," who was "crusading virtually alone to save the Yugoslav state, even as the political leadership he served was acting in ways that could only carve it apart." And in memoirs, Bosnian president Alija Izetbegović stated that Kadijević was "a Yugoslav by conviction; . . . Kadijević tried to preserve Yugoslavia." Sources: Testimony of Aleksander Vasljević, ICTY, February 6, 2003, 15860, *www.icty.org*; Jović's testimony is discussed in note 42; and James Bissett, "Scapegoat, RIP," *National Post*, March 15, 2006. The next to last quote is from US Central Intelligence Agency [USCIA], *Balkan Battlegrounds: A Military History of the Yugoslav Conflict, 1990–1995*, vol. 1 (Washington, D.C.: CIA Office of Russian and European Analysis, 2002), 46. And the last quote is from Alija Izetbegović, *Inescapable Questions: Autobiographical Notes* (Leicester, UK: Islamic Foundation, 2003), 87.

40. Alex N. Dragnich, "The Dayton Accords: Symbol of Great Power Failings," *Mediterranean Quarterly* 17, no. 2, 2006, 49. The previous air force commander, also a Croat, was Gen. Anton Tus. General Tus had resigned as the war began and returned to his native Croatia. The JNA carefully replaced Tus with another Croat, General Jurjević. See "Internal Disputes Tear Yugoslav Army," *Toronto Star*, July 1, 1991. Marko Hoare provides the following misleading statement: "The two most senior JNA officers . . . Veljko Kadijević and . . . Blagoje Adžić were a Croatian Serb and a Bosnia Serb respectively (though Kadijević had a Croat mother). They ensured the JNA would act as Serbia's Army." Hoare neglects to mention Kadijević's deputy, Admiral Brovet, who was a Slovene, nor does he mention the JNA Air Force commander, General Jurjević, who was a Croat. From Hoare, *The History of Bosnia: From the Middle Ages to the Present Day* (London: Saqi Books, 2007), 349.

41. "Sacked General Admits Errors in Slovenia," Associated Press, July 10, 1991.

42. Quoted in "Defense Secretary Says Army Supports Democratic Transformation of Yugoslavia," Yugoslav News Agency, in BBC Summary of World Broadcasts, June 26, 1991. V. P. Gagnon states that there was an agreement among Kadijević, Milošević, and Yugoslav president Borisav Jović to "throw Slovenia and Croatia out" of Yugoslavia through the use of military force. Gagnon cites the (Serbian-language) memoirs of Jović. The existence of such an agreement, and especially General Kadijević's assent to it, seems doubtful. Jović later distanced himself from such claims. In 2003, as a prosecution witness at the Milošević trial, he testified for three days and he discussed extensively the politics of the period immediately preceding the war. In the course of this testimony, Jović made no mention of any agreement to throw out the secessionists, nor did he say that General Kadijević would have been receptive to such an agreement. On the contrary, Jović described the general as a Yugoslav nationalist: Kadijević's "orientation was a traditional one, that is to say in favor of Yugoslavia and having a mixed ethnic composition in the Army." Jović also noted that General "Kadijević made persistent insistence on defending the whole of Yugoslavia. Milošević [in contrast] considered that we ought not to force the Croats and Slovenes who wished to step down from Yugoslavia to remain within Yugoslavia." Sources: Gagnon, *The Myth of Ethnic War: Serbia and Croatia in the 1990s* (Ithaca: Cornell University Press, 2004), 92; and Borisav Jović, testimony before the ICTY, November 18, 2003, 29154, and November 19, 2003, 29284, *www.icty.org*.

43. The central government was indeed multiethnic, though the top figures were predominantly Croat at the time. As noted, Marković himself was an ethnic Croat,

while his foreign minister, Budimir Lončar, also was a Croat. And Defense Minister Kadijević was of mixed Croat and Serb descent. See Slobodan Lekic, "Yugoslav Federal Government Trying to Avert All-Out Civil War," Associated Press, June 27, 1991.

44. The order is quoted in Zimmermann, *Origins of a Catastrophe*, 143. Zimmermann added that Marković's order "implicitly condoned [the JNA's use of] force." During the Milošević trial, Marković tried to disassociate himself from the army's decision to use force. However, the substance of the cross-examination leaves little doubt that Marković initially approved the JNA's intervention in Slovenia. See testimony and cross-examination of Ante Marković, ICTY, October 23, 2003, 28075–81, and January 15, 2004, 30843–44, *www.icty.org*.

45. Janša, *Making of the Slovenian State,* 249, 164, 186.

46. Bissett, "Scapegoat, RIP," 14.

47. On the Slovenian military preparations, see USCIA, *Balkan Battlegrounds*, vol. 1, chap. 3.

48. Casualty estimate from USCIA, *Balkan Battlegrounds*, vol. 1, 68–69. For an even lower estimate of deaths in the Slovene war, see Zimmermann, *Origins of a Catastrophe*, 144–45. For information on the military aspects of the war, see Viktor Meier, *Yugoslavia: A History of Its Demise* (London: Routledge, 1999), 170–80.

49. Bissett, "Scapegoat, RIP," 14.

50. Zimmermann, *Origins of a Catastrophe*, 143, 145.

51. Quoted in "Hearings of the House International Relations Committee," Federal News Service, January 12, 1995, 20.

52. Bissett, "Scapegoat, RIP," 14.

53. "Slovenia's Self Defense," *Economist*, July 6, 1991, 46.

54. "No Union by Force," *Financial Times*, July 4, 1991.

55. See, for example, Aryeh Neier, "Inconvenient Facts: Review of Noam Chomsky's *The New Military Humanism,*" *Dissent* 47, no. 2, 2000; and Ewa Tabeau and Jakub Bijak, "War Related Deaths in the 1992–1995 Armed Conflicts in Bosnia and Herzegovina: A Critique of Previous Estimates and Recent Results," *European Journal of Population* 21, nos. 2/3, 2005, 188.

56. Bissett, "Balkan War" ("Slovenian Independence" section).

57. Government Liaison Office, Republic of Slovenia, "Military Occupation of Slovenia by Communist-led Yugoslav Forces: Status Report," July 2, 1991, Bush Presidential Records, NSC, Robert Hutchings Files, Yugoslavia—General—Hutchings—1991–Yugoslavia, OA/ID CFO 1412 [3 of 6], George H. W. Bush Presidential Library.

58. Quoted in Cohen, *Broken Bonds*, 221. For further analysis of the JNA's failure in Slovenia, see USCIA, *Balkan Battlegrounds*, vol. 1, chap. 5.

59. Kitty McKinsey, "How Did a Few Slovenes Humiliate the Federal Army?" *Ottawa Citizen*, July 10, 1991.

60. Zimmermann, *Origins of a Catastrophe*, 153.

61. Dusan Stojanovic, "Tension Increasing as Serbs in Croatia Vote on Secession," Associated Press, May 12, 1991.

62. S. Woodward, *Balkan Tragedy*, 133.

63. Ivan Zvonimir Cičak of Helsinki Watch, Croatia, quoted in David Binder, "Croatia Forced Thousands from Homes, Rights Group Says," *New York Times*, December 8, 1993.

64. For purposes of this discussion, the term "Krajina" refers to all the Serb-held territory in border areas of eastern Croatia.

65. S. Woodward, *Balkan Tragedy*, 102.

66. United Nations, "Report on the Historical Background of the Civil War in the Former Yugoslavia, United Nations Commission of Experts, Security Council Resolution 780 (1992), Professor M. Cherif Bassiouni, Chairman," March 1994, 34.

67. Misha Glenny, *The Fall of Yugoslavia: The Third Balkan War* (New York: Penguin, 1996), 16–19.

68. See Babić's lengthy testimony as a prosecution witness during the Milošević trial, ICTY, November 18, 2002–December 9, 2002, *www.icty.org*. During the course of this testimony, Babić emphasized the role of Milošević in encouraging and supporting the Krajina Serbs in their efforts to resist the Croatian government.

69. See Laura Silber and Allan Little, *The Death of Yugoslavia* (London: Penguin, 1997), 151–54, 188–89.

70. Lazar Macura, information minister of Krajina, quoted in Steve Crawshaw, "Bloody Path to a 'Greater Serbia,'" *Independent*, August 6, 1991.

71. Regarding Arkan's role, see Paul Wood, "Gangster's Life of Serb Warlord," BBC News, January 15, 2000, *news.bbc.co.uk/2/hi/europe/605266.stm*.

72. Zimmermann, *Origins of a Catastrophe*, 153. One of the key figures among the group of "young colonels" that Zimmermann referred to was Ratko Mladić, who was organizing Serb nationalists within the JNA and also in the Krajina region during this period. See Louis Sell, *Slobodan Milošević and the Destruction of Yugoslavia* (Durham, N.C.: Duke University Press, 2002), 123.

73. USCIA, *Balkan Battlegrounds*, vol. 1, 91–92. The later testimony of ICTY prosecution witness Gen. Aleksander Vasiljević confirms the initial neutrality of the JNA with regard to the Serb-Croat conflict in Krajina. Vasiljević testified that the JNA's "first and basic objective during the first stage [of war in Croatia was to] separate the parties in conflict. This is a conflict that the JNA did not take part in." Vasiljević testimony before the ICTY, February 5, 2003, 15770, *www.icty.org*.

74. Anthony Robinson and Laura Silber, "Yugoslav Army Loses Its Sense of Direction," *Financial Times*, September 21, 1991.

75. Bogdan Denitch, *Ethnic Nationalism: The Tragic Death of Yugoslavia* (Minneapolis: University of Minnesota Press, 1996), 41.

76. See Milan Babić, prosecution witness at the Milošević trial, ICTY, November 20, 2002, 13064, *www.icty.org*.

77. The expansion of the war was followed by a Croat decision to blockade preexisting JNA fortifications within Croatia, a move taken in September 1991. Sabrina Petra Ramet, "Review Essay—Views from Inside: Memoirs Concerning the Yugoslav Breakup and War," *Slavic Review* 61, no. 3, 2002, 570–71. On the JNA offensive more generally, see USCIA, *Balkan Battlegrounds*, vol. 1, chap. 11.

78. Excerpts from a JNA document, read by an attorney at the Milošević trial during the testimony of Aleksander Vasiljević, ICTY, February 5, 2003, 15771, *www.icty.org*.

79. This new role for the JNA appears to have begun in late August. Krajina Serb leader Milan Babić later claimed that beginning in "August 1991, the Yugoslav People's Army [the JNA] entered into the war with Croatia." Appearing as a prosecution witness at the Milošević trial, Babić confirmed that the JNA participated in ethnic cleansing campaigns against Croatian inhabitants in the course of its armed activity. See Babić testimony before the ICTY, November 20,

2002, 13064, *www.icty.org*. Croatian nationalist Tomac claims that the JNA did not give up entirely the possibility of reintegrating Croatia back into Yugoslavia. According to Tomac, the JNA worked throughout the summer of 1991 to force Croatia to give up its de facto independence; even as late as October 1991, the federal army considered an all-out attack on the Republic, a plan derailed through the intervention of Mikhail Gorbachev, who restrained the JNA. See Tomac, *The Struggle for the Croatian State*, 86, 155–57. For a similar claim that the JNA sought to reintegrate Croatia, see USCIA, *Balkan Battlegrounds*, vol. 1, 97–98.

80. See "Marković Reportedly Demands Resignation of Kadijević and Brovet from FEC," Trajug report, BBC Summary of World Broadcasts, September 21, 1991; and Robinson and Silber, "Yugoslav Army Loses Its Sense of Direction." Marković resigned as prime minister in December 1991, and later left the country.

81. USCIA, *Balkan Battlegrounds*, vol. 1, 93–105; James Gow, *The Serbian Project and Its Adversaries* (Montreal: McGill-Queen's University Press, 2003), 159.

82. "There Never Was a Good War," *Economist*, November 16, 1991, 59; and Silber and Little, *Death of Yugoslavia*, 205–6.

83. Glenny, *Fall of Yugoslavia*, 136.

84. See Jack H. Geiger, "Balkan War Crimes Indictment," *Lancet*, March 9, 1996.

85. Chris Hedges, "Croatian's Confession Describes Torture and Killing on Vast Scale," *New York Times*, September 5, 1997.

86. Carlotta Gall, "A Croat's Killing Prods Action on War Atrocities," *New York Times*, September 17, 2000.

87. Quote from unnamed diplomat in "Croats Accused of Atrocities," *Washington Post*, February 6, 1992. The total number of deaths in the Croatian war has been estimated at twenty thousand. Tim Judah, "Milošević's Legacy of Discord," BBC News, March 11, 2006, *news.bbc.co.uk/2/hi/europe/4797564.stm*.

88. Silber and Little, *Death of Yugoslavia*, 218.

89. David Israelson, "Europe's Leaders Crow over Mediation Bid," *Toronto Star*, June 30, 1991.

90. Jacques Delors quoted in Owen Harris, "The Collapse of 'The West,'" *Foreign Affairs* 72, no. 4, 1993, 49.

91. S. Woodward, *Balkan Tragedy*, 160; and Jelena Pejic, "Yugoslavia: Prime Minister Sends Clear Message to Republics," Inter Press Service, June 21, 1991

92. Eduardo Cue, "Yugoslav Crisis Reveals Split within European Community," UPI, July 6, 1991; and Jonathan Kaufman, "Yugoslav Strife Spoils Europe's Unity Party," *Boston Globe*, July 7, 1991.

93. Quoted in S. Woodward, *Balkan Tragedy*, 1995, 158.

94. Quoted in Silber and Little, *Death of Yugoslavia*, 177.

95. Mary Curtius, "US, Allies Eye Halting Arms to Yugoslavia," *Boston Globe*, July 4, 1991.

96. William Drozdiak, "EC Halts Aid, Bans Arms Sales to Yugoslavia," *Washington Post*, July 6, 1991; and Henri de Bresson, "M. François Mitterrand Souligne qu'on ne Peut pas Sauver une Fédération par la Force," *Le Monde*, July 25, 1991.

97. See Daniel Vernet, "La Poudrière Yougoslave: Les Pays Européens ont Tort de ne pas Assez se Préoccuper des Risques d'Eclatement de la Fédération," *Le Monde*, May 24, 1991.

98. See Silber and Little, *Death of Yugoslavia*, 180.

99.   Silber and Little, *Death of Yugoslavia*, 179.
100. Richard Ingham, "World Consensus Shatters as Germany Threatens to Recognize Breakaways," Agence France Presse, July 3, 1991.
101. "When Tanks Dictate," *Guardian*, July 4, 1991.
102. "The Yugoslavian Crisis," *Eurobarometer*, December 1991. The full question, as noted in *Eurobarometer*: EC "citizens were asked 'whether the most important thing is to preserve Yugoslavia's territorial integrity (also in order to prevent the breakup of states elsewhere in Europe) or whether the most important thing is respect for democracy and for each people's right to self determination, including possible independence for certain republics.'"
103. Among EC member states, only Greece had a higher proportion of respondents who favored Yugoslavia's territorial integrity over the right to self-determination. On Greece's role in Yugoslavia's breakup, see Takis Michas, *Unholy Alliance: Greece and Milošević's Serbia* (College Station: Texas A&M University Press, 2002).
104. Glenny, *Fall of Yugoslavia*, 103.
105. James Steinberg, "International Involvement in the Yugoslavia Conflict," in Lori Fisler Damrosch, ed., *Enforcing Restraint: Collective Intervention in Internal Conflicts* (New York: Council on Foreign Relations, 1993), 36; Ahrens, *Diplomacy on the Edge*, 42–43; and Zimmermann, *Origins of a Catastrophe*, 148–49. Regarding the actual text of the agreement, see "Joint Declaration of the EC Troika and the Parties Directly Concerned with the Yugoslav Crisis, the So-Called 'Brioni Accord,' Brioni, 7 July 1991," in Snežana Trifunovska, ed., *Yugoslavia through Documents: From Its Creation to Its Dissolution* (Dordrecht, Netherlands: Martinus Nijhoff, 1994), 311–15. Though the text emphasized Slovenia, the Brioni agreement was intended to apply to Croatia as well.
106. Quotes from the text of the Brioni agreement in Trifunovska, *Yugoslavia through Documents*, 311.
107. This quote is from an account by two BBC reporters, Silber and Little, *Death of Yugoslavia*, 181.
108. Quoted in Sarah Lambert, "Yugoslavia in Crisis: Netherlands Calls for Twelve to Speak as One," *Independent*, July 10, 1991.
109. Tomac states that the "Slovenian government did not actually adhere to it [the Brioni agreement]. . . . Slovenia in spite of the [Brioni agreement] was realizing its sovereignty and independence." Tomac, *The Struggle for the Croatian State*, 126. There is also little evidence that Croatia had any intention of stepping back from its initial move toward independence.
110. Libal, *Limits of Persuasion*, 21.
111. Zimmermann, *Origins of a Catastrophe*, 148–49.
112. This mediation was provided under the rubric of the International Conference on Yugoslavia (later, International Conference on the Former Yugoslavia), which Lord Carrington chaired. A collection of papers from this conference appears in B. G. Ramcharan, ed., *The International Conference on the Former Yugoslavia: Official Papers* (The Hague: Kluwer Law International, 1997). In September 1991, the Security Council imposed an arms embargo on all of former Yugoslavia. However, Slovenia and Croatia managed to acquire considerable arms surreptitiously from a variety of sources. See UN Security Council Resolution 713, September 25, 1991, in Daniel Bethlehem and Marc Weller, eds., *The Yugoslav Crisis in International Law* (New

York: Cambridge University Press, 1997), 1; and Diana Johnstone, *Fools' Crusade: Yugoslavia, NATO, and Western Delusions* (New York: Monthly Review Press, 2002), 139–42.

113. The Badinter Commission's legal "opinions" are reprinted verbatim in Ramcharan, *International Conference on the Former Yugoslavia*, vol. 2, 1259–1302. They are also available in David Owen, ed., *Balkan Odyssey* [Academic Edition], CD-ROM document collection (Princeton: Electric Company, 1996).

114. Quoted from "Peace Conference on Yugoslavia, Carrington Draft Convention for a General Settlement, 18 October, 1991," in Marc Weller, ed., *The Crisis in Kosovo: 1989–1999* (Cambridge: Documents and Analysis Publishing, 1999), 80. See also a later proposal: "Treaty Provisions for the Convention of 4 November 1991," reprinted in Ramcharan, *International Conference on the Former Yugoslavia*, vol. 1, 13–23; and discussion in Goulding, *Peacemonger*, 293. To a large extent, the economic union plan was a revival of "confederation" plans put forward in 1990, shortly before the beginning of war.

115. Silber and Little, *Death of Yugoslavia*, 210.

116. Zimmermann, *Origins of a Catastrophe*, 161. Regarding Europe's shift in favor of eventual recognition for the independent republics, see Richard Caplan, *Europe and the Recognition of New States in Yugoslavia* (Cambridge: Cambridge University Press, 2005), 16–22.

117. Ahrens, *Diplomacy on the Edge*, 87.

118. James Gow, *The Triumph of the Lack of Will: International Diplomacy and the Yugoslav War* (New York: Columbia University Press, 1997), 57.

119. Zimmermann, *Origins of a Catastrophe*, 159.

120. Jean Manas, "The Impossible Trade-Off: 'Peace' versus 'Justice' in Settling Yugoslavia's Wars," in Richard H. Ullman, ed., *The World and Yugoslavia's Wars* (New York: Council on Foreign Relations, 1996), 47.

121. "There Never Was a Good War," 59.

122. In this respect, see Sabrina Petra Ramet, *Balkan Babel: The Disintegration of Yugoslavia from the Death of Tito to Ethnic War* (Boulder, Colo.: Westview, 1996); and Noel Malcolm, *Bosnia: A Short History* (New York: New York University Press, 1996).

123. "India Does What It Had to Do," *Economist*, June 9, 1984, 43.

124. A legal analysis notes: "Professor Rupert Emerson has recently written that 'the room left for self-determination in the sense of the attainment of independent statehood is very slight, with the great current exception of decolonization.' The United Nations practice supports Professor Emerson's conclusions." From Ved P. Nanda, "Self-Determination in International Law: The Tragic Tale of Two Cities—Islamabad (West Pakistan) and Dacca (East Pakistan)," *American Journal of International Law* 66, no. 2, 1972, 326.

125. During the postcolonial period, the only major case of secession that was internationally accepted was that of Bangladesh, which was created in 1971 after separation from Pakistan. However, the Bangladesh precedent is of little use in analyzing Yugoslavia; international recognition of Bangladesh's secession was based on the violent repression that Pakistan created, which in turn justified Bangladesh's secession. In Yugoslavia's case there was no violent repression by the central government against Slovenia and Croatia during the months preceding secession.

The Bangladesh case offers little support for secessionist arguments in Yugoslavia. On the Bangladesh case, see Nanda, "Self-Determination in International Law."

126. Quoted in Rupert Emerson, "Self-Determination," *American Journal of International Law* 65, no. 3, 1971, 464. On this issue in general, see also Raju Thomas, "Sovereignty, Self-Determination, and Secession: Principles and Practice," in Thomas, ed., *Yugoslavia Unraveled: Sovereignty, Self-Determination, Intervention* (Lanham, Md.: Lexington Books, 2003); and Thomas, "Self-Determination and International Recognition Policy," *World Affairs* 160, no. 1, 1997.

127. According to Yugoslavia's 1974 constitution, republics could not secede unless they gained consent from the various regional units in the federation. The specific wording (from art. 5): "The frontiers of the Socialist Federal Republic of Yugoslavia may not be altered without the consent of all Republics and Autonomous Provinces." Slovenia's and Croatia's 1991 secessions clearly altered Yugoslavia's frontiers, but this was done without the permission of the other republics and autonomous provinces—and hence was illegal. See "Constitution of the Socialist Federal Republic of Yugoslavia," in William B. Simons, ed., *Constitutions of the Communist World* (Alphen ann den Rijn, Netherlands: Sijthoff and Noordhoff, 1980), 428, 445. Also, note that in January 1991, Yugoslavia's Constitutional Court declared that Slovenia's efforts at secession were illegal. See USCIA, *Balkan Battlegrounds*, vol. 1, 45. German diplomats would later make the inaccurate claim that the 1974 constitution provided an unqualified right to secede. See Ahrens, *Diplomacy on the Edge*, 87; and Genscher, *Rebuilding a House Divided*, 493.

128. One could argue that the independence of Slovenia and Croatia was *later* justified by the fact that Yugoslavia had effectively ceased to exist as an integral country. Such an argument was in fact made on November 29, 1991, by the EC Arbitration Commission under Robert Badinter. The Commission issued a statement that Yugoslavia was in a "process of dissolution," with the implication that the Yugoslav state had effectively ceased functioning, and that the independence of Slovenia and Croatia was therefore legitimate at that time. The Commission's argument may have had some merit, since by November 1991, the Yugoslav central government had indeed ceased to function effectively, and the federation was on the brink of disintegration. Some sources claim, however, that the Commission's judgment justified the *initial* secessionist acts by Slovenia and Croatia in June 1991. This argument is erroneous. The Badinter Commission did not justify the initial secessions, and it did not make any claim to such a justification. In reading the Badinter Commission's statement, it is important to bear in mind the distinction between the conditions that prevailed at the time of writing, in late November 1991; and the conditions that prevailed at the time the secessions began, in June 1991. The distinction between these two periods is crucial, since in June, the central government was functioning, and it sought to stop the secessions. We have seen that Prime Minister Marković and the multiethnic military command tried to reassert central authority. Marković signed an order for the JNA to establish control in Slovenia, and the army sought to implement this order. The process of general dissolution later cited by the Commission did not prevail when the secessions initially occurred. Regarding the Arbitration Commission's view of secession, see "Conference on Yugoslavia Arbitration Commission, Opinion No. 1," November 29, 1991, in Owen, *Balkan Odyssey*, CD-ROM. On inaccurate claims that the Badinter Commission

had justified Slovenia and Croatia's initial acts of secession, see statement by Herbert Okun, prosecution witness at the Milošević trial, ICTY, February 27, 2003, 17085, and February 28, 2003, 17089, *www.icty.org*.

129. The general point that human rights must take precedence over legality became widely accepted by the end of the 1990s. See, for example, Independent International Commission on Kosovo, *Kosovo Report: Conflict, International Response, Lessons Learned* (Oxford: Oxford University Press, 2000), 4.

130. On the issue of *uti possidetis* and the Krajina, see "Conference on Yugoslavia Arbitration Commission, Opinion No. 3," January 11, 1992, in Owen, *Balkan Odyssey*, CD-ROM. Legal experts have generally been critical of the Commission's use of *uti possidetis*. See the following: Marc Weller, "International Response to the Dissolution of the Socialist Federal Republic of Yugoslavia," *American Journal of International Law* 86, no. 3, 1992; Matthew Craven, "The European Community Arbitration Commission on Yugoslavia," in *The British Yearbook of International Law, 1995* (Oxford: Clarendon Press, 1996), 385–90; Michla Pomerance, "The Badinter Commission: The Use and Misuse of the International Court of Justice's Jurisprudence," *Michigan Journal of International Law* 20, no. 1, 1998, 51–58; Peter Radan, "Post-Secession International Borders: A Critical Analysis of the Opinions of the Badinter Arbitration Commission," *Melbourne University Law Review* 24, no. 1, 2000; Caplan, *Europe and the Recognition of New States*, 70–71; and Steven R. Ratner, "Drawing a Better Line: *Uti Possidetis* and the Borders of New States," *American Journal of International Law* 90, no. 4, 1996, 613–14.

131. International Court of Justice, "Case Concerning the Frontier Dispute (Burkina Faso and Republic of Mali)," December 22, 1986, 566. I thank Professor Matthew Craven for providing me with a copy of this document.

132. "Europe's Duty to Intervene," *Independent*, July 4, 1991.

133. See, for example, Vernet, "La Poudeière Yougoslave."

134. On the role of European Left parties, see Peter Gowan, "Western Economic Diplomacy and the New Eastern Europe," *New Left Review*, no. 182, 1990, 79; and "Engholm Verlangt Entschlosseneres Vorgehen der Bundesregierung," *Frankfurter Allgemeine Zeitung*, August 7, 1991. On Catholics (especially in Bavaria) responding to the Vatican's lead on the Yugoslav issue, see Bissett, "Balkan War" ("Slovenian Independence" section).

135. "Republic with Eyes Fixed on the West," *Daily Telegraph*, June 29, 1991.

136. Manas, "Impossible Trade-Off," 47.

137. George H. W. Bush, "Remarks to the Supreme Soviet of the Republic of the Ukraine in Kiev, Soviet Union," August 1, 1991, in John Woolley and Gerhard Peters, eds., American Presidency Project, *www.presidency.ucsb.edu/ws/index. php?pid=19864andst=andst1=*. On the administration's initial reluctance to adopt a policy of breaking up communist states, see also Maynard Glitman, "US Policy in Bosnia: Rethinking a Flawed Approach," *Survival* 38, no. 4, 1996–97, 67. The policy of holding the USSR together was probably not very strong to begin with, and it weakened over time. According to Bush's memoirs, Defense Secretary Dick Cheney advocated policies that (if adopted) would have entailed "a thinly disguised effort to encourage the breakup of the USSR." Bush and Scowcroft, *A World Transformed*, 541. For a similar account, see also the memoirs of the former CIA director Robert M.

Gates, *From the Shadows: The Ultimate Insider's Story of Five Presidents and How They Won the Cold War* (New York: Simon and Schuster, 1996), 529.

138. David Binder, "Eagleburger Anguishes over Yugoslav Upheaval," *New York Times*, June 19, 1992. Eagleburger also had significant investments in Yugoslavia. While president of Kissinger Associates, he sat on the board of directors of the Yugo car manufacturers and also a bank in Slovenia. These investments would seem to bias Eagleburger to favor Yugoslav unity; but we will see that Eagleburger was ultimately influenced by the anticommunist objective, which favored breaking up the federation. Regarding claims that Eagleburger was biased by his investment interests, see Gregory Peroche, *Histoire de la Croatie et des Nations Slaves du Sud: 395–1992* (Paris: F.X. de Guibert, OEIL, 1992), 506–7.

139. As recounted in his memoirs, James A. Baker III, *The Politics of Diplomacy: Revolution, War, and Peace, 1989–1992* (New York: Putnam, 1995), 482.

140. "State Department Regular Briefing, Briefer: Margaret Tutwiler," Federal News Service, June 27, 1991, 1 (electronic version available through Lexis-Nexis).

141. David Binder, "Some Western Nations Split Off on Yugoslavia," *New York Times*, July 3, 1991.

142. See newsletter sent to constituents of Sen. Bob Dole, "Yugoslavia: International Community Must Bring Pressure to End Aggression against Freedom-Minded Republics," August 30, 1992, Bush Presidential Records, WHORM Subject File, General, Scanned Records, CO 176 [277593–55], George H. W. Bush Presidential Library. See also speeches by Dole on the Senate floor, including "Condemnation of Violence in Yugoslavia," *Congressional Record*, September 10, 1991. Note that under congressional pressure, the United States suspended its five-million-dollar economic aid program—a relic of Cold War assistance—for twenty days. The aid was resumed on May 25, 1991. See David Binder, "US Resumes Aid It Suspended to Yugoslavia," *New York Times*, May 25, 1991.

143. James Jatras, defense witness at the Milošević trial, ICTY, September 8, 2004, 32594–95, *www.icty.org*.

144. Binder, "Eagleburger Anguishes over Yugoslav Upheaval."

145. A document from the American Croatian Society noted: "Communist hardliners in the Yugoslav Army and in Serbia brutally attacked the new democracies," i.e., Slovenia and Croatia. See "Recognize Croatia: The Only Solution," November 25, 1991. This is a typescript version of a presentation made to the White House and the Department of State. From Bush Presidential Records, Public Liaison, James Schaefer Files, Croatia/Croatian Americans, OA/ID 07549, George H. W. Bush Presidential Library.

146. Descriptions of Letica are from Robert Musial, "Lawyer Named Envoy to New Croatian Nation," *Detroit Free Press*, September 18, 1992; and "Correction on Mara Letica," *New York Times*, November 19, 1992. Letica was never confirmed by the Senate and did not, in fact, serve as ambassador.

147. The meeting is described and Eagleburger is paraphrased in Halberstam, *War in a Time of Peace*, 29. Halberstam notes that Eagleburger's statement constituted a "green light" for secession. And CIA director Gates's memoirs note: "Nearly everyone in the [Bush] administration believed that the breakup of former communist states risked violence and instability *if not carried out in an orderly, peaceful way and through a political-legal process.* . . . This would be Bush's policy on both the Soviet Union and Yugoslavia" (emphasis added). Gates, *From the Shadows*, 529.

148. That Eagleburger's 1990 statement encouraged the secessionist forces was the opinion

of US diplomat Louis Sell (who served in the US embassy in Belgrade at this point), as described in Halberstam, *War in a Time of Peace*, 29.

149. Zimmermann, *Origins of a Catastrophe*, 151. Regarding the ambiguous signals that the United States and European states were sending during the period immediately preceding war—which left some doubt as to whether the West would support Yugoslav unity—see discussion in Paul Shoup, "The Disintegration of Yugoslavia and Western Foreign Policy in the 1980s," in Lenard J. Cohen and Jasna Dragović-Soso, eds., *State Collapse in South-Eastern Europe: New Perspectives on Yugoslavia's Disintegration* (West Lafayette, Ind.: Purdue University Press, 2008), 344–45.

150. David Binder, "Conflict in Yugoslavia: United Yugoslavia Is US Policy Aim," *New York Times*, July 1, 1991. US officials had consistently opposed any use of force against secession, and this policy existed before the war began. See US Department of State, Bureau of Public Affairs, letter from Joan Colbert to Hal Zimmerman, April 9, 1991, Bush Presidential Records, WHORM Subject File, General Scanned Records, CO176 [219365], George H. W. Bush Presidential Library; Warren Zimmermann, "The Last Ambassador: A Memoir on the Collapse of Yugoslavia," *Foreign Affairs* 74, no. 2, 1995, 11; and Sell, *Slobodan Milošević*, 143.

151. Eagleburger quoted in Edward Mortimer and Lionel Barber, "Crisis in Yugoslavia: Diplomacy Tested by Territorial Integrity," *Financial Times*, July 4, 1991.

152. Such plans had been put forward by Slovenia and Croatia before they seceded, and later by EC mediator Lord Carrington during the International Conference on Yugoslavia in the fall of 1991. For a critique of the confederation plans, see Robert Hayden, *Blueprints for a House Divided: The Constitutional Logic of Yugoslav Conflicts* (Ann Arbor: University of Michigan Press, 1999), chap. 3.

153. Mortimer and Barber, "Crisis in Yugoslavia."

154. Within the Bush administration, there was a tendency to deemphasize Yugoslav events evident from the first year of Bush's tenure. In 1989, the State Department was receiving substantial correspondence about Serb repression in Kosovo. An internal State Department memorandum noted: "We have tried to avoid giving too high a profile to such a contentious issue [i.e., repression in Kosovo]." See Memorandum for Brent Scowcroft, March 21, 1989, FG 006-06, National Security Council [035014–035055], George H. W. Bush Presidential Library.

155. Baker, *Politics of Diplomacy*, 636. The general theme that the United States initially encouraged Europe to take the lead in Yugoslavia is also emphasized by Hutchings, *American Diplomacy*, 303–21; Glitman, "US Policy in Bosnia," 68; and Vernet and Gonin, *La Rêve Sacrifié*, 52–53.

156. On US support for Carrington, see "State Department Regular Briefing, Briefer: Richard Boucher," Federal News Service, September 26, 1991.

157. Zimmermann, *Origins of a Catastrophe*, 172–73.

158. See Pérez de Cuéllar's own account in *Pilgrimage for Peace*, 492–94; David Binder, "UN Fights Bonn's Embrace of Croatia," *New York Times*, December 14, 1991; and Goulding, *Peacemonger*, 302, 306. Pérez de Cuéllar's letter to German foreign minister Genscher is reprinted (in French) in Merlino, *Vérités Yougoslaves*, 245–46.

159. "EEC/Yugoslavia: Recognizing the Independence of the Republics," *European Report*, December 17, 1991. See also Gow, *Triumph of the Lack of Will*, 63–64.

160. Tom Walker, "Doubts Emerge on EC Recognition of Breakaway Croatia," *Times* (London), January 11, 1992.

161. The EC politics that attended recognition are explored in Goulding, *Peacemonger*, 302.

162. On the Krajina peace agreement, see Pérez de Cuéllar, *Pilgrimage for Peace*, 486–91; and United Nations, *The Blue Helmets: A Review of United Nations Peacekeeping* (New York: United Nations, Department of Public Information, 1996), 488, 513–14. The basis for UN peacekeeping in Croatia appears to be the following document: "Concept for a United Nations Peace-Keeping Operation in Yugoslavia," in Ramcharan, *International Conference on the Former Yugoslavia*, vol. 1, 447–53. No exact date is given for the document.

163. "Yugoslavia: Wreckognition," *Economist*, January 18, 1992, 48.

164. "Yugoslavia: Wreckognition." The persecution of Serb minorities continued, despite Croatia's assurances. See Binder, "Croatia Forced Thousands from Homes." Nevertheless, the Badinter Commission validated the decision to recognize Croatia. See International Conference on Yugoslavia Arbitration Commission, "Opinion no. 5," January 11, 1992, in Owen, *Balkan Odyssey*, CD-ROM.

165. Steinberg, "International Involvement in the Yugoslav Conflict," 38. Similarly, EC mediator Peter Carrington would later note that "Croatia had designed a constitution that contained 'very inadequate' safeguards for the Serb minority." Carrington is paraphrased in a National Security Council e-mail, March 12, 1992, in Bush Presidential Records, NSC, Jane Holl Files, Yugoslavia—February 1992 OA/ID CFO1401 [1 of 2], George H. W. Bush Presidential Library.

166. UN official Marrack Goulding would later note that "at a meeting of EC foreign ministers on 15–16 December, Genscher browbeat his colleagues" on the issue of recognizing the secessionist republics. Goulding also noted that Britain, France, and the United States "allowed Germany to get its way" on the issue of recognition. Goulding, *Peacemonger*, 302, 306. Regarding the international politics of recognition, see also Caplan, *Europe and the Recognition of New States*, 45–48.

167. David Binder, "As Bonn Talks Louder, Some in the US Wince," *New York Times*, January 7, 1992.

168. Ian Traynor, "Independence Is Top of the Zagreb Hit Parade," *Guardian*, January 16, 1992.

169. Zimmermann writes that Slovenian official "Janez Drnovšek credits American pressure with diverting a JNA tank column from moving on Slovenia." Zimmermann, *Origins of a Catastrophe*, 151. Regarding international pressures against the use of force, and how they restrained the JNA, see also Woodward, *Balkan Tragedy*, 257; and Robert J. Donia and John V. A. Fine Jr., *Bosnia and Herzegovina: A Tradition Betrayed* (New York: Columbia University Press, 1994), 218–19.

170. David Binder, "As Bonn Talks Louder, Some in the US Wince." On US nervousness about the German role, see also Hubert Védrine, *Les Mondes de François Mitterrand: A l'Elysée, 1981–1995* (Paris: Fayard, 1996), 605.

171. Officials from several European states also expressed irritation at Germany's domineering style. See "Lord Carrington Erläutert Serbien de Anerkennungsbescluff der EG," *Frankfurter Allgemeine Zeitung*, December 19, 1991; and Stark, "Dissonances Franco-Allemandes," 346.

172. The most immediate US reaction to the EC recognition debacle was one of spite: The United States refused to recognize Slovenia and Croatia for two months after the EC did so. "Washington Maintient son Refus de Reconnaître les Républiques Sécessionistes," *Le Monde,* January 18, 1992; and "US Rebuffs Slovenia on Trade Privileges," *Journal of Commerce*, February 20, 1992.

Chapter 5

Epigraph: George Tomashevich, "Hands Off Post-Tito Yugoslavia," letter to the editor, *New York Times*, April 1, 1980.

1. On paper, the Socialist Federal Republic of Yugoslavia continued until April 1992, when it was officially abolished. Regarding Marković's resignation, see "Ante Marković Explains His Resignation as President of FEC," from Belgrade Radio in BBC Summary of World Broadcasts, December 23, 1991.

2. Quote from Lexis-Nexis abstract, "Punishing Serbia," *Philadelphia Inquirer*, August 11, 1992.

3. Anthony Lewis, "Abroad at Home: Weakness and Shame," *New York Times*, June 14, 1992.

4. See, for example, Jane Sharp, "Dayton Report Card," *International Security* 22, no. 3, 1997–1998, 101–2.

5. Gen. Philippe Morillon, *Croire et Oser: Chronique de Sarajevo* (Paris: Bernard Grasset, 1993), 95. Translated from the French.

6. Richard Holbrooke, *To End a War* (New York: Random House, 1998), 35.

7. David Binder, "Thoughts on United States Policy towards Yugoslavia," *South Slav Journal* 16, nos. 61–62, 1995.

8. George Kenney interviewed in the documentary film *Yugoslavia: The Avoidable War*, 2002, directed by George Bogdanich.

9. Zimmermann quoted in David Binder, "US Policymakers on Bosnia Admit Errors in Opposing Partition in 1992," *New York Times*, August 29, 1993.

10. US National Security Council, "US Actions in the Yugoslav Crisis—Checklist," August 4, 1992, Presidential Records, NSC, Jane Holl Files, Bosnia-Herzegovina, August 1992, OA/ID CFO 1475 [4 of 9]. In public, US policy continued to favor European leadership. See Letter from Brent Scowcroft to Lee Hamilton, December 28, 1991, Bush Presidential Records, WHORM Subject File, General, Scanned Records, CO176 [287233]; and letter from Janet Mullins, Department of State, to Glenn Anderson, February 28, 1992, Bush Presidential Records, WHORM Subject File, General, Scanned Records, CO176 [300946]. Documents from George H. W. Bush Presidential Library.

11. Louis Sell, *Slobodan Milošević and the Destruction of Yugoslavia* (Durham, N.C.: Duke University Press, 2002), 164.

12. Genscher interviewed in documentary film *Yugoslavia: The Avoidable War*.

13. Quote from David Owen in "The Future of the Balkans: An Interview with David Owen," *Foreign Affairs* 72, no. 2, 1993, 6.

14. For a description of this plan see Netherlands Institute for War Documentation [NIOD], "Srebrenica—A 'Safe' Area: Reconstruction, Background, Consequences, and Analyses of the Fall of a Safe Area," 2003, part 1, chap. 5, sec. 3, *srebrenica.brightside.nl/ srebrenica/*. See also "Statement on Principles for New Constitutional Arrangement for Bosnia and Herzegovina, Lisbon, 23 February, 1992," in Snežana Trifunovska, ed., *Yugoslavia through Documents* (Dortrecht, Netherlands: Martinus Nijhoff, 1994), 517–19.

15. NIOD, "Srebrenica," part 1, chap. 5, sec. 1.

16. Binder, "US Policymakers on Bosnia Admit Errors."

17. It is apparent that all three ethnic groups agreed to Cutileiro's plan (although there is some confusion about whether they formally signed the document). See Steven L. Burg and Paul S. Shoup, *The War in Bosnia-Herzegovina: Ethnic Conflict and*

International Intervention (Armonk, N.Y.: M. E. Sharp, 1999), 110; and James Bissett, "Balkan War, Balkan Peace, Balkan Future?" no date ("Bosnia" section), *www.deltax. net/bissett/western/bosnia.htm.*

18. Robert Hayden, *Blueprints for a House Divided: The Constitutional Logic of the Yugoslav Conflicts* (Ann Arbor: University of Michigan Press, 1999), 100. Note that the Croats actually withdrew from the agreement first; the Muslims withdrew the next day.

19. Binder, "US Policymakers on Bosnia Admit Errors." In response to Binder's article, Zimmermann wrote a letter to the editor in which he denied having opposed the Cutileiro plan (although Zimmermann did not challenge the factual accuracy of the quotes in the article). See Warren Zimmermann, "Bosnian About-Face," letter to the editor, *New York Times*, September 30, 1993. In his public statements, Ambassador Zimmermann nominally supported the EC diplomacy. See Burg and Shoup, *War in Bosnia-Herzegovina*, 114–15. A considerable body of evidence contradicts Zimmermann's claims. This chapter provides extensive evidence that Zimmermann *did* in fact oppose Cutileiro's plan.

20. Kenney interviewed in documentary film *Yugoslavia: The Avoidable War*.

21. Bissett, "Balkan War" ("Bosnia" section).

22. NIOD, "Srebrenica," part 1, chap. 5, sec. 3.

23. José Cutileiro, "Pre-War Bosnia," letter to the editor, *Economist*, December 9, 1995. Cutileiro also notes that some feeble efforts were made in the summer of 1992 to rescue the agreement, but these were unsuccessful. For further information on US opposition to this plan, see also Saadia Touval, *Mediation in the Yugoslav Wars: The Critical Years, 1990–95* (New York: Palgrave, 2002), 108–10.

24. Carrington interviewed in documentary film *Yugoslavia: The Avoidable War*.

25. Quoted in Brendan Simms, *Unfinest Hour: Britain and the Destruction of Bosnia* (London: Allen Lane, 2001), 66.

26. Marko Hoare misleadingly implies that Izetbegović rejected the Lisbon agreement on his own initiative; but Hoare neglects to mention the US role in encouraging Izetbegović's decision. Hoare, *The History of Bosnia: From the Middle Ages to the Present Day* (London: Saqi Books, 2007), 376.

27. Binder, "US Policymakers on Bosnia Admit Errors."

28. Warren Zimmermann, *Origins of a Catastrophe: Yugoslavia and Its Destroyers—America's Last Ambassador Tells What Happened and Why* (New York: Times Books, 1996), 190.

29. Sell, *Slobodan Milošević*, 164.

30. This is the view expressed in Zimmermann, *Origins of a Catastrophe*, 190–91.

31. Karadžić quoted in Binder, "US Policymakers on Bosnia Admit Errors."

32. US Central Intelligence Agency [USCIA], *Balkan Battlegrounds: A Military History of the Yugoslav Conflict, 1990–1995*, vol. 1 (Washington, D.C.: CIA Office of Russian and European Analysis, 2002), 140.

33. Sell, *Slobodan Milošević*, 164.

34. Kenney quoted in the documentary film *Yugoslavia: The Avoidable War*.

35. See "EC Declaration on Recognition of Bosnia and Herzegovina," April 6, 1992; and "President Bush's Statement [on the Recognition of Bosnia and Herzegovina, Croatia, and Slovenia]," April 7, 1992; both in Trifunovska, *Yugoslavia through Documents*, 521–22.

36. "Base Force Idea Is 'Tailored to New and Enduring Strategic Reality,'" *Aerospace Daily*, October 9, 1990. On the base force plan and other projects aimed at keeping military

spending close to Cold War levels, see Michael Klare, *Rogue States and Nuclear Outlaws: America's Search for a New Foreign Policy* (New York: Hill and Wang, 1995), 30–34.

37. The neoconservatives were especially enthusiastic about the idea of lifting the arms embargo and arming the Muslims. "See No Evil," *New Republic*, October 25, 1993.

38. See analysis in Alain Frachon, "S'Alignant sur la Communauté Européene: Washington Reconnaît la Slovénie, la Croatie, et la Bosnie-Herzégovine," *Le Monde*, April 9, 1992.

39. See discussion in Chapter 2 of this study.

40. Quoted in Christopher Layne, "From Preponderance to Offshore Balancing: America's Future Grand Strategy," *International Security* 22, no. 1, 1997, 100. Also see William Odom, *America's Military Revolution: Strategy and Structure after the Cold War* (Washington, D.C.: American University Press, 1993), 36–37.

41. Lugar quoted in "Raising the Ante," MacNeil/Lehrer NewsHour, May 6, 1993.

42. See Alija Izetbegović, *Inescapable Questions: Autobiographical Notes* (Leicester, UK: Islamic Foundation, 2003).

43. Thomas Gjelton, *Sarajevo Daily: A City and Its Newspaper under Siege* (New York: HarperCollins, 1995), 76.

44. "Alija Izetbegović, Politician, Was Born on August 8, 1925," *Times* (London), October 20, 2003; and David Binder, "Alija Izetbegović, Muslim Who Led Bosnia, Dies at 78," *New York Times*, October 20, 2003.

45. Alija Izetbegović, *The Islamic Declaration*, unpublished ms, 1970, 3, 16, 49, available through the University of Washington Library.

46. Alija Izetbegović, *Islam between East and West* (Indianapolis: American Trust Publications, 1993).

47. NIOD, "Srebrenica," part 1, chap. 3, sec., 3 .

48. This Iranian arms supply appears to have begun on a small scale during the fall of 1992. Cees Wiebes, *Intelligence and the War in Bosnia: 1992–1995* (Münster: Lit, 2003), 159–60.

49. The importance of nationalist propaganda is the main conclusion of Franke Wilmer, *The Social Construction of Man, the State, and War: Identity, Conflict, and Violence in Former Yugoslavia* (New York: Routledge, 2002).

50. Zulfikarpašić's role is discussed in "Ex-Yugoslavs on Yugoslavia: As They See It," *Economist*, March 16, 1996, R5.

51. Adil Zulfikarpašić, Milovan Djilas, and Nadeža Gaće, *The Bosniak* (London: Hurst, 1998), 141, 163.

52. Zulfikarpašić, Djilas, and Gaće, *Bosniak*, 137.

53. Regarding the World War II period, see Chapter 3 of this study.

54. USCIA, *Balkan Backgrounds*, vol. 1, 122.

55. Quoted in Lenard J. Cohen, *Broken Bonds: Yugoslavia's Disintegration and Balkan Politics in Transition* (Boulder, Colo.: Westview, 1995), 145.

56. Susan L. Woodward, *Balkan Tragedy: Chaos and Dissolution after the Cold War* (Washington, D.C.: Brookings, 1995), 133.

57. Zulfikarpašić commented that there were "three nationalist, totalitarian parties in Bosnia . . . all of them essentially undemocratic." Zulfikarpašić, Djilas, and Gaće, *Bosniak*, 152.

58. This apt phrase is from Hayden, *Blueprints for a House Divided*, 92.

59. NIOD, "Srebrenica," part 1, chap. 3, sec. 6.

60. The popular image of a multicultural Bosnian state did not reflect reality. Military correspondent Tim Ripley observed: "The real power in the Bosnian state lay not with the multi-ethnic collective presidency or cabinet but with the executive committee of the Muslim Party for Democratic Action." Ripley, *Operation Deliberate Force: The UN and NATO Campaign in Bosnia, 1995* (Lancaster, UK: Centre for Defence and International Security Studies, 1999), 27.

61. Ashdown paraphrased in Stephen Castle, "Bosnian Leader Was Suspected of War Crimes," *Independent*, October 23, 2003.

62. Bernard Kouchner, *Les Guerriers de la Paix: Du Kosovo à l'Irak* (Paris: Grasset, 2004), 375. Translated from the French.

63. Wayne Burt, *The Reluctant Superpower: United States' Policy in Bosnia, 1991–95* (New York: St. Martin's, 1997), 30; Roy Gutman, *A Witness to Genocide: The 1993 Pulitzer Prize–Winning Dispatches on the "Ethnic Cleansing" of Bosnia* (New York: Macmillan, 1993), xxviii. Slavoj Zizek presents a similarly skewed view of the Izetbegović regime, while he mentions none of its negative features. See Zizek, *Did Somebody Say Totalitarian? Five Interventions in the (Mis)use of a Notion* (London: Verso, 2001), 232.

64. Laura Silber and Allan Little, *The Death of Yugoslavia* (New York: Penguin, 1997), 233.

65. The UN secretary-general had urged Germany not to push for early recognition of Slovenian and Croatian independence, fearing that such recognition would sabotage mediation efforts and might provoke war in Bosnia. See letter from Javier Pérez de Cuéllar to Hans-Dietrich Genscher, December 14, 1991, reprinted in Jacques Merlino, *Les Vérités Yougoslaves Ne Sont Pas Toutes Bonnes à Dire* (Paris: Albin Michel, 1993), 245–46; and Pérez de Cuéllar, *Pilgrimage for Peace: A Secretary-General's Memoir* (New York: St. Martin's, 1997), 492–94.

66. Technically, the resolution stated that Bosnia would cease participating in Yugoslav institutions if other republics ceased to participate. Given the circumstances, this must be viewed as a move toward independence. See Hayden, *Blueprints for a House Divided*, 92–94.

67. On the legally questionable means that the Muslim and Croat parties used to pass their resolution, see testimony by Robert Hayden as a defense witness in the trial of Duško Tadić, International Criminal Tribunal for the Former Yugoslavia (ICTY), September 11, 1996, 5676–79, 5695–97, *www.icty.org*; and United Nations, "Report on the Historical Background of the Civil War in the Former Yugoslavia: United Nations Commission of Experts, Security Council Resolution 780 (1992), Professor M. Cherif Bassiouni, Chairman," March 1994, 37.

68. Hayden, *Blueprints for a House Divided*, 92–94.

69. See Burg and Shoup, *War in Bosnia and Herzegovina*, 117–20.

70. "Belgrade Purges Military," *Times* (London), February 29, 1992. Three months after the first purge, there was a second purge, in which another forty officers were removed. See Ian Traynor, "Belgrade Sacks Generals in Military Purge," *Guardian*, May 9, 1992. In the course of these events, the Yugoslav National Army was renamed simply the Yugoslav Army. Officially, Kadijević resigned.

71. According to the account by retired JNA general Aleksander Vasiljević, prosecution witness at the Milošević trial, ICTY, February 12, 2003, 15911–15, *www.icty.org*.

72. However, some accounts suggest that elements of the army sought to act as mediators and peacekeepers among Bosnia's ethnic groups. See General Vasiljević, testimony at the ICTY, February 5, 2003, 15769–72, *www.icty.org*. A CIA account states that the

JNA initially followed a "schizophrenic, two-track policy [in Bosnia], of attempting to defuse hostilities and arrange negotiations among the three ethnic groups, while continuing to provide practical support to the Bosnian Serbs." USCIA, *Balkan Battleground*, vol. 1, 136.

73. See "Declaration on a New Yugoslavia," April 27, 1992, in Trifunovska, *Yugoslavia through Documents*, 532–34.

74. Lenard J. Cohen, *Serpent in the Bosom: The Rise and Fall of Slobodan Milošević* (Boulder, Colo.: Westview, 2002), 209–14.

75. Sell, *Slobodan Milošević*, 161.

76. See Snežana Trifunovska, ed., *Former Yugoslavia through Documents: From Its Dissolution to the Peace Settlement* (The Hague: Martinus Nijhoff, 1999), 180.

77. Quoted in NIOD, "Srebrenica," part 1, chap. 3, sect. 4.

78. USCIA, *Balkan Battlegrounds*, vol. 1, 128.

79. Milošević met with Franjo Tudjman to coordinate the partition of Bosnia into Croat- and Serb-controlled zones. Even as late as 1995, Tudjman was still planning for a "Greater Croatia." See Silber and Little, *Death of Yugoslavia*, 213; Misha Glenny, *The Fall of Yugoslavia* (New York: Penguin, 1996), 149; and testimony by Paddy Ashdown, prosecution witness at the Milošević trial, ICTY, March 14, 2002, 2333–35, *www.icty.org*. On Tudjman's long-standing hostility toward Bosnian Muslims, see account by France's ambassador to Croatia, Georges-Marie Chenu, preface to Renéo Lukic, *L'Agonie Yougoslave (1986–2003): Les Etats-Unis et l'Europe Face aux Guerres Balkaniques* (Quebec: Presse de l'Université de Laval, 2003), xxxi–xxxii.

80. Gen. Philippe Morillon, prosecution witness at the Milošević trial, ICTY, February 12, 2004, 31963, *www.icty.org*. For additional information on intervention by the Republic of Serbia, see testimony by Herbert Okun, ICTY, February 27, 2003, 17062, *www.icty.org*.

81. Okun testimony, February 27, 2003, 17061.

82. US National Security Council, "German Generals on Yugoslavia," August 20, 1992, Bush Presidential Records, NSC, Jane Holl Files, Electronic Messages—Yugoslavia, OA/ID CFO 1428 [13 of 17], George H. W. Bush Presidential Library.

83. The greater Serb culpability was widely recognized by UN peacekeepers on the ground. See, for example, Maj. Gen. Lewis MacKenzie, *Peacekeeper: The Road to Sarajevo* (Vancouver: Douglas and McIntyre, 1993), 193–94.

84. "Bosnia's Future," *Financial Times*, January 22, 1993.

85. The Greek Civil War of the late 1940s, though long forgotten, also involved a large loss of life.

86. See Vincent Browne, "When Is Slaughter of Innocents Not an Outrage?" *Irish Times*, June 16, 1999.

87. On atrocities in the Bosnia war, see US Congress, *The Betrayal of Srebrenica: Why Did the Massacre Happen? Will It Happen Again?* (Washington, D.C.: US Government Printing Office, 1998); Chuck Sudetic, *Blood and Vengeance: One Family's Story of the War in Bosnia* (New York: Norton, 1998); Thomas Cushman and Stjepan G. Meštrović, eds., *This Time We Knew: Western Responses to Genocide in Bosnia* (New York: New York University Press, 1996); Michael Sells, *The Bridge Betrayed: Religion and Genocide in Bosnia* (Berkeley: University of California Press, 1996); Gutman, *A Witness to Genocide*; David Rhode, *Endgame: The Betrayal and Fall of Srebrenica, Europe's Worst Massacre since World War II* (New York: Farrar, Straus, and Giroux, 1997); Norman L. Cigar,

Genocide in Bosnia: The Policy of "Ethnic Cleansing" (College Station: Texas A&M University Press, 1995); US Congress, *Genocide in Bosnia-Herzegovina* (Washington, D.C.: US Government Printing Office, 1995); Roger Cohen, *Hearts Grown Brutal: Sagas of Sarajevo* (New York: Random House, 1998); US Congress, *Human Rights, Refugees, and War Crimes: The Prospects for Peace in Bosnia* (Washington, D.C.: US Government Printing Office, 1996); Alexandra Stiglmayer, *Mass Rape: The War against Women in Bosnia-Herzegovina* (Lincoln: University of Nebraska Press, 1994); Beverly Allen, *Rape Warfare: The Hidden Genocide in Bosnia-Herzegovina and Croatia* (Minneapolis: University of Minnesota Press, 1996); James Gow, *The Serbian Project and Its Adversaries* (Montreal: McGill-Queen's University Press, 2003); David Rieff, *Slaughterhouse: Bosnia and the Failure of the West* (New York : Simon and Schuster, 1995); Jan Willem Honig and Norbert Both, *Srebrenica: Record of a War Crime* (London: Penguin, 1996); Stevan M. Weine, *When History Is a Nightmare: Lives and Memories of Ethnic Cleansing in Bosnia-Herzegovina* (New Brunswick, N.J.: Rutgers University Press, 1999).

88. The Pulitzer Prize winners are John Burns of the *New York Times* (1993), Roy Gutman of *Newsday* (1993), and David Rhode of the *Christian Science Monitor* (1996). See the official Pulitzer Web site, *www.pulitzer.org/*. For critical analyses of press coverage of the Bosnia war, see the following: Michel Collon, *Poker Menteur: Les Grandes Puissances, la Yougoslavie, et les Prochaines Guerres* (Bruxelles: EPO, 1998); Peter Brock, *Media Cleansing, Dirty Reporting: Journalism and Tragedy in Yugoslavia* (Los Angeles: GM Books, 2005); Diana Johnstone, *Fools' Crusade: Yugoslavia, NATO, and Western Delusions* (New York: Monthly Review Press, 2002); and Merlino, *Vérités Yougoslaves*.

89. Kjell Arild Nilson, "102,000 Drept i Bosnia," Norwegian Press Service, November 14, 2004. An English translation is available at *grayfalcon.blogspot.com/2004/11/bosnia-death-toll-revealed.html*. I have had the translation checked by Vilja Hülden, a graduate student in history at the University of Arizona and a speaker of Norwegian, who verified that the online translation is accurate.

90. Nedim Dervisbegovic, "Bosnia War Death Toll Put at Less Than 150,000," Reuters, December 10, 2004.

91. These death-toll figures are based on a Lexis-Nexis search of "News, All (English, full text)," for the period 1992–2000. The search parameters were: the word "Bosnia" in the headline or first paragraph and either "200,000 dead" or "250,000 dead" anywhere in the full text. A total of 422 hits resulted. The search was undertaken on May 25, 2008. It is evident in retrospect that these death-toll numbers are exaggerations. Some sources exaggerate even further and suggest that between 200,000 and 250,000 people were *murdered* in the Bosnia war. See Dick Morris, *Because He Could* (New York: Regan Books, 2004), 62–63.

92. Nilson, "102,000 Drept i Bosnia." The ICTY's 110,000 figure is noted in "Bosnia War Dead Figure Announced," BBC News, June 21, 2007, *news.bbc.co.uk/2/hi/europe/6228152.stm*. For a discussion of the methodology used in the ICTY study, see Ewa Tabeau and Jakub Bijak, "War Related Deaths in the 1992–1995 Armed Conflicts in Bosnia and Herzegovina: A Critique of Previous Estimates and Recent Results," *European Journal of Population* 21, nos. 2–3, 2005; and also Ewa Tabeau, prosecution witness at the Milošević trial, ICTY, October 7, 2003, *www.icty.org*.

93. Quoted from the translation of Nilson, "102,000 Drept i Bosnia.

94. "Bosnia War Dead Figure Announced."

95. See interview with Mirsad Tokača in "Genocide Is Not a Matter of Numbers," *Bosnia*

Report, December–March 2006, *www.bosnia.org.uk/bosrep/report_format.cfm?articleid=3 055andreportid=170.*

96. "A Guide to the War in Bosnia," *Toronto Star*, July 15, 1995.

97. NIOD, "Srebrenica," part 1, chap. 3, sec. 2. The report states: "Prior to the 1992 conflict, 56 percent of Bosnian territory was in Serb hands."

98. See USCIA, *Balkan Battlegrounds*, vol. 1, 124.

99. Gutman, *A Witness to Genocide*, xiv.

100. Kouchner, *Les Guerriers de la Paix*, 374–375. Translated from the French. I thank Michel Collon for drawing my attention to this source.

101. With regard to the allegations on Serb-run camps, Samantha Power takes a self-contradictory position: On the one hand, she acknowledges that Serb detention centers "were not extermination camps." Three pages later, on the other hand, she approvingly quotes Gutman's claim that the detention centers were "like Auschwitz." She thus reaffirms the misperception that Serb camps were indeed extermination camps— immediately after denying that this was the case. See Power, *"A Problem from Hell": America and the Age of Genocide* (New York: HarperCollins, 2002), 269, 272.

102. David Owen, *Balkan Odyssey: An Uncompromising Personal Account of the International Peace Efforts Following the Breakup of the Former Yugoslavia* (Orlando, Fla.: Harcourt, Brace, 1995), 112.

103. Charles Boyd, "Making Peace with the Guilty: The Truth about Bosnia," *Foreign Affairs* 74, no. 5, 1995, 28. In addition, UN official Lieut. Gen. Satish Nambiar, an Indian national, reported that Bosnian forces were intentionally firing on UN peacekeeping troops. Nambiar is quoted in "Visit by Co-Chairmen of Steering Committee to Zagreb, Sarajevo, and Belgrade, 9–12, September, 1992," COREU document, in David Owen, ed., *Balkan Odyssey* [Academic Edition], CD-ROM document collection (Princeton: Electric Company, 1996). See also Nambiar, "NATO Celebrates Its Fiftieth Anniversary by Destroying Yugoslavia," *Mediterranean Quarterly* 10, no. 3, 1999.

104. Lieut. Gen. Michael Rose, *Fighting for Peace: Bosnia 1994* (London: Harvill Press, 1998), 172.

105. Peter Andreas, "The Clandestine Political Economy of War and Peace in Bosnia," *International Studies Quarterly* 48, no. 1, 2004, 40; and Ripley, *Operation Deliberate Force*, 32.

106. Ripley, *Operation Deliberate Force*, 32–33. Similarly, UNPROFOR commander General Rose stated: "In the view of some extremists in the SDA [Izetbegović's party], it was better to keep the shells falling on their own people in the hope that the US would one day enter the war on their side." Rose, *Fighting for Peace*, 45. The memoir of Bernard-Henri Lévy mentions a conversation with Bosnian official Haris Silajdžić, in which Silajdžić emphasized the "propaganda" value of the genocide claims. Lévy, *Le Lys et la Cedre: Journal d'un Ecrivain au Temps de la Guerre de Bosnie* (Paris: Grasset, 1996), 426.

107. From Rochelle Stanfield, "Balkans Wars on K Street," *National Journal*, August 15, 1992. The Serbs made a feeble effort to fight back with their own propaganda campaign, but this was largely ineffectual. For a brief period in 1992, two public relations firms represented Serb interests overseas: the British firm of Ian Greer, and the US firm Wise Communications. Serbia worked with these firms because its leaders realized that (in the words of one lobbyist) the Serbs were "getting killed in terms of public perception." Both firms ended their contracts with Serbia in June 1992, due to concerns that further service would violate UN-imposed economic sanctions. After 1992, the Serb side of the conflict relied entirely on Serb emigrés in Europe and the

United States to direct public relations. The principal Serb emigré group was the Serbian Unity Congress (SUC), which was, according to Paul Hockenos, "never a big nor particularly well endowed organization." The one alliance that the SUC was able to establish was with the Greek American community, where there was significant sympathy for the Serb cause. The Greek American public relations firm Manatos and Manatos agreed to provide the SUC with professional lobbying assistance. The Serbs hired the Manatos firm because "it was the only reputable PR firm that would take their business." Sources: Tom O'Sullivan, "Truth Is the First Casualty in PR Offensive," *Independent*, August 21, 1992; Carol Matlack and Zoran B. Djordjevic, "Serbian–Croatian PR War," *National Interest*, March 14, 1992; and Paul Hockenos, *Homeland Calling: Exile Patriotism and the Balkan Wars* (Ithaca: Cornell University Press, 2003), 137.

108. The English version of the transcript appears in Yohanan Ramati, "Stopping the War in Yugoslavia," *Midstream: A Monthly Jewish Review*, April 1994. The original interview appeared in French in Merlino, *Vérités Yougoslaves*, 126–29.

109. Ed Vulliamy, " 'Neutrality' and the Absence of Reckoning: A Journalist's Account," *Journal of International Affairs* 52, no. 2, 1999, 604; see also Vulliamy, "Bosnia: The Crime of Appeasement," *International Affairs* 74, no. 1, 1998. Samantha Power also adopted a partisan stance, according to a friendly profile of her early career as a journalist: "Power [wanted to make] a contribution toward raising awareness of the ethnic cleansing policy of the Bosnian Serbs." Apparently, Power engaged in a one-sided effort to publicize *Serb* atrocities—rather than atrocities committed by all parties. Ken Gewertz, "Speaking Truth with Power," *Harvard Gazette*, March 6, 2003.

110. Amanpour quoted in Sherry Ricchiardi, "Over the Line? Journalists as Advocates in the Bosnian War," *American Journalism Review*, September 1996, 3 (electronic version available through Lexis-Nexis). BBC correspondent Martin Bell notes that in Bosnia: "Maggie O'Kane of the *Guardian* and John Burns of the *New York Times* . . . went on crusades." Bell, *In Harm's Way: Reflections of a War Zone Thug* (London: Penguin, 1996), 39.

111. Rieff quoted in a review of his book *Slaughterhouse*, in *Kirkus Review*, December 15, 1994, 1548.

112. NIOD, "Srebrenica," part 1, chap. 5, sec. 5. Note that Topalović's atrocities (and atrocities perpetrated by Bosnian government forces more generally) received little notice in contemporary or retrospective accounts. The widely noted study by James Gow, for example, does not include Topalović in the index. See Gow, *The Serbian Project and Its Adversaries*.

113. Regarding Muslim atrocities, the memoir of UNPROFOR commander General Rose states: "We flew north towards Tuzla, [and] our US embassy escort repeatedly pointed down at destroyed villages high in the Zvijezda mountains; . . . the mosques in the area were still standing while the churches in the neighboring villages had been destroyed, [and] it was obvious that Muslim forces had been responsible for most of the ethnic cleansing in this region of Bosnia. The conflict had occurred in 1993." At another point, Rose's memoir reads: "The Bosnian army offensive in the Ozren region of central Bosnia had caused 3,000 Serb civilians to flee." Rose, *Fighting for Peace*, 82, 142. On Muslim attacks against Croat civilians, see NIOD, "Srebrenica," part 1, chap. 12, sec. 3.

114. Gen. Colin L. Powell, *My American Journey* (New York: Random House, 1995), 558.

115. Quoted in "Colin Luther Powell: Reluctant Warrior," *Observer* (London), September 30, 2001.

116. McPeak's hawkish views were supported by his predecessor as air force chief of staff, Gen. Michael Dugan. See George Kenney and Michael Dugan, "Operation Balkan Storm: Here's a Plan," *New York Times,* November 29, 1992. Note that Kenney would later revise his pro-interventionist stance, as discussed in Kenney, "The Bosnia Calculation," *New York Times Magazine,* May 14, 1995.

117. David Halberstam, *War in a Time of Peace: Bush, Clinton, and the Generals* (New York: Simon and Schuster, 2002), 40–41.

118. Eagleburger's pro-interventionist role during this phase of the conflict is described in Halberstam, *War in a Time of Peace,* 135–42; and David Binder, "Why the US Now Leans on Belgrade," *New York Times,* May 27, 1992. However, some sources contradict this view and suggest that Eagleburger was still reluctant to intervene. See David Rothkopf, *Running the World: The Inside Story of the National Security Council and the Architects of American Power* (New York: Public Affairs, 2005), 317. One source claims that Eagleburger was an active "friend of Serbia," but this seems exaggerated. See Gregory Peroche, *Histoire de la Croatie et des Nations Slaves du Sud* (Paris: F. X. de Guibert, OEIL, 1992), 506. Quote translated from the French.

119. Anthony Lewis, "Closing Our Eyes?" *New York Times,* November 27, 1992.

120. A leading advocate of intervention was Senate Republican leader Bob Dole. See Dole, letter to George Bush, September 5, 1991, Bush Presidential Records, WHORM Subject File, General, Scanned Records, CO 176 [269969], George H. W. Bush Presidential Library.

121. Quoted in Ted Galen Carpenter, "Foreign Policy Masochism: The Campaign for US Intervention in Yugoslavia," Cato Foreign Policy Briefing Paper 19 (Washington, D.C.: Cato Institute, 1992), *www.cato.org/pub_display.php?pub_id=1544.* The NATO factor in US policy is also emphasized in Sean Gervasi, "Why Is NATO in Yugoslavia?" in Ramsey Clark, ed., *NATO in the Balkans* (New York: International Action Center, 1998).

122. This reluctance is noted by former National Security Council staffer David C. Gompert, "The United States and Yugoslavia's Wars," in Richard Ullman, ed., *The World and Yugoslavia's Wars* (New York: Council on Foreign Relations, 1996), 128.

123. On Bush's opposition, see NIOD, "Srebrenica," part 1, chap. 3, sec. 12.

124. "Remarks by Secretary of Defense Dick Cheney," Federal News Service, October 1, 1992.

125. James A. Baker III, *The Politics of Diplomacy: Revolution, War, and Peace, 1989–1992* (New York: Putnam, 1995), 651.

126. The UNPROFOR force in Bosnia-Herzegovina was part of a larger UN peacekeeping presence that extended into Croatia and Macedonia. See description in United Nations, *The Blue Helmets: A Review of United Nations Peacekeeping* (New York: United Nations, Department of Public Information, 1996), 485–566, 744–52.

127. In 1992, State Department official John Bolton stated: "I would characterize our view [in the Bush administration] toward the United Nations as a *competitor* in the marketplace of international problem-solving" (emphasis added). Quoted in Mary Curtius, "Some Nations Uneasy with UN's New Clout," *Boston Globe,* January 27, 1992. On US hostility, see also Boutros Boutros-Ghali, *Unvanquished: A US-UN Saga* (New York: Random House, 1999), 198.

128. UN Security Council Resolution 757, May 30, 1992, and Resolution 760, June 18, 1992. Both available at *www.un.org/documents/sc/res/1992/scres92.htm.*

129. NIOD, "Srebrenica," part 1, chap. 5, sec. 10.

130. Technically, this arms embargo was an extension of the 1991 embargo imposed on all parties in the Balkan conflict. See UN Security Council Resolution 713, September 25, 1991, *www.un.org/Docs/scres/1991/scres91.htm*.

131. Hella Pick, "WEU and NATO to Enforce UN Sea Blockade against Rump Yugoslavia," *Guardian*, November 21, 1992.

132. Peter Grier, "Washington Takes Leading Role in Seeking to Stem Yugoslav Strife," *Christian Science Monitor*, June 2, 1992.

133. David Binder, "US Is Backing Serbian President's Internal Foes," *New York Times*, November 19, 1992.

134. In 1992, US officials had a significant opportunity to influence Yugoslav politics. In that year, Milan Panić became prime minister of the Federal Republic of Yugoslavia, a newly created post for a newly created state. Panić held this position from June 1992 until February 1993. Milošević retained his position as president of Serbia (though in reality he remained the main political force in Yugoslavia as well). Panić unsuccessfully challenged Milošević for president of Serbia during elections in December 1992; shortly thereafter, Panić left his post as federal prime minister. Panić was in fact a US citizen (though he was born in Yugoslavia). He was also a multimillionaire through his firm ICN pharmaceuticals. And Panić was politically well connected: The vice president of ICN's Serbia affiliate, ICN-Galenika, was John Scanlon, a former US ambassador to Yugoslavia. However, there is no real evidence to suggest that Panić was acting in concert with or being supported by the US government. Regarding Panić's role, see Michael Kaufman, "Yugoslavs Offer Post to American," *New York Times*, June 17, 1992; Florence Hartmann, "Premières Evaluations Contradictoires: Les Elections en Serbie ont été Marquées par de Nombreuses Irrégularités," *Le Monde*, December 22, 1992; and US National Security Council, e-mail, July 27, 1992, Bush Presidential Record, NSC, Jane Holl Files, Electronic Messages—Yugoslavia, OA/ID CFO 1428 [12 of 17], George H. W. Bush Presidential Library.

135. Martin Fletcher, "Serbia Opens Rift between Allies," *Times* (London), May 30, 1992. Note that the policy of publicly attacking the European Community over Bosnia represented a shift in policy. At least through February 1992, US officials publicly supported European diplomatic efforts. See the following: Letter from Brent Scowcroft to Lee Hamilton, December 28, 1991, Bush Presidential Records, WHORM Subject File, General, Scanned Records, CO176 [287233]; and Letter from Janet Mullins to Glenn Anderson, February 28, 1992, Bush Presidential Records, WHORM Subject File, General, Scanned Records, CO176 [300946]. Both documents from George H. W. Bush Presidential Library.

136. By late 1992, the base force remained the cornerstone of the military's planning during this period, despite some modifications. "Base Force Review," *Aviation Week and Space Technology*, September 14, 1992.

137. Halberstam, *War in a Time of Peace*, 41–42. The quote is directly from Halberstam, which paraphrases McPeak.

138. For a general description of Operation Restore Hope and subsequent international interventions in Somalia, see United Nations, *The United Nations and Somalia, 1992–1996* (New York: United Nations Department of Public Information, 1996).

139. Jon Western, "The Sources of Humanitarian Intervention: Beliefs, Information, and Advocacy in the US Decisions on Somalia and Bosnia," *International Security* 26, no. 4, 2002, 112.

140. Western, "Sources of Humanitarian Intervention," 113.

141. Stephen Smith, *Somalie: La Guerre Perdue de l'Humanitaire* (Paris: Calmann-Lévy, 1993), 168. Translated from the French.

142. Alex de Waal, "US War Crimes in Somalia," *New Left Review*, no. 230, 1998, 132; and Keith Richburg, "US Envoy in Somalia Viewed as Linchpin of Reconciliation," *Washington Post*, February 2, 1993.

143. See Steven Livingston and Todd Eachus, "Humanitarian Crises and US Foreign Policy: Somalia and the CNN Effect Reconsidered," *Political Communication* 12, no. 4, 1995.

144. On Clinton's support for the December 1992 troop landing, see Clinton, "Address to the Nation on Somalia," October 7, 1993," in John Woolley, and Gerhard Peters, eds., American Presidency Project Document Archive, *www.presidency.ucsb.edu/ws/index.php?pid=47180andst=Address+to+the+Nation+on+Somaliaandst1=.*

145. Elizabeth Drew, *On the Edge: The Clinton Presidency* (New York: Simon and Schuster, 1994), 139.

146. Sidney Blumenthal, "Why Are We in Somalia?" *New Yorker*, October 25, 1993, 53. The quoted official is not named.

147. Gallucci quoted in Rothkopf, *Running the World*, 317.

148. Western, "Sources of Humanitarian Intervention," 136–38. According to Halberstam: "Sending troops to Somalia . . . was Powell's way of doing something humanitarian but, equally important, of *not* sending troops to Bosnia." Halberstam, *War in a Time of Peace*, 251.

149. Recall that Powell had emphasized a preference for intervention in desert zones.

150. Regarding the oil factor in Somalia, see David Gibbs, "Realpolitik and Humanitarian Intervention: The Case of Somalia," *International Politics* 37, no. 1, 2000, *www.gened.arizona.edu/dgibbs/somalia.pdf.* See also recently declassified US government documents on Conoco's role, available through Keith Yearman, ed., "The Conoco-Somalia Declassification Project," *www.cod.edu/people/faculty/yearman/somalia.htm.* Kevin Phillips states that the 1992 troop landing in Somalia was "substantially oil driven." Phillips, *American Theocracy: The Peril and Politics of Radical Religion, Oil, and Borrowed Money in the Twenty-First Century* (New York: Viking, 2006), 81.

151. Powell quoted in John Morrocco, "Somalia to Impact Debate on Reshaping of US Forces," *Aviation Week and Space Technology*, December 14–21, 1992, 23. See also Powell's comments in "Cheney Says Somalia Relief Will Cost Pentagon $200-$300 Million," *Aerospace Daily*, December 7, 1992.

152. Christy Fisher, "Uncle Sam Banks on Somalia PR: Military Hopes Publicity Makes Up for Ad Cutback," *Advertising Age*, December 14, 1992.

153. Morrocco, "Somalia to Impact Debate," 23.

154. George H. W. Bush, "Address to the Nation on the Situation in Somalia," in Woolley and Peters, American Presidency Project, Document Archive, December 4, 1992, *www.presidency.ucsb.edu/ws/index.php?pid=21758andst=andst1=.*

155. "Number of Foreign Troops in Somalia Nears 30,000," Agence France Presse, January 6, 1993.

156. US forces withdrew from Somalia in 1994; the remaining UN forces withdrew in 1995.

157. At the time of his death in 2003, Izetbegović was being investigated by the ICTY. He died before any indictment was issued. See "UN War Crimes Court Was Investigating Late Bosnian President Izetbegović," Agence France Presse, October 22, 2003.

158. Quoted in Halberstam, *War in a Time of Peace*, 91–92.

159. Quoted in Michael Sherry, "The Military," *American Quarterly* 35, nos. 1–2, 1983, 73.

Chapter 6

Epigraph: Boutros Boutros-Ghali, *Unvanquished: A US-UN Saga* (New York: Random House, 1999), 198. Boutros-Ghali's observation was not made specifically with respect to Bosnia.

1.   Richard Holbrooke, *To End a War* (New York: Random House, 1998), 50. Holbrooke quotes from a memorandum he wrote on January 13, 1993.

2.   Clinton quoted in Elizabeth Drew, *On the Edge: The Clinton Presidency* (New York: Simon and Schuster, 1994), 146.

3.   The anti-Serb proclivity of US policy resulted, in part, from a perception that "those in power in Serbia still represented the communists," in the eyes of US officials. Quote from Netherlands Institute for War Documentation [NIOD], "Srebrenica—A 'Safe' Area: Reconstruction, Background, Consequences, and Analyses of the Fall of a Safe Area," 2003, part 1, chap. 9, sec. 8, *srebrenica.brightside.nl/srebrenica/*. The Dutch report paraphrases the views of US officials during the Bush administration. See similar anticommunist comments by British official Peter Carrington, as noted in Javier Pérez de Cuéllar, *Pilgrimage for Peace: A Secretary-General's Memoir* (New York: St. Martin's, 1997), 481; and by a former US military attaché, Alan Parrington, in "Clinton Had a Chance to Avoid Kosovo Bombing," *Colorado Springs Gazette*, October 11, 2000, *www.commondreams.org/views/101300-107.htm*.

4.   Regarding the percentage figures, see John Callcott, "Croat and Muslim Slav Leaders Sign Truce," UPI, January 27, 1993. For discussions of the peace plan, see the following: David Owen, *Balkan Odyssey: An Uncompromising Personal Account of the International Peace Efforts Following the Breakup of the Former Yugoslavia* (Orlando, Fla.: Harcourt, Brace, 1995), chap. 3; Robert Hayden, "The Partition of Bosnia and Herzegovina, 1990–1993," *RFE/RL Research Report* 2, no. 22, 1993; Steven L. Burg and Paul S. Shoup, *The War in Bosnia-Herzegovina: Ethnic Conflict and International Intervention* (Armonk, N.Y.: M. E. Sharp, 1999), 214–30; and James Gow, *The Triumph of the Lack of Will: International Diplomacy and the Yugoslav War* (New York: Columbia University Press, 1997), chap. 9. For access to various drafts of the Vance-Owen plan, see David Owen, ed, *Balkan Odyssey* [Academic Edition], CD-ROM (Princeton: Bureau of Electronic Publishing, 1996).

5.   Steve Coll, "Balkans Face New Test: Splitting Spoils of War," *Washington Post*, March 7, 1993.

6.   David Owen, testimony before the International Criminal Tribunal for the Former Yugoslavia [ICTY], November 4, 2003, 28525, *www.icty.org*. Marko Hoare criticizes Owen because he "refused to testify against Milošević at the latter's trial at The Hague." See Hoare, *The History of Bosnia: From the Middle Ages to the Present Day* (London: Saqi Books, 2007), 379. In fact, the ICTY Web site lists Owen as a prosecution witness.

7.   David Halberstam, *War in a Time of Peace: Bush, Clinton, and the Generals* (New York: Simon and Schuster, 2002), 198.

8.   Burg and Shoup, *War in Bosnia-Herzegovina*, 234. Burg and Shoup cite a "senior diplomat" as their source.

9.   Albright quoted in Hella Pick and Alan Travis, "US to Press Allies on Bosnia," *Guardian*, January 23, 1993.

10. John Major, *John Major: The Autobiography* (London: HarperCollins, 1999), 540.

11. Gow, *Triumph of the Lack of Will*, 242. Norbert Both notes that the Netherlands also opposed the Vance-Owen proposals during this period and generally acted to back up

the US position. Both, *From Indifference to Entrapment: The Netherlands and the Yugoslav Crisis, 1990–1995* (Amsterdam: Amsterdam University Press, 2000), 151–59.

12. Christopher's views paraphrased in Margaret Warner, "Putting Clinton in a Bind on Bosnia," *Newsweek*, February 15, 1993. Regarding US objections to the 43 percent allocation of land to Serb-controlled areas, see comments by Warren Christopher in Alan Ferguson, "Serbs 'Punished' by Plan, Officials Say," *Toronto Star*, February 4, 1993.

13. NIOD, "Srebrenica," part 1, chap. 5, sec. 1.

14. NIOD, "Srebrenica," part 1, chap. 9, sec. 11.

15. British foreign minister Douglas Hurd also noted US tensions with Owen. Hurd, *Memoirs* (London: Little, Brown, 2003), 463. The Clinton foreign policy team also held negative views of Vance, even though he was a former secretary of state; one reason for this negative view was that Vance was associated with the "failed" Carter presidency. This was the observation of EU diplomat David Ludlow, who served as an aide to David Owen. See Ludlow's report, "Direct Governmental Involvement in the Search for a Negotiated Settlement to the Conflict in Bosnia and Herzegovina with Special Reference to the Work of the Contact Group, September 1992–July 1994" ("Notes and References" section), no date. Available in Owen, *Balkan Odyssey*, CD-ROM.

16. Warren Zimmermann, *Origins of a Catastrophe: Yugoslavia and Its Destroyers—America's Last Ambassador Tells What Happened and Why* (New York: Times Books, 1996), 222.

17. As told to Boutros-Ghali and recounted in his memoir *Unvanquished*, 52. The quote is directly from Boutros-Ghali's memoir, which paraphrases the Serb official. The name of the official is not mentioned. See also Owen, *Balkan Odyssey*, 111.

18. Halberstam claims that Bush's acting secretary of state, Lawrence Eagleburger, took the position that the administration "would not formally endorse it [the Vance-Owen plan] but they would not attack it either." See Halberstam, *War in a Time of Peace*, 198.

19. Paraphrased in John Pomfret, "Bosnian President Accuses Serbs of Playing Games with Talks," *Washington Post*, January 8, 1993.

20. NIOD, "Srebrenica," part 1, chap. 9, sec. 6.

21. NIOD, "Srebrenica," part 1, chap. 9, sec. 11.

22. Thomas Friedman, "U.S. Will Not Push Muslims to Accept Bosnia Peace Plan," *New York Times*, February 4, 1993. Burg and Shoup note that in late January, the negotiators had "secured the agreement of all three sides to a set of constitutional principles . . . only by separating them from the [proposed] map. The Croat and Serb leaders . . . also signed the military agreement. But Izetbegović now refused to do so." Burg and Shoup, *War in Bosnia-Herzegovina*, 225–27.

23. See Owen, *Balkan Odyssey*, 111. Owen's optimism at this point was based on Karadžić's apparent willingness to accept a proposed map as an integral part of the settlement.

24. NIOD, "Srebrenica," part 1, chap. 9, sec. 12.

25. Ludlow, "Direct Governmental Involvement," part 1, in Owen, *Balkan Odyssey*, CD-ROM.

26. NIOD, "Srebrenica," part 1, chap. 9, sec. 12.

27. Coll, "Balkans Face New Test." Coll quotes an anonymous UN official who paraphrased discussions with Serb leaders.

28. Regarding Milošević's conduct during this period, see Owen, testimony before the ICTY, November 3, 2003, 28415, 28474, 28475, *www.icty.org*; and NIOD, "Srebrenica," part 1, chap. 9, sec. 7; and part 1, chap. 9, sec. 11. Both sources believe that Milošević did cooperate in pressuring the Bosnian Serb leadership, up to a point; they also agree that he could have done considerably more in terms of eliciting Bosnian Serb cooperation.

See also "COREU from Lord Owen to Foreign Ministers, 27 April, 1993," in Owen, *Balkan Odyssey*, CD-ROM.

29. Gow, *Triumph of the Lack of Will*, 247. The referendum had produced a 96 percent "no" vote, and Gow rightly finds this number too high to be plausible.

30. Owen testimony, ICTY, November 4, 2003, 28560, *www.icty.org*. British foreign minister Hurd implies that US opposition to Vance-Owen contributed to the plan's failure. Hurd, *Memoirs*, 458. Simms writes: "Bizarrely, Owen blamed the failure of the [Vance-Owen plan] on the Americans." Simms downplays the considerable body of evidence that supports Owen's contention. Brendan Simms, *Unfinest Hour: Britain and the Destruction of Bosnia* (London: Allen Lane, 2001), 150.

31. This lack of support is repeatedly emphasized by Owen, who concludes: "Two US administrations [both Bush and Clinton] neither pressurized nor even cajoled the parties to accept, let alone threatened to impose any one of the four successive peace proposals: the Carrington-Cutileiro plan of March 1992, the VOPP [Vance-Owen Peace Plan] in May 1993, the EU action plan in December 1993, and the Contact Group plan in July 1994." Owen, *Balkan Odyssey*, 221, 399. In the course of the international negotiation efforts, there were "over 30 cease fires and agreements in Bosnia." Richard Holbrooke, foreword to Derek Chollet, *The Road to the Dayton Accords: A Study of American Statecraft* (New York: Palgrave Macmillan, 2005), ix. One of the more effective cease-fires was brokered by Jimmy Carter; it lasted for five months, December 1994 to May 1995. The former president's mediation activities are discussed in his memoir: Carter, *Beyond the White House: Waging Peace, Fighting Disease, Building Hope* (New York: Simon and Schuster, 2007), 71.

32. Owen, *Balkan Odyssey*, 400–401.

33. During the 1992 campaign, both Clinton and Gore emphasized the need for US military action in Bosnia, and they sounded "more interventionist than any Democratic ticket in recent memory." Scot Lehigh, "Clinton Backs Military Action in Bosnia over Genocide," *Boston Globe*, August 6, 1992.

34. Bill Clinton, "The President's News Conference, April 23rd, 1993," in John Woolley and Gerhard Peters, eds., American Presidency Project, Document Archive, *www.presidency.ucsb.edu/ws/index.php?pid=46472andst=bosniaandst1=holocaust*.

35. See for example, "Press Briefing by Michael McCurry, August 11th, 1995," in Woolley and Peters, American Presidency Project, Document Archive, *www.presidency.ucsb.edu/ws/index.php?pid=59608andst=genocideandst1=bosnia*.

36. Regarding the bureaucratic politics of this period, see Halberstam, *War in a Time of Peace*, 195–99; Gail Sheehy, *Hillary's Choice* (New York: Ballantine Books, 2000), 345; Hillary Rodham Clinton, *Living History* (New York: Simon and Schuster, 2003), 241; Dick Morris, *Behind the Oval Office: Winning the Presidency in the Nineties* (New York: Random House, 1997), 251–55; and George Stephanopoulos, *All Too Human: A Political Education* (Boston: Little, Brown, 1999), 380–84.

37. Bob Dole, "Holocaust/Armenian Genocide," *Congressional Record*, April 21, 1993. Paul Wolfowitz, who later served as an advisor to Dole, was critical of Clinton for not using direct US force in Bosnia. See Wolfowitz, "Clinton's First Year," *Foreign Affairs* 73, no. 1, 1994, 31.

38. See, for example, Anthony Lewis, "No Place to Hide," *New York Times*, April 9, 1993.

39. Sidney Blumenthal, *The Clinton Wars* (New York: Farrar, Straus, and Giroux, 2003), 63–64. On Powell's role on the Bosnia issue, also see Andrew J. Bacevich, *The New*

American Militarism: How Americans Are Seduced by War (New York: Oxford University Press, 2005), 49. Despite high-level deadlock, the military bureaucracy was actively preparing for intervention in the Balkans. In April 1993, army intelligence advertised for 125 Serbo-Croatian speakers who would "support US forces in Yugoslavia." James Bamford, *Body of Secrets: Anatomy of the Ultra-Secret National Security Agency from the Cold War through the Dawn of a New Century* (New York: Doubleday, 2001), 554.

40. "Into Bosnia?" *Economist*, May 15, 1993, 57.

41. Major, *John Major*, 540. Regarding European objections to lift and strike, see also Hubert Védrine, *Les Mondes de François Mitterrand: A l'Elysée, 1981–1995* (Paris: Fayard, 1996), 656.

42. The European position is well summarized in F. Stephen Larrabee, "La Politique Américaine et la Crise Yougoslave," *Politique Etrangère* 59, no. 4, 1994, 1045–47.

43. Drew, *On the Edge*, 156–57.

44. President Bill Clinton, "The President's News Conference," June 17, 1993, in Woolley and Peters, American Presidency Project Document Archive, *www.presidency.ucsb.edu/ws/index.php?pid=46708andst=bosniaandst1=*.

45. Kornblum quoted in David Rothkopf, *Running the World: The Inside Story of the National Security Council and the Architects of American Power* (New York: Public Affairs, 2005), 365.

46. US Central Intelligence Agency [USCIA], *Balkan Battlegrounds: A Military History of the Yugoslav Conflict, 1990–1995*, vol. 1 (Washington, D.C.: CIA Office of Russian and European Analysis, 2002), chaps. 39–40.

47. By September 1993, the unity of the Bosnian state faced yet another challenge: A renegade Muslim faction established control in part of the Bihać region of western Bosnia and set up a separate state, which called itself the Autonomous Province of Western Bosnia. This new autonomous province was led by Fikret Abdić, a Muslim politician who had been a member of Izetbegović's government. Thus, by the end of 1993, the war in Bosnia had become a four-way conflict among the Muslims (still nominally constituting the central government), the Serbs, the Croats, and Abdić's breakaway state in Bihać. On Abdić's role see: "Bosnie: Musulmans contre Musulmans à Bihać," *Le Monde*, October 6, 1993; and USCIA, *Balkan Battlegrounds*, vol. 1, 187–89, 293–95.

48. Charles Shrader, *The Muslim-Croat Civil War in Central Bosnia: A Military History, 1992–1994* (College Station: Texas A&M University Press, 2003), 3–4, 66–70.

49. Shrader, *Muslim-Croat Civil War*, 160.

50. NIOD, "Srebrenica," part 1, chap. 12, sec. 3.

51. USCIA, *Balkan Battlegrounds*, vol. 1, chap. 44. Tudjman's interest in a Greater Croatia was expressed intermittently throughout the Bosnia war. And even after the Muslim-Croat war was settled in 1994, Tudjman held on to the idea of a Greater Croatia, including parts of Bosnia. See Paddy Ashdown testimony before the ICTY, March 14, 2002, 2333–35, *www.icty.org*.

52. Shrader, *Muslim-Croat Civil War*, 159.

53. Marcus Tanner, "Croats and Serbs Launch Joint Attack," *Independent*, June 28, 1993.

54. Both quotes from Ganić appear in Burg and Shoup, *War in Bosnia-Herzegovina*, 270.

55. Paul Lewis, "Clashes Cloud US Policy on Bosnia," *New York Times*, May 11, 1993.

56. The principal resolutions authorizing the safe areas are UN Security Council Resolution 819, April 16, 1993; Resolution 824, May 6, 1993; and Resolution 836, June 4, 1993. All three are at *www.un.org/Docs/scres/1993/scres93.htm*.

57. Such air strikes required the prior approval of both UNPROFOR and NATO officials. This cumbersome bureaucratic process (termed the "dual key" system) was the source of complaint among hawks in the United States. The politics of the dual key are described in Phillip Corwin, *Dubious Mandate: A Memoir of the UN in Bosnia, Summer 1995* (Durham, N.C.: Duke University Press, 1999), 44.

58. The no-fly zone was authorized by UN Security Council Resolution 816, March 31, 1993, *www.un.org/Docs/scres/1993/scres93.htm*.

59. United Nations, "Report of the Secretary-General Pursuant to Security Council Resolutions 982 (1995) and 987 (1995)," S/1995/444, May 30, 1995, 11, *www.un.org/Docs/secu95.htm*. And at the Milošević trial, a British general testified that the safe areas "were certainly used [by Muslim forces] as a base of operations into the Serb areas." From cross-examination of Gen. Rupert Smith, prosecution witness at the Milošević trial, ICTY, October 9, 2003, 27378, *www.icty.org*.

60. The idea of UN impartiality was emphasized by Dag Hammarskjöld in "The International Civil Service in Law and Fact," in A. W. Cordier and W. Foote, eds., *Public Papers of the Secretaries-General of the United Nations*, vol. 5 (New York: Columbia University Press, 1975). See also M. W. Zacher, *Dag Hammarskjöld's United Nations* (New York: Columbia University Press, 1970), 13–15, 39–47.

61. Gen. Philippe Morillon, prosecution witness, Milošević trial, ICTY, February 12, 2004, 31965, 31966, *www.icty.org*. After the war, Orić was tried before the ICTY and initially convicted of war crimes. In 2008, however, the conviction was overturned on appeal. The appeal chamber acknowledged that "it had no doubt that grave crimes were committed against Serbs" in the Srebrenica area, but there was insufficient evidence to prove Orić's personal guilt "beyond reasonable doubt." Legalities aside, it seems highly probable that Orić did direct war crimes. On the appeal, see ICTY, "Appeals Chamber Acquits Naser Orić," July 3, 2008, *www.icty.org*.

62. This was the wording of the French representative to the United Nations. Similar statements were also made by the UN representatives of China and Britain. Quoted in United Nations, "Report of the Secretary-General Pursuant to General Assembly Resolution 53/35: The Fall of Srebrenica," November 15, 1999, *www.un.org/Depts/dpko/dpko/reports.htm*.

63. Owen, *Balkan Odyssey*, 190.

64. Specific reference is made to the "Joint Program of Action" presented by both the EU and the United States, which proposed the idea of safe areas. See NIOD, "Srebrenica," part 1, chap. 11, sec. 8; and part 1, chap. 11, sec. 18. When discussing the safe-area policy in his memoirs, Boutros-Ghali states that the Americans wanted to use the UN "as a scapegoat for problems created by the great powers' unwillingness to act." Boutros-Ghali, *Unvanquished*, 84. See also Lieut. Gen. Satish Nambiar, "NATO Celebrates its Fiftieth Anniversary by Destroying Yugoslavia," *Mediterranean Quarterly* 10, no. 3, 1999, 17.

65. The shift at the JCS and its importance for Bosnia is noted in Cees Wiebes, *Intelligence and the War in Bosnia: 1992–1995* (Münster: Lit, 2003), 165.

66. The central importance of NATO credibility in US decision making on Bosnia is repeatedly noted. See Warren Christopher, *In the Stream of History: Shaping Foreign Policy for a New Era* (Stanford: Stanford University Press, 1998), 357–59, and *Chances of a Lifetime: A Memoir* (New York: Scribner, 2001), 260; Holbrooke, *To End a War*, 50; Strobe Talbott, "US Leadership and the Balkan Challenge," *Department of State*

Dispatch, November 20, 1995; Ivo Daalder, *Getting to Dayton: The Making of America's Bosnia Policy* (Washington, D.C.: Brookings, 2000), 187–88; Ashton B. Carter and William J. Perry, *Preventive Defense: A New Security Strategy for America* (Washington, D.C.: Brookings, 1999), 22; Védrine, *Les Mondes de François Mitterrand*, 657; and US Department of State [USDOS], "The Road to Dayton: US Diplomacy and the Bosnia Peace Process," 1997, 11, 38–39, *www.gwu.edu/~nsarchiv/NSAEBB/NSAEBB171/index. htm.*

67. Chollet, *Road to the Dayton Accords*, 185. This book was based in part on an official State Department history, which Chollet had helped to research and write (USDOS, "Road to Dayton").

68. Quote from Robert Hayden, *Blueprints from a House Divided: The Constitutional Logic of the Yugoslav Conflicts* (Ann Arbor: University of Michigan Press, 1999), 112. George Rudman, who served as a translator for the Croat delegation, stated that negotiations on the drafting of the Federation constitution "were guided by State Department lawyers." See Rudman, "Backtracking to Reformulate: Establishing the Bosnian Federation," *International Negotiation* 1, no. 3, 1996, 540.

69. The constitution is analyzed in Hayden, *Blueprints from a House Divided*, 113–21. For the text of the agreement, see "Washington Agreement," March 1, 1994, in Peter Galbraith, ed., *The United States and Croatia: A Documentary History, 1992–1997* (Washington, D.C.: US Department of State, 1997), 29–37. For the text of the constitution that followed the agreement, see "Federation Constitution," March 13, 1994, in Owen, *Balkan Odyssey*, CD-ROM.

70. "Balkan Wars," *Economist*, April 24, 1999.

71. Ludlow, "Direct Governmental Involvement," part 2, in Owen, *Balkan Odyssey,* CD-ROM.

72. On European perceptions that the United States was trying to dominate the negotiation process, see Rudman, "Backtracking to Reformulate," 534. For pro forma statements of European support, see "ICFY Bosnia Memo 2 March, 1994: Lord Owen's Conversation with Redman on Muslim-Croat Federation," in Owen, *Balkan Odyssey*, CD-ROM.

73. The quote paraphrases the opinion of EU diplomat Michael Steiner, who worked closely with the Vance-Owen peace efforts. "Washington Negotiations: Report to the Co-Chairmen of Conversations with Szasz and Steiner from David Ludlow," February 12, 1994, in Owen, *Balkan Odyssey*, CD-ROM. During this period, mediation efforts were undertaken by a Contact Group of five states—the United States, United Kingdom, France, Germany, and Russia—which was formed in 1994. The United States helped create the Contact Group but sought to deemphasize its role. On the Contact Group, see Chollet, *Road to the Dayton Accords*, 68; USDOS, "Road to Dayton," 84; and David Ludlow, "Direct Governmental Involvement," part 2, in Owen, *Balkan Odyssey*, CD-ROM.

74. Wiebes, *Intelligence and the War in Bosnia*, 164–67.

75. Clinton's authorization for this program is described in Wiebes, *Intelligence and the War in Bosnia*, chap. 4.

76. The statements were intentionally vague in order to establish plausible deniability, but Wiebes's account leaves little doubt that the Americans initiated the whole project. Wiebes, *Intelligence and the War in Bosnia*, 167–68.

77. State Department legal opinion, as paraphrased by Holbrooke and quoted in Wiebes, *Intelligence and the War in Bosnia*, 172.

78. Wiebes, *Intelligence and the War in Bosnia*, 177.

79. Wiebes, *Intelligence and the War in Bosnia*, 194. The British researcher that Wiebes refers to is not cited by name.

80. In hearings before the US Senate, Holbrooke testified about allegations of direct US arms shipments to Bosnia and stated: "I am here again today, under oath, Mr. Chairman, to assure you that the stories were obviously not true. Had they been true, we would have been in violation of the law, and we don't do that sort of thing." US Senate, *U.S. Actions Regarding Iranian and Other Arms Transfers to the Bosnian Army* (Washington, D.C.: US Government Printing Office, 1996), *www.fas.org/irp/congress/1996_rpt/bosnia.htm*. These denials seem unpersuasive, given the evidence provided by the Wiebes study, which suggests that the United States probably did play a direct role.

81. Regarding the CIA's disapproval of the arms shipments, see US Senate, *U.S. Actions Regarding Iranian and Other Arms Transfers*; and John Prados, *Safe for Democracy: The Secret Wars of the CIA* (Chicago: Ivan R. Dee, 2006), 610.

82. Richard Holbrooke, foreword to Chollet, *Road to the Dayton Accords*, ix. Regarding the Bosnia connection to Islamic terrorist groups, see Evan Kohlmann, *Al-Qaida's Jihad in Europe: The Afghan-Bosnian Network* (Oxford: Berg, 2004); John Schindler, *Unholy Terror: Bosnia, Al-Qaeda, and the Rise of Global Jihad* (Osceola, Wis.: Zenith Press, 2007); and Christopher Deliso, *The Coming Balkan Caliphate: The Threat of Radical Islam to Europe and the West* (Westport, Conn.: Praeger, 2007). Marko Hoare is dismissive about the possibility of an Al Qaeda role in Bosnia; he refers to the "'Bosnia-Bin Laden' conspiracy theory," which "belongs in this category of the farcical." Hoare, *How Bosnia Armed* (London: Saqi Books and Bosnia Institute, 2004), 134, 135. In fact, Holbrooke has since confirmed the Al Qaeda role in Bosnia.

83. The Croatian buildup was covered in the press. See, for example, Andrzej Jeziorski, "Croatia's Cocked Hammer: Despite Sanctions, Croatia Has Been Able to Build Up Its Air Force," *Flight International*, February 1, 1995.

84. Tim Ripley, *Operation Deliberate Force* (Lancaster, UK: Centre for Defense and International Security Studies, 1999), 82; and Stan Crock, "Trouble Is Our Business," *Business Week*, November 20, 1995.

85. Regarding the military significance of the MPRI training team, see the range of views expressed in Halberstam, *War in a Time of Peace*, 334–35; Wiebes, *Intelligence and the War in Bosnia*, 216; Burg and Shoup, *War in Bosnia-Herzegovina*, 339–40, 379; and "Croatian Atrocities Being Forgotten: Cdn. Officers," Canadian Broadcasting Corporation, July 21, 2003, *www.cbc.ca/news/story/2003/07/21/croatia_030721.html*.

86. Ripley, *Operation Deliberate Force*, 62. Despite his close connections to the Tudjman regime, Galbraith moralistically emphasized human rights in his speeches. See a collection of his speeches and public statements in Galbraith, *The United States and Croatia*.

87. Barbara Starr, "US Navy to Let through Bosnia Bound Arms," *Jane's Defense Weekly*, November 19, 1994.

88. Corwin, *Dubious Mandate*, 177–78.

89. Regarding French antagonism toward US policy, see William Drozdiak, "US and Europe in Serious Rift over Bosnia War," *Washington Post*, November 27, 1994; T. Claire, "Paris Estime que l'Attitude Américaine en Bosnia Conduit à la 'Catastrophe,'" *Le Monde*, January 26, 1994; and Jacques Isnard, "Une Guerre du Soupçon entre Etats-Majors Français et Américain," *Le Monde*, November 23, 1994.

90. Frédéric Bozo, "Organisations de Sécurité et Insécurité en Europe," *Politique Étrangère* 58, no. 2, 1993, 453. Translated from the French.

91. Major, *John Major*, 540.

92. Corwin, *Dubious Mandate*, 54.

93. Quoted in Ed Vulliamy, "Bosnia—The Secret War," *Guardian*, May 21, 1996. The quoted official is identified only as "a senior official in the US State Department."

94. Charles Dick, "Kosovo's Legacy for the Future of NATO," *Jane's Intelligence Review*, July 1, 1999

95. "America versus Europe," *Economist*, April 24, 1999. See also Carl Bildt, *Peace Journey: The Struggle for Peace in Bosnia* (London: Weidenfeld and Nicolson, 1998), 39.

96. NIOD, "Srebrenica," part 3, chap. 1, sec. 16. See also Ripley, *Operation Deliberate Force*, 96, 140–41.

97. Bildt, *Peace Journey*, 57. For the record, Sacirbey added perfunctorily that "he was deeply concerned about the humanitarian situation" in Srebrenica. The quotes are directly from Bildt, who paraphrases Sacirbey's statements.

98. Ripley, *Operation Deliberate Force*, 145. A UN report presents (uncorroborated) evidence that Izetbegović foresaw the scale of the massacre in Srebrenica should the Serbs capture the town. The UN report describes a meeting that took place in 1993 between a group of Bosnian Muslims who lived in Srebrenica at the time and President Izetbegović and notes: "Some surviving members of the Srebrenica delegation have stated that President Izetbegović . . . told them he had learned that a NATO intervention in Bosnia and Herzegovina was possible, but could only occur if the Serbs were to break into Srebrenica, killing at least 5,000 of its people. President Izetbegović has flatly denied making such a statement." United Nations, "Report of the Secretary-General Pursuant to General Assembly Resolution 53/35."

99. The vast majority of victims were males over the age of fifteen. See NIOD, "Srebrenica," part 4, chap. 2, sec. 3.

100. See NIOD, "Srebrenica," "Summary for the Press."

101. The genocide designation received endorsement from the ICTY in its August 2, 2001, decision in the Radislav Krstić case. However, I agree with Katherine Southwick's criticism of the ICTY judgment, which was published in the *Yale Human Rights and Development Law Journal*: "In diluting the meaning of genocide as it does, the trial chamber [the ICTY] may have reduced the authority of the international tribunal and weakened the distinctions between genocide and crimes against humanity, consequently reducing the capacity of the word 'genocide' to evoke a unique form of devastation. This effect offends the memory of extreme instances of genocide, affects perceptions of survivors, distorts history, and complicates attempts to prevent or mitigate genocide through effective policy-making." Certainly, the murder of eight thousand people is a grave crime, but to call it "genocide" needlessly exaggerates the scale of the crime. Sources: On judicial determinations that the Srebrenica massacre was genocide, see ICTY, Judgment in the Case of Radislav Krstić, August 2, 2001, *www.icty.org*; and International Court of Justice, "Application of the Convention on the Prevention and Punishment of the Crime of Genocide (Bosnia and Herzegovina v. Serbia and Montenegro), Final Judgment of 26 February, 2007," *www.icj-cij.org/docket/ files/91/13685.pdf*. For the criticism of ICTY, see Katherine Southwick, "Srebrenica as Genocide? The Krstić Decision and the Language of the Unspeakable," *Yale Human Rights and Development Law Journal* 8, 2005, 226–27. For another critical review of court decisions, see also Fran Pilch, "Prosecution of the Crime of Genocide in the

ICTY: The Case of Radislav Krstić," *Journal of Legal Studies (United States Air Force Academy)* 12, 2002–2003, 57–58.

102. Quoted in USDOS, "Road to Dayton," 193. For a similar view, see International Court of Justice, "Application of the Convention on the Prevention and Punishment of the Crime of Genocide." In his ICTY testimony, David Owen implied that Milošević bore *indirect* guilt for Srebrenica—because of his long-term support for Serb militias—but no direct guilt. See Owen, November 3, 2003, 28411–15, 28471, 28478, and November 4, 2003, 28524, 28543, *www.icty.org*.

103. A US State Department analysis from this period noted that Milošević still retained ties to Serb forces in Bosnia as late as the fall of 1995, but he had only limited influence with those forces. See USDOS, "Road to Dayton," 76, 92, 98, 135.

104. "Foreign Ministry Criticizes UN for Failing to Defend Zepa," TRT TV, Ankara, in BBC Summary of World Broadcasts, July 28, 1995.

105. The bureaucratic politics are discussed in Vulliamy, "Bosnia."

106. Beginning in mid-June 1995—before the Srebrenica massacre—National Security Advisor Lake organized a study group to generate a detailed plan for military action in Bosnia. President Clinton supported these efforts. See Halberstam, *War in a Time of Peace*, 312–13; Rothkopf, *Running the World*, 367–68; and Anthony Lake, *Six Nightmares: Real Threats in a Dangerous World and How America Can Meet Them* (Boston: Little, Brown, 2000), 145–49.

107. Quoted from Chollet, *Road to the Dayton Accords*, 23.

108. One factor that influenced presidential decision making during this period was pressure from Congress. On June 8, 1995, the House of Representatives voted overwhelmingly to end the arms embargo with respect to the Izetbegović government. House Speaker Newt Gingrich also criticized the president for a lack of decisiveness with respect to the Balkans. See Elizabeth Drew, *Showdown: The Struggle between the Gingrich Congress and the Clinton White House* (New York: Simon and Schuster, 1996), 248. The vote mattered little from a policy standpoint, since Clinton was already disregarding the embargo. But the congressional criticism was surely important from a political standpoint. Another factor influencing US policy was military operational planning: In June 1995, President Clinton approved OPLAN 40104, which committed the administration to sending ground troops into Bosnia in the event that this might be necessary to extricate UN peacekeepers. Thus the president had already accepted the idea of sending US troops to the Balkans, at least in principle. See Bob Woodward, *The Choice: How Bill Clinton Won* (New York: Simon and Schuster, 1996), 256–57.

109. Michael Ignatieff, "They Are All Baddies at Odds in Bosnia," *Observer* (London), January 31, 1993. Ignatieff would later shift his views and support an intervention in Kosovo.

110. A previous (though much smaller) Croat offensive in May 1995 had captured Serb-controlled Western Slavonia. Other sections of Serb-controlled territory, including Eastern Slavonia, were later reintegrated into the Republic of Croatia as part of a negotiated settlement, the Erdut Agreement. See "The Erdut Agreement," November 12, 1995, in Galbraith, *The United States and Croatia*, 270–71; Galbraith, "Negotiating Peace in Croatia: A Personal Account of the Road to Erdut," in Brad Blitz, ed., *War and Change in the Balkans: Nationalism, Conflict, and Cooperation* (New York: Cambridge University Press, 2006); and United Nations, *The Blue Helmets: A Review*

of United Nations Peacekeeping (New York: United Nations, Department of Public Information, 1996), 496, 549.

111. For military details of Operation Storm, see USCIA, *Balkan Battlegrounds*, vol. 1, chaps. 88–89.

112. Bildt, *Peace Journey*, 73. See also John Pomfret, "In Knin, Clues to Croat Rout of Serbs," *Washington Post*, August 13, 1995.

113. This is acknowledged in a volume edited by Ambassador Galbraith. See "A Short History of United States–Croatian Relations, 1991–1997," in Galbraith, *The United States and Croatia*, xviii–xix. Galbraith strongly criticizes the Croat atrocities, but he neglects to mention his own role in laying the groundwork for the offensive. For a similar whitewash of the US role in Krajina, see the account by Galbraith's State Department colleague John Shattuck, *Freedom on Fire: Human Rights Wars and America's Response* (Cambridge, Mass.: Harvard University Press, 2003), 167–71.

114. There were still military units from the Republic of Serbia in Krajina at the time of the Croat attack. However, these units offered no support to the local population. See account in Burg and Shoup, *War in Bosnia-Herzegovina*, 331–33. The withdrawal of Milošević's support elicited great bitterness among Krajina Serbs. Their leader, Milan Babić, was sufficiently angry that he became a prosecution witness at Milošević's postwar trial. See Babić's extensive testimony before the ICTY, November 18–December 12, 2002, *www.icty.org*.

115. On Serb refugees, the higher figure is offered by Bildt, *Peace Journey*, 398. The lower figure is from Charles Krauthammer, "Ethnic Cleansing That's Convenient," *Washington Post*, August 11, 1995.

116. On Croat atrocities in Krajina, see the following: International Helsinki Federation for Human Rights, "Report to the OSCE: The International Helsinki Federation for Human Rights Fact-Finding Mission to the Krajina 17–19 August 1995," Vienna, August 25, 1995, *www.ihf-hr.org/*; Amnesty International, "Croatia: Impunity for Killings after Storm," August 1, 1998, *web.amnesty.org/library/Index/ENGEUR640041998?openandof=ENG-2EU*; Raymond Bonner, "War Crimes Panel Finds Croat Troops 'Cleansed' the Serbs," *New York Times*, March 21, 1999; and Mark Danner, "Operation Storm," *New York Review of Books*, October 22, 1998. Most credible sources suggest that Serb civilian deaths from Operation Storm ranged in the hundreds. However, several sources suggest that the death toll might have been even higher. According to a 1996 article in *Le Monde*: "Officials at the Zagreb office of the Helsinki Human Rights Committee believe that 'perhaps 6,000 persons may have disappeared during Operation Storm and 1,000 [additional persons] since.'" "How Croatia Reclaimed Its Accursed Land," reprinted in *Manchester Weekly Guardian*, March 31, 1996. For additional estimates of more than one thousand Serb deaths see "Tribunal to Issue Indictments Soon for Crimes in Croatian 'Storm,'" Tanjug report, reprinted in English in *Yugoslav Daily Survey*, April 10, 1998, *www.hri.org/news/balkans/yds/1998/98-04-10.yds.html*; and "Croatian Atrocities Being Forgotten."

117. Bildt, *Peace Journey*, 76.

118. Minutes of the Council for Defense and National Security of the Republic of Croatia, September 12, 1993, translated and reprinted verbatim in "Planning Croatia's Final Solution," *Harper's*, December 2001.

119. At one point, Galbraith appeared to justify Operation Storm. He stated that Storm had helped alleviate a Serb threat to the Bihać region, where there was danger of a

Srebrenica-style massacre. Galbraith claimed that forty thousand might have died if the Serbs had overrun Bihać, a tragedy that had been averted by Storm. However, Ripley claims that the Bosnian government was exaggerating the threat to Bihać during this period as part of its propaganda campaign to generate Western support. And the forty thousand predicted killings cited by Galbraith seems an implausibly high figure. For Galbraith's statements about Bihać, see his testimony before the ICTY, June 26, 2003, 23100, *www.icty.org*; and Ripley, *Operation Deliberate Force*, 177.

120. An example of US official distancing occurred during Galbraith's testimony at the ICTY, when he made the following (misleading) statement: "We did . . . not approve any kind of [Croat] military action." And he added: "We neither supported or opposed" the Croat attacks. See Galbraith, testimony at the Milošević trial, June 25, 2003, 23100, 23113, *www.icty.org*.

121. The quote from General Boyd is taken from an interview in the documentary film *Yugoslavia: The Avoidable War*, directed by George Bogdanich, 2002. On the US role, see also David Binder, "The Role of the United States in the Krajina Issue," *Mediterranean Quarterly* 8, no. 4, 1997.

122. Croatian foreign minister Mate Granić is quoted in "Bill Clinton Cherche à Reprendre l'Initiative à propos de l'ex-Yougoslavie," *Le Monde*, August 12, 1995. Translated from the French.

123. Bonner, "War Crimes Panel."

124. NIOD, "Srebrenica," part 1, chap. 15, sec. 4.

125. Bill Clinton, *My Life* (New York: Knopf, 2004), 667. See also "4 Navy Jets Bomb Serb Missile Sites," *Navy Times*, August 21, 1995.

126. Robert Frasure quoted in Holbrooke, *To End a War*, 73.

127. Bonner, "War Crimes Panel."

128. Holbrooke, *To End a War*, 86, 160. Hillary Clinton would later write glowingly of victories by "the Croat-Muslim coalition *that the US had helped support*" (emphasis added). Clinton, *Living History*, 241.

129. Ripley, *Operation Deliberate Force*, 303. The officer quoted was Lieut. Col. Jim Baxter, who served as an aide to Gen. Rupert Smith, UNPROFOR commander.

130. On Mistral and a series of later Bosnian offensives, see USCIA, *Balkan Battlegrounds*, vol. 1, chaps. 91–94; and USDOS, "Road to Dayton," 146. The offensives were finally halted on October 20, due to US pressure.

131. Holbrooke, *To End a War*, 160. For further discussion of US policy in the Banja Luka case, see USDOS, "Road to Dayton," 110, 115; and Daalder, *Getting to Dayton*, 124.

132. Ripley, *Operation Deliberate Force*, 316.

133. Ripley, *Operation Deliberate Force*, 316. These Muslims were supporters of Fikret Abdić's rebel state in Bihać, which was crushed by the combined Bosnian and Croat offensives.

134. Bildt, *Peace Journey*, 112.

135. Clinton paraphrased in Chollet, *Road to the Dayton Accords*, 27. NATO officials in Brussels strongly supported the idea of a bombing campaign. See Ryan Hendrickson, "Leadership at NATO: Secretary General Manfred Woerner and the Crisis in Bosnia," *Journal of Strategic Studies* 27, no. 3, 2004, and "NATO's Secretary General and the Use of Force: Willy Claes and the Air Strikes in Bosnia," *Armed Forces and Society* 31, no. 1, 2004.

136. Chollet, *Road to the Dayton Accords*, 41.

137. French president Chirac also was moving in an interventionist direction at this time.

See Chollet, *Road to the Dayton Accords*, 14–16. However, it seems doubtful that Chirac had in mind the US-dictated intervention that emerged with Deliberate Force. France's reservations about the domineering US manner during this period were discussed by British UNPROFOR officer Baxter, whose account was read during the testimony of Rupert Smith at the Milošević trial, ICTY, October 9, 2003, 27339–40, *www.icty.org*.

138. On Russia's opposition to the use of armed force, Chrystia Freeland, "NATO Strikes in Bosnia: Yeltsin Condemns 'Cruel Bombardment,'" *Financial Times*, August 31, 1995; USDOS, "Road to Dayton," 103; and Strobe Talbott, *The Russia Hand: A Memoir of Presidential Diplomacy* (New York: Random House, 2002), 72–79.

139. See Boutros-Ghali, "Bosnia Statement," August 30, 1995, and "Bosnia Statement," September 2, 1995, both in Charles Hill, ed., *The Papers of United Nations Secretary-General Boutros Boutros-Ghali* (New Haven: Yale University Press, 2003), vol. 3, 1661, 1672–73; and Boutros-Ghali, *Unvanquished*, 240–45.

140. Boutros-Ghali, *Unvanquished*, 245. The new UNPROFOR commander, British general Rupert Smith, was more willing than previous commanders to support air strikes. Holbrooke, *To End a* War, 187. See also Smith, *The Utility of Force: The Art of War in the Modern World* (London: Allen Lane, 2005), chap. 9.

141. Officially, the operation was triggered by a Serb mortar attack on Sarajevo, but this was probably just a pretext. Ripley provides the following account: "The real reason for the [mortar] attack is still unexplained, although [British UNPROFOR officer] Baxter believes it was a Serb revenge attack for a Muslim shelling of a Serb funeral. . . . 'The whole thing in Sarajevo was tit for tat. The Bosnian Serbs overreacted,' [states Baxter]." Ripley, *Operation Deliberate Force*, 231.

142. See the description in NATO Regional Headquarters, Allied Forces Southern Europe, "Operation Deliberate Force," December 16, 2002, *www.afsouth.nato.int/factsheets/DeliberateForceFactSheet.htm*. Deliberate Force appears to have produced few civilian casualties, according to Ripley, *Operation Deliberate Force*, 255, 257.

143. Regarding the air strikes' limited military effectiveness, see Ripley, *Operation Deliberate Force*, chap. 26; and Piers Robinson, "Misperception in Foreign Policy Making: Operation 'Deliberate Force' and the Ending of War in Bosnia," *Civil Wars* 4, no. 4, 2001.

144. This was implicitly conceded by Gen. Wesley Clark, when he recounted a conversation with Milošević during the Dayton conference. Milošević stated: "Well, General Clark, you must be pleased that NATO won this war." Clark responded: "Mr. President, NATO didn't even fight this war. You lost it to the Croats and Muslims." Clark, *Waging Modern War: Bosnia, Kosovo, and the Future of Combat* (New York: Public Affairs, 2002), 67.

145. William Pfaff, quoted in Holbrooke, *To End a War*, 102–3.

146. From the Lausanne publication *24 Heures*, quoted in translation in "Viewpoints: Redrawing Bosnia's Map," *World Press Review*, November 1995, 6.

147. Bildt quoted in Colum Lynch, "Holbrooke Faces Challenge at UN," *Washington Post*, August 24, 1999.

148. Quote from Robert Gallucci in USDOS, "Road to Dayton," 217. For similar views regarding US dominance of the Dayton talks, see Clark, *Waging Modern War*, 59; Pauline Neville-Jones, "Dayton, IFOR, and Alliance Relations in Bosnia," *Survival* 38, no. 4, 1996–1997, 48; Alain Franchon, "Bosnie: Divergences Euro-Américaines," *Le Monde*, November 29, 1995; " 'Greift den Strohhalm': Die Deutsche Rolle bei den

Friedensgesprächen in Dayton," *Der Spiegel*, November 27, 1995, 148; and Talbott, *The Russia Hand*, 187.

149. Michael Ignatieff, "After the Balkan Failure, Who Will Ever Believe in Europe Again?" *Independent*, November 22, 1995.

150. On US-European tensions, see USDOS, "Road to Dayton," 141, 157, 158, 216, 217.

151. Bosnian foreign minister Muhamed Sacirbey quoted in " 'Greift den Strohhalm,' " 148. Translated from the German.

152. From USDOS, "Road to Dayton," 194–95. See also Bildt, *Peace Journey*, 128.

153. The formal signing ceremony took place in Paris. The text of the Dayton Accords is in Owen, *Balkan Odyssey*, CD-ROM.

154. For a general description of the Dayton settlement and the IFOR peacekeeping force, see European Defense, "Military Operations: Bosnia-Herzegovina, December 2007," *www.european-defence.co.uk/thebalkans.html*.

155. "Europe's Yugoslav Lesson," *Foreign Report*, October 10, 1996. Several non-NATO states from the former Eastern Bloc also participated in the IFOR peacekeeping force, through NATO's Partnership for Peace. See Ronald Asmus, *Opening NATO's Door: How the Alliance Remade Itself for the New Era* (New York: Columbia University Press, 2002), 125; and Talbott, *The Russia Hand*, 186.

156. Regarding the post-Dayton political situation, see the following: Sumantra Bose, *Bosnia after Dayton: Nationalist Partition and International Intervention* (New York: Oxford University Press, 2002); David Chandler, *Bosnia: Faking Democracy after Dayton* (London: Pluto, 2000); Paula Pickering, *Peacebuilding in the Balkans: The View from the Ground Floor* (Ithaca: Cornell University Press, 2007); and Gen. Charles Boyd, "Making Bosnia Work," *Foreign Affairs* 77, no. 1, 1998.

157. Bildt, *Peace Journey*, 196.

158. Bildt, *Peace Journey*, 198.

159. In memoirs, British MP Paddy Ashdown provides a misleading account of the violence that immediately followed Dayton; he neglects to mention that it was the Serbs who were the victims of attacks, and that it was forces backed by NATO who were the perpetrators. See Ashdown, *Swords and Ploughshares: Peace to the Twenty-First Century* (London: Weidenfeld and Nicolson, 2007), 68.

160. IFOR was later replaced by a Stabilization Force and then, in 2004, by a European Union Force. See US Congressional Research Service, "Bosnia and the European Union Military Force (EUFOR): Post-NATO Peacekeeping," December 5, 2006, *www.fas.org/sgp/crs/row/RS21774.pdf*.

161. Holbrooke, *To End a War*, 359.

162. Christopher, *Stream of History*, 358–59.

163. See John Harris, *The Survivor: Bill Clinton in the White House* (New York: Random House, 2005), 221. The Republicans did, however, manage to influence the negotiation process through Richard Perle, a neoconservative intellectual with close ties to the Republican party. Perle acted as an advisor to the Bosnian delegation at the Dayton conference. See Michael Dobbs, "US Starts Process of Army Aid: Some Allies Resist Bosnian Project," *Washington Post*, December 21, 1995.

164. Michael Ignatieff, "Europe's Utter Failure," *Independent*; Ameen Izzadeen, "An Uneasy Peace in Bosnia," *Sunday Times* (Colombo Sri Lanka); and Alain Frachon, "The US Ruffles Gallic Feathers [translation]," *Le Monde*, November 29, 1995, all reprinted in *World Press Review*, February 1995, 12–15.

165. John Bolton in "Hearings of the House International Relations Committee, Subject: Sending US Troops into Bosnia," *Federal News Service*, December 7, 1995, 8 (electronic version available through Lexis-Nexis).

166. "Balkan Wars," *Economist*, April 24, 1999, 14.

167. See Frederick Kemp, "NATO Leaders Prepare to Expand Ties to Ex-Warsaw Pact Countries," *Wall Street Journal*, November 4, 1991.

168. Chollet, *Road to the Dayton Accords*, 200. This quote is actually Chollet paraphrasing the views of former State Department official Ronald Asmus. See also Asmus's own account, *Opening NATO's Door*, 124–25. Similar conclusions about Bosnia's significance for NATO prestige are noted in James Goldgeier, *Not Whether but When: The U.S. Decision to Enlarge NATO* (Washington, D.C.: Brookings, 1999), 98, 121.

169. This was noted repeatedly by both EU and UN personnel. See, for example, Boutros-Ghali, *Unvanquished*, 247. See also comments by Alain Juppé quoted in Holbrooke, *To End a War*, 318; and Owen, *Balkan Odyssey*, 367.

170. See Chapter 2 for a fuller discussion of the 1992 Defense Planning Guidance document.

Chapter 7

Epigraphs: Letter from Brent Scowcroft to Vin Weber, May 4, 1992, Bush Presidential Records, NSC, Jane Holl Files, Yugoslavia, April 1992, OA/ID CFO 1402 [1 of 6], from the George H. W. Bush Presidential Library; and Thomas Friedman, "Stop the Music," *New York Times*, April 23, 1999.

1. The alleged altruistic and Wilsonian aspects of this war are argued, for example, in David Fromkin, *Kosovo Crossing: The Reality of American Intervention in the Balkans* (New York: Free Press, 2002).

2. "Running Out of Puff," *Financial Times*, January 2, 1999.

3. Helmut Schmidt quoted in William Drozdiak, "Even Allies Resent US Dominance," *Washington Post*, November 4, 1997.

4. "It's Bigger Than Bananas," *Business Week*, March 22, 1999, 64.

5. Charles Dick, "Kosovo's Legacy for the Future of NATO," *Jane's Intelligence Review*, July 1, 1999, 3 (electronic version available through Lexis-Nexis).

6. Jacques Isnard, "Les Limites d'une Concértation Opérationnelle entre les Etats-Majors," *Le Monde*, December 7, 1998; Michael Evans, "Britain and France Sign up to Defend Europe," *Times* (London), December 5, 1998; and Alexander Moens, "EDSP, the United States, and the Atlantic Alliance," in Jolyon Howorth and John T. S. Keeler, eds., *Defending Europe: The EU, NATO, and the Quest for European Autonomy* (New York: Palgrave, 2003), 26.

7. See "Dr Jeffrey Gedmin Resident Scholar American Enterprise Institute, testimony before the Senate Foreign Relations European Affairs," *Federal Document Clearing House*, March 24, 1999, 4–5 (electronic version available through Lexis-Nexis).

8. S. Neil MacFarlane, "Challenges to Euro-Atlantic Security," in Pierre Martin and Mark R. Brawley, eds., *Alliance Politics, Kosovo, and NATO's War: Allied Force or Forced Allies?* (New York: Palgrave, 2000).

9. Gen. Wesley Clark, "The United States and NATO: The Way Ahead," *Parameters: Journal of the US Army War College* 29, no. 4, 1999–2000, 2–3. Clark also mentioned briefly the importance of EU and US humanitarian aid.

10. See "Checks and Balances," *Economist*, April 24, 1999, 17–18; and Sidney Blumenthal, *The Clinton Wars* (New York: Farrar, Straus, and Giroux, 2003), 643.

11. Tim Smart, "Count Corporate America among NATO's Staunchest Allies," *Washington Post*, April 13, 1999.

12. See J. Lewis, "French Barbs Target US," *Jane's Defense Weekly*, April 14, 1999; Karl-Heinz Kamp, "L'OTAN après le Kosovo: L'Ange de Paix ou Gendarme du Monde?" *Politique Etrangère* 64, no. 2, 1999, 249.

13. Daniel Bensaid, "Leur Logique et Nôtre," *Le Monde*, April 9, 1999. Translated from the French. The article also acknowledged humanitarian interest as a second motivation; I deal with the plausibility of this motive later in this chapter. See also "A New Look NATO," *Foreign Report*, April 29, 1999; and Gen. Mike Jackson, *Soldier: The Autobiography of General Sir Mike Jackson* (London: Bantam Press, 2007), 230.

14. President Bill Clinton, "Remarks at the Legislative Convention of the American Federation of State, County, and Municipal Employees," March 23, 1999, in John Woolley and Gerhard Peters, eds., American Presidency Project, Document Archive, *www.presidency.ucsb.edu/ws/index.php?pid=57294andst=genocide+in+the+heart+of+Europeandst1=*. Clinton also claimed that humanitarianism was an additional motivation.

15. With regard to the larger issue of pretexts in US foreign policy, see Bruce Cumings, "The American Way of Going to War: Mexico (1846) to Iraq (2003)," *Orbis* 51, no. 2, 2007; and David Gibbs, "Pretexts and US Foreign Policy: The War on Terrorism in Historical Perspective," *New Political Science* 26, no. 3, 2004, *www.gened.arizona.edu/dgibbs/pretexts.pdf*.

16. Noel Malcolm, *Kosovo: A Short History* (New York: New York University Press, 1999), 322–25.

17. On the 1966 party shakeup, see Dennison Rusinow, *The Yugoslav Experiment: 1948–1974* (Berkeley: University of California Press, 1977), 183–91.

18. Tim Judah, *Kosovo: War and Revenge* (New Haven: Yale University Press, 2002), 38.

19. Alex Dragnich N. and Slavco Todorovich, *The Saga of Kosovo: Focus on Serbian-Albanian Relations* (New York: Columbia University Press, 1984), 161–62.

20. "Yugoslavia: Is Fair Unfair?" *Economist*, November 9, 1985, 66. The 1966 figure includes both Serbs and Montenegrins.

21. Malcolm, *Kosovo*, 325.

22. Dan Morgan, "One Nation under Tito," *Washington Post*, June 16, 1999.

23. Elizabeth Pond, "Why Turbulent Kosovo Has Marble Sidewalks but Troubled Industries," *Christian Science Monitor*, December 15, 1981.

24. See discussion in Diana Johnstone, *Fools' Crusade: Yugoslavia, NATO, and Western Delusions* (New York: Monthly Review Press, 2002), 209–13.

25. Morgan, "One Nation under Tito." With regard to intimidation of Serbs in Kosovo, see Chris Hedges, "Kosovo's Next Masters?" *Foreign Affairs* 78, no. 3, 1999, 38; and Independent International Commission on Kosovo [IICK], *Kosovo Report: Conflict, International Response, Lessons Learned* (Oxford: Oxford University Press, 2000), 38–39.

26. Derek Brown, "The Bad Blood of Kosovo," *Guardian*, October 14, 1991.

27. Susan L. Woodward, *Balkan Tragedy: Chaos and Dissolution after the Cold War* (Washington, D.C.: Brookings, 1995), 53.

28. Eric Bourne, "Economic Woes Worsen Ethnic Tensions in Yugoslavia," *Christian Science Monitor*, July 29, 1986.

29. See Jim Naureckas, "Rescued from the Memory Hole: The Forgotten Background

of the Serb/Albanian Conflict," *Extra*, May–June 1999. For critical perspectives on
Western press reporting on Kosovo, see Phil Hammond and Edward S. Herman,
eds., *Degraded Capability: The Media and the Kosovo Crisis* (London: Pluto, 2000);
Michael Parenti, *To Kill a Nation: The Attack on Yugoslavia* (London: Verso, 2002),
chap. 13; and Edward S. Herman and David Peterson, "The Dismantling of
Yugoslavia," *Monthly Review* 59, no. 5, 2007.

30. Randy Hodson, Dusko Sekulic, and Garth Massey, "National Tolerance in
the Former Yugoslavia," *American Journal of Sociology* 99, no. 6, 1994, 1551. This
generalization applied to Albanians in both Kosovo and Macedonia.

31. Franke Wilmer, *The Social Construction of Man, the State, and War: Identity, Conflict,
and Violence in Former Yugoslavia* (New York: Routledge, 2002), 161; and IICK,
Kosovo Report, 39.

32. There was an effort to formalize Serbian dominance through vaguely worded
constitutional amendments. See "1989 Amendments of the Serbian Constitution,"
in Heike Krieger, ed., *The Kosovo Conflict and International Law: An Analytical
Documentation, 1974–1999* (Cambridge: Cambridge University Press, 2001), 8–9.

33. Quotes from UN General Assembly Resolution 48/153, February 7, 1994, *www.
un.org/Depts/dhl/res/resa48.htm*.

34. See "Amendment to the University Law, 1990," "Elementary School Law, 1992,"
"Secondary School Law, 1992," and "High School Law, 1992," all from the *Official
Gazette of the Socialist Republic of Serbia*, all in Marc Weller, ed., *The Crisis in Kosovo,
1989–1999* (Cambridge: Documents and Analysis Publishing, 1999), 60, 63. See also
Judah, *Kosovo*, 62–63.

35. UK House of Commons [UKHOC], "Foreign Affairs, Fourth Report: Kosovo,"
May 23, 2000, sec. 18, *www.publications.parliament.uk/pa/cm199900/cmselect/
cmfaff/28/2802.htm*.

36. See Ibrahim Rugova, prosecution witness, testimony at the Milošević trial,
International Criminal Tribunal for the Former Yugoslavia [ICTY], May 3, 2002,
and May 6, 2002, *www.icty.org*.

37. UKHOC, "Foreign Affairs, Fourth Report," sec. 22.

38. According to a 1995 survey, virtually all ethnic Albanians in Kosovo favored either
unification with the Republic of Albania or independence. Ivo H. Daalder and
Michael E. O'Hanlon, *Winning Ugly: NATO's War to Save Kosovo* (Washington,
D.C.: Brookings, 2000), 8. On Albanian secessionist sentiment, see also "Letter
from the Chargé d'Affaires of the Permanent Mission of Yugoslavia to the United
Nations, Addressed to the Secretary-General, 18 December, 1995," in Krieger, *The
Kosovo Conflict and International Law*, 13.

39. "Kosova Report: 24 May Multiparty Elections for Parliament and President
of Kosova, 15 June, 1992," in Weller, *Crisis in Kosovo*, 73; and Zoran Kusovac,
"Different Realities Wrestle for Kosovo," *Jane's Intelligence Review*, September 1,
1998.

40. Tim Judah quoted in Noam Chomsky, *The New Military Humanism: Lessons from
Kosovo* (Monroe, Me.: Common Courage Press, 1999), 27.

41. Miranda Vickers, *Between Serb and Albanian: A History of Kosovo* (London: Hurst,
1998), 289.

42. As noted in US National Security Council Memorandum, "Rugova and Bukoshi
Talk Trade with GOA Leaders," July 17, 1992, Bush Presidential Records, NSC,

Beth Sanner Files, Electronic Messages—Kosovo, OA/IA CFO 01521, George H. W. Bush Presidential Library.

43. Quoted in Judah, *Kosovo*, 73–74, 150.

44. On Senator Dole's long-standing interest in Kosovo, see his speech in "Tragedy in Kosovo," *Congressional Record*, March 22, 1990; and Johnstone, *Fools' Crusade*, 230–31.

45. James Harff, president of Ruder-Finn, quoted in Matthew C. Via, "Secret Weapon: US Public Relations Firm Sells Serbs as Bad Guys," *Atlanta Journal and Constitution*, February 28, 1993. See also "Opération Médiatique aux USA," *Le Monde du Renseignement*, June 3, 1993.

46. The text of the Dayton Accords appears in David Owen, ed., *Balkan Odyssey* [Academic Edition], CD-ROM (Princeton: Bureau of Electronic Publishing, 1996).

47. Stacy Sullivan, *Be Not Afraid for You Have Sons in America: How a Brooklyn Roofer Helped Lure the US into the Kosovo War* (New York: St. Martin's, 2004), 90–91. The weaknesses of the 1995 Dayton Accords, and their failure to address Serb repression in Kosovo, are emphasized in Alex Bellamy, *Kosovo and International Society* (New York: Palgrave Macmillan, 2002), 48–56.

48. Another factor in Rugova's declining popularity was a 1997 breakdown of civil order in the Republic of Albania. This freed up a large quantity of arms, which were smuggled across the border; this in turn encouraged Rugova's political rivals, who favored armed revolt. UKHOC, "Foreign Affairs, Fourth Report," sec. 23.

49. On the Albanian diaspora, see Paul Hockenos, *Homeland Calling: Exile Patriotism and the Balkan Wars* (Ithaca: Cornell University Press, 2003), chaps. 8–11.

50. UKHOC, "Foreign Affairs, Fourth Report," sec. 25.

51. See Roger Boyes and Eske Wright, "Drugs Money Linked to the Kosovo Rebels," *Times* (London), March 24, 1999; Christophe Chiclet, "Aux Origines de l'Armée de Libération du Kosovo," *Le Monde Diplomatique*, May 1999; and Paddy Ashdown testimony before the ICTY, March 14, 2002, 2341, *www.icty.org*.

52. Marcia Christoff Kurop, "European Jihads: Al Qaeda's Balkan Links," *Wall Street Journal* (European edition), November 1, 2001. The article also claims that Al Qaeda operated "factories for weapons of mass destruction" in the Balkans, but this claim would seem exaggerated.

53. For purposes of this study, we will accept the following definition of terrorism: "politically-motivated violence perpetrated against noncombatant targets by sub-national groups or clandestine agents." US Congressional Research Service, "Terrorism and National Security," December 21, 2004, 4, *www.fas.org/irp/crs/IB10119. pdf*.

54. UKHOC, "Foreign Affairs, Fourth Report," sec. 25.

55. Ashdown testimony, ICTY, March 15, 2002, 2401–02, *www.icty.org*.

56. Sullivan, *Be Not Afraid*, 157.

57. UKHOC, testimony of Defence Secretary George Robertson before the Select Committee on Defence, March 24, 1999, sec. 391, *www.parliament.the-stationery-office.co.uk/pa/cm199899/cmselect/cmdfence/39/9032403.htm*. The specific event that Robertson referred to in January 1999 was the Račak massacre, a Serb-perpetrated atrocity. British foreign minister Robin Cook confirmed Robertson's contention when he stated on January 18, 1999: "[The Kosovo] Liberation Army . . . until this weekend was responsible for more deaths than the [Serb] security forces." The Cook quotation was read by Milošević during his trial before the ICTY, in the course of testimony

by Paddy Ashdown, March 15, 2002, 2418–20, *www.icty.org*. The authenticity of the quotations was not contested.

58. Thaçi quoted in the documentary film by the BBC, *Moral Combat: NATO at War*, which aired March 12, 2000, 2, *news.bbc.co.uk/hi/english/static/events/panorama/transcripts/transcript_12_03_00.txt*.

59. British officials believed that the KLA was "just looking to NATO to be their defense arm and bomb Milošević." Views of Tony Blair and Robin Cook are paraphrased in Alastair Campbell, *The Blair Years: The Alastair Campbell Diaries* (New York: Knopf, 2007), 362.

60. David Halberstam, *War in a Time of Peace* (New York: Simon and Schuster, 2002), 397.

61. Madeleine Albright, *Madam Secretary: A Memoir* (New York: Miramax, 2003), 386. President Clinton's memoirs provide extended discussion of the Kosovo war but reveal little of importance. See Bill Clinton, *My Life* (New York: Knopf, 2004), 848–60.

62. See discussion in Mine Aysen Doyran, "Financial Crisis and Hegemony: An Investigation into the Declinist Paradigm," PhD thesis, Department of Political Science, State University of New York, Albany, 2007, chaps. 7–8.

63. V. Anantha-Nageswaren, Credit Suisse Private Banking, letter to the editor, *Financial Times*, September 2, 1998.

64. Albright, *Madam Secretary*, 378.

65. Timothy Crawford, "Pivotal Deterrence and the Kosovo War: Why the Holbrooke Agreement Failed," *Political Science Quarterly* 116, no. 4, 2001, 506.

66. UN Security Council Resolution 1160, March 31, 1998, *www.un.org/Docs/scres/1998/scres98.htm*. On the Contact Group see Stefan Troebst, *Conflict in Kosovo: Failure of Prevention? An Analytical Documentation, 1992–1998* (Flensburg, Germany: European Centre for Minority Issues, 1998), 40–41.

67. Anticommunism remained a significant aspect of US policy in the Balkans, as suggested in Alan Parrington, "Clinton Had a Chance to Avoid Kosovo Bombing," *Colorado Springs Gazette*, October 12, 2000, *www.commondreams.org/views/101300-107.htm*. Parrington was a US military attaché in London at the time, and his article refers to Milošević as Europe's "last reigning communist."

68. Justin Brown, "The Players in Kosovo Face Off," *Christian Science Monitor*, March 10, 1998.

69. "Kosovo—The Untold Story: How the War Was Won," *Observer* (London), July 18, 1999.

70. "Statement by the Contact Group," March 9, 1998, in Philip E. Auerswald, David P. Auerswald, and Christian Duttweiler, eds., *The Kosovo Conflict: A Diplomatic History through Documents* (Cambridge: Kluwer Law International, 2000), 111.

71. Crawford, "Pivotal Deterrence," 507.

72. Crawford, "Pivotal Deterrence," 509.

73. See Albright, *Madam Secretary*, 385.

74. Daalder and O'Hanlon, *Winning Ugly*, 23.

75. On the bureaucratic politics, see Halberstam, *War in a Time of Peace*, 376, 377, 388, 389, 422; Gail Sheehy, *Hillary's Choice* (New York: Ballantine Books, 2000), 345; and Sally Bedell Smith, *For Love of Politics: Inside the Clinton White House* (New York: Random House, 2007), 382. John Prados cites evidence that in 1998 President Clinton approved a covert operation "against Serbian President Slobodan Milošević," presumably aimed at Milošević's overthrow. See Prados, *Safe for Democracy: The Secret Wars of the CIA* (Chicago: Ivan R. Dee, 2006), 624.

76. Crawford, "Pivotal Deterrence," 511.

77. Gen. Wesley Clark, *Waging Modern War: Bosnia, Kosovo, and the Future of Combat* (New York: Public Affairs, 2002), 144–45.

78. Clark, *Waging Modern War*, 148. On NATO threats, see also "Statement by NATO Secretary-General following ACTWARN Decision, Vilamoura, 24 September, 1998," in Weller, *Crisis in Kosovo*, 277.

79. On the Holbrooke agreement see the following documents: "Serbian Government Endorses Accord Reached by President Milošević, Belgrade, 13 October, 1998"; "NATO-FRY Kosovo Verification Mission Agreement, FRY, 15 October, 1998"; "Record of NATO-Serbia/FRY Meeting in Belgrade, 25 October, 1998"; and "Understanding between KDOM and the Ministry of Interior of the Republic of Serbia, 25 October, 1998," all in Weller, *Crisis in Kosovo*, 279–84.

80. On the KLA's reaction, see Crawford, "Pivotal Deterrence," 512.

81. The Kosovo Verification Mission was preceded by the Kosovo Diplomatic Observer Mission, which had been established in July 1998. IICK, *Kosovo Report*, 73–74.

82. Javier Solana, "NATO's Success in Kosovo," *Foreign Affairs* 78, no. 6, 1999, 116.

83. Gen. Klaus Naumann, prosecution witness at the Milošević trial, ICTY, June 13, 2002, 6994–95, *www.icty.org*. During a 2000 interview, General Naumann also stated that Milošević "really did what we asked him to do [with regard to the Holbrooke agreement]; he withdrew within 48 hours some 6,000 police officers and the military back into the barracks. This [withdrawal] was also confirmed by the OSCE Verification Mission." Quoted in *Moral Combat*, 6. Naumann made this same point yet again in testimony before a British parliamentary committee. Naumann is paraphrased by MP Mike Gapes in UKHOC, "Minutes of Evidence taken before the Defence Committee, Tuesday, 20 June 2000," question 1086, *www.publications.parliament.uk/pa/cm199900/cmselect/cmdfence/347/0062001.htm*.

84. IICK, *Kosovo Report*, 78. Sabrina Ramet distorts the record when she notes "Milošević's failure to live up to the commitments he had made to Ambassador Richard Holbrooke in October 1998." Sabrina Ramet, "Kosovo: A Liberal Approach," *Society* 36, no. 6, 1999, 62.

85. Quoted in *Moral Combat*, 6–7. Naumann later stated with regard to the fighting after the Holbrooke agreement that "many of the incidents were triggered by the [KLA], who obviously tried to exploit the vacuum created by the withdrawn Serb security forces. . . . They also I think launched provocations." Naumann testimony, ICTY, June 13, 2002, 6995, *www.icty.org*.

86. Barton Gellman, "The Path to Crisis: How the United States and Its Allies Went to War," *Washington Post*, April 18, 1999. Gellman cites "US intelligence" sources.

87. Kissinger's views are paraphrased in Boris Johnson, "Cold Warrior Scorns 'New Morality,'" *Daily Telegraph*, June 28, 1999.

88. Agim Ceku, quoted in *Moral Combat*, 6.

89. Yugoslav Defense Minister Pavle Bulatović paraphrased in "Belgrade Urges West to Put Pressure on Kosovo Rebels," Agence France Presse, November 1, 1998.

90. Quote from Naumann, testimony before the ICTY, June 14, 2002, 7080, *www.icty.org*.

91. Tom Walker and Aidan Laverty, "CIA Aided Kosovo Guerrilla Army," *Sunday Times* (London), March 12, 2000. When the *Sunday Times* asked Verification Mission director William Walker if the CIA might have infiltrated the mission, Walker stated: "Sure they could. It's their job. But nobody told me." It would seem likely that much

of the training was undertaken by military contracting firms, notably DynCorp and Military Personnel Resources Inc. (MPRI), both of which had personnel in Kosovo during this period, according to the news story. When asked about any possible role the MPRI might have had in Kosovo, Walker was evasive: "In Kosovo, I don't remember coming across MPRI, but this is not to say that they weren't there." Walker, testimony before the ICTY, June 12, 2002, 6904, *www.icty.org*.

92. Marcia Christoff Kurop, "European Jihads: Al Qaeda's Balkan Links," *Wall Street Journal* [European edition], November 1, 2001.

93. Quoted in *Moral Combat*, 7. On the CIA role see also Peter Beaumont, Ed Vulliamy, and Paul Beaver, " 'CIA's Bastard Army Ran Riot in Balkans,'" *Observer* (London), March 11, 2001.

94. Walker and Laverty, "CIA Aided Kosovo Guerrilla Army." For the record, General Clark would later state: "NATO has no relationship with the KLA, period." The statement seems implausible in light of the *Sunday Times* information just mentioned. Also British general Rupert Smith notes that the NATO states established "common cause . . . with the KLA." Smith, *The Utility of Force: The Art of War in the Modern World* (London: Allen Lane, 2005), 304. For the Clark quote, see his testimony at the ICTY, December 16, 2003, 30510, *www.icty.org*.

95. BBC reporter Alan Little, in *Moral Combat*, 7.

96. See account in Organization for Security and Cooperation in Europe [OSCE], "Kosovo/Kosova, as Seen, as Told: An Analysis of the Human Rights Findings of the OSCE Kosovo Verification Mission," 1999, parts 3 and 4, *www.osce.org/item/17755. html*.

97. President Clinton distorted the circumstances of the Račak massacre when he stated that "innocent men, women, and children [were] taken from their homes to a gully, forced to kneel in the dirt, [and] sprayed with gunfire." In addition, media reports incorrectly suggested that the Serbs had tortured the victims or had disfigured the bodies posthumously. However, a Finnish forensics investigation concluded that all but one of the victims had been shot at a distance, not at close range. And (contrary to Clinton's claims) the victims included only one women and one child under the age of sixteen. Also, the disfigurement of the bodies was probably caused by feral dogs after the massacre, not by Serb forces. See J. Rainio, K. Lalu, and A. Penttilä, "Independent Forensic Autopsies in an Armed Conflict: Investigation of the Victims from Račak, Kosovo," *Forensic Science International* 116, no. 2, 2001, 178, 179, 183. Regarding the exaggerated allegations, see President Clinton, "The President's News Conference," March 19, 1999, Woolley and Peters, American Presidency Project, Document Archive, *www.presidency.ucsb.edu/ws/index.php?pid=57287andst=racakandst1=children*; and "Helsinki Commission Leaders Call Milosevic Responsible for 'Barbaric' Kosovo Massacre," *PR Newswire*, January 21, 1999. However, it seems likely that a massacre did occur at Račak (despite the exaggerations), and that the deaths did not result from active combat. See testimony by Helena Ranta, prosecution witness at the Milošević trial, ICTY, March 12, 2003, *www.icty.org*; and Human Rights Watch, "Yugoslav Government War Crimes at Račak," 1999, *www.hrw.org/campaigns/kosovo98/racak. shtml*.

98. Human Rights Watch, "Yugoslav Government War Crimes at Račak."

99. For detailed accounts of the Rambouillet conference, see Albright, *Madam Secretary*, chap. 24; Clark, *Waging Modern War*, chap. 7; James Rubin, "The Promise of Freedom:

A Very Personal War, Part II," *Financial Times*, October 7, 2000, and "A Very Personal War [Part I]," *Financial Times*, September 30, 2000; Marc Weller, "The Rambouillet Conference on Kosovo," *International Affairs* 75, no. 2, 1999, and *Crisis in Kosovo*.

100. Louis Sell, *Slobodan Milošević and the Destruction of Yugoslavia* (Durham, N.C.: Duke University Press, 2002), 296.

101. "Opening Remarks by Robin Cook, UK Secretary of State, Rambouillet, 6 February, 1999," in Weller, *Crisis in Kosovo*, 419–20.

102. Rubin, "Very Personal War [Part I]."

103. Kevin Cullen, "A Call for Limits on 'Hyperpower' US: At Kosovo Talks, French Aide Urges Blunting of Nation's Will," *Boston Globe*, February 9, 1999. Note that the KLA delegation at Rambouillet was being coached by US personnel, according to the *Christian Science Monitor*: "Advising the ethnic Albanians are private American consultants: Morton Abramowitz, a former ambassador and close friend of US Secretary of State Madeleine Albright; Marshall Harris of the Washington, D.C.-based human rights group Freedom House, a former US diplomat who resigned to protest US policy on Bosnia; and Paul Williams, a former State Department lawyer." Jonathan Landay, "Inside the Kosovo Peace Talks," *Christian Science Monitor*, February 10, 1999. For various drafts of the proposed Rambouillet agreement presented by the Contact Group, see Weller, *Crisis in Kosovo*, chap. 15.

104. "Kosovo—The Untold Story."

105. The pro-Albanian proclivity is apparent in Rubin, "Very Personal War, [Part I]."

106. "Secretary of State Albright, Briefing Following Contact Group Meeting, 14 February, 1999," in Weller, *Crisis in Kosovo*, 431.

107. See comments by Albright in *Moral Combat*, 7; and Christopher Layne, "Blunder in the Balkans: The Clinton Administration's Bungled War against Serbia," *Policy Analysis*, May 20, 1999, 5.

108. Commentary by Weller, *Crisis in Kosovo*, 475. See also Paul-Marie de la Gorce, "Histoire Secrète des Négotiations de Rambouillet," *Le Monde Diplomatique*, May 1999. Regarding Weller's role as advisor to the Albanians, see Judah, *Kosovo*, 205.

109. Rubin, "Very Personal War, Part II."

110. Albright stated on February 20 that the Serbs "basically, I think, were not focusing that much on the political agreement, and felt that on the whole they could accept that." "Excerpts from Remarks by Secretary of State Albright, February 20, 1999," in Auerswald, Auerswald, and Duttweiler, *The Kosovo Conflict*, 518–21. Regarding the positive progress of the negotiations and the receptiveness of the Serb delegation to a settlement, also see comments by Wolfgang Petritsch, an Austrian diplomat involved in the negotiations. Though Petritsch expressed concern that Milošević was not present at Rambouillet, he also stated that the Serb delegation consisted of "well-versed, excellent experts" who "knew up to the minutest detail all the problems and issues." Christopher Hill, a US diplomat, stated that "Milošević was open to the Rambouillet political deal." Sources: Petritsch's comments were made as a prosecution witness at the Milošević trial, ICTY, July 2, 2002, 7218–20, *www.icty.org*. Hill is quoted in IICK, *Kosovo Report*, 157.

111. Barry Posen, "The War for Kosovo: Serbia's Political-Military Strategy," *International Security* 24, no. 4, 2000, 47.

112. Samantha Power, *"A Problem from Hell": America and the Age of Genocide* (New York: HarperCollins, 2002), 448.

113. "Appendix B: Status of Multinational Military Implementation Force" (see especially

sec. 8), in Weller, *Crisis in Kosovo*, 468–69. The Military Annex was first noted by British journalist John Pilger in "Revealed: The Amazing NATO Plan, Tabled at Rambouillet, to Occupy Yugoslavia," *New Statesman*, May 17, 1999.

114. During his trial in The Hague, Milošević emphasized the importance of the Military Annex as a provocation against Serbia. See Milošević's statements during the cross-examination of Paddy Ashdown at the ICTY trial, March 15, 2002, 2478, *www.icty.org*. See also Milošević's comments in Posen, "War for Kosovo," 48. Another factor that may have provoked the Serb delegation was a letter drafted by Secretary Albright's staff for the Albanian delegation at Rambouillet that promised US support for a referendum on a permanent status for Kosovo. It was understood that such a referendum would have led to a vote for full independence—an outcome that was unacceptable to the Serbs. Note that this letter constituted a shift in the US position, which had previously opposed independence for Kosovo. The UN Security Council had already passed a resolution that affirmed "the commitment of all member states to the sovereignty and territorial integrity of the Federal Republic of Yugoslavia"—which at that time still included Kosovo. Sources: Regarding the international consensus against Kosovar independence, see UN Security Council Resolution 1160, March 31, 1998, *www.un.org/Docs/scres/1998/scres98.htm*. On the Albright letter, see Judah, *Kosovo*, 215. For the actual text of the draft letter, see "Draft for Chapter 8, Article 1 (3), 22 February 1999, 0.525hrs, and Proposed Draft Side Letter," in Weller, *Crisis in Kosovo*, 452.

115. UKHOC, "Foreign Affairs, Fourth Report," sec. 65.

116. Posen, "War for Kosovo," 44. Political scientist James Kurth also found the Military Annex suspicious. See Kurth, "First War of the Global Era: Kosovo and US Grand Strategy," in Andrew J. Bacevich and Eliot A. Cohen, eds., *War over Kosovo: Politics and Strategy in a Global Age* (New York: Columbia University Press, 2001), 77.

117. Quoted in Johnson, "Cold Warrior Scorns 'New Morality.'"

118. UKHOC, "Foreign Affairs, Fourth Report," sec. 65. Similarly, the Independent International Commission on Kosovo stated that the inclusion of this clause was "widely viewed in retrospect as a blunder." IICK, *Kosovo Report*, 156. Alex Bellamy dismisses the idea that the Military Annex was a deliberate provocation—but he also concedes: "There is no doubt that the Annex was unfortunately worded." Bellamy, *Kosovo and International Society*, 138.

119. Clark, *Waging Modern War*, 162–63. Regarding Clark's reputation for meticulous preparation, see Halberstam, *War in a Time of Peace*, chap. 39.

120. Quoted in Johnson, "Cold Warrior Scorns 'New Morality.'" Regarding the possibility that Western powers were seeking a pretext, see also Oskar Lafontaine, *Das Herz Schlägt Links* (Munich: Econ, 1999), 243; Maj. Gen. Lewis MacKenzie, "Time to Stop the Mr. Nice Guy Act," *Ottawa Citizen*, March 20, 2001; and David Binder, "A Balkan Balance Sheet," *Mediterranean Quarterly* 11, no. 1, 2000, 50–51.

121. Patrick Wintour, "Ex-Minister Attacks Kosovo War Tactics," *Guardian*, July 21, 2000. This quote is directly from the *Guardian*, which paraphrased the statement of British official John Gilbert.

122. Testimony of John Gilbert before the UK House of Commons Defence Committee, June 20, 2000, paragraph 1086, *www.publications.parliament.uk/pa/cm199900/cmselect/cmdfence/347/0062001.htm*. Additional evidence that the United States avoided a peaceful settlement in Kosovo is provided by a retired US Air Force colonel who served as a military attaché at the US embassy in London. See Parrington, "Clinton Had a Chance to Avoid Kosovo Bombing." James Gow is dismissive regarding allegations

that the United States or other Western powers were seeking a pretext for war against Serbia, and he states that such allegations were "utterly ridiculous." Gow neglects to mention the testimony of Lord Gilbert, which suggests that certain powers *were* seeking a pretext for war. See Gow, *The Serbian Project and Its Adversaries: A Strategy of War Crimes* (Montreal: McGill-Queen's University Press, 2003), 284.

123. The Military Annex was presented on the last day of the Rambouillet conference, February 23, and the talks adjourned, to be followed up in Paris on March 15. Even before the talks reconvened in Paris, it is evident that the Serbs had lost confidence in the idea of a negotiated settlement. Several days after the Military Annex was presented, Serb forces began massing for an offensive against the KLA, probably on the assumption that war was inevitable. The follow-up talks took place in Paris in March as scheduled, and produced nothing. The circumstances of the Serb military buildup are (inaccurately) discussed in a Human Rights Watch report that claims: "*Throughout the [Rambouillet] conference*, Serbian and Yugoslav forces were observed positioning themselves around the Kosovo border with Serbia proper, a clear indication—coupled with the Serbian delegation's intransigence—that a military offensive was in preparation. According to the OSCE, 'a significant build-up of [Yugoslav] forces' was taking place throughout Kosovo" (emphasis added). The only source cited for this claim is a previous OSCE report from which the embedded quote was drawn. When one checks the original OSCE document itself, however, it clear that the excerpt constitutes a quote out of context. A more complete quote from the OSCE document reads: "*Following the talks in Rambouillet*, France (6–23 February 1999), there was a significant buildup of [Yugoslav] forces" (emphasis added). In other words, the Serbs began to build up their forces *after* (not before) the Rambouillet conference had ended. Sources: Human Rights Watch, "Under Orders: War Crimes in Kosovo," 2001 ("Background" section, "The Rambouillet Conference" subsections), *www.hrw.org/ reports/2001/kosovo/*; and OSCE, "Kosovo/Kosova," part 2, chap. 3 ("Security Situation December 1998 to mid-March 1999" section, "Open Hostilities" subsection). For documentation on the Paris phase of the peace talks, see Weller, *Crisis in Kosovo*, chap. 16.

124. See commentary by Weller, *Crisis in Kosovo*, 475.

125. Quoted from commentary by Weller, *Crisis in Kosovo*, 475. Weller implies that this incident reflected a basic Serb intransigence, while he ignores the provocations that virtually guaranteed a negative Serb reaction. Defenders of US/NATO policy nevertheless insist that the Military Annex was innocuous and could not have caused the breakdown in negotiations. Their principal claim is that the Contact Group negotiators would have happily withdrawn the offending clause (regarding the occupation of all Yugoslavia) if the Serbs had requested it; but the Serbs did not so request. Given the absence of a Serb request to remove the clause, it is claimed, the Serbs could not have been greatly bothered by it. And therefore the Annex could not have caused the breakdown of negotiations. This argument seems implausible in light of Lord Gilbert's testimony (that demands on the Serbs were "absolutely intolerable," and that this was done deliberately because "certain people were spoiling for a fight"). It is true that the Serb delegation failed to lodge any *formal* complaint about the Military Annex during the negotiations; but this proves little since the Serbs had already lost confidence in the negotiation process. There is no doubt that the Serbs were angered by the Annex, as indicated by their pungent question to Contact Group

mediators ("Have you come to fuck us again?"), which was posed after the Annex was presented. And there is another problem: If the negotiators would have willingly changed the Annex—as some now claim—this begs the question of *why* such obviously objectionable demands as those contained in the Annex were presented in the first place. The following sources defend the Military Annex as a harmless detail: Stephen Hosmer, *The Conflict over Kosovo: Why Milošević Decided to Settle When He Did* (Santa Monica, Calif.: Rand, 2001), 15; Bellamy, *Kosovo and International Society*, 138; Rubin, "Very Personal War, Part II."; Daalder and O'Hanlon, *Winning Ugly*, 87; Clark, *Waging Modern War*, 162–63; and Weller, *Crisis in Kosovo*, 413.

126. Quoted in Barton Gellman, "In the End, Allies See No Credible Alternative," *Washington Post*, March 23, 1999.

127. Naumann, ICTY testimony, June 13, 2002, 7020, *www.icty.org*.

128. An anonymous US official quoted in Thomas Lippman, "Albright Misjudged Milošević on Kosovo," *Washington Post*, April 7, 1999.

129. Blair's view is paraphrased by his press spokesperson, in Campbell, *The Blair Years*, 362. Campbell states that this was also the view of Foreign Minister Robin Cook.

130. The idea that Milošević would not negotiate in good faith is strongly implied in Albright, *Madam Secretary*, chaps. 23–24.

131. See Susan Bell, " 'Ethnic Cleansing' Plans Laid Years Ago," *Times* (London), April 9, 1999; Daniel Vernet, "Ce Plan Fér à Cheval qui Programmait des Déportation des Kosovars," *Le Monde*, April 8, 1999, and "Bonn Confirme l'Existence du Plan Fér à Cheval de Néttoyage Ethnique," *Le Monde*, April 9, 1999.

132. John Goetz and Tom Walker, "Serbian Ethnic Cleansing Scare Was a Fake, Says General," *Times* (London), April 2, 2000. The quotes are directly from the article, which paraphrases Loquai. See also "German Lawmakers Say Minister Misled Them over Kosovo," Agence France Presse, March 30, 2000. An earlier article in the German press also cast doubt on the Horseshoe report. See Karl Grobe, "Das 'Hufeisen' Läft Fragen Offen," *Frankfurter Rundschau*, May 19, 1999.

133. According to Judah: "A senior US State Department source says that 'Bulgaria and some other states in the region' had passed some information to the US about Operation Horseshoe or 'Operation Winter,' before the bombing but implied that it was extremely vague and certainly not taken too seriously." Judah, *Kosovo*, 141. During the Milošević war crimes trial, the prosecution sought to revive allegations of a plan to remove the Albanians. This allegation was made by Ratomir Tanić, who was presented as a Serb security official, part of Milošević's "inner circle." The prosecution was sufficiently eager to gain Tanić's testimony that they agreed to place him in a witness protection program, presumably in a third country. Tanić claimed that, in 1997, Milošević made a specific decision to reduce the number of ethnic Albanians living in Kosovo through mass expulsions. However, Tanić's reputation did not survive cross-examination. According to Agence France Presse, Tanić's "credibility was easily undermined by Milošević, when the political party Tanić said he belonged to denied he was a member." After this, little more was heard about Tanić. After Tanić was discredited, the prosecution made yet another effort to establish a secret Serb plan, this time one to allegedly murder the Albanians. Specifically, Wesley Clark testified that Milošević had admitted the existence of such a plan during a conversation Clark had with Milošević in October 1998. General Clark's testimony contained the following specific claims: "He [Milošević] turned to me and said, 'Gen. Clark . . . we

know how to handle these murderers, these rapists, these criminals [a reference to Kosovar Albanians]. . . . We've done this before . . . [in] Drenica in 1946. . . . *We killed them all.'* . . . I remember how chilling it was to recognize that what lay underneath the signature of the agreement [Milošević's signature of the Holbrooke agreement] seemed to be a clear determination to eliminate the problem of resistance by *killing them all.*" In separate testimony, General Naumann stated that he was present during the Clark-Milošević meeting, and he corroborated the substance of Clark's account. These claims are contradicted by the known record of events. In fact the Serbs never attempted a plan of mass extermination, even when they had the opportunity to do so. It is true that the Serbs committed selective atrocities, resulting in many deaths, but there was nothing that could be termed "killing them all." Even during the 1999 air war with NATO—when Serb atrocities reached horrific levels—the main technique was not mass *murder* (as implied by Clark), but mass *expulsion*. And the record of events contradicts Clark's claims in other ways: As we have seen, Milošević implemented the terms of the Holbrooke agreement. It was attacks by the KLA that were the main cause of the agreement's failure. These facts seem inconsistent with Clark's testimony, which implies that Milošević had signed the agreement in bad faith and never intended to implement it. And finally, the testimony is inconsistent with what is known about Milošević's character. By all accounts, Milošević was sophisticated and experienced in dealing with Western officials, and it seems unlikely he would have made such self-incriminating statements to NATO generals who were threatening to bomb him. Sources: On Ratomir Tanić, see his testimony before the ICTY, May 14, 2002, and May 16, 2002, at *www.icty.org*; Vesna Peric Zimonjic, "The West Backed Milošević 'Until He Targeted Civilians,'" *Independent*, May 15, 2002; "Milošević Trial Enters Second Year with Top Insider Witness," Agence France Presse, February 12, 2002. Regarding testimony that Milošević "admitted" he had a plan to murder the Albanians, see Clark testimony before the ICTY, December 15, 2003, 30396, 30510, and December 16, 2003, 30510 (emphasis added in quotes); and Naumann testimony, June 13, 2002, 6989–92, all from *www.icty.org*. Regarding the widespread perception of Milošević as a sophisticated operator, see William Walker testimony, June 11, 2002, 6785, *www.icty.org*; and Lenard J. Cohen, *Serpent in the Bosom: The Rise and Fall of Slobodan Milošević* (Boulder, Colo.: Westview, 2001), 50–51.

134. Clinton, "Remarks at the Legislative Convention." Some academic studies also claim that the Serbs committed genocide in Kosovo. See, for example, Peter Ronayne, "Genocide in Kosovo," *Human Rights Review* 5, no. 4, 2004.

135. International Criminal Tribunal for the Former Yugoslavia, Initial Indictment against Milošević—Kosovo, May 24, 1999; First Amended Indictment—Kosovo, June 29, 2001; and Second Amended Indictment—Kosovo, October 29, 2001; all from *www.icty.org*. Note that genocide was alleged for Milošević's conduct during the 1992–1995 Bosnia war. These allegations were dealt with in separate indictments that specifically addressed Bosnia. On the genocide allegation with respect to Bosnia, see Chapter 6 of this study.

136. Garentina Kraja, "UN-Run Court Says Acts Committed during Milošević's Regime in Kosovo Were Not Genocide," Associated Press, September 7, 2001. Quote is directly from the article, which paraphrases the court's decision.

137. Testimony by Ashdown before the ICTY, March 15, 2002, 2402, *www.icty.org*. See

similar comments by Naumann, ICTY testimony, June 13, 2002, 6984, 6995–96, *www.icty.org.*

138. On excessive force see Lionel McPherson, "Excessive Force in War: A 'Golden Rule' Test," *Theoretical Inquiries in Law* 7, no. 1, 2006.

139. Judah, *Kosovo*, 226.

140. On numbers of dead and refugees, see Craig Whitney, "In New Talks on Kosovo, NATO's Credibility Is at Stake," *New York Times*, March 14, 1999. See also Judah, *Kosovo*, 177.

141. Bruce Cumings, *The Origins of the Korean War*, vol. 2, *The Roaring of the Cataract, 1947–1950* (Princeton: Princeton University Press, 1990), 258.

142. The epigraph quote is from Rubin, "Very Personal War, Part I."

143. Jonathan Landay, "US Threatens Force: Why Now?" *Christian Science Monitor*, October 15, 1998.

144. Madeleine Albright, "US and NATO Policy toward the Crisis in Kosovo: Testimony before the Senate Foreign Relations Committee," *Department of State Dispatch*, May 1999.

145. Alexander Nicoll, "Cracks Still Appear in NATO's Collective Will for Air Strikes," *Financial Times*, October 9, 1998. The salience of NATO credibility as a motive for US intervention is also emphasized by James Steinberg, who was Clinton's deputy national security advisor at the time. Steinberg, "A Perfect Polemic: Blind to Reality on Kosovo," *Foreign Affairs* 78, no. 6, 1999, 131; and John Kampfner, *Blair's Wars* (New York: Free Press, 2003), 44.

146. Blair lobbied the Americans to consider using ground troops against Serbia. Kampfner, *Blair's Wars*, 47–50, 53.

147. Rubin, "Very Personal War [Part I]." Note that the Italian foreign minister Lamberto Dini challenged some of Rubin's comments with regard to the specific issue of Italian actions during Rambouillet. See James Blitz, "Italian Minister Disputes Version of Kosovo Talks," *Financial Times*, October 2, 2000.

148. Kevin Cullen, "US, Europeans in Discord on Kosovo," *Boston Globe*, February 22, 1999; "OSCE Official Critical of US Kosovo Policy," DDPADN News Agency, Berlin, in BBC Monitoring Service, January 19, 1999; and Smith, *Utility of Force*, 381. General Smith was a British officer and deputy NATO commander during the 1999 war. In his memoir, Smith reveals that he doubted the legality of the war and participated with reluctance.

149. Martin Walker and Stephen Bates, "Battle Underway to Replace Santer," *Guardian*, March 18, 1999.

150. "French Unease over the New Germany," *Economist*, March 6, 1999, 48. Regarding the party politics of intervention in Europe more generally, see Brian Rathbun, *Partisan Interventions: European Party Politics and Peace Enforcement in the Balkans* (Ithaca: Cornell University Press, 2004), especially chaps. 3–5.

151. Alan Henrikson, "The Constraint of Legitimacy: The Legal and Institutional Framework of Euro-Atlantic Security," in Pierre Martin and Mark R. Brawley, eds., *Alliance Politics, Kosovo, and NATO's War* (New York: Palgrave, 2000), 50. Note that this was the position of Germany and Britain, though in retrospect it appears to have been the dominant position of NATO more generally. The official US position was more unilateral: It asserted that UN approval for US intervention was desirable but not necessary.

152. Clinton authorized the attack without an explicit vote of approval from Congress. The Senate had approved a resolution that allowed the use of force, but the House of Representatives failed to do so. Regarding the legal issues associated with Clinton's decision to use force, see John Yoo, "Kosovo, War Powers, and the Multilateral Future," *University of Pennsylvania Law Review* 148, no. 5, 2000; Tom Campbell, "Kosovo: An Unconstitutional War," *Mediterranean Quarterly* 11, no. 1, 2000; and Kenneth Moss, *Undeclared War and the Future of US Foreign Policy* (Baltimore: Johns Hopkins University Press, 2008), 99–100. See also Sen. Joseph Biden, *Promises to Keep: On Life and Politics* (New York: Random House, 2007), 285–86.

153. See Solana's account: Solana, "NATO's Success in Kosovo."

154. Pierre Glachant, "Kosovo Crisis Leaves NATO Allies Wary of Future Interventions," Agence France Presse, June 11, 1999.

155. Daalder and O'Hanlon, *Winning Ugly*, 91.

156. The military aspects of the war are described in Posen, "War for Kosovo"; Benjamin S. Lambeth, *NATO's Air War for Kosovo: A Strategic and Operational Assessment* (Santa Monica, Calif.: Rand, 2001); Anthony H. Cordesman, *The Lessons and Non-Lessons of the Air and Missile Campaign in Kosovo* (Westport, Conn.: Praeger, 2001), chap. 2; Gian Gentile, *How Effective Is Strategic Bombing? Lessons Learned from World War II to Kosovo* (New York: New York University Press, 2001), afterword; and Grant Hammond, "Myths of the Air War over Serbia," *Aerospace Power Journal* 14, no. 4, 2000.

157. "Bombs over Belgrade, Diplomatic as well as Military," *Economist*, May 8, 1999, 50–51. Rubin claims that the heightened ethnic cleansing had in fact begun shortly before the air attacks, and therefore the air attacks could not have been the main cause of the augmented ethnic cleansing. However Rubin neglects to mention that the Serb attacks began after the collapse of peace talks, when NATO air strikes were clearly imminent. Rubin, "Promise of Freedom"; and US Department of State, "Kosovo Chronology," May 21, 1999, *www.state.gov/www/regions/eur/fs_kosovo_timeline.html*.

158. The 90 percent figure is from UKHOC, "Foreign Affairs, Fourth Report," sec. 94; the 850,000 figure is from Judah, *Kosovo*, 241.

159. The Serb-directed ethnic cleansing campaign of this period certainly entailed central government direction, as argued by statistician Patrick Ball. The campaign might also have entailed some degree of prior planning (although there is no hard evidence of this). However, Ball's conclusion—that "NATO bombing was not the cause of the [Albanian] migration"—does not follow from his facts. Ball, "Policy or Panic? The Flight of Ethnic Albanians from Kosovo, March-May 1999," American Association for the Advancement of Science, 2000, *shr.aaas.org/kosovo/policyorpanic/*.

160. From "NATO Attacks," *Sunday Times* (London), March 28, 1999.

161. See New Strategic Concept, as approved: North Atlantic Treaty Organization, "The Alliance's Strategic Concept Approved by the Heads of State and Government Participating in the Meeting of the North Atlantic Council in Washington D.C. on 23rd and 24th April 1999," *www.nato.int/docu/pr/1999/p99-065e.htm*. The wording is somewhat vague as to the exact nature of NATO's out-of-area role, apparently reflecting European concerns. However, the later NATO intervention in post-2001 Afghanistan leaves little doubt, in retrospect, that the alliance has indeed embraced a global agenda.

162. David Buchan and Stephen Fidler, "An Uneasy Anniversary," *Financial Times*, April 23, 1999.

163. Both quoted in Frank Viviano, "Bitter Debate in Europe on US Role: Washington's Dominance of NATO Creates Wave of Anti-Americanism," *San Francisco Chronicle*, April 15, 1999. It is clear that the French government was also developing doubts about the war, though only in private. Campbell's diaries note repeated instances of US-French and UK-French tensions over the handling of the war. Campbell, *The Blair Years*, 379, 381.

164. Noted in UKHOC, "Kosovo: Operation 'Allied Force,'" Research Paper 99/48, April 29, 1999, 15, *www.parliament.uk/commons/lib/research/rp99/rp99-048.pdf*. On this issue, see US Congressional Research Service, "Kosovo: Lessons Learned from Operation Allied Force," November 19, 1999, 20–22, *www.au.af.mil/au/awc/awcgate/crs/rl30374.pdf*.

165. "At Daggers Drawn," *Economist*, May 8, 1999, 17.

166. Maxim Yusin, "Sea Blockade of Yugoslavia Will Lead NATO to Conflict with Moscow," *Izvestia*, translation in *Russian Press Digest*, April 27, 1999.

167. Bell, "Ethnic Cleansing Plans Laid Years Ago."

168. Paraphrase of German general Loquai in Goetz and Walker, "Serbian Ethnic Cleansing Scare."

169. Cohen quoted in Phil Davison, "War in the Balkans: '100,000 Albanian Men Are Missing,'" *Independent*, May 17, 1999. For uncritical press acceptance of the 100,000 figure, see "Messy War, Messy Peace," *Economist*, June 12, 1999.

170. Scheffer presented these points in "NATO Daily Morning Briefing, Re Kosovo," Federal News Service, May 18, 1999, 2–3 (electronic version available through Lexis-Nexis).

171. During the Milošević trial, statistician Patrick Ball testified as a prosecution witness, and he stated that 10,366 was his best estimate of Albanians killed. See Ball's testimony before the ICTY, March 13, 2002, 2166, *www.icty.org*; Richard Stone, "Statistical Analysis Provides Key Links in Milošević Trial," *Science*, March 22, 2002; and Tim Judah, "Milošević's Legacy of Discord," BBC News, March 11, 2006, *news.bbc.co.uk/2/hi/europe/4797564.stm*.

172. Smith, *Utility of Force*, 5.

173. The London *Observer* presented persuasive evidence that the embassy attack was preplanned and deliberate. See John Sweeney, Jens Holsoe, and Ed Vulliamy, "Revealed: NATO Bombed Chinese Deliberately," *Observer*, October 17, 1999; and John Sweeney, Paul Beaver, Jens Holsoe, Ed Vulliamy, Helena Smith, and John Henley, "The Raid on Belgrade: Why America Bombed the Chinese Embassy," *Observer*, November 28, 1999. See also discussion of the embassy bombing in UKHOC, "Foreign Affairs, Fourth Report," secs. 153–55. For a self-exculpatory account by the CIA director, see George Tenet, *At the Center of the Storm: My Years at the CIA* (New York: HarperCollins, 2007), 46–47, 503. Regarding the attacks on the Zastava factory and the television station, see: Uli Schmetzer, "NATO Bombs Deal Fatal Blow to Once-Proud Automaker," *Chicago Tribune*, July 16, 1999; and interview with Wesley Clark by Jeremy Scahill, *Democracy Now* radio program, January 26, 2004, *www.democracynow.org/2004/1/26/exclusive_democracy_now_confronts_wesley_clark*.

174. Brian Brady, "NATO Comes Clean on Cluster Bombs: Eight Years On, Serbia Is Finally Told Where Munitions Fell," *Independent*, September 16, 2007.

175. The ineffectiveness of the NATO strikes against Serb ground targets is one conclusion of Lambeth, *NATO's Air War for Kosovo*. See also Jackson, *Soldier*, 245.

176. Jannine di Giovanni, "War in the Balkans, 'It Is Impossible to Tell Who Is Killing Us—the Serbs or NATO,'" *Sunday Telegraph*, May 16, 1999; and Tim Butcher and Patrick Bishop, "NATO Admits Air Campaign Failed," *Daily Telegraph*, July 22, 1999.

177. Andrew Stigler argues persuasively that a ground invasion was never a realistic possibility, and that the Serbs did not take seriously NATO threats to invade. Stigler, "A Clear Victory for Air Power: NATO's Empty Threat to Invade Kosovo," *International Security* 27, no. 3, 2002–2003. See also Posen, "War for Kosovo," 74.

178. Thomas Friedman, "Stop the Music," *New York Times*, April 23, 1999.

179. Posen, "War for Kosovo," 72–73. See also Vincent Jauvert, "Kosovo: Rien ne s'est Passé comme Prévu," *Le Nouvel Observateur*, January 7, 1999. The Jauvert article refers to "the third phase [of the bombing], which was to be a total war, according to a French military figure. Without limitation, or close to it." Translated from the French.

180. LeMay quoted in Public Broadcasting Service, "The Korean War," *www.pbs.org/wgbh/amex/bomb/peopleevents/pandeAMEX58.html.*

181. Maj. Gen. Emmett O'Donnell Jr. quoted in I. F. Stone, *The Hidden History of the Korean War* (New York: Monthly Review Press, 1969), 312.

182. Pressure from Russia helped persuade Milošević to capitulate. However, given Russia's inability to provide substantial material support for Serbia during the war, it would seem likely that Russian pressure was only a secondary influence on Milošević; the danger of massive NATO bombing was a more significant factor in Milošević's capitulation. On Russia's role, see the memoirs by two former State Department officials: John Norris, *Collision Course: NATO, Russia, and Kosovo* (Westport, Conn.: Praeger, 2005); and Strobe Talbott, *The Russia Hand* (New York: Random House, 2002), chap. 12.

183. Hosmer, *The Conflict over Kosovo*, xvii.

184. For the full text of the agreements that ended the air war, see "Kosovo Peace Plan, June 3, 1999," and "Military-Technical Agreement between NATO and the Federal Republic of Yugoslavia and the Republic of Serbia, June 9, 1999." Both documents in Auerswald, Auerswald, and Duttweiler, *Kosovo Conflict*, 1079–81, 1101–6. See also analysis in Posen, "War for Kosovo," 76–77, 80. Regarding the political aspects of the settlement, the June 3 agreement referred to the previous draft agreement from Rambouillet. Note that Finnish President Martti Ahtisaari was involved in the events that led to the settlement of the Kosovo war. There is no evidence that Ahtisaari played any role in causing Serbia to agree to NATO terms, or that he had any significant impact on the settlement. However, the participation of Ahtisaari—as a high-profile figure from a traditionally neutral country—lent legitimacy to the war's settlement and also to the war itself.

185. KFOR also contained troops from Russia, a non-NATO state. See Global Security, "Operation Joint Guardian Kosovo Force (KFOR)," *www.globalsecurity.org/military/ops/joint_guardian.htm.*

186. See "United Nations Security Council Resolution 1244, June 10, 1999," in Auerswald, Auerswald, and Duttweiler, *Kosovo Conflict*, 1126–32.

187. "Who Controls Kosovo?" *Economist*, June 26, 1999, 57–58; and "Kosovo Resurgent," *Economist*, September 25, 1999, 57.

188. Iain King and Whit Mason, *Peace at Any Price: How the World Failed Kosovo* (Ithaca: Cornell University Press, 2006), 52–53. King and Mason both worked for the multinational peacekeeping administration in Kosovo. These atrocities are whitewashed in an account by British MP Paddy Ashdown; he briefly alludes to atrocities after the end of war but neglects to mention that Albanians were the perpetrators and Serbs

were the victims. Ashdown, *Swords into Ploughshares: Bringing Peace to the Twenty-First Century* (London: Weidenfeld and Nicolson, 2007), 68.

189. Tom Walker, "West Abandons Dream of a Unified Kosovo," *Sunday Times* (London), February 13, 2000. In 2008, new information emerged regarding alleged atrocities in Kosovo, including claims that Albanian nationalists had murdered Serbs and then sold their internal organs. This allegation was made in a recently published memoir by Carla Del Ponte, who served as the chief prosecutor at the ICTY and is described in the *Guardian* as follows: "Del Ponte . . . has unleashed a storm of recrimination with allegations of a trade in human body parts in Kosovo and Albania after NATO bombed Serbia in 1999. Del Ponte claims, based on what she describes as credible reports and witnesses, that Kosovan Albanian guerrillas transported hundreds of Serbian prisoners into northern Albania where they were killed, and their organs 'harvested' and trafficked out of Tirana airport. The Kosovan government, now headed by the former guerrilla leader Hashim Thaçi, dismisses the claims as untrue, while Serbia and Russia are demanding a war crimes investigation into the allegations. Del Ponte, now a Swiss ambassador, has been ordered to keep silent by the Swiss government. . . . While there is widespread skepticism about the veracity of the claims, Human Rights Watch said Del Ponte had supplied 'sufficiently grave evidence' to warrant an investigation by the Kosovo and Albanian authorities." Ian Traynor, "Former War Crimes Prosecutor Alleges Kosovan Army Harvested Organs from Serb Prisoners," *Guardian*, April 12, 2008. The Del Ponte memoir is currently available only in Italian.

190. United Nations, "Two Months After Its Return to Kosovo, UNHCR Says 750,000 Refugees Have Been Brought Home Safely," August 13, 1999, *www.un.org/peace/ kosovo/news/99/aug99_2.htm.*

191. Raymond Whitaker, "Liberation of Kosovo: Milošević's Victims—Dispossessed Prepare to Uproot Again," *Independent*, July 1, 1999.

192. Cited in "Kosovo Minorities 'Under Threat,'" BBC News, April 28, 2003, *news.bbc. co.uk/2/hi/europe/2983509.stm.*

193. Estimate provided by Judah, *Kosovo*, 264; see also Human Rights Watch, "Civilian Deaths in the NATO Air Campaign," February 2000, *www.hrw.org/reports/2000/nato.* In addition, some 576 Serb soldiers and police were killed in the war. See Kampfner, *Blair's Wars*, 58.

194. Once again, the total number of deaths from the war before the NATO bombing began was two thousand. This figure includes Albanian and Serb deaths (civilians as well as soldiers). It would therefore seem likely that the total number of Albanian civilians killed during this phase ranged in the hundreds.

195. Quoted in William Drozdiak, "Once Again, Europe Follows America's Lead," *Washington Post*, March 26, 1999.

196. Laurent Zecchini, "L'Amérique Veut-elle d'une Défense Européenne?" *Le Monde*, November 19, 1999. Translated from the French. See also Denis Duclos, "Guerre Contre les Serbes ou Contre l'Europe?" *Le Monde*, April 22, 1999.

197. Rachel Sylvester, "NATO Chief Tipped for New Role as 'Voice of Europe,'" *Independent*, May 30, 1999.

198. "Javier Solana Appointed WEU Secretary-General," *European Report*, November 27, 1999.

199. "Outlook: EU/US Summit to Focus on Kosovo Rebuilding, Not Trade Disputes," *AFX News*, June 17, 1999.

200. The term "empire of bases" is from Chalmers Johnson, *The Sorrows of Empire: Militarism, Secrecy, and the End of the Republic* (New York: Metropolitan Press, 2004), chap. 6. The importance of Camp Bondsteel is also emphasized by Charles Simic, "The Troubled Birth of Kosovo," *New York Review of Books*, April 3, 2008.

201. These include the Baku-Ceyhan pipeline, to terminate in Turkey, as well as a proposed Albanian Macedonian Bulgarian Oil pipeline, to terminate in Albania. See Bulent Gokay, "Introduction: Oil, War, and Geopolitics from Kosovo to Afghanistan," *Journal of Southern Europe and the Balkans* 4, no. 1, 2002; and Keith Fisher, "A Meeting of Blood and Oil: The Balkan Factor in Western Energy Security," *Journal of Southern Europe and the Balkans* 4, no. 1, 2002.

202. Leslie Wayne, "Weapons Makers Seek Rise in Pentagon Spending," *New York Times*, May 19, 1999.

203. Jeffrey E. Garten, "The West Needs to Forge a Weapons Alliance," *Business Week*, June 14, 1999, 31. See also Annie Kahn, "Des Contrats pour les Occidentaux?" *Le Monde*, April 6, 1999; and Richard Bassett, "Kosovo War Spurs Industry Rethink," *Jane's Defense Weekly*, June 30, 1999.

204. William Pesek Jr., "Euro = Dollar? It Looks as If the Euro Will Be Equal to the Greenback in Value, If Not Stature," *Barrons*, May 31, 1999, 13.

205. Jonathan Eyal, "Conflict with Milošević Has Resolved Many—But Not All—of the Conflicts within the Alliance," *Irish Times*, April 26, 1999. Though the article was written before the US triumph, it surely reflected the attitude afterward as well.

Chapter 8

Epigraph: Maj. Gen. Smedley Butler, *War Is a Racket: The Anti-War Classic by America's Most Decorated General* (Los Angeles: Feral House, 2003), 23.

1. George W. Bush, "Remarks at Carl Harrison High School in Kennesaw, Georgia," February 20, 2003, in John Woolley and Gerhard Peters, eds., American Presidency Project, Document Archive, *www.presidency.ucsb.edu/ws/index.php?pid=147andst=iraqandst1=liberate*.

2. See, for example, George Packer, "The Liberal Quandary over Iraq," *New York Times Magazine*, December 8, 2002; and Thomas Cushman, ed., *A Matter of Principle: Humanitarian Arguments for War in Iraq* (Berkeley: University of California Press, 2005).

3. Fernando R. Tesón, "Ending Tyranny in Iraq," *Ethics and International Affairs* 19, no. 2, 2005, 8.

4. For varied estimates of the death toll that followed the 2003 US invasion, see the following: Iraq Family Health Survey Study Group, "Violence-Related Mortality in Iraq from 2002 to 2006," *New England Journal of Medicine* [online edition], January 31, 2008, *content.nejm.org/cgi/reprint/358/5/484.pdf*; Gilbert Burnham, Riyadh Lafta, Shannon Doucy, and Les Roberts, "Mortality after the 2003 Invasion of Iraq: A Cross-Sectional Cluster Sample Survey," *Lancet* 368, no. 9545, 2006, *www.thelancet.com/webfiles/images/journals/lancet/s0140673606694919.pdf*; and Opinion Research Business, "New Analysis 'Confirms' 1 Million Iraq Casualties," January 28, 2008, *www.globalresearch.ca/index.php?context=va&aid=7950*.

5. Jeffrey Sachs, *The End of Poverty: Economic Possibilities for Our Time* (New York: Penguin, 2005), 127.

6. Testimony of John Gilbert before the UK House of Commons Defence Committee,

June 20, 2000, paragraph 1086, *www.publications.parliament.uk/pa/cm199900/cmselect/ cmdfence/347/0062001.htm*. Quoted at greater length in Chapter 7.

7. Quoted from James Traub, "Their High Brow Hatred of Us," *New York Times Magazine*, October 30, 2005.

8. On the neoconservatives and the Bosnia conflict, see Chapters 5 and 6 of this study, as well as Albert Wohlstetter, "Bosnia as Future," in Zalmay Khalilzad, ed., *Lessons from Bosnia* (Santa Monica, Calif.: Rand Corporation, 1993). From the United Kingdom, neoconservative writers have been influential in promoting retrospectively benign views of the Bosnia/Kosovo interventions. See David Aaronovitch, "Why the Left Must Tackle the Crimes of Saddam," *Observer* (London), February 2, 2003; Nick Cohen, *What's Left? How Liberals Lost Their Way* (London: Fourth Estate, 2007); Oliver Kamm, *Anti-Totalitarianism: The Left-Wing Case for a Neoconservative Foreign Policy* (London: Social Affairs Unit, 2005); and Marko Hoare, "Chomsky's Genocidal Denial," *FrontPage Magazine*, November 23, 2005.

9. US Office of the President, "National Security Strategy of the United States," September 2002, see especially chap. 5, *www.whitehouse.gov/nsc/nss.pdf*.

10. Thomas Friedman, "A War for Oil?" *New York Times*, January 5, 2003.

11. David Buchan and Stephen Fidler, "An Uneasy Anniversary," *Financial Times*, April 23, 1999. See also Paul Latawski and Martin A. Smith, *The Kosovo Crisis and the Evolution of Post-Cold War European Security* (Manchester: Manchester University Press, 2003), 56–60.

12. Hubert Védrine, *Les Mondes de François Mitterrand: A l'Elysée, 1981–1995* (Paris: Fayard, 1996), 602. Translated from the French.

13. The supposed reluctance to intervene in Yugoslavia is frequently emphasized. See Samantha Power, *"A Problem from Hell": America and the Age of Genocide* (New York: HarperCollins, 2002), chaps. 9, 11, 12.

14. On the importance of "credibility" in US policy more generally, see Robert J. McMahon "Heisse Kriege im Kalten Krieg," in Bernd Greiner, Christian Müller, and Dierk Walter, eds., *Heisse Kriege im Kalten Krieg* (Hamburg: Hamburger Edition, 2006).

15. Andrew Bacevich, *The New American Militarism: How Americans Are Seduced by War* (New York: Oxford University Press, 2005), 19, 199.

16. And sometimes interventions are used as test cases to accomplish larger objectives. Regarding Bosnia as a test case to reaffirm NATO's credibility, see 1995 statements by Lee Hamilton in "Congressional Panel: US Troops in Bosnia," CNN, October 19, 1995.

17. Epigraph quote from Gil Scott-Heron, "Work for Peace," 1994, *lyricwiki.org/Gil_Scott-Heron:Work_For_Peace*.

18. I have evaluated the intellectual history of this concept in David N. Gibbs, "The 'Military-Industrial Complex,' Sectoral Conflict, and the Study of US Foreign Policy," in Ronald Cox, ed., *Business and the State in International Relations* (Boulder, Colo.: Westview, 1996).

19. Chalmers Johnson, *Blowback: The Costs and Consequences of American Empire* (New York: Metropolitan Books, 2000).

20. Alan Abelson, "Up and Down on Wall Street: Gun Boat Rally," *Barron's*, March 29, 1999, 3.

21. Tim Smart, "Count Corporate America among NATO's Staunchest Allies," *Washington Post*, April 13, 1999.

22. Madeleine Albright, *Madam Secretary: A Memoir* (New York: Miramax Books, 2003), 182. Albright's question was addressed to Colin Powell in 1993.

23. Bacevich, *New American Militarism,* 57.

24. Yet *Serb* atrocities committed in Kosovo during this early period were repeatedly condemned by Western journalists. See, for example, Robert McCartney, "Crackdown on Kosovo Riots Harms Yugoslavia's Unity," *Washington Post,* April 3, 1989.

25. It is true that the US ambassador to Croatia, Peter Galbraith, criticized the atrocities— but he made no serious effort to stop them.

26. Charles Krauthammer, "Ethnic Cleansing That's Convenient," *Washington Post,* August 11, 1995. For a similar view, see Gen. Rupert Smith, *The Utility of Force: The Art of War in the Modern World* (London: Allen Lane, 2005), 362.

27. Many writers minimize the Krajina atrocities. Thus Power's book barely mentions the 1995 Croat offensives. Power also describes Ambassador Peter Galbraith—who played a key role in orchestrating US support for the Croat offensives—as a hero and a passionate defender of human rights. During the Milošević trial, Galbraith himself denied that the Krajina Serbs had been ethnically cleansed. Brendan Simms's lengthy study gives Operation Storm and the resulting atrocities only the briefest discussion. And others acknowledge that the Krajina Serbs were ethnically cleansed, but they take a *positive* view of this action. Thus, NATO spokesperson Jamie Shea made the following statement in 1999, in response to a question from the press: "When you spoke about the Serbs who were driven from the Krajina, this is absolutely true. But . . . do not forget that there were many, many Croats who were persecuted and also driven from their homes in that part of the world, when the Yugoslav National Army moved there in 1991. Vukovar is obviously a testimony to that experience." Shea came close to endorsing the Krajina expulsions as justified revenge for previous Serb atrocities. Sources: Power, *"A Problem from Hell,"* 179–85, 412–18; Galbraith made his comments as a prosecution witness at the Milošević trial, International Criminal Tribunal for the Former Yugoslavia, June 25, 2003, 23113, *www.icty.org*; and Brendan Simms, *Unfinest Hour: Britain and the Destruction of Bosnia* (London: Allen Lane, 2001), 329. Shea's statements appear in "Special NATO Briefing from Brussels," Federal News Service, May 14, 1999.

28. See the full interview with Izetbegović in Chapter 5.

29. See interview with Harff in Chapter 5.

30. Regarding the dubious Operation Horseshoe, see Chapter 7. The Horseshoe allegations are cited uncritically in the following: Jon C. Pevehouse and Joshua S. Goldstein, "Serbian Compliance or Defiance in Kosovo? Statistical Analysis and Real-Time Predictions," *Journal of Conflict Resolution* 43, no. 4, 1999, 541–42; Power, *"A Problem from Hell,"* 449; and Peter Ronayne, "Genocide in Kosovo," *Human Rights Review* 5, no. 4, 2004, 63. These provide good examples of how propaganda can influence mainstream scholarship. In fairness to Pevehouse and Goldstein, their article appeared before Operation Horseshoe was discredited.

31. See details in Chapter 7. Sabrina Ramet advances the claim of relativism against all her academic adversaries: "On the one side [of the Yugoslavia debate] are those who have taken a moral universalist perspective, holding that there are universal norms in international politics. . . . On the other side are authors who reject the universalist framework . . . and who, in their accounts, embrace one or another version of moral relativism." Ramet, *Thinking about Yugoslavia: Scholarly Debates about the Yugoslav Breakup and the Wars in Bosnia and Kosovo* (Cambridge: Cambridge University Press,

2005), 1–2. Ramet confuses criticism of moral *double standards* with moral relativism; the two are not the same. For a similar misuse of the term "moral relativism," see Simms, *Unfinest Hour*, 308.

32. On death tolls for the Bosnian, Croatian, and Kosovar wars, see Tim Judah, "Milošević's Legacy of Discord," BBC News, March 11, 2006, *news.bbc.co.uk/2/hi/europe/4797564.stm*.

33. During the post-1989 period, the worst war in terms of lives lost was certainly not in Croatia, Bosnia, or Kosovo. The worst probably was the civil war in the Congo from 1997 to 2003, which killed approximately four million people. See Benjamin Coghlan et al., "Mortality in the Democratic Republic of the Congo: A Nationwide Survey," *Lancet* 367, no. 9504, 2006. Yet this conflict, inexplicably, received only a minute portion of the attention that was accorded the Balkan wars.

34. Quoted in Tariq Ali, "Introduction: After the War," in Ali, ed., *Masters of the Universe? NATO's Balkan Crusade* (London: Verso, 2000), xv–xvi.

35. "Iraqi Incubator Horror Story False," *Pediatrics* 91, no. 4, 1993; and Arthur Rowse, "How to Build Support for War," *Columbia Journalism Review*, September–October 1992.

36. German atrocities did occur in Belgium, and they included some 6,500 Belgian and French civilians killed; but the scale of these atrocities was greatly exaggerated by Allied war propaganda. Spanish atrocities in Cuba were even more substantial but, once again, they were exaggerated and inaccurately reported. On Cuba, see John Lawrence Tone, *War and Genocide in Cuba, 1895–1898* (Chapel Hill: University of North Carolina Press, 2006), chaps. 14, 16. The exaggeration of German atrocities during World War I is conceded (grudgingly) by Power in *"A Problem from Hell,"* 524.

37. I surveyed *New York Times* coverage over a nine-year time frame, 1991–1999, using the *New York Times* database, available through ProQuest. I selected the "Advanced Search" menu, and for search category 1, I selected "1" and "Page" for the entire time frame (1991–1999). For year 1991, I also used the search term "Yugoslavia" ("citation and abstract") for search category 2, and left search category 3 blank; for 1992, I used "Bosnia" OR "Yugoslavia" ("citation and abstract") for search categories 2 and 3; for 1993–1996, I used "Bosnia" OR "Croatia" ("citation and abstract") for search categories 2 and 3; and for 1997–1999, I used "Bosnia" OR "Kosovo" ("citation and abstract") for search categories 2 and 3. Search performed on September 27, 2007. I have checked each article title individually to confirm that it appeared on the front page of the first section of the paper, and that the article's main topic was Yugoslavia or one of its successor states.

38. Again using the ProQuest/*New York Times* database, I surveyed the period 1991–1999, to keep the time frame consistent with my previously noted survey regarding Yugoslavia. For search category 1, I selected "1" and "Page." For search categories 2, I selected "AIDS" ("citation and abstract"); and for search category 3, I selected "Africa" ("citation and abstract"). I checked each title individually and omitted hits that did not appear on the first page of the first section, or that did not focus primarily on AIDS in Africa. This produced a total of 13 hits for the nine-year period—just over 1 percent of the 1,020 hits for the Yugoslavia topics. Search on AIDS performed September 27, 2007.

39. The link between underdevelopment and political instability is argued in Paul Collier, "Economic Causes of Civil Conflict and Their Implications for Policy," World Bank, Development Research Group, June 15, 2000.

40. The economic aspects of the Rwanda case are discussed Michel Chossudovsky, *The*

Globalization of Poverty: Impacts of IMF and World Bank Reforms (London: Zed Books, 1997), chap. 5. See also Isaac Kamola, "The Global Coffee Economy and the Production of Genocide in Rwanda," *Third World Quarterly* 28, no. 3, 2007.

41.   A good distillation of the conventional wisdom on the Rwanda case appears in Power, *"A Problem from Hell,"* chap. 10.

42.   Dwight D. Eisenhower, " 'The Chance for Peace,' Delivered before the American Society of Newspaper Editors," April 16, 1953, in John Woolley and Gerhard Peters, eds., American Presidency Project, Document Archive, *www.presidency.ucsb.edu/ws/index.php?pid=9819andst=peaceandst1=*.

43.   Regarding the Iraq war, Joseph Stiglitz has estimated the long-term costs will reach $3 trillion. From US Congress, Testimony of Joseph Stiglitz before the Joint Economic Committee, February 28, 2008, *www2.gsb.columbia.edu/faculty/jstiglitz/download/papers/Stiglitz_testimony.pdf*. Regarding the cost of intervention in Yugoslavia, see Chapter 3 of this study, note 153.

44.   Jeffrey Sachs, "A Better Use of Our $87 Billion," *Boston Globe*, September 13, 2003.

45.   See Tariq Ali, "Afghanistan: Mirage of the Good War," *New Left Review*, no. 50, 2008.

Bibliography

Transcripts from the International Criminal Tribunal for the Former Yugoslavia (ICTY) *www.icty.org*

Witnesses for the Prosecution, Trial of Slobodan Milošević

Paddy Ashdown, March 14 and 15, 2002
Milan Babić, November 18–December 9, 2002
Patrick Ball, March 13, 2002
Gen. Wesley Clark, December 15 and 16, 2003
Peter Galbraith, June 25 and 26, 2003
Borisav Jović, November 18–20, 2003
Milan Kučan, May 21, 2003
Jeri Laber, December 10 and 11, 2002
Ante Marković, October 23, 2003, and January 15, 2004
Stjepan Mesić, October 2, 2002
Gen. Philippe Morillon, February 12, 2004
Gen. Klaus Naumann, June 13 and 14, 2002
Herbert Okun, February 27 and 28, 2003
David Owen, November 3 and 4, 2003
Wolfgang Petritsch, July 2, 2002
Helena Ranta, March 12, 2003
Ibrahim Rugova, May 3 and 6, 2002
Gen. Rupert Smith, October 9, 2003
Ewa Tabeau, October 7, 2003
Ratomir Tanić, May 14–16, 2002
Gen. Aleksander Vasiljević, February 6 and 12, 2003
William Walker, June 11 and 12, 2002

Witness for the Defense, Trial of Slobodan Milošević

James Jatras, September 8, 2004

Witness for the Defense, Trial of Duško Tadić

Robert M. Hayden, September 11, 1996

Articles of Indictment against Slobodan Milošević, Pertaining to Kosovo
Initial Indictment, May 24, 1999
First Amended Indictment, June 29, 2001
Second Amended Indictment, October 29, 2001

Judgment in the Case of Radislav Krstić
August 2, 2001

Newspapers, Magazines, and Media Sources (Select List)

Advertising Age
Aerospace Daily
American Journalism Review
Air Force Magazine
Aviation Week and Space Technology
The Banker
Barron's
BBC Summary of World Broadcasts
Blueprint
Bosnia Report
Bulletin of the Atomic Scientists
Business Week
Columbia Journalism Review
Defense and Foreign Affairs Strategic Policy
Department of State Dispatch
Deutsche Presse–Agentur
DOD News
East European Energy Report
Economic and Political Weekly
Eurobarometer
European Report
Federal Document Clearing House
Federal News Service
Flight International
Foreign Report
Frankfurter Allgemeine Zeitung
Frankfurter Rundschau

International Defense Review
Irish Times
Jane's Defense Weekly
Jane's Intelligence Review
Japan Times
Jerusalem Post
Journal of Commerce
Mideast Mirror
Le Monde
Le Monde de Renseignement
Le Monde Diplomatique
Navy Times
Norwegian Press Service
Le Nouvel Observateur
PR Newswire
Le Quotidien de Paris
Radio Free Europe/Radio Liberty Reports
Report on Eastern Europe
Review of International Affairs (Belgrade)
Russian Press Digest
Science
Der Spiegel
World Press Review
Yugoslav Daily Survey
Yugoslav Survey

Document Collections and Archives

Auerswald, Philip E., David P. Auerswald, and Christian Duttweiler, eds., *The Kosovo Conflict: A Diplomatic History through Documents* (Cambridge: Kluwer Law International, 2000).

Bethlehem, Daniel, and Marc Weller, eds., *The Yugoslav Crisis in International Law* (New York: Cambridge University Press, 1997).

Clinton Presidential Library, online public documents, *www.clintonlibrary.gov/archivesearch-advanced.html.*

Declassified Documents Reference System (Thomson-Gale databases).

Galbraith, Peter, ed., *The United States and Croatia: A Documentary History, 1992–1997* (Washington, D.C.: US Department of State, 1997). Obtained through Widener Library, Harvard University.

George H. W. Bush Presidential Library, College Station, Texas. Files consulted include White House and National Security Council collections. See especially FOIA Release no. 1998–0102-F ("Bosnia and the Former Yugoslavia"). A detailed breakdown of document categories is at: *bushlibrary.tamu.edu/research/pdfs/foia/1998-0102-F.html.*

Hill, Charles, ed., *The Papers of United Nations Secretary-General Boutros Boutros-Ghali*, 3 vols. (New Haven: Yale University Press, 2003).

Krieger, Heike, ed., *The Kosovo Conflict and International Law: An Analytical Documentation, 1974–1999* (Cambridge: Cambridge University Press, 2001).

Owen, David, ed., *Balkan Odyssey* [Academic Edition], CD-ROM document collection (Princeton: Electric Company, 1996).

Ramcharan, B. G., ed., *The International Conference on the Former Yugoslavia: Official Papers*, 2 vols. (The Hague: Kluwer Law International, 1997).

Simons, William B., ed., *Constitutions of the Communist World* (Alphen ann den Rijn, Netherlands: Sijthoff and Noordhoff, 1980).

Trifunovska, Snežana, ed., *Former Yugoslavia through Documents: From Its Dissolution to the Peace Settlement* (The Hague: Martinus Nijhoff, 1999).

———, *Yugoslavia through Documents: From Its Creation to Its Dissolution* (Dortrecht, Netherlands: Martinus Nijhoff, 1994).

Troebst, Stefan, *Conflict in Kosovo: Failure of Prevention? An Analytical Documentation, 1992–1998* (Flensburg, Germany: European Centre for Minority Issues, 1998).

United Nations, Official Document System, *www.un.org/documents/.*

Weller, Marc, ed., *The Crisis in Kosovo, 1989–1999* (Cambridge: Documents and Analysis Publishing, 1999).

Woolley, John, and Gerhard Peters, eds., American Presidency Project, Document Archive, *www.presidency.ucsb.edu/ws.*

Yearman, Keith, ed., "The Conoco-Somalia Declassification Project," *www.cod.edu/people/faculty/yearman/somalia.htm.*

Reports by Governments, International Organizations, and Non-Governmental Organizations

Amnesty International, "Croatia: Impunity for Killings after Storm," August 1, 1998, *web. amnesty.org/library/Index/ENGEUR640041998?openandof=ENG-2EU.*

Amnesty International Report, 1993 (London: Amnesty International Publications, 1993).

Amnesty International Report, 1994 (London: Amnesty International Publications, 1994).

Amnesty International Report, 1995 (London: Amnesty International Publications, 1995).

Ball, Patrick, "Policy or Panic? The Flight of Ethnic Albanians from Kosovo, March–May

1999," American Association for the Advancement of Science, 2000, *shr.aaas.org/kosovo/policyorpanic/*.

Center for Strategic and Budgetary Assessments, "After the War: Kosovo Peacekeeping Costs," June 7, 1999, *www.csbaonline.org*.

———, "Total Cost of Allied Force Air Campaign: Preliminary Estimate," June 10, 1999, *www.csbaonline.org*.

Collier, Paul, "Economic Causes of Civil Conflict and Their Implications for Policy," World Bank, Development Research Group, June 15, 2000.

European Parliament, "Draft Report: On the Alleged Use of European Countries by the CIA for the Transportation and Illegal Detention of Prisoners," November 24, 2006, *abcnews.go.com/images/International/european_report2_clean.pdf*.

Freedom House, "Country Reports: Yugoslavia (Serbia and Montenegro)," in *Freedom in the World: The Annual Survey of Political Rights and Civil Liberties, 1998–1999* (New Brunswick, N.J.: Transaction Publishers, 1999).

Human Rights Watch, "Civilian Deaths in the NATO Air Campaign," February 2000, *www.hrw.org/reports/2000/nato/*.

———, "Under Orders: War Crimes in Kosovo," 2001, *www.hrw.org/reports/2001/kosovo/*.

———, "Yugoslav Government War Crimes at Račak," 1999, *www.hrw.org/campaigns/kosovo98/racak.shtml*.

Independent International Commission on Kosovo [IICK], *Kosovo Report: Conflict, International Response, Lessons Learned* (Oxford: Oxford University Press, 2000).

International Court of Justice, "Application of the Convention on the Prevention and Punishment of the Crime of Genocide (Bosnia and Herzegovina v. Serbia and Montenegro), Final Judgment of 26 February, 2007," *www.icj-cij.org/docket/files/91/13685.pdf*.

———, "Case Concerning the Frontier Dispute (Burkina Faso and Republic of Mali)," December 22, 1986.

International Helsinki Federation for Human Rights, "Report to the OSCE: The International Helsinki Federation for Human Rights Fact-Finding Mission to the Krajina, 17–19 August 1995," Vienna, August 25, 1995, *www.ihf-hr.org/*.

Netherlands Institute for War Documentation [NIOD], "Srebrenica—A 'Safe' Area: Reconstruction, Background, Consequences, and Analyses of the Fall of a Safe Area," 2003, *srebrenica.brightside.nl/srebrenica/*. Independent analysis commissioned by the government of the Netherlands.

North Atlantic Treaty Organization, "The Alliance's Strategic Concept Approved by the Heads of State and Government Participating in the Meeting of the North Atlantic Council in Washington D.C. on 23rd and 24th April 1999," *www.fas.org/man/nato/natodocs/99042411.htm*.

Organization for Security and Cooperation in Europe [OSCE], "Kosovo/Kosova, As Seen, As Told: An Analysis of the Human Rights Findings of the OSCE Kosovo Verification Mission," 1999, *www.osce.org/item/17755.html*.

Organization of American States, "Charter of the Organization of American States," as amended, 1997, *www.oas.org/juridico/English/charter.html#ch4*.

Sloan, Stanley, "US-West European Relations and Europe's Future," in Glennon J. Harrison, ed., *Europe and the United States: Competition and Cooperation in the 1990s* (Armonk, N.Y.: M.E. Sharpe, 1994). Study submitted to the US Congressional Committee on Foreign Affairs.

UK House of Commons [UKHOC], "Foreign Affairs, Fourth Report: Kosovo," May 23, 2000, *www.publications.parliament.uk/pa/cm199900/cmselect/cmfaff/28/2802.htm*.

———, "Kosovo: Operation 'Allied Force,'" Research Paper 99/48, April 29, 1999, *www.parliament.uk/commons/lib/research/rp99/rp99-048.pdf*.

———, Testimony by Defense Minister of State Lord John Gilbert, before the parliamentary Defence Committee, June 20, 2000, *www.publications.parliament.uk/pa/cm199900/cmselect/cmdfence/347/0062001.htm*.

———, Testimony by Defence Secretary George Robertson before the Select Committee on Defence, March 24, 1999, *www.parliament.the-stationery-office.co.uk/pa/cm199899/cmselect/cmdfence/39/9032403.htm*.

United Nations, *The Blue Helmets: A Review of United Nations Peacekeeping* (New York: United Nations, Department of Public Information, 1996).

———, "Convention on the Prevention and Punishment of the Crime of Genocide, Adopted by Resolution 260 (III) A of the United Nations General Assembly on 9 December 1948," *www.un.org/millennium/law/iv-1.htm*.

———, "Report on the Historical Background of the Civil War in the Former Yugoslavia: United Nations Commission of Experts, Security Council Resolution 780 (1992), Professor M. Cherif Bassiouni, Chairman," March 1994.

———, *The United Nations and Somalia, 1992–1996* (New York: United Nations Department of Public Information, 1996).

US Central Intelligence Agency [USCIA], *Balkan Battlegrounds: A Military History of the Yugoslav Conflict, 1990–1995*. 2 vols. (Washington, D.C.: CIA Office of Russian and European Analysis, 2002).

US Congress, *The Betrayal of Srebrenica: Why Did the Massacre Happen? Will It Happen Again?* (Washington, D.C.: US Government Printing Office, 1998).

———, *Genocide in Bosnia-Herzegovina* (Washington, D.C.: US Government Printing Office, 1995).

———, *Human Rights, Refugees, and War Crimes: The Prospects for Peace in Bosnia* (Washington, D.C.: US Government Printing Office, 1995).

———, *Quota Increase of the International Monetary Fund* (Washington, D.C.: US Government Printing Office, 1991).

———, Testimony of James Baker before the House International Relations Committee, Federal News Service, January 12, 1995.

———, Prepared Statement of John R. Bolton, Senior Vice President, American Enterprise Institute, before the House Committee on International Relations, Federal News Service, November 10, 1999.

———, Testimony of Joseph Stiglitz before the Joint Economic Committee, February 28, 2008, *www2.gsb.columbia.edu/faculty/jstiglitz/download/papers/Stiglitz_testimony.pdf*.

———, *The Use of Force in the Post–Cold War Era* (Washington, D.C.: US Government Printing Office, 1993).

US Congressional Research Service, "Bosnia and the European Union Military Force (EUFOR): Post-NATO Peacekeeping," December 5, 2006, *www.fas.org/sgp/crs/row/RS21774.pdf*.

———, "Kosovo: Lessons Learned from Operation Allied Force," November 19, 1999, *www.au.af.mil/au/awc/awcgate/crs/rl30374.pdf*.

———, "Terrorism and National Security: Issues and Trends," December 21, 2004, *www.fas.org/irp/crs/IB10119.pdf*.

US Department of Defense, *United States–Vietnam Relations, 1945–1967* (Washington, D.C.: US Government Printing Office, 1971).

US Department of State [USDOS], "The Road to Dayton: US Diplomacy and the Bosnia Peace Process," 1997 (declassified 2003). This report is a nine-chapter internal study of the processes that led to the 1995 Dayton Accords, as compiled by State Department staff. The National Security Archive has digitized the whole document: *www.gwu.edu/~nsarchiv/NSAEBB/NSAEBB171/index.htm*.

US General Accounting Office, "Bosnia: Operational Decisions Needed before Estimating DOD's Costs," February 1998, *www.fas.org/man/gao/nsiad98077.htm*.

US Office of the President, "The National Security Strategy of the United States of America," September 2002, *www.whitehouse.gov/nsc/nss.pdf*.

US Senate, *US Actions Regarding Iranian and Other Arms Transfers to the Bosnian Army, 1994–1995* (Washington, D.C.: US Government Printing Office, 1996), *www.fas.org/irp/congress/1996_rpt/bosnia.htm*.

Memoirs, Diaries, and Accounts by Participants

Ahrens, Geert-Hinrich, *Diplomacy on the Edge: Containment of Ethnic Conflict and the Minorities Working Group of the Conferences on Yugoslavia* (Baltimore: Johns Hopkins University Press, 2007). Ahrens was a German diplomat, with extensive Yugoslav experience.

Albright, Madeleine, *Madam Secretary: A Memoir* (New York: Miramax Books, 2003).

Ashdown, Paddy, *Swords and Ploughshares: Bringing Peace to the Twenty-First Century* (London: Weidenfeld and Nicolson, 2007). As a member of the British parliament, Lord Ashdown was involved in the diplomacy of both the Bosnia and Kosovo wars.

Asmus, Ronald, *Opening NATO's Door: How the Alliance Remade Itself for the New Era* (New York: Columbia University Press, 2002). Asmus was the deputy assistant secretary of state for European affairs during the Clinton administration, and he worked on US policy vis-à-vis NATO.

Baker, James A., III, *The Politics of Diplomacy: Revolution, War, and Peace, 1989–1992* (New York: Putnam, 1995). Baker was secretary of state under George H. W. Bush.

Bell, Martin, *In Harm's Way: Reflections of a War Zone Thug* (London: Penguin, 1996). Bell was a BBC correspondent in Bosnia-Herzegovina.

Biden, Sen. Joseph, *Promises to Keep: On Life and Politics* (New York: Random House, 2007).

Bildt, Carl, *Peace Journey: The Struggle for Peace in Bosnia* (London: Weidenfeld and Nicolson, 1998). Bildt was an EU mediator in Bosnia and a Swedish prime minister.

Bissett, James, "Balkan War, Balkan Peace, Balkan Future?" no date, *www.deltax.net/bissett/western.htm*. Bissett was the Canadian ambassador to Yugoslavia at the time of breakup.

———, "Scapegoat, RIP," *National Post*, March 15, 2006.

Blumenthal, Sidney, *The Clinton Wars* (New York: Farrar, Straus, and Giroux, 2003). Blumenthal was a presidential advisor.

Both, Norbert, *From Indifference to Entrapment: The Netherlands and the Yugoslav Crisis, 1990–1995* (Amsterdam: Amsterdam University Press, 2000). Both worked as an assistant to EC/EU mediator David Owen.

Boutros-Ghali, Boutros, *Unvanquished: A US-UN Saga* (New York: Random House, 1999). Boutros-Ghali was UN secretary-general during the Bosnia war.

Boyd, Gen. Charles G., "Making Bosnia Work," *Foreign Affairs* 77, no. 1, 1998. Boyd was an air force general who served as deputy chief of the US European Command in 1995.

————, "Making Peace with the Guilty: The Truth about Bosnia," *Foreign Affairs* 74, no. 5, 1995.

Brown, Michael Barratt, *From Tito to Milošević: Yugoslavia, the Lost Country* (London: Merlin, 2005). Brown worked as a UN official in the Balkans during the 1940s.

Bush, George H. W., and Brent Scowcroft, *A World Transformed* (New York: Knopf, 1998).

Campbell, Alastair, *The Blair Years: The Alastair Campbell Diaries* (New York: Knopf, 2007). Campbell was press spokesperson for Tony Blair.

Carter, Ashton B., and William J. Perry, *Preventive Defense: A New Security Strategy for America* (Washington, D.C.: Brookings, 1999). Carter served as assistant secretary of defense for international security policy during the Bosnia war; Perry served as deputy secretary of defense and then as secretary of defense.

Carter, Jimmy, *Beyond the White House: Waging Peace, Fighting Disease, Building Hope* (New York: Simon and Schuster, 2007). Carter worked with the Contact Group to broker a five-month cease-fire in Bosnia during 1994–1995.

Chenu, Georges-Marie, preface to Renéo Lukic, *L'Agonie Yougoslave (1986–2003): Les Etats-Unis et l'Europe Face aux Guerres Balkaniques* (Québec: Presse de l'Université de Laval, 2003). Chenu served as the first French ambassador to independent Croatia.

Christopher, Warren, *Chances of a Lifetime: A Memoir* (New York: Scribner, 2001). Christopher was Clinton's first secretary of state.

————, *In the Stream of History: Shaping Foreign Policy for a New Era* (Palo Alto, Calif.: Stanford University Press, 1998).

Clark, Gen. Wesley, "The United States and NATO: The Way Ahead," *Parameters: Journal of the US Army War College* 29, no. 4, 1999–2000. Clark served as NATO commander during the Kosovo war.

————, *Waging Modern War: Bosnia, Kosovo, and the Future of Combat* (New York: Public Affairs, 2002).

Clinton, Bill, *My Life* (New York: Knopf, 2004).

Clinton, Hillary Rodham, *Living History* (New York: Simon and Schuster, 2003).

Corwin, Phillip, *Dubious Mandate: A Memoir of the UN in Bosnia, Summer 1995* (Durham, N.C.: Duke University Press, 1999). Corwin was a senior civilian official with the UN force in Bosnia.

Daalder, Ivo H., *Getting to Dayton: The Making of America's Bosnia Policy* (Washington, D.C.: Brookings, 2000). Daalder served on the National Security Council staff at the time of the Dayton conference.

Delors, Jacques, "European Integration and Security," *Survival* 33, no. 2, 1991. Delors was president of the EC Commission.

Drnovšek, Janez, "Riding the Tiger," *World Policy Journal* 17, no. 1, 2000. Drnovšek was a Slovenian representative to Yugoslavia's federal presidency, 1989–1990.

Eagleburger, Lawrence S., "NATO in a Corner," *New York Times*, April 4, 1999. Eagleburger was a State Department official and, briefly, secretary of state during the George H. W. Bush presidency.

Galbraith, Peter, "Negotiating Peace in Croatia: A Personal Account of the Road to Erdut," in Brad K. Blitz, ed., *War and Change in the Balkans: Nationalism, Conflict, and Cooperation* (New York: Cambridge University Press, 2006). Galbraith was the first US ambassador to Croatia.

Gates, Robert M., *From the Shadows: The Ultimate Insider's Story of Five Presidents and How They Won the Cold War* (New York: Simon and Schuster, 1996). Gates was CIA director during the George H. W. Bush presidency.

Genscher, Hans-Dietrich, *Rebuilding a House Divided: A Memoir by the Architect of Germany's Reunification* (New York: Broadway Books, 1998). Genscher was Germany's foreign minister.

Glitman, Maynard, "US Policy in Bosnia: Rethinking a Flawed Approach," *Survival* 38, no. 4, 1996–97. Glitman was the US ambassador to Belgium at the time of Yugoslavia's breakup.

Goldgeier, James M., *Not Whether but When: The US Decision to Enlarge NATO* (Washington, D.C.: Brookings, 1999). Goldgeier served in both the State Department and the National Security Council during the Clinton presidency.

Gompert, David C., "How to Defeat Serbia," *Foreign Affairs* 77, no. 4, 1994. Gompert served on the National Security Council during the George H. W. Bush presidency.

———, "The United States and Yugoslavia's Wars," in Richard Ullman, ed., *The World and Yugoslavia's Wars* (New York: Council on Foreign Relations, 1996).

Goulding, Marrack, *Peacemonger* (Baltimore: Johns Hopkins University Press, 2003). Goulding was the overall director of UN peacekeeping during the early phases of the Yugoslav war.

Holbrooke, Richard, *To End a War* (New York: Random House, 1998). Holbrooke served as assistant secretary of state for European and Canadian affairs, and he directed the 1995 Dayton conference.

Hurd, Douglas, *Memoirs* (London: Little, Brown, 2003). Hurd served as British foreign minister during the early phases of Yugoslavia's breakup.

Hutchings, Robert L., *American Diplomacy and the End of the Cold War: An Insider's Account of US Policy in Europe, 1989–1992* (Baltimore: Johns Hopkins University Press, 1997). Hutchings served on the National Security Council staff during the George H. W. Bush administration.

Izetbegović, Alija, *Inescapable Questions: Autobiographical Notes* (Leicester, UK: Islamic Foundation, 2003). Izetbegović was president of Bosnia-Herzegovina.

———, *Islam between East and West* (Indianapolis: American Trust Publications, 1993).

———, *The Islamic Declaration*, unpublished ms, 1970. Obtained from the University of Washington Library.

Jackson, Gen. Mike, *Soldier: The Autobiography of General Sir Mike Jackson* (London: Bantam Press, 2007). Jackson was a British officer who worked under NATO command during the Kosovo war.

Janša, Janez, *The Making of the Slovenian State, 1988–1992: The Collapse of Yugoslavia* (Ljubljana: Založba Mladinska Knjiga, 1994). Janša was the Slovene defense minister at the time of secession.

Kenney, George, "The Bosnia Calculation," *New York Times Magazine*, May 14, 1995. Kenney headed the State Department's Yugoslavia desk at the time of the country's breakup.

King, Iain, and Whit Mason, *Peace at any Price: How the World Failed Kosovo* (Ithaca: Cornell University Press, 2006). Both King and Mason served in Kosovo with the multinational peacekeeping forces after the NATO bombing campaign.

Kouchner, Bernard, *Les Guerriers de la Paix: Du Kosovo à l'Irak* (Paris: Grasset, 2004). During the Bosnia war, Kouchner held several positions in the French government.

Lafontaine, Oskar, *Das Herz Schlägt Links* (Munich: Econ, 1999). Lafontaine, the German finance minister, left the government shortly before the Kosovo war began.

Lake, Anthony, *Six Nightmares: Real Threats in a Dangerous World and How America Can Meet Them* (Boston: Little, Brown, 2000). Lake was Clinton's first national security advisor.

Lévy, Bernard-Henri, *Le Lys et la Cedre: Journal d'un Ecrivain au Temps de la Guerre de Bosnie*

(Paris: Grasset, 1996). Lévy traveled to Bosnia and wrote extensively in favor of Western intervention.

Libal, Michael, *Limits of Persuasion: Germany and the Yugoslav Crisis, 1991–1992* (Westport, Conn.: Praeger, 1997). Libal was an official in the West German Foreign Ministry during the period of Yugoslavia's breakup.

MacKenzie, Maj. Gen. Lewis, *Peacekeeper: The Road to Sarajevo* (Vancouver: Douglas and McIntyre, 1993). MacKenzie, a Canadian national, served with UN forces in Bosnia.

Major, John, *John Major: The Autobiography* (London: HarperCollins, 1999).

Marković, Mira [Mirjana], *Night and Day: A Diary, December 1992–July 1994* (Kingston, Ont.: Quarry Press, 1996). Marković was Milošević's wife.

Mesić, Stipe [Stjepan], *The Demise of Yugoslavia: A Political Memoir* (Budapest: Central European University Press, 2004). Mesić served as president of Yugoslavia during the early phases of the breakup.

Moral Combat: NATO at War, March 12, 2000, BBC documentary, directed by Allan Little. Includes interviews with Gen. Klaus Naumann, James Rubin, Lieut. Gen. Michael Short, Hashim Thaçi, Madeleine Albright, Richard Holbrooke, Robin Cook, William Walker, and Gen. Wesley Clark. Transcript at: *news.bbc.co.uk/hi/english/static/events/panorama/transcripts/transcript_12_03_00.txt*.

Morillon, Gen. Philippe, *Croire et Oser: Chronique de Sarajevo* (Paris: Bernard Grasset, 1993). Morillon was a French general assigned to the UN peacekeeping force in Bosnia.

Morris, Dick, *Because He Could* (New York: Regan Books, 2004). Morris served as a political advisor to President Clinton.

———, *Behind the Oval Office: Winning the Presidency in the Nineties* (New York: Random House, 1997).

Nambiar, Lieut. Gen. Satish, "NATO Celebrates Its Fiftieth Anniversary by Destroying Yugoslavia," *Mediterranean Quarterly* 10, no. 3, 1999. Nambiar was an Indian general with the UN peacekeeping force in Bosnia.

Neville-Jones, Pauline, "Dayton, IFOR, and Alliance Relations in Bosnia," *Survival* 38, no. 4, 1996–1997. Neville-Jones was a senior British diplomat and a participant in the 1995 Dayton conference.

Norris, John, *Collision Course: NATO, Russia, and Kosovo* (Westport, Conn.: Praeger, 2005). Norris was a State Department official during the Kosovo war.

Owen, David, *Balkan Odyssey: An Uncompromising Personal Account of the International Peace Efforts Following the Breakup of the Former Yugoslavia* (Orlando, Fla.: Harcourt, Brace, 1995). Owen, a former British foreign minister, was the chief EU mediator during the Balkan conflict.

Parrington, Alan J., "Clinton Had a Chance to Avoid Kosovo Bombing," *Colorado Springs Gazette*, October 12, 2000, *www.commondreams.org/views/101300-107.htm*. Parrington was an air force colonel and a military attaché at the US Embassy in London during the Kosovo war.

Pérez de Cuéllar, Javier, *Pilgrimage for Peace: A Secretary-General's Memoir* (New York: St. Martin's, 1997).

Powell, Gen. Colin L., *My American Journey* (New York: Random House, 1995).

Rose, Lieut. Gen. Michael, *Fighting for Peace: Bosnia 1994* (London: Harvill Press, 1998). Rose served with UN peacekeeping forces in Bosnia.

Rubin, James P., "The Promise of Freedom: A Very Personal War, Part II," *Financial Times*, October 7, 2000. Rubin was the State Department press spokesperson during the Kosovo war.

———, "A Very Personal War [Part I]," *Financial Times*, September 30, 2000.

Rudman, George, "Backtracking to Reformulate: Establishing the Bosnian Federation," *International Negotiation* 1, no. 3, 1996. Rudman served as a translator for the Croatian delegation during the negotiations that led to the 1994 Muslim-Croat Federation.

Sachs, Jeffrey D., *The End of Poverty: Economic Possibilities for Our Time* (New York: Penguin, 2005). Sachs worked as an economic advisor to the Yugoslav central government and then to the Republic of Slovenia.

Schindler, John R., *Unholy Terror: Bosnia, Al-Qaeda, and the Rise of Global Jihad* (Osceola, Wis.: Zenith Press, 2007). Schindler worked as a Balkan specialist at the US National Security Agency.

Sell, Louis, *Slobodan Milošević and the Destruction of Yugoslavia* (Durham, N.C.: Duke University Press, 2002). Sell was a diplomat at the US Embassy in Belgrade, during the Yugoslav breakup.

Shattuck, John, *Freedom on Fire: Human Rights Wars and America's Response* (Cambridge, Mass.: Harvard University Press, 2003). Shattuck served as Clinton's assistant secretary of state for democracy, human rights, and labor.

Shea, Jamie, "NATO—Upholding Ethics in International Security Policy," *Cambridge Review of International Affairs* 15, no. 1, 2002. Shea was the NATO press spokesperson during the Kosovo war.

Smith, General Sir Rupert, *The Utility of Force: The Art of War in the Modern World* (London: Allen Lane, 2005). Smith commanded UN peacekeeping forces in Bosnia and served as deputy NATO commander during the Kosovo war.

Solana, Javier, "NATO's Success in Kosovo," *Foreign Affairs* 78, no. 6, 1999. Solana was the NATO secretary-general during the Kosovo war.

Steinberg, James B., "A Perfect Polemic: Blind to Reality on Kosovo," *Foreign Affairs* 78, no. 6, 1999. Steinberg was deputy national security advisor to President Clinton during the Kosovo war.

Stephanopoulos, George, *All Too Human: A Political Education* (Boston: Little, Brown, 1999). Stephanopoulos served as a political advisor to President Clinton.

Talbott, Strobe, *The Russia Hand: A Memoir of Presidential Diplomacy* (New York: Random House, 2002). Talbott was a State Department official during the Bosnia and Kosovo wars.

Tenet, George, *At the Center of the Storm: My Years at the CIA* (New York: HarperCollins, 2007). Tenet was CIA director toward the end of the Clinton presidency.

Tomac, Zdravko, *The Struggle for the Croatian State: Through Hell to Democracy* (Zagreb: Prokifon, 1993). Tomac was a Croatian nationalist politician and a member of Tudjman's government.

Védrine, Hubert, *Les Mondes de François Mitterrand: A l'Elysée, 1981–1995* (Paris: Fayard, 1996). Védrine was an advisor to the French president.

Weller, Marc, "The Rambouillet Conference on Kosovo," *International Affairs* 75, no. 2, 1999. Weller served as an advisor to the Albanian delegation at Rambouillet.

Yugoslavia: The Avoidable War, documentary film, directed by George Bogdanich, 2002. Includes filmed interviews with Peter Carrington, James Baker, George Kenney, Lawrence Eagleburger, Gen. Charles G. Boyd, and Hans-Dietrich Genscher.

Zelikow, Philip, and Condoleezza Rice, *Germany Unified and Europe Transformed: A Study in Statecraft* (Cambridge, Mass.: Harvard University Press, 1995). Zelikow and Rice served on the National Security Council during the George H. W. Bush presidency.

Zimmermann, Warren, "The Last Ambassador: A Memoir on the Collapse of Yugoslavia," *Foreign Affairs* 74, no. 2, 1995.

———, *Origins of a Catastrophe: Yugoslavia and Its Destroyers—America's Last Ambassador Tells What Happened and Why* (New York: Times Books, 1996).

Zulfikarpašić, Adil, Milovan Djilas, and Nadeža Gaće, *The Bosniak* (London: Hurst, 1998). Zulfikarpašić was a cofounder of the Party of Democratic Action in Bosnia-Herzegovina.

Secondary Sources

Adeli, Lisa, "From Jasenovac to Yugoslavism: Ethnic Persecution in Croatia during World War II," PhD thesis, Department of History, University of Arizona, 2004.

Aho, C. Michael, " 'Fortress Europe': Will the EU Isolate Itself from North America and Asia?" *Columbia Journal of World Business* 29, no. 3, 1994.

Ali, Rabia, and Lawrence Lifschultz, "Why Bosnia?" *Monthly Review* 45, no. 10, 1994.

Ali, Tariq, "Afghanistan: Mirage of the Good War," *New Left Review*, no. 50, 2008.

———, "Introduction: After the War," in Ali, ed., *Masters of the Universe? NATO's Balkan Crusade* (London: Verso, 2000).

Allcock, John B., *Explaining Yugoslavia* (London: Hurst, 2000).

Allen, Beverly, *Rape Warfare: The Hidden Genocide in Bosnia-Herzegovina and Croatia* (Minneapolis: University of Minnesota Press, 1996).

Alonzo-Maizlish, David, "In Whole or in Part: Group Rights, the Intent Element of Genocide, and the 'Quantitative Criterion,' " *New York University Law Review* 77, no. 5, 2002.

Andreas, Peter, "The Clandestine Political Economy of War and Peace in Bosnia," *International Studies Quarterly* 48, no. 1, 2004.

Anzulovic, Branimir, *Heavenly Serbia: From Myth to Genocide* (New York: New York University Press, 1999).

Bacevich, Andrew J., *The New American Militarism: How Americans Are Seduced by War* (New York: Oxford University Press, 2005).

Balassa, Bela, and Trent J, Bertrand, "Growth Performance of Eastern European Economies and Comparable Western European Countries," *American Economic Review* 60, no. 2, 1970.

Bamford, James, *Body of Secrets: Anatomy of the Ultra-Secret National Security Agency from the Cold War through the Dawn of a New Century* (New York: Doubleday, 2001).

Bamyeh, Mohammed A., "The New Imperialism: Six Theses," *Social Text* 18, no. 1, 2000.

Banac, Ivo, "Historiography of the Countries of Eastern Europe: Yugoslavia," *American Historical Review* 97, no. 4, 1992.

———, *The National Question in Yugoslavia: Origins, History, Politics* (Ithaca: Cornell University Press, 1988).

———, "Yugoslavia," in Joel Krieger, ed., *Oxford Companion to Politics of the World* (New York: Oxford University Press, 1993).

Barnes, Trevor, "The Secret Cold War: The CIA and American Foreign Policy in Europe, 1946–1956, Part I," *Historical Journal* 24, no. 2, 1981.

———, "The Secret Cold War: The CIA and American Foreign Policy in Europe, 1946–1956, Part II," *Historical Journal* 25, no. 3, 1982.

Barry, Charles, "Combined Joint Task Forces in Theory and Practice," in Philip H. Gordon, ed., *NATO's Transformation: The Changing Shape of the Atlantic Alliance* (Lanham, Md.: Rowman and Littlefield, 1997).

Bass, Gary Jonathan, *Stay the Hand of Vengeance: The Politics of War Crimes Tribunals* (Princeton: Princeton University Press, 2000).

Bellamy, Alex J., *Kosovo and International Society* (New York: Palgrave Macmillan, 2002).

Berman, Paul, *Power and the Idealists: The Passion of Joschka Fischer and Its Aftermath* (Brooklyn: Soft Skull Press, 2005).

Bergsten, C. Fred, "America and Europe: Clash of the Titans?" *Foreign Affairs* 78, no. 2, 1999.

Betts, Richard K., "The Delusion of Impartial Intervention," *Foreign Affairs* 73, no. 6, 1994.

Binder, David, "A Balkan Balance Sheet," *Mediterranean Quarterly* 11, no. 1, 2000.

———, "The Role of the United States in the Krajina Issue," *Mediterranean Quarterly* 8, no. 4, 1997.

———, "Thoughts on United States Policy towards Yugoslavia," *South Slav Journal* 16, nos. 61–62, 1995.

Bingham, Laura, "Strategy or Process? Closing the International Criminal Tribunals for the Former Yugoslavia and Rwanda," *Berkeley Journal of International Law* 24, no. 3, 2006.

Blum, William, *Killing Hope: US Military and CIA Interventions since World War II* (Monroe, Me.: Common Courage Press, 2003).

Bose, Sumantra, *Bosnia after Dayton: Nationalist Partition and International Intervention* (New York: Oxford University Press, 2002).

Botev, Nikolai, "Where East Meets West: Ethnic Intermarriage in the Former Yugoslavia, 1962 to 1989," *American Sociological Review* 59, no. 3, 1994.

Bougarel, Xavier, *Bosnie: Anatomie d'un Conflit* (Paris: La Découverte, 1996).

Brands, H. W., *The Devil We Knew: Americans and the Cold War* (New York: Oxford University Press, 1993).

Brayton, Steven, "Outsourcing War: Mercenaries and the Privatization of Peacekeeping," *Journal of International Affairs* 55, no. 2, 2002.

Bricmont, Jean, *Humanitarian Imperialism: Using Human Rights to Sell War* (New York: Monthly Review Press, 2006).

Brock, Peter, *Media Cleansing, Dirty Reporting: Journalism and Tragedy in Yugoslavia* (Los Angeles: GM Books, 2005).

Brown, Michael Barratt, "The Role of Economic Factors in Social Crisis: The Case of Yugoslavia," *New Political Economy* 2, no. 2, 1997.

Buchanan, Allen, "Reforming the International Law of Humanitarian Intervention," in J. L. Holzgrefe and Robert Keohane, eds., *Humanitarian Intervention: Ethical, Legal, and Political Dilemmas* (Cambridge: Cambridge University Press, 2003).

Burg, Steven L., and Michael L. Berbaum, "Community, Integration, and Stability in Multinational Yugoslavia," *American Political Science Review* 83, no. 2, 1989.

Burg, Steven L., and Paul S. Shoup, *The War in BosniaHerzegovina: Ethnic Conflict and International Intervention* (Armonk, N.Y.: M. E. Sharp, 1999).

Burnham, Gilbert, Riyadh Lafta, Shannon Doucy, and Les Roberts, "Mortality after the 2003 Invasion of Iraq: A Cross-Sectional Cluster Sample Survey," *Lancet* 368, no. 9545, 2006, *www.thelancet.com/webfiles/images/journals/lancet/s0140673606694919.pdf.*

Burt, Wayne, *The Reluctant Superpower: United States' Policy in Bosnia, 1991–95* (New York: St. Martin's, 1997).

Butler, Maj. Gen. Smedley, *War Is a Racket: The Anti-War Classic by America's Most Decorated General* (Los Angeles: Feral House, 2003).

Buzzanco, Robert, "What Happened to the New Left? Toward a Radical Reading of American Foreign Relations," *Diplomatic History* 23, no. 4, 1999.

Calleo, David P., "Restarting the Marxist Clock? The Economic Fragility of the West," *World Policy Journal* 13, no. 2, 1996.

Campbell, Tom, "Kosovo: An Unconstitutional War," *Mediterranean Quarterly* 11, no. 1, 2000.

Caplan, Richard, *Europe and the Recognition of New States in Yugoslavia* (Cambridge: Cambridge University Press, 2005).

Carpenter, R. Charli, "Surfacing Children: Limitations of Genocidal Rape Discourse," *Human Rights Quarterly* 22, no. 2, 2000.

Carpenter, Ted Galen, "Foreign Policy Masochism: The Campaign for US Intervention in Yugoslavia," Cato Foreign Policy Briefing Paper 19 (Washington, D.C.: Cato Institute, 1992), *www.cato.org/pub_display.php?pub_id=1544*.

———, *A Search for Enemies: America's Alliances after the Cold War* (Washington, D.C.: Cato Institute, 1992).

Carr, E. H., *The Twenty Years' Crisis, 1919–1939: An Introduction to the Study of International Relations* (New York: Harper and Row, 1964).

Chalmers, Malcolm, and Lutz Unterseher, "Is There a Tank Gap? Comparing NATO and Warsaw Pact Tank Fleets," *International Security* 13, no. 1, 1988.

Chandler, David, *Bosnia: Faking Democracy after Dayton* (London: Pluto, 2000).

———, *From Kosovo to Kabul: Human Rights and International Intervention* (London: Pluto, 2002).

Chollet, Derek, *The Road to the Dayton Accords: A Study of American Statecraft* (New York: Palgrave Macmillan, 2005).

Chomsky, Noam, *The New Military Humanism: Lessons from Kosovo* (Monroe, Me.: Common Courage Press, 1999).

Chossudovsky, Michel, *The Globalization of Poverty: Impacts of IMF and World Bank Reforms* (London: Zed, 1997).

Chua, Amy *World on Fire: How Exporting Free Market Democracy Breeds Ethnic Hatred and Global Instability* (New York: Doubleday, 2003).

Cigar, Norman L., *Genocide in Bosnia: The Policy of "Ethnic Cleansing"* (College Station: Texas A&M University Press, 1995).

Clarke, Jonathan, "Replacing NATO," *Foreign Policy*, no. 93, 1993–94.

Coghlan, Benjamin, Richard J. Brennan, Pascal Ngoy, David Dofara, Brad Otto, Mark Clements, and Tony Stewart, "Mortality in the Democratic Republic of the Congo: A Nationwide Survey," *The Lancet* 367, no. 9504, 2006.

Cohen, Lenard J., *Broken Bonds: Yugoslavia's Disintegration and Balkan Politics in Transition* (Boulder, Colo.: Westview, 1995).

———, *Serpent in the Bosom: The Rise and Fall of Slobodan Milošević* (Boulder, Colo.: Westview, 2001).

Cohen, Nick, *What's Left? How Liberals Lost their Way* (London: Fourth Estate, 2007).

Cohen, Roger, *Hearts Grown Brutal: Sagas of Sarajevo* (New York: Random House, 1998).

Collon, Michel, *Poker Menteur, Les Grandes Puissances, la Yougoslavie, et les Prochaines Guerres* (Brussels: EPO, 1998).

Cordesman, Anthony H., *The Lessons and Non-Lessons of the Air and Missile Campaign in Kosovo* (Westport, Conn.: Praeger, 2001).

Cox, Ronald W., "Corporate Coalitions and Industrial Restructuring: Explaining Regional Trade Agreements," *Competition and Change* 1, no. 1, 1995.

Cox, Ronald W., and Daniel Skidmore-Hess, *US Politics and the Global Economy: Corporate Power, Conservative Shift* (Boulder, Colo.: Lynne Rienner, 1999).

Crawford, Timothy, "Pivotal Deterrence and the Kosovo War: Why the Holbrooke Agreement Failed," *Political Science Quarterly* 116, no. 4, 2001.

Cumings, Bruce, "The American Way of Going to War: Mexico (1846) to Iraq (2003)," *Orbis* 51, no. 2, 2007.

———, "Global Realm with No Limit, Global Realm with No Name," *Radical History Review*, no. 57, 1993.

———, *The Origins of the Korean War*, vol. 2, *The Roaring of the Cataract, 1947–1950* (Princeton: Princeton University Press, 1990).

Curtis, Glenn E., ed., *Yugoslavia: A Country Study* (Washington D.C., US Government Printing Office, 1992), *lcweb2.loc.gov/frd/cs/yutoc.html.*

Cushman, Thomas, ed., *A Matter of Principle: Humanitarian Arguments for War in Iraq* (Berkeley: University of California Press, 2005).

Cushman, Thomas, and Stjepan G. Meštrović, eds., *This Time We Knew: Western Responses to Genocide in Bosnia* (New York: New York University Press, 1996).

Cviić, Christopher, "Croatia," in David A. Dyker and Ivan Vejvoda, eds., *Yugoslavia and After: A Study in Fragmentation, Despair, and Rebirth* (New York: Longman, 1996).

Daalder, Ivo H., and Michael E. O'Hanlon, *Winning Ugly: NATO's War to Save Kosovo* (Washington, D.C.: Brookings, 2000).

Dahl, Robert Alan, *After the Revolution: Authority in a Good Society* (New Haven: Yale University Press, 1970).

———, *A Preface to Economic Democracy* (Berkeley: University of California Press, 1985).

David, Dominique, "La Communauté entre la Paix et la Guerre," *Politique Etrangère* 58, no. 2, 1993.

Dawidowicz, Lucy W., *The War against the Jews* (New York: Holt, Rinehart, and Winston, 1975).

Deliso, Christopher, *The Coming Balkan Caliphate: The Threat of Radical Islam to Europe and the West* (Westport, Conn.: Praeger, 2007).

Denitch, Bogdan, *Ethnic Nationalism: The Tragic Death of Yugoslavia* (Minneapolis: University of Minnesota Press, 1996).

De Waal, Alex, "US War Crimes in Somalia," *New Left Review*, no. 230, 1998.

DiPrizio, Robert C., *Armed Humanitarians: US Interventions from Northern Iraq to Kosovo* (Baltimore: Johns Hopkins University Press, 2002).

Djilas, Alexa, *The Contested Country: Yugoslav Unity and Communist Revolution, 1919–1953* (Cambridge, Mass.: Harvard University Press, 1991).

Doder, Dusko, and Louise Branson, *Milošević: Portrait of a Tyrant* (New York: Free Press, 1999).

Donia, Robert J., and John V. A. Fine Jr., *Bosnia and Herzegovina: A Tradition Betrayed* (New York: Columbia University Press, 1994).

Downs, Anthony, *Inside Bureaucracy* (Boston: Little, Brown, 1967).

Doyran, Mine Aysen, "Financial Crisis and Hegemony: An Investigation into the Declinist Paradigm," PhD thesis, Department of Political Science, State University of New York, Albany, 2007.

Dragnich, Alex N., "The Anatomy of a Myth: Serbian Hegemony," *Slavic Review* 50, no. 3, 1991.

———, "The Dayton Accords: Symbol of Great Power Failings," *Mediterranean Quarterly* 17, no. 2, 2006.

Dragnich, Alex N., and Slavco Todorovich, *The Saga of Kosovo: Focus on Serbian-Albanian Relations* (New York: Columbia University Press, 1984).

Dragović-Soso, Jasna, *Saviours of the Nation: Serbia's Intellectual Opposition and the Revival of Nationalism* (Montreal: McGill-Queen's University Press, 2002).

Drakulić, Slavenka, *How We Survived Communism and Even Laughed* (London: Hutchinson, 1992).

Drew, Elizabeth, *On the Edge: The Clinton Presidency* (New York: Simon and Schuster, 1994).

———, *Showdown: The Struggle between the Gingrich Congress and the Clinton White House* (New York: Simon and Schuster, 1996).

Duffield, John S., "NATO's Function after the Cold War," *Political Science Quarterly* 109, no. 5, 1994–95.

Dukic, Slavoljub, *Milošević and Marković: A Lust for Power* (Montreal: McGill-Queen's University Press, 2001).

Dyker, David A., *Yugoslavia: Socialism, Development, and Debt* (London: Routledge, 1990).

Eisenberg, Carolyn, "Working Class Politics and the Cold War: American Intervention in the German Labor Movement, 1945–49," *Diplomatic History* 7, no. 4, 1983.

Elshtain, Jean Bethke, "Just War and Humanitarian Intervention," *American University International Law Review* 17, no. 1, 2001.

Emerson, Rupert, "Self-Determination," *American Journal of International Law* 65, no. 3, 1971.

Engel, Jeffrey A., *Cold War at 30,000 Feet: The Anglo-American Fight for Aviation Supremacy* (Cambridge, Mass.: Harvard University Press, 2007).

Evangelista, Matthew, "Second Guessing the Experts: Citizens' Group Criticism of the Central Intelligence Agency's Soviet Military Estimates," *International History Review* 19, no. 3, 1997.

Falk, Richard, "The Complexities of Humanitarian Intervention: A New World Order Challenge," *Michigan Journal of International Law* 17, no. 2, 1996.

Feldstein, Martin, "EMU and International Conflict," *Foreign Affairs* 76, no. 6, 1997.

Fisher, Keith, "A Meeting of Blood and Oil: The Balkan Factor in Western Energy Security," *Journal of Southern Europe and the Balkans* 4, no. 1, 2002.

Finnemore, Martha, *The Purpose of Intervention: Changing Beliefs about the Use of Force* (Ithaca: Cornell University Press, 2003).

Fordham, Benjamin O., *Building the Cold War Consensus: The Political Economy of US National Security Policy, 1949–51* (Ann Arbor: University of Michigan Press, 1998).

Friend, Julius W., "US Policy toward Franco-German Cooperation," in Patrick McCarthy, ed., *France-Germany, 1983–1993: The Struggle to Cooperate* (New York: St. Martin's, 1993).

Fromkin, David, *Kosovo Crossing: The Reality of American Intervention in the Balkans* (New York: Free Press, 2002).

Gagnon, V. P., Jr., *The Myth of Ethnic War: Serbia and Croatia in the 1990s* (Ithaca: Cornell University Press, 2004).

Gebhard, Paul R. S., *The United States and European Security*, Adelphi Paper no. 286 (London: IISS/Brassey's, 1994).

Gendzier, Irene L., *Notes from the Minefield: United States Intervention in Lebanon and the Middle East, 1945–1958* (New York: Columbia University Press, 1997).

Gentile, Gian P., *How Effective Is Strategic Bombing? Lessons Learned from World War II to Kosovo* (New York: New York University Press, 2001).

Gervasi, Sean, "Why Is NATO in Yugoslavia?" in Ramsey Clark, ed., *NATO in the Balkans* (New York: International Action Center, 1998).

Gibbs, David N., "The 'Military-Industrial Complex,' Sectoral Conflict, and the Study of US

Foreign Policy," in Ronald W. Cox, ed., *Business and the State in International Relations* (Boulder, Colo.: Westview, 1996).

———, "Political Parties and International Relations: The United States and the Decolonization of Sub-Saharan Africa," *International History Review* 17, no. 2, 1995.

———, "Pretexts and US Foreign Policy: The War on Terrorism in Historical Perspective," *New Political Science* 26, no. 3, 2004, *www.gened.arizona.edu/dgibbs/pretexts.pdf.*

———, "Realpolitik and Humanitarian Intervention: The Case of Somalia," *International Politics* 37, no. 1, 2000, *www.gened.arizona.edu/dgibbs/somalia.pdf.*

———, "Reassessing Soviet Motives for Invading Afghanistan: A Declassified History," *Critical Asian Studies* 38, no. 2, 2006, *www.gened.arizona.edu/dgibbs/Afghan-coldwar.pdf.*

———, "The United Nations, International Peacekeeping, and the Question of 'Impartiality': Revisiting the Congo Operation," *Journal of Modern African Studies* 38, no. 3, 2000.

Gjelton, Thomas, *Sarajevo Daily: A City and Its Newspaper under Siege* (New York: HarperCollins, 1995).

Glenny, Misha, *The Fall of Yugoslavia: The Third Balkan War* (New York: Penguin, 1996).

Gokay, Bulent, "Introduction: Oil, War, and Geopolitics from Kosovo to Afghanistan," *Journal of Southern Europe and the Balkans* 4, no. 1, 2002.

Goldstein, Joshua S., and Jon C. Pevehouse, "Reciprocity, Bullying, and International Cooperation: Time-Series Analysis of the Bosnia Conflict," *American Political Science Review* 91, no. 3, 1997.

Gordon, Philip H, "The Western European Union and NATO's 'Europeanisation,'" in Gordon, ed., *NATO's Transformation: The Changing Shape of the Atlantic Alliance* (Lanham, Md.: Rowman and Littlefield, 1997).

Gow, James, *The Serbian Project and Its Adversaries: A Strategy of War Crimes* (Montreal: McGill-Queen's University Press, 2003).

———, *The Triumph of the Lack of Will: International Diplomacy and the Yugoslav War* (New York: Columbia University Press, 1997).

Gowan, Peter, *The Global Gamble: Washington's Faustian Bid for World Dominance* (London: Verso, 1999).

———, "Western Economic Diplomacy and the New Eastern Europe," *New Left Review*, no. 182, 1990.

Grant, Robert P., "France's New Relationship with NATO," in Philip H. Gordon, ed., *NATO's Transformation: The Changing Shape of the Atlantic Alliance* (Lanham, Md.: Rowman and Littlefield, 1997).

Greider, William, *Fortress America: The American Military and the Consequences of Peace* (New York: Public Affairs Press, 1998).

Griffin, Larry J., Joel A. Devine, and Michael Wallace, "Monopoly Capital, Organized Labor, and Military Expenditures in the United States, 1949–1976," *American Journal of Sociology* 88, no. 3, 1982.

Gumz, Jonathan, "German Counterinsurgency Policy in Independent Croatia, 1941–1944," *Historian* 61, no. 1, 1998.

Gutman, Roy, "The Collapse of Serbia?" *World Policy Journal* 16, no. 1, 1999.

———, *A Witness to Genocide: The 1993 Pulitzer Prize–Winning Dispatches on the "Ethnic Cleansing" of Bosnia* (New York: Macmillan, 1993).

Halberstam, David, *The Best and the Brightest* (New York: Fawcett-Crest, 1972).

———, *War in a Time of Peace: Bush, Clinton, and the Generals* (New York: Simon and Schuster, 2002).

Hallin, Daniel C., "The Media, the War in Vietnam, and Political Support: A Critique of the Thesis of an Oppositional Media," *Journal of Politics* 46, no. 1, 1984.

Hammarskjöld, Dag, "The International Civil Service in Law and Fact," in A. W. Cordier and W. Foote, eds., *Public Papers of the Secretaries-General of the United Nations*, vol. 5 (New York: Columbia University Press, 1975).

Hammond, Grant T., "Myths of the Air War over Serbia," *Aerospace Power Journal* 14, no. 4, 2000.

Hammond, Phil, and Edward S. Herman, eds. *Degraded Capability: The Media and the Kosovo Crisis* (London: Pluto, 2000).

Hardt, Michael, and Antonio Negri, *Empire* (Cambridge, Mass.: Harvard University Press, 2000).

Harris, John F., *The Survivor: Bill Clinton in the White House* (New York: Random House, 2005).

Harris, Owen, "The Collapse of 'The West,'" *Foreign Affairs* 72, no. 4, 1993.

Hartmann, Ralph, *"Die Ehrlichen Makler": Die Deutsche Aussenpolitik und der Bürgerkrieg in Jugoslawien* (Berlin: Dietz, 1998).

Harvey, David, *A Brief History of Neo-Liberalism* (Oxford: Oxford University Press, 2005).

Havel, Václav, *To the Castle and Back* (New York: Knopf, 2007).

Hayden, Robert M., *Blueprints for a House Divided: The Constitutional Logic of the Yugoslav Conflicts* (Ann Arbor: University of Michigan Press, 1999).

Hechter, Michael, *Internal Colonialism: The Celtic Fringe in British National Development* (New Brunswick, N.J.: Transaction Publishers, 1999).

Hedges, Chris, "Kosovo's Next Masters?" *Foreign Affairs* 78, no. 3, 1999.

Hendrickson, Ryan C., "Leadership at NATO: Secretary General Manfred Woerner and the Crisis in Bosnia," *Journal of Strategic Studies* 27, no. 3, 2004.

———, "NATO's Secretary General and the Use of Force: Willy Claes and the Air Strikes in Bosnia," *Armed Forces and Society* 31, no. 1, 2004.

Henrikson, Alan K., "The Constraint of Legitimacy: The Legal and Institutional Framework of Euro-Atlantic Security," in Pierre Martin and Mark R. Brawley, eds., *Alliance Politics, Kosovo, and NATO's War: Allied Force or Forced Allies?* (New York: Palgrave, 2000).

Henwood, Doug, "Impeccable Logic: Trade, Development, and Free Markets in the Clinton Era," *NACLA Report on the Americas* 26, no. 5, 1993.

Herman, Edward S., and David Peterson, "The Dismantling of Yugoslavia," *Monthly Review* 59, no. 5, 2007.

Hirschman, Albert O., *National Power and the Structure of Foreign Trade* (Berkeley: University of California Press, 1980).

Hitchens, Christopher, *A Long Short War: The Postponed Liberation of Iraq* (New York: Plume Books, 2003).

Hoare, Marko Attila, *The History of Bosnia: From the Middle Ages to the Present Day* (London: Saqi Books, 2007).

———, *How Bosnia Armed* (London: Saqi Books and Bosnia Institute, 2004).

Hockenos, Paul, *Homeland Calling: Exile Patriotism and the Balkan Wars* (Ithaca: Cornell University Press, 2003).

Hodson, Randy, Dusko Sekulic, and Garth Massey, "National Tolerance in the Former Yugoslavia," *American Journal of Sociology* 99, no. 6, 1994.

Hoffmann, Stanley, "Yugoslavia: Implications for Europe and for European Institutions," in Richard Ullman, ed., *The World and Yugoslavia's Wars* (New York: Council on Foreign Relations, 1996).

Holmes, John W., *The United States and Europe after the Cold War: A New Alliance?* (Columbia: University of South Carolina Press, 1997).

Holzgrefe, J. L., and Robert Keohane, eds., *Humanitarian Intervention: Ethical, Legal, and Political Dilemmas* (Cambridge: Cambridge University Press, 2003).

Honig, Jan Willem, and Norbert Both, *Srebrenica: Record of a War Crime* (London: Penguin, 1996).

Horowitz, Shale, "War after Communism: Effects on Political and Economic Reform in the Former Soviet Union and Yugoslavia," *Journal of Peace Research* 40, no. 1, 2003.

Hosmer, Stephen T., *The Conflict over Kosovo: Why Milošević Decided to Settle When He Did* (Santa Monica, Calif.: Rand, 2001).

Howe, Russell Warren, *Along the Afric Shore* (New York: Barnes and Noble, 1975).

Hudson, Kate, *Breaking the South Slav Dream: The Rise and Fall of Yugoslavia* (London: Pluto, 2003).

Hudson, Michael, *Super Imperialism: The Economic Strategy of American Empire* (New York: Holt, Rinehart, and Winston, 1972).

Huntington, Samuel P., "The Erosion of American National Interests," *Foreign Affairs* 76, no. 5, 1997.

———, "The Lonely Superpower," *Foreign Affairs* 78, no. 2, 1999.

Ignatieff, Michael, *Virtual War: Kosovo and Beyond* (London: Chatto and Windus, 2000).

Iraq Family Health Survey Study Group, "Violence-Related Mortality in Iraq from 2002 to 2006," *New England Journal of Medicine* [online edition], January 31, 2008, *content.nejm. org/cgi/reprint/358/5/484.pdf.*

Irvine, Jill, "Ultranationalist Ideology and State Building in Croatia, 1990–1996," *Problems of Post-Communism* 44, no. 4, 1997.

James, Alan, *Peacekeeping in International Politics* (New York: St. Martin's, 1990).

Johnsen, William T., and Thomas-Durell Young, "France's Evolving Policy toward NATO," *Strategic Review*, Summer 1995.

———, "Franco-German Security Accommodation: Agreeing to Disagree," *Strategic Review*, Winter 1993.

Johnson, Chalmers, *Blowback: The Costs and Consequences of American Empire* (New York: Metropolitan Books, 2000).

———, *The Sorrows of Empire: Militarism, Secrecy, and the End of the Republic* (New York: Metropolitan Books, 2004).

Johnson, Robert H., *Improbable Dangers: US Conceptions of Threat in the Cold War and After* (New York: St. Martin's, 1997).

Johnstone, Diana, *Fools' Crusade: Yugoslavia, NATO, and Western Delusions* (New York: Monthly Review Press, 2002).

Joly, Hervé, "Les Investissements Directs des Groupes Industriels Allemands en Europe du Centre-Est entre 1919 et 1945," in François Bafoil, ed., *Les Stratégies Allemandes en Europe Central et Orientale: Une Géopolitiques des Investissements Directs* (Paris: Harmattan, 1997).

Jones, Adam, "Gender and Genocide in Rwanda," *Journal of Genocide Research* 4, no. 1, 2002.

Judah, Tim, *Kosovo: War and Revenge* (New Haven: Yale University Press, 2002).

Juneau, Jean-François, "La Politique de l'Allemagne à l'Egard de la Croatie, 1991–2006," in Renéo Lukic, ed., *La Politique Etrangère de la Croatie: De son Indépendance à nos Jours, 1991–2006* (Quebec: Les Presses de l'Université de Laval, 2006).

Kaldor, Mary, "A Response [to David Rieff]," *Journal of Human Rights* 1, no. 1, 2002.

Kamm, Oliver, *Anti-Totalitarianism: The Left-Wing Case for a Neoconservative Foreign Policy* (London: Social Affairs Unit, 2005).

Kamola, Isaac, "The Global Coffee Economy and the Production of Genocide in Rwanda," *Third World Quarterly* 28, no. 3, 2007.

Kamp, Karl-Heinz, "L'OTAN après le Kosovo: L'Ange de Paix ou Gendarme du Monde?" *Politique Etrangère* 64, no. 2, 1999.

Kampfner, John, *Blair's Wars* (New York: Free Press, 2003).

Kaplan, Lawrence S., *NATO and the United States: The Enduring Alliance* (New York: Twayne Publishers, 1994).

Katzenstein, Peter J., "The Smaller European States, Germany, and Europe," in Katzenstein, ed., *Tamed Power: Germany in Europe* (Ithaca: Cornell University Press, 1998).

Kegley, Charles W., "The Neo-Idealist Moment in International Studies? Realist Myths and the New International Realities," *International Studies Quarterly* 37, no. 2, 1993.

Kissinger, Henry, *Diplomacy* (New York: Simon and Schuster, 1994).

Klare, Michael T., *Rogue States and Nuclear Outlaws: America's Search for a New Foreign Policy* (New York: Hill and Wang, 1995).

Kohlmann, Evan, *Al-Qaida's Jihad in Europe: The Afghan-Bosnian Network* (Oxford: Berg, 2004).

Kolko, Joyce, and Gabriel Kolko, *The Limits of Power: The World and United States Foreign Policy, 1945–1954* (New York: Harper and Row, 1972).

Korzeniewicz, Roberto Patricio, and Timothy Patrick Moran, "World Economic Trends in the Distribution of Income, 1965–1992," *American Journal of Sociology* 102, no. 4, 1997.

Kouchner, Bernard, "The Right to Intervention: Codified in Kosovo," *New Perspectives Quarterly* 16, no. 4, 1999.

Kraft, Evan, "Evaluating Regional Policy in Yugoslavia, 1966–1990," *Comparative Economic Studies* 34, no. 3–4, 1992.

Kupchan, Charles A., "After Pax Americana: Benign Power, Regional Integration, and the Sources of a Stable Multipolarity," *International Security* 23, no. 2, 1998.

Kuperman, Alan J., "Suicidal Interventions and Humanitarian Intervention," *Ethnopolitics* 4, no. 2, 2005.

Kurth, James, "First War of the Global Era: Kosovo and US Grand Strategy," in Andrew J. Bacevich and Eliot A. Cohen, eds., *War over Kosovo: Politics and Strategy in a Global Age* (New York: Columbia University Press, 2001).

Lacorne, Denis, Jacques Rupnik, and Marie-France Toinet, *The Rise and Fall of Anti-Americanism: A Century of French Perception* (Basingstoke: Macmillan, 1990).

Lambeth, Benjamin S., *NATO's Air War for Kosovo: A Strategic and Operational Assessment* (Santa Monica, Calif.: Rand, 2001).

Lampe, John, *Yugoslavia as History: Twice There Was a Country* (Cambridge: Cambridge University Press, 1996).

Larrabee, F. Stephen, "La Politique Américaine et la Crise Yougoslave," *Politique Etrangère* 59, no. 4, 1994.

Latawski, Paul, and Martin A. Smith, *The Kosovo Crisis and the Evolution of Post–Cold War European Security* (Manchester: Manchester University Press, 2003).

Laughland, John, *Travesty: The Trial of Slobodan Milošević and the Corruption of International Justice* (London: Pluto, 2006).

Layne, Christopher, "Blunder in the Balkans: The Clinton Administration's Bungled War against Serbia," *Policy Analysis*, May 20, 1999.

————, "From Preponderance to Offshore Balancing: America's Future Grand Strategy," *International Security* 22, no. 1, 1997.

————, *The Peace of Illusions: American Grand Strategy from 1940 to the Present* (Ithaca: Cornell University Press, 2006).

————, "Rethinking American Grand Strategy," *World Policy Journal* 15, no. 2, 1998.

Layne, Christopher, and Benjamin Schwarz, "American Hegemony—Without an Enemy," *Foreign Policy*, no. 92, 1993.

Lebor, Adam, *"Complicity with Evil": The United Nations in the Age of Modern Genocide* (New Haven: Yale University Press, 2006).

————, *Milošević: A Biography* (London: Bloomsbury, 2002).

Leffler, Melvyn P., *A Preponderance of Power: The Truman Administration and the Cold War* (Stanford: Stanford University Press, 1992).

Lindblom, Charles A., *Politics and Markets: The World's Political-Economic Systems* (New York: Basic Books, 1977).

Livingston, Steven, and Todd Eachus, "Humanitarian Crises and US Foreign Policy: Somalia and the CNN Effect Reconsidered," *Political Communication* 12, no. 4, 1995.

Lukic, Renéo, *L'Agonie Yougoslave (1986–2003): Les Etats-Unis et l'Europe Face aux Guerres Balkaniques* (Québec: Presse de l'Université de Laval, 2003).

Lundestad, Geir, " 'Empire by Invitation' in the American Century," *Diplomatic History* 23, no. 2, 1999.

MacDonald, David Bruce, *Balkan Holocausts? Serbian and Croatian Victim-Centred Propaganda and the War in Yugoslavia* (Manchester: Manchester University Press, 2002).

MacFarlane, S. Neil, "Challenges to Euro-Atlantic Security," in Pierre Martin and Mark R. Brawley, eds., *Alliance Politics, Kosovo, and NATO's War: Allied Force or Forced Allies?* (New York: Palgrave, 2000).

Magaš, Branka, *The Destruction of Yugoslavia: Tracing the Break-Up, 1980–92* (London: Verso, 1993).

Malcolm, Noel, *Bosnia: A Short History* (New York: New York University Press, 1996).

————, *Kosovo: A Short History* (New York: New York University Press, 1999).

Manas, Jean E., "The Impossible Trade-Off: 'Peace' versus 'Justice' in Settling Yugoslavia's Wars," in Richard H. Ullman, ed., *The World and Yugoslavia's Wars* (New York: Council on Foreign Relations, 1996).

Mandel, Michael, *How America Gets Away with Murder: Illegal Wars, Collateral Damage, and Crimes against Humanity* (London: Pluto, 2004).

Mandelbaum, Michael, *The Case for Goliath: How America Acts as the World's Government in the Twenty-First Century* (New York: Public Affairs, 2005).

Mann, James, *The Rise of the Vulcans: The History of Bush's War Cabinet* (New York: Viking, 2004).

Markovits, Andrei S., Simon Reich, and Frank Westermann, "Germany: Hegemonic Power and Economic Gain?" *Review of International Political Economy* 3, no. 4, 1996.

McCoy, Alfred W., Jr., *The Politics of Heroin in Southeast Asia* (Harper and Row, 1972).

McMahon, Robert J., "Heisse Kriege im Kalten Krieg," in Bernd Greiner, Christian Müller, and Dierk Walter, eds, *Heisse Kriege im Kalten Krieg* (Hamburg: Hamburger Edition, 2006).

McPherson, Lionel K., "Excessive Force in War: A 'Golden Rule' Test," *Theoretical Inquiries in Law* 7, no. 1, 2006.

Meggle, Georg, ed., *Ethics of Humanitarian Intervention* (Frankfort: Ontos, 2004).

Meier, Viktor, *Yugoslavia: A History of Its Demise* (London: Routledge, 1999).

Merlino, Jacques, *Les Vérités Yougoslaves Ne Sont Pas Toutes Bonnes à Dire* (Paris: Albin Michel, 1993).

Mertus, Julie A., *War's Offensive on Women: The Humanitarian Challenge in Bosnia, Kosovo, and Afghanistan* (Bloomfield, Conn.: Kumarian Press, 2000).

Mežnaric, Sliva, "Sociology of Migration in Yugoslavia," *Current Sociology* 32, no. 2, 1984.

Michas, Takis, *Unholy Alliance: Greece and Milošević's Serbia* (College Station: Texas A&M University Press, 2002).

Milanovic, Branko, "The Two Faces of Globalization: Against Globalization as We Know It," *World Development* 31, no. 4, 2003.

Miller, Nicholas J., "Search for a Serbian Havel," *Problems of Post-Communism* 44, no. 4, 1997.

Moens, Alexander, "EDSP, the United States, and the Atlantic Alliance," in Jolyon Howorth and John T. S. Keeler, eds., *Defending Europe: The EU, NATO, and the Quest for European Autonomy* (New York: Palgrave, 2003).

Moffitt, Michael, *The World's Money: International Banking from Bretton Woods to the Brink of Insolvency* (New York: Simon and Schuster, 1983).

Morgenthau, Hans J., "To Intervene or Not to Intervene," *Foreign Affairs* 45, no. 3, 1967.

Morris, Benny, *The Birth of the Palestinian Refugee Problem Revisited* (Cambridge: Cambridge University Press, 2004).

Mortimer, Edward, *European Security after the Cold War: An Assessment of the Dangers to Peace in Europe since the Soviet Collapse, and of the Western Responses They Require* (London: Brassey's/IISS, 1992).

Moss, Kenneth B., *Undeclared War and the Future of US Foreign Policy* (Baltimore: Johns Hopkins University Press, 2008).

Muravchik, Joshua, *The Imperative of American Leadership: A Challenge to Neo-Isolationism* (Washington, D.C.: AEI Press, 1996).

Nanda, Ved P., "Self-Determination in International Law: The Tragic Case of Two Cities— Islamabad (West Pakistan) and Dacca (East Pakistan)," *American Journal of International Law* 66, no. 2, 1972.

Neier, Aryeh, "Inconvenient Facts: Review of Noam Chomsky's *The New Military Humanism*," *Dissent* 47, no. 2, 2000.

Nelson, Mark M., "Transatlantic Travails: Europe and America," *Foreign Policy*, no. 92, 1993.

Nye, Joseph S., Jr, "Soft Power," *Foreign Policy*, no. 80, 1990.

Nyrop, Richard F., ed., *Yugoslavia: A Country Study* (Washington, D.C.: US Government Printing Office, 1982).

O'Brien, Conor Cruise, *To Katanga and Back: A UN Case History* (New York: Universal Library, 1962).

Odom, William E., *America's Military Revolution: Strategy and Structure after the Cold War* (Washington, D.C.: American University Press, 1993).

Opinion Research Business, "New Analysis 'Confirms' 1 Million Iraq Casualties," January 28, 2008, *www.globalresearch.ca/index.php?context=va&aid=7950*.

Orford, Ann, *Reading Humanitarian Intervention: Human Rights and the Use of Force in International Law* (Cambridge: Cambridge University Press, 2004).

Orwell, George, "Benefit of Clergy: Some Notes on Salvador Dali," 1944, *www.orwell.ru/library/reviews/dali/english/e_dali*.

———, "Toward European Unity," *Partisan Review* 14, no. 4, 1947.

Owen, David, "Atlantic Partnership or Rivalry?" in Henry Brandon, ed., *In Search of a New World Order: The Future of US-European Relations* (Washington, D.C.: Brookings, 1992).

————, "The Future of the Balkans: An Interview with David Owen," *Foreign Affairs* 72, no. 2, 1993.

Palmer, John, *Europe without America?* (Oxford: Oxford University Press, 1987).

Panitch, Leo, "The New Imperial State," *New Left Review*, no. 2, 2000.

Pappé, Ilan, *The Ethnic Cleansing of Palestine* (Oxford: OneWorld Press, 2006).

Parenti, Michael, *To Kill a Nation: The Attack on Yugoslavia* (London: Verso, 2002).

Pateman, Carole, *Participation and Democratic Theory* (Cambridge: Cambridge University Press, 1970).

Peroche, Gregory, *Histoire de la Croatie et des Nations Slaves du Sud: 395–1992* (Paris: F. X. de Guibert, OEIL, 1992).

Petras, James, and Morris Morley, "Contesting Hegemons: US-French Relations in the 'New World Order,'" *Review of International Studies* 26, no. 1, 2000.

Petras, James, and Steven Vieux, "Bosnia and the Revival of US Hegemony," *New Left Review*, no. 218, 1996.

Pevehouse, Jon C., and Joshua S. Goldstein, "Serbian Compliance or Defiance in Kosovo? Statistical Analysis and Real-Time Predictions," *Journal of Conflict Resolution* 43, no. 4, 1999.

Phillips, Kevin, *American Theocracy: The Peril and Politics of Radical Religion, Oil, and Borrowed Money in the Twenty-First Century* (New York: Viking, 2006).

————, *Wealth and Democracy: A Political History of the American Rich* (New York: Broadway Books, 2002).

Phillips, Robert L., and Duane L. Cady, *Humanitarian Intervention: Just War versus Pacifism* (Lanham, Md.: Rowman and Littlefield, 1996).

Pickering, Paula M., *Peacebuilding in the Balkans: The View from the Ground Floor* (Ithaca: Cornell University Press, 2007).

Pilch, Fran, "Prosecution of the Crime of Genocide in the ICTY: The Case of Radislav Krstić," *Journal of Legal Studies (United States Air Force Academy)* 12, 2002–2003.

Pomerance, Michla, "The Badinter Commission: The Use and Misuse of the International Court of Justice's Jurisprudence," *Michigan Journal of International Law* 20, no. 1, 1998.

Posen, Barry R., "The War for Kosovo: Serbia's Political-Military Strategy," *International Security* 24, no. 4, 2000.

Posen, Barry R., and Andrew L. Ross, "Competing US Grand Strategies," in Robert J. Lieber, ed., *Eagle Adrift: American Foreign Policy at the End of the Century* (New York: Longman, 1997).

Power, Samantha, *"A Problem from Hell": America and the Age of Genocide* (New York: HarperCollins, 2002).

Prados, John, *Safe for Democracy: The Secret Wars of the CIA* (Chicago: Ivan R. Dee, 2006).

Prasnikar, Janez, and Zivko Pregl, "Economic Development in Yugoslavia in 1990 and Prospects for the Future," *American Economic Review* 81, no. 2, 1991.

Pugh, Michael "Peacekeeping and IR Theory: Phantom of the Opera?" *International Peacekeeping* 10, no. 4, 2003.

Radan, Peter, "Post-Secession International Borders: A Critical Analysis of the Opinions of the Badinter Arbitration Commission," *Melbourne University Law Review* 24, no. 1, 2000.

Rainio, J., K. Lalu, and A. Penttilä, "Independent Forensic Autopsies in an Armed Conflict: Investigation of the Victims from Račak, Kosovo," *Forensic Science International* 116, no. 2, 2001.

Ramet, Sabrina Petra, *Balkan Babel: The Disintegration of Yugoslavia from the Death of Tito to Ethnic War*, 2d ed. (Boulder, Colo.: Westview, 1996).

———, "Kosovo: A Liberal Approach," *Society* 36, no. 6, 1999.

———, "Review Essay—Views from Inside: Memoirs Concerning the Yugoslav Breakup and War," *Slavic Review* 61, no. 3, 2002.

———, *Thinking about Yugoslavia: Scholarly Debates about the Yugoslav Breakup and the Wars in Bosnia and Kosovo* (Cambridge: Cambridge University Press, 2005).

Ramet, Sabrina Petra, and Letty Coffin, "German Foreign Policy toward the Yugoslav Successor States, 1991–1999," *Problems of Post-Communism* 48, no. 1, 2001.

Ramsbotham, Oliver, and Tom Woodhouse, *Humanitarian Intervention in Contemporary Conflict: A Re-Conceptualization* (Cambridge: Polity Press, 1996).

Rathbun, Brian C., *Partisan Interventions: European Party Politics and Peace Enforcement in the Balkans* (Ithaca: Cornell University Press, 2004).

Ratner, Steven R., "Drawing a Better Line: *Uti Possidetis* and the Borders of New States," *American Journal of International Law* 90, no. 4, 1996.

Rhode, David, *Endgame: The Betrayal and Fall of Srebrenica, Europe's Worst Massacre since World War II* (New York: Farrar, Straus, and Giroux, 1997).

Rieff, David, "Denying Moral Equivalence," *Foreign Affairs* 74, no. 6, 1995.

———, "On the Wishful Thinking of Eminent Persons: The Independent Commission's Kosovo Report," *Journal of Human Rights* 1, no. 1, 2002.

———, *Slaughterhouse: Bosnia and the Failure of the West* (New York: Simon and Schuster, 1995).

Ripley, Tim, *Operation Deliberate Force: The UN and NATO Campaign in Bosnia, 1995* (Lancaster, UK: Centre for Defense and International Security Studies, 1999).

Robin, Gabriel, "A Quoi Sert l'OTAN?" *Politique Etrangère* 60, no. 1, 1995.

Robinson, Piers, "Misperception in Foreign Policy Making: Operation 'Deliberate Force' and the Ending of War in Bosnia," *Civil Wars* 4, no. 4, 2001.

Robinson, William I., *A Theory of Global Capitalism: Production, Class, and State in a Transnational World* (Baltimore: Johns Hopkins University Press, 2004).

Roemer, John E., *A Future for Socialism* (Cambridge, Mass.: Harvard University Press, 1994).

Ronayne, Peter, "Genocide in Kosovo," *Human Rights Review* 5, no. 4, 2004.

Rothkopf, David J., *Running the World: The Inside Story of the National Security Council and the Architects of American Power* (New York: Public Affairs, 2005).

Rothschild, Joseph, *East Central Europe between the Two World Wars* (Seattle: University of Washington Press, 1983).

Ruggie, John G., "The United Nations and the Collective Use of Force: Whither or Whether?" *International Peacekeeping* 3, no. 4, 1996.

Rusinow, Dennison I., *The Yugoslav Experiment, 1948–1974* (Berkeley: University of California Press, 1977).

Samary, Cathérine, *Yugoslavia Dismembered* (New York: Monthly Review Press, 1995).

Saunders, Frances Stoner, *Who Paid the Piper? The CIA and the Cultural Cold War* (London: Granta Books, 1999).

Scahill, Jeremy, *Blackwater: The Rise of the World's Most Powerful Mercenary Army* (New York: Nation Books, 2007).

Schmidt-Eenboom, Erich, *Der Schattenkrieger: Klaus Kinkel und der BND* (Dusseldorf: ECON, 1995).

Schmitz, David F., *The United States and Right-Wing Dictatorships* (New York: Cambridge University Press, 2006).

Schnabel, Albrecht, and Ramesh Thakur, eds., *Kosovo and the Challenge of Humanitarian Intervention: Selective Indignation, Collective Action, and International Citizenship* (Tokyo: United Nations University Press, 2000).

Schraeder, Peter J., *African Politics and Society: A Mosaic in Transformation* (Boston: Bedford/St. Martin's, 2000).

Schweizer, Peter, "The Growth of Economic Espionage: America Is Target Number One," *Foreign Affairs* 75, no. 1, 1996.

Sells, Michael Anthony, *The Bridge Betrayed: Religion and Genocide in Bosnia* (Berkeley: University of California Press, 1996).

Sharp, Jane M. O., "Dayton Report Card," *International Security* 22, no. 3, 1997–1998.

Shawcross, William, *Allies: The US, Britain, Europe, and the War in Iraq* (New York: Public Affairs, 2004).

Sheehy, Gail, *Hillary's Choice* (New York: Ballantine Books, 2000).

Sherry, Michael S., "The Military," *American Quarterly* 35, nos. 1–2, 1983.

Shoup, Paul, "The Disintegration of Yugoslavia and Western Foreign Policy in the 1980s," in Lenard J. Cohen and Jasna Dragović-Soso, eds., *State Collapse in South-Eastern Europe: New Perspectives on Yugoslavia's Disintegration* (West Lafayette, Ind.: Purdue University Press, 2008).

Shrader, Charles R., *The Muslim-Croat Civil War in Central Bosnia: A Military History, 1992–1994* (College Station: Texas A&M University Press, 2003).

Silber, Laura, and Allan Little, *The Death of Yugoslavia* (London: Penguin, 1995).

Simms, Brendan, *Unfinest Hour: Britain and the Destruction of Bosnia* (London: Allen Lane, 2001).

Singleton, Fred, *A Short History of the Yugoslav Peoples* (Cambridge: Cambridge University Press, 1985).

Slaughter, Anne-Marie, *The Idea That Is America: Keeping Faith with Our Values in a Dangerous World* (New York: Basic Books, 2007).

Smith, Sally Bedell, *For Love of Politics: Inside the Clinton White House* (New York: Random House, 2007).

Smith, Stephen, *Somalie: La Guerre Perdue de l'Humanitaire* (Paris: Calmann-Lévy, 1993).

Solomon, Robert, *The International Monetary System, 1945–1976: An Insider's View* (New York: Harper and Row, 1977).

Southwick, Katherine C., "Srebrenica as Genocide? The Krstić Decision and the Language of the Unspeakable," *Yale Human Rights and Development Law Journal* 8, 2005.

Spiro, David, *The Hidden Hand of American Hegemony: Petrodollar Recycling and International Markets* (Ithaca: Cornell University Press, 1999).

Stark, Hans, "Dissonances Franco-Allemendes sur Fond de Guerre Serbo-Croate," *Politique Etrangère* 57, no. 2, 1992.

Steel, Ronald, *Temptations of a Superpower* (Cambridge, Mass.: Harvard University Press, 1995).

Steinberg, James B., "International Involvement in the Yugoslavia Conflict," in Lori Fisler Damrosch, ed., *Enforcing Restraint: Collective Intervention in Internal Conflicts* (New York: Council on Foreign Relations, 1993).

Stevanovic, Vidosav, *Milošević: The People's Tyrant* (New York: St. Martin's, 2004).

Stigler, Andrew L. "A Clear Victory for Air Power: NATO's Empty Threat to Invade Kosovo," *International Security* 27, no. 3, 2002–2003.

Stiglmayer, Alexandra, *Mass Rape: The War against Women in Bosnia-Herzegovina* (Lincoln: University of Nebraska Press, 1994).

Stone, I. F., *The Hidden History of the Korean War* (New York: Monthly Review Press, 1969).

Strange, Susan, "The Defective State," *Daedalus* 124, no. 2, 1995.

Sudetic, Chuck, *Blood and Vengeance: One Family's Story of the War in Bosnia* (New York: Norton, 1998).

Sullivan, Stacy, *Be Not Afraid for You have Sons in America: How a Brooklyn Roofer Helped Lure the US into the Kosovo War* (New York: St. Martin's, 2004).

Tabeau, Ewa, and Jakub Bijak, "War Related Deaths in the 1992–1995 Armed Conflicts in Bosnia and Herzegovina: A Critique of Previous Estimates and Recent Results," *European Journal of Population* 21, nos. 2–3, 2005.

Tanner, Marcus, *Croatia: A Nation Forged in War* (New Haven: Yale University Press, 2001).

Tesón, Fernando R., "Ending Tyranny in Iraq," *Ethics and International Affairs* 19, no. 2, 2005.

———, *Humanitarian Intervention: An Inquiry into Law and Morality* (Ardsley-on-Hudson, N.Y.: Transnational Publishers, 1988).

Thomas, Raju, "Self-Determination and International Recognition Policy," *World Affairs* 160, no. 1, 1997.

———, "Sovereignty, Self-Determination, and Secession: Principles and Practice," in Thomas, ed., *Yugoslavia Unraveled: Sovereignty, Self-Determination, Intervention* (Lanham, Md.: Lexington Books, 2003).

Thompson, John A., "The Exaggeration of American Vulnerability: The Anatomy of a Tradition," *Diplomatic History* 16, no. 1, 1992.

Thompson, Mark R., and Philipp Kuntz, "Stolen Elections: The Case of the Serbian October," *Journal of Democracy* 15, no. 4, 2004.

Todorovic, Ilija Ika, "Regional Economic Nationalism in the Former Yugoslavia," in Raju G. C. Thomas and H. Richard Friman, eds., *The South Slav Conflict: History, Religion, Ethnicity, and Nationalism* (New York: Garland, 1996).

Tomasevich, Jozo, *War and Revolution in Yugoslavia, 1941–1945: Occupation and Collaboration* (Stanford: Stanford University Press, 2001).

Tone, John Lawrence, *War and Genocide in Cuba, 1895–1898* (Chapel Hill: University of North Carolina Press, 2006).

Touval, Saadia, *Mediation in the Yugoslav Wars: The Critical Years, 1990–95* (New York: Palgrave, 2002).

Tuathail, Gearóid O., "Geopolitical Discourses: Paddy Ashdown and the Tenth Anniversary of the Dayton Peace Accords," *Geopolitics* 11, no. 1, 2006.

Van Der Pijl, Kees, "From Gorbachev to Kosovo: Atlantic Rivalries and the Re-Incorporation of Eastern Europe," *Review of International Political Economy* 8, no. 2, 2001.

———, *Global Rivalries from the Cold War to Iraq* (London: Pluto, 2006).

Van Der Wee, Herman, *Prosperity and Upheaval: The World Economy, 1945–1980* (Berkeley: University of California Press, 1987).

Veneroso, Frank, and Robert Wade, "The Asian Crisis: The High Debt Model versus the Wall Street-Treasury-IMF Complex," *New Left Review*, no. 228, 1998.

Vernet, Daniel, and Jean-Marc Gonin, *La Rêve Sacrifié: Chroniques des Guerres Yougoslaves* (Paris: Editions Odile Jacob, 1994).

Vetlesen, Arne Johan, "Genocide: A Case for the Responsibility of the Bystander," *Journal of Peace Research* 37, no. 4, 2000.

Vickers, Miranda, *Between Serb and Albanian: A History of Kosovo* (London: Hurst, 1998).

Vulliamy, Ed, "Bosnia: The Crime of Appeasement," *International Affairs* 74, no. 1, 1998.

———, " 'Neutrality' and the Absence of Reckoning: A Journalist's Account," *Journal of International Affairs* 52, no. 2, 1999.

Walzer, Michael, *Just and Unjust Wars: A Moral Argument with Historical Illustrations* (New York: Basic Books, 1977).

———, "The Triumph of Just War Theory (and the Dangers of Success)," *Social Research* 69, no. 4, 2002.

Weine, Stevan M., *When History Is a Nightmare: Lives and Memories of Ethnic Cleansing in Bosnia-Herzegovina* (New Brunswick, N.J.: Rutgers University Press, 1999).

Weiss, Thomas G., "Triage: Humanitarian Interventions in a New Era," *World Policy Journal* 11, no. 1, 1994.

Weller, Marc, "International Response to the Dissolution of the Socialist Federal Republic of Yugoslavia," *American Journal of International Law* 86, no. 3, 1992.

Welsh, Jennifer M., ed., *Humanitarian Intervention and International Relations* (Oxford: Oxford University Press, 2006).

Western, Jon, "The Sources of Humanitarian Intervention: Beliefs, Information, and Advocacy in the US Decisions on Somalia and Bosnia," *International Security* 26, no. 4, 2002.

Wheeler, Nicholas J., *Saving Strangers: Humanitarian Intervention in International Society* (New York: Oxford University Press, 2000).

Whitehead, Laurence, "The European Union and the Americas," in Victor Bulmer-Thomas and James Dunkerley, eds., *The United States and Latin America: The New Agenda* (Cambridge, Mass.: Harvard University Press, 1999).

Wiebes, Cees, *Intelligence and the War in Bosnia: 1992–1995* (Münster: Lit, 2003), *srebrenica. brightside.nl/srebrenica/*.

Wilmer, Franke, *The Social Construction of Man, the State, and War: Identity, Conflict, and Violence in Former Yugoslavia* (New York: Routledge, 2002).

Wohlstetter, Albert, "Bosnia as Future," in Zalmay Khalilzad, ed., *Lessons from Bosnia* (Santa Monica, Calif.: Rand, 1993).

Wolfowitz, Paul D., "Clinton's First Year," *Foreign Affairs* 73, no. 1, 1994.

Woodward, Bob, *The Choice: How Bill Clinton Won* (New York: Simon and Schuster, 1996).

Woodward, Susan L., *Balkan Tragedy: Chaos and Dissolution after the Cold War* (Washington, D.C.: Brookings, 1995).

———, "Costly Disinterest: Missed Opportunities for Preventive Diplomacy in Croatia and Bosnia and Herzegovina, 1985–1991," in Bruce W. Jentleson, ed., *Opportunities Missed, Opportunities Seized: Preventive Diplomacy in the Post–Cold War World* (Lanham, Md.: Rowman and Littlefield, 2000).

———, "Orthodoxy and Solidarity: Competing Claims and International Adjustment in Yugoslavia," *International Organization* 40, no. 2, 1986.

Yoo, John C., "Kosovo, War Powers, and the Multilateral Future," *University of Pennsylvania Law Review* 148, no. 5, 2000.

Zacher, M. W., *Dag Hammarskjöld's United Nations* (New York: Columbia University Press, 1970).

Zakaria, Fareed, "When Switching Channels Isn't Enough: The Rise of Illiberal Democracy," *Foreign Affairs* 76, no. 6, 1997.

Žižek, Slavoj, *Did Somebody Say Totalitarian? Five Interventions in the (Mis)use of a Notion* (London: Verso, 2001).

Index